The Tyranny of the Federal Reserve

Brian O'Brien

THE TYRANNY OF THE FEDERAL RESERVE

Copyright © 2015 by Brian O'Brien

All Rights Reserved

No part of this book may be reproduced in any form by photocopying or by any electronic or mechanical means, including information storage or retrieval systems, without permission in writing from the copyright owner.

Published 2015

thetyrannyofthefederalreserve@yahoo.com

Cover art is an alteration of a drawing by Alfred Owen Crozier that appeared in his book *U.S. Money Vs Corporation Currency* in 1912.

Table of Contents

Introduction	1
Ben Franklin's Money	22
The Tyranny of Debt	37
On the hook	41
Debt cycle	44
The Tyranny of Usury	50
The Tyranny of Fractional Reserve Banking	72
Compound interest	74
The multiplier effect	75
Bank runs	79
The bankers' solution	82
The Tyranny of Gold	92
The Tyranny of Central Banks	106
A (not so modest) Proposal for a New American Monetary System	123
A United States Monetary Council	126
Taxing and spending	128
Public loan offices	130
Monetary policy	134
The Road to the Great Depression	140
The Great Confiscation	157
The Tyranny of World War II	164
What do the Bankers Want?	213
The Tyranny of Free Trade	239
The tyranny of the petro dollar	266
The tyranny of the Trilateral Commission	270
The tyranny of Wall Street	282
Climate change and global governance	300

The Tyranny of Mass Immigration	**310**
The tyranny of poverty	341
The Tyranny of War	**354**
The tyranny of the draft	367
The rise of China	380
Don't tread on me	389
The Tyranny of the Media	**395**
The Tyranny of Public Education	**419**
Re-awakening the American Spirit	**423**
What is to be done?	427
Saving the republic	432

THE TYRANNY OF THE FEDERAL RESERVE

Introduction

God has blessed America. We Americans are a blessed people. We are truly fortunate to live here.

Of all nations, the United States of America occupies the most favorable portion of the planet. We call the best part of the North American continent our home.

No other nation is situated on such a large and variegated landmass that overflows with such an abundance of resources. No other nation has such variety and beauty—from the autumn foliage of the New England woodlands; the pines, Spanish moss, wetlands and warm coastal waters of the South; the fertile Heartland; the prairies and amber waves of grain of the Great Plains; the colored deserts of the Southwest; the purple mountain majesties of the Rockies; the golden California coast; the misty mountains of the Pacific Northwest; our vast and untamed Alaskan frontier; and, of course, the tropical paradise of Hawaii. From sea to shining sea, God has truly shed his grace on us.

The continent is ours. More so than any other people, we are blessed to call such a large and bountiful land our home.

Our Founders recognized long ago that the United States is situated in a very geographically advantageous position on the globe.

In the early days of the Republic, control of the continent was disputed with the American Indian nations and the great empires of Europe. The dispute was decided in our favor. The continent was conquered and today our advantageous position could not be more favorable.

No other nation is so easily defended. With Canada to our north and Mexico to our south, we border two nations that do not rival us either economically, militarily or in population. We have had friendly relations with both nations for more than a century.

To our east is the Atlantic Ocean and to our west is the

Pacific, separating us by vast distances from any potential enemy.

When our situation is compared to the other great nations—China, Russia and India—our advantages become obvious. Those nations have long borders that are often in dispute, even with each other.

And when we look to Europe, a continent that has seen so much bloodshed and destruction over the centuries, it too is bordered on its east, southeast and south by rivals that could someday overrun it.

From a strategic standpoint, the United States can be easily defended at a fraction of the cost the other great powers must expend for their own security.

Not only are we blessed by geography, but also by our history and the rich tradition that has been passed down to us. In the Colonial Era, the first American colonists were reliant upon no one but themselves. They hacked their way through the wilderness and built their homes and farms with their own hands and defended themselves in a hostile land. The vastness and the abundance of the land offered pioneers and adventurers the opportunity to better themselves through personal initiative and through their own hard work. The fire of self-reliance burned brightly inside them. Because of this heritage, we Americans have long valued our liberty and our independence, both as a nation and as individuals.

The circumstances of their time caused them to value self-rule, liberty and independence. When the tyranny of their English king infringed on their liberty and became too heavy a burden to bear, they united and rebelled against him.

They declared their independence. They declared to the world their unalienable rights to life, liberty and the pursuit of happiness. They fought to the death to secure those rights. Their rebellion against a tyrannical king was hard fought against overwhelming odds and was ultimately successful. The rebellious colonists won their independence and created a new form of government that was designed to derive its power from the consent of the governed. This government was organized under a separation of powers with checks and balances designed to protect the rights and liberty of the American people. This system was made the law of the land when the U.S. Constitution was ratified in 1789. Its results were startling and far-reaching. America began to quickly grow into the most prosperous and powerful nation in all human history.

In the two centuries after the founding, the American Republic expanded across the continent and advanced to become one of the greatest and most remarkable civilizations ever to exist on Earth.

We Americans are truly a blessed people. We are fortunate to be alive now at the height of our American civilization. We have inherited a grand legacy.

But there is a sense across this land that something is wrong—that our country is changing, and not for the better. There is a sense that all is not well in the United States. As we look around us, many are feeling an uneasiness, as if something is being lost—we feel the rot that has set in. We see around us the corruption, we feel the decline and smell the decay that is advancing on us and affecting our daily lives. Our old values and way of life seem to be slipping away as new alien values and a new diminished way of life take hold. Forces that are mysterious and beyond our control seem to be determining the course of events and making changes that are altering our nation beyond recognition from the old America we knew and loved.

Yes, we Americans are still a blessed people and we are fortunate to live in a prosperous nation founded on great principles. But, unfortunately, we Americans have been cursed with a monetary system that was purposefully designed to siphon off the wealth of our nation and concentrate it into the grasping hands of a small number of usurers and speculators. This monetary system was put in place a century ago under false pretenses. Its architects made grand promises that their system would end the cycle of booms and busts that had been plaguing American families, farms and businesses. They designed a system that appeared to be aligned with American values, but this was a deception. The Federal Reserve Act of 1913 was a rejection of American values. It put in place a system that was unaccountable to the people, without checks and balances, and which concentrated power into the hands of a few who were given the authority to make decisions in secrecy that affect the lives of all of us. This system was purposefully designed to operate without the consent of the governed.

The entire rationale for why our current monetary system was put in place was to protect the American people from the bank panics that periodically afflicted the nation and caused widespread chaos and misery.

One hundred years after the passage of the Federal Reserve Act, by any objective measure, the Federal Reserve has failed to protect us from the very thing its architects told us it was designed to prevent. Only five years after the passage of the act, the United States was struck by a severe depression when World War I came to a close. Sixteen years after the passage of the act, our nation suffered the most devastating and catastrophic depression in our history—the Great Depression. Since the founding of the Federal Reserve, we have lurched from economic boom to bust at regular intervals. These booms and busts have been just as chaotic and have caused just as much misery for the American people as they did prior to the founding of the Federal Reserve. One economic crisis has followed another. The past 20 years have seen us lurch from bust to boom to bust over and over again. Since the crash of 2007, we have seen working Americans lose ground while a handful of rich people grows ever richer. The rich have never been richer. The wealth gap in 2015 between the rich and the poor is greater than any time in our history, greater than during the Gilded Age or the Roaring Twenties. A small group of rich people is monopolizing the wealth of our nation like no other time in the history of the Republic.

Since the founding of the Federal Reserve, we have seen our industries that had been built up over generations flee from our shores. We've watched the greatest middle class in the history of the world collapse around us as more and more of us struggle to maintain the same level of prosperity as the generations that came before us. We've seen the prosperity of the American nation concentrated more and more into the grasping, rent-seeking, interest-collecting hands of a transnational elite that we share little in common with in outlook or in lifestyle.

Since the founding of the Federal Reserve, our nation has been drawn into overseas wars, one after the other, again and again, which have taken the lives of hundreds of thousands of American citizens whose blood has been spilled on foreign soil. After all these wars, we still do not have peace. Our media alarms us day in and day out about enemies on the other side of the planet who seek to do us harm.

Since the founding of the Federal Reserve, we have gone from being a creditor nation into becoming the biggest debtor nation in the history world. Our nation is being buried under a national debt that increases exponentially year upon year and which can never be paid back. Before the founding of the Federal Reserve, we had no income tax. Now our tax burden grows heavier and heavier as our debt burden expands. Our government taxes our wages to pay back huge debts owed to banks and foreign nations.

And now, 239 years after the Founders of this nation took up arms and declared their independence from a tyrannical king, our government, which was designed to serve us, is spying on our every move, collecting and storing information on us, attempting to do the very things that the American colonists rebelled against.

As an American citizen, surely you must feel that something is wrong, that we have lost our way as a nation and as a people. But what is the cause of our misfortunes? You will not find the answers from our political leaders, our media or our academics. They have been corrupted and are servants of the very system that was put in place a century ago.

In 1912 during the height of the debate about monetary policy in the United States before the Federal Reserve Act was passed, a Midwestern attorney named Alfred Owen Crozier published a book titled *U.S. Money vs. Corporation Currency*. In his book, Crozier suggested that the Panic of 1907, which had caused such fear and misery, had been engineered by Wall Street bankers to scare the government and the people into accepting the monetary reforms that the bankers craved. The bankers had a plan, called the Aldrich Plan named after its backer Senator Nelson Aldrich, to create a central bank that they said would put a stop to crises like the Panic of 1907. But Crozier called the Aldrich Plan a "money trust" that would give Wall Street control of the bank reserves of the American people. He warned us that Wall Street bankers were attempting to seize control of the American money supply for private profit and power, and if they were successful, no good would come of it for American workers, farmers and small businessmen.

Crozier warned that if the bankers were successful, the United States government would be corrupted and our economy would fall under the control of the corporations that would spring up around Wall Street's central bank. Crozier warned us that our government would become subservient to Wall Street banks and their corporations.

Crozier wrote that if Wall Street got its way, "Then we shall have only corporate currency, and a government of the corporations, by the corporations and for the corporations—a 'soulless' corporate republic."

What Crozier advocated for was a "U.S. Monetary Council" created by an amendment to the Constitution. The council he envisioned consisted of 75 members. The Chief Justice of the Supreme Court, Vice-President, Speaker of the House, Secretary of the Treasury, Secretary of Commerce and Labor (the Secretary of Commerce and Labor was a single person in 1912) would serve as members. Twenty-two members would be appointed with the advice and consent of the Senate. The governor or vote of the people would nominate one member from each of the states (there were 48 states in Crozier's day). All would then be appointed to the council by the president. Each member would serve a term of four years with the appointed members so arranged that one-half of those nominated by the states and one-half of those confirmed by the Senate would go out of office each two years, the president in the same manner appointing their successors and filling any vacancies. Each member could be impeached for cause. A majority vote of the people of any state could recall and replace their representative on the council. This Monetary Council would be responsible for regulating the American money supply.

Crozier wanted every dollar of the currency guaranteed by the government, redeemable in gold, backed by an adequate gold reserve and always kept equal in value with gold, "and so made sound."

His Monetary Council was intended to be a public institution, not a private corporation. Forty-eight of its representatives would serve each of the 48 states of his day with the rest representing the federal government. He wanted his council to have the power to regulate the banking system, fix the general discount rate, and issue and determine the volume of the public currency, under strict regulations and legal safeguards. His vision was to have a council that would establish and maintain a "square deal" between the banks and the public.

His hope was that his plan would insure against politics or partisanship in monetary policy because both parties would have members serving that could block by publicity any attempt to improperly use the powers of the council. He imagined his council would guard against Wall Street influences and instead create monetary policy to serve the interests of the public, commerce and the nation at large.

In the Crozier plan, every state had representation, and thus Crozier imagined his council would establish a sound, stable, permanent and elastic system of banking and currency adapted to the changing needs of the country. The council would protect the country and commerce from the panics and evils of excessive currency and credit inflations and contractions.

While perhaps Crozier's plan for monetary reform was not perfect, what he envisioned was a government body created under American principles—separation of powers, checks and balances and accountability to the people.

Unfortunately, the monetary reform we got in 1913 under the Federal Reserve Act was in no way, shape or form designed using American principles. Quite the opposite. The system we got is not subject to a separation of powers, or checks and balances, and it is in no way accountable to the people. The system we got was designed to act independently from the will of the people and of our representatives in Congress. Policy was not intended to be made transparently but in secret behind closed doors. Accountability was not to the American people but to Wall Street banks.

The system we have today was the one Crozier warned us against—a corporate monetary system controlled by private bankers, designed not to serve American citizens, but to fleece us.

The origins of the Federal Reserve System were unknown to all but a few Americans until recently when writers, journalists and members of the Fed began openly discussing the institution's secretive inception. After the Panic of 1907, Congress formed the National Monetary Commission to search for solutions that would avoid another banking collapse. Senator Nelson Aldrich was a founding member of this council, which he took on a trip to Europe to study the central banks there.

Aldrich had deep ties to the New York banking clique. He was a personal friend of J.P. Morgan, and Aldrich's daughter was married to John D. Rockefeller Jr.

Upon his return from Europe, Aldrich organized a meeting at the exclusive Jekyll Island Club on the Georgia coast. In November of 1910, a group of men all with ties to Wall Street banks arrived at Jekyll Island wearing disguises to keep the press from knowing who they were.

The men Aldrich assembled at Jekyll Island were Abram Piatt Andrew, assistant secretary of the Treasury; Henry P. Davison, a J.P Morgan senior partner; Charles D. Norton, president of J.P. Morgan's First National Bank of New York; Benjamin Strong, a close Morgan friend and vice president of Bankers Trust Co.; Frank A. Vanderlip, president of National City

Bank; and the German citizen Paul M. Warburg, a partner in Kuhn, Loeb & Co.

In a February 12, 2012 article in *Bloomberg News*, Gregory D.L. Morris described the meeting. "Of course, the Jekyll Island conference, which met that month, was dodgy even by the standards of the Gilded Age: a self-selected handful of plutocrats secretly meeting at a private resort island to draw up a new framework for the nation's banking system," Morris wrote. "The Jekyll Island collaborators knew that public reports of their meeting would scupper their plans. The idea of senior officials from the Treasury, Congress, major banks and brokerages (along with one foreign national) slipping off to design a new world order has struck generations of Americans as distasteful at best and undemocratic at worst—and would have been similarly received at the time. So the meeting of the minds was planned under the ruse of a gentlemen's duck-hunting expedition."

These men knew that a populist spirit of reform was in the air. The American people wanted change. They wanted something done about the booms and busts and bank failures that had been plaguing the country.

The men at Jekyll Island wanted a central bank along the lines of the Bank of England and the other central banks of Europe. But Americans had long distrusted central banks. Three times before a central bank had been set up in the United States, and three times before they were shut down. Allegations were made that these central banks were engaged in fraud and corruption, that they concentrated wealth and power into the hands of their shareholders, that they were servants of plutocrats and foreign financiers. The Bank of North America, the First Bank of the United States and the Second Bank of the United States had each been formed and later shut down.

President Andrew Jackson famously clashed with the Second Bank of the United States in what was called the Bank War. "The Bank, Mr. Van Buren, is trying to kill me, but I shall kill it," Jackson wrote to his former Secretary of State.

Jackson won the Bank War and in 1836 ended the charter

of the Second Bank of the United States. He killed the bank.

Seventy-four years later the bankers were once again making their move to seize control of the issuance and volume of the American money supply.

They devised the Aldrich Plan, which placed the money supply under the control of the largest Wall Street banks, but they had to appease populist sentiment, so they made their monetary reform appear decentralized and under government oversight.

Their system placed 12 Federal Reserve Banks in regions distributed across the country—in San Francisco, Atlanta, Richmond, Chicago, Dallas, Philadelphia, Cleveland, Boston, Kansas City, St. Louis, Minneapolis and New York. The 12 banks were organized as private corporations with board members selected by private banks that own stock in the regional Federal Reserve Banks. The Federal Reserve Bank shareholders earn a guaranteed 6 percent dividend on their stock. Even foreign-owned bank branches in the regions can be member banks.

These 12 Federal Reserve Banks control the money supply in their regions. They increase or contract the amount of money their member banks have available to them for lending to businesses, governments and the public. They are wholly owned and operated by private bankers. And, with New York being home to Wall Street and the world's largest banks, the Federal Reserve Bank of New York is far and away the most powerful of the Federal Reserve's regional banks. The amount of assets it controls dwarfs that of the other regional banks. The Federal Reserve Bank of New York is the nexus of power over the American money supply.

There is no starker example of the fact that the 12 regional banks are privately run corporations than the fact that the banker Jamie Dimon was serving on the board of the Federal Reserve Bank of New York during the 2007 financial crisis while also serving as the president, chairman and chief executive officer of JPMorgan Chase, Wall Street's largest bank. While Dimon was serving on the board of the Federal Reserve Bank of New York, JPMorgan Chase received more than $390 million in emergency loans from the Federal Reserve.

How did the Federal Reserve Act, which gave private bankers control over our money supply, get passed by Congress? To get it passed, the men at Jekyll Island had to give their system the appearance of government control.

They put the regional banks under the oversight of the Federal Reserve Board of Governors in Washington, D.C. The Board of Governors sets monetary policies and oversees the regional banks.

Members of the Board of Governors are appointed by the President of the United States and approved by the Senate. By having the president and the Senate appoint the Board, the men of Jekyll Island gave the Federal Reserve System the appearance of being a government institution that is controlled by elected representatives of the American people.

But the goal of the bankers was for the Federal Reserve System to operate independently from the will of the people and from elected politicians who might be influenced by public pressure. The architects of the Federal Reserve designed the system so that monetary policy decisions would not be approved by the president or anyone else in the executive or legislative branches of government. The Federal Reserve does not receive funding appropriated by Congress, and the terms of the members of the Board of Governors span multiple presidential and congressional terms.

The only power elected officials have over the Federal Reserve System is the power to select the seven members of the Board of Governors every 14 years in staggered terms.

The Chairman of the Board can be called before congressional committees and asked questions, which he or she can answer or not; but otherwise, the members of the Board have a free hand to make decisions that affect the lives of hundreds of millions of people without oversight by anyone.

In 2007 on PBS's News Hour, Alan Greenspan, who served as Fed Chairman from 1987 to 2006, clarified the relationship between the government and the Fed. "Well, first of all, the Federal Reserve is an independent agency, and that means, basically, that there is no other agency of government which can overrule actions that we take."

Basically, the Fed can operate freely, without transparency nor accountability. No one can overrule its actions.

How does the president choose whom to appoint to the Board of Governors? As recent history shows, the bankers give a list of a few of their own for the president to choose from. These people are always insiders, people who have spent their whole lives connected to high finance as Wall Street investment bankers or as economists who have spent their careers promoting the interests of high finance.

The argument given in 1913, and which you can still read in the opinion pages of newspapers today, is that the Fed must remain independent of congressional influence so that its financial decisions are not influenced by partisan politics. The bankers do not want Congress meddling in their affairs. Their argument was that monetary decisions must be made on sound economics and should not be subordinate to members of Congress who are up for election every two years. The bankers insist that monetary policy must be free from the interests and concerns of representatives elected by the American people.

The bankers would have us believe that bankers who sit on the boards of the Federal Reserve Banks are somehow benevolent economists who put monetary policy above self-interest, and that if their decisions were not made in private and instead were made transparent and open, it would hinder their ability to make sound monetary decisions. These arguments for secrecy and for lack of democratic control go against every principle this country was founded on.

Article I, Section 8, Clause 5 of the U.S. Constitution, called the Coinage Clause, states, "The Congress shall have Power To...coin Money, regulate the Value thereof, and of foreign Coin..."

The Constitution makes Congress the body that regulates the money supply, not private bankers or the executive branch. By passing the Federal Reserve Act, Congress delegated away its constitutional authority to private bankers while giving the executive branch the power to appoint members to the Federal Reserve Board. Congress neutered itself of its constitutional responsibility to regulate our money.

Many people today believe that monetary policy is too important a matter to be left in the hands of elected congressmen. But if monetary decisions are too important to be left to our elected representatives, what about other important decisions, such as the decision to go to war? Isn't going to war just as important as deciding what interest rates should be? Under the logic of the bankers, we should create a board to decide when we go to war, and not leave this important decision to our elected representatives. Following the example of the Fed, a War Board could be created made up of members chosen by the top companies in the military-industrial complex. This War Board should be given the decision to take the country to war in secret and without oversight and without meddling from people worried about electoral cycles. Of course, following the Fed's example, it would never be called a War Board. It would be called the National Peace Board or the Federal Defense Board or some other Orwellian euphemism.

Under the Fed's logic, why should any important decision at all be left to Congress?

Isn't the whole point of the electoral cycle to make our representatives accountable to the public—so that we can throw them out of office and replace them if they are making decisions that are adversely affecting our lives?

Congress was designed by the Founders to represent the interests of the states and of the American people at large. Before the 17th Amendment was ratified in 1913, senators were appointed by state legislatures to represent in the federal government the interests of the states. Congress members in the House of Representatives then and now are directly elected by the people in their districts to give we the people our most direct voice in the federal government.

Congress represents us, for better or worse. It is the voice of the people and of the states in the federal government, yet it is often maligned in our media, while the executive branch amasses more and more power. The Founders knew that war and monarchical tyranny were most likely to manifest themselves in the executive branch, so they gave Congress the power to declare war, write laws, control the monetary system and the budget, and to serve as a check and a balance over the actions of the president.

Under the current monetary system, when monetary policy set by the Fed results in economic hardship for the American people, we use the power of the ballot box to throw the bums out of Congress and throw the bum out of the White House; but the bums who set the monetary policy remain entrenched at the Fed safe from the electorate, free from blame, and free from the threat of losing their jobs. There is no accountability for their actions.

It is Congress that created the Fed and it is in Congress where the Fed's biggest critics speak out against it today. Congress, impelled by the will of the people, has the power to kill the Fed. The bankers and the owners of the media know this. A strong anti-Congress propaganda effort has been at work to turn the people against any congressional action that would weaken the Fed's power. In a February 3, 2015 article in *USA Today,* business columnist Darrell Delamaide wrote that an audit of the Fed by Congress would result in legislators manipulating policy for politically expedient goals, which he said would be detrimental to the economy.

"We really don't want the posturing blowhards who have brought us government shutdowns, mindless cuts in government services and six years of legislative gridlock in charge of managing our money," Delamaide wrote. Delamaide does not want elected representatives of the people taking a look at the Fed's books. He prefers that unelected bankers be allowed to continue making decisions behind closed doors, manipulating policy without democratic controls.

But obviously, the Fed's actions have clearly been detrimental to the economy and to the well-being of the majority of the American people. The Fed was sold to the public and the

Congress under the logic that it would stop economic crises, like the Panic of 1907, yet today we still have economic crises that are every bit as damaging as the Panic of 1907.

The designers of the Fed were clever. They understood that money is power. They understood that whoever controls the creation and volume of money in a country would be seizing the reins of power. But they also understood the character of the American people and knew that they had to create a system that gave the appearance of serving our interests and being under our control. They disguised their system just enough to fool the public into believing that the Federal Reserve is not a central bank like those found in Europe.

What our Founders understood was that power corrupts and absolute power corrupts absolutely. They designed our government with checks and balances and made it decentralized with power shared by our municipalities, states and the federal government—each with its own areas of responsibility. They did not want power concentrated in any one branch or region.

Money is power. The Federal Reserve has the ability to create money out of thin air behind closed doors without oversight and without checks and balances. Imagine having this power. Imagine sitting at a computer behind closed doors and secretly creating as much money as you like, say a trillion dollars, and then wiring it anywhere in the world with no one being the wiser.

On November 4, 2010, a collection of Federal Reserve officials, bankers and economists convened at Jekyll Island to commemorate the 100-year anniversary of the secret meeting that resulted in the creation of the Federal Reserve. According to a November 8, 2010 article in *Bloomberg News* by Scott Lanman, attendees checked in at the Jekyll Island Club Hotel's Federal Reserve Room. The room was adorned with portraits of the "Six Men From the Elite of the Banking and Financial World" who 100 years prior had avoided reporters, retreated to the isolated resort and devised a plan for an American central bank.

The commemoration, which included a four-day

conference on the past, present and future of monetary policy, was held on an indoor tennis court turned into a banquet hall named after J.P. Morgan. Attendees included Fed Chairman of the day, Ben Bernanke, former Fed Chairman Alan Greenspan and several governors from the various Federal Reserve Banks. Former Fed Chair Paul Volcker did not attend but addressed the assembled luminaries through a videotaped message.

Much of the discussion at the 2010 Jekyll Island conference was about economic crises, such as the Great Depression, the runaway inflation of the 1970s, the 1990-91 recession, and the deep recession of 2007, which the Fed was still struggling to cope with when the conference was being held.

Just think that over for a moment. The rationale for founding the Federal Reserve was to put a stop to economic crises, such as the Panic of 1907. One hundred years after the blueprints for the Fed were drawn up at Jekyll Island, Federal Reserve officials were on the island conducting panel discussions about economic crises since the founding of the Fed that were far worse than the Panic of 1907. These men were commemorating the foundation of an institution that had totally failed to achieve the stated objective of providing us with a safer, more stable monetary and financial system.

Depression, recession, booms and busts. This has been the economic history of our nation since the founding of the Fed. We have watched as the rich have gotten far richer than at any point in our history while the middle class barely treads water and the ranks of the poor continue to grow.

Back in 1912, Crozier warned us that nothing good would come from the creation of a new central bank in the United States. Since the time of Crozier's writing, in each generation critics of the Fed have spoken out. But the Fed's defenders in the media have drowned out and ridiculed their voices. However, today, like never before, due to the Internet and the ready accessibility of information, more and more people are figuring out that there is a man behind the curtain pulling the levers of credit, not for the benefit of the American people, but to enrich and empower a small clique of usurers and speculators who do not have the best interests of this nation in mind.

Alfred Crozier warned us in 1912 that if we turned over control of the money supply to private bankers, it would corrupt our government and threaten our sovereignty and our prosperity.

Have his warnings not come to pass? Has our government not been corrupted? Is our sovereignty and our Constitution not being undermined? Is our prosperity not being taken from us and hoarded by a small clique of insiders? All those things the American revolutionaries fought for—liberty, freedom, justice, independence—are they not being lost?

We Americans are still a fortunate people. We still live in a prosperous nation. We still have the ability to speak out and organize. We come from a great nation with people who follow a proud tradition of standing up against tyranny and fighting for justice, freedom and liberty. The Spirit of 1776 still lives inside us.

But today our great nation has fallen into a sorry state. We are fighting undeclared foreign wars around the world. Tens of millions of our citizens are unemployed. Our great and modern economy is being deindustrialized and made dependent on the economic production of foreign nations. The prosperity of the American people is in decline. A police and surveillance state is being erected around us. We are being buried under a massive debt that has been promised to be paid to bankers and foreign governments through the confiscation of the wages of working Americans. Our culture is in decline and is growing increasingly morally bankrupt. Our rights to privacy under the Fourth Amendment are now lost as intelligence agencies and corporations have taken a free hand to spy on us and watch our every move. Our borders are wide open and our sovereignty has been eroded with each trade treaty that our government passes. The attacks on our Constitution and our traditions by the corporate media, academia and our politicians continue relentlessly.

In 1834, President Andrew Jackson allegedly stood before a group of Philadelphia bankers and spoke his mind about the

Fed of his day, the Second Bank of the United States.

"Gentlemen!" Jackson said. "I too have been a close observer of the doings of the Bank of the United States. I have had men watching you for a long time, and am convinced that you have used the funds of the bank to speculate in the breadstuffs of the country. When you won, you divided the profits amongst you, and when you lost, you charged it to the bank. You tell me that if I take the deposits from the bank and annul its charter I shall ruin ten thousand families. That may be true, gentlemen, but that is your sin! Should I let you go on, you will ruin fifty thousand families, and that would be my sin! You are a den of vipers and thieves. I have determined to rout you out, and by the eternal God, I will rout you out!"

Jackson routed them out, killed the bank and paid off the national debt. However, he did not go far enough. The fractional reserve banking system that had enriched and empowered the bankers was left in place.

The bankers were patient. They waited and plotted until the time was right. Seventy-seven years later, a new central bank, the Fed, arose from Jekyll Island, stronger, more pervasive, and better disguised from the public.

From any objective point of view, the Fed has utterly failed to fulfill the reasons for its founding. It has been a disaster for the American people. But it has been a smashing success for the small clique of people it serves. The big bankers who are its beneficiaries are richer and more powerful than ever.

In his monumental historical work *Tragedy and Hope*, Georgetown historian Carroll Quigley stated that great civilizations pass through a process of evolution that begins with a slow start, followed by an Age of Expansion, then an Age of Crisis, followed by an Age of Universal Empire. It is in the Age of Universal Empire that civilizations grow corrupt.

"Racked by internal struggles of a social and constitutional character, weakened by loss of faith in its older ideologies and by the challenge of newer ideas incompatible with its past nature, the civilization grows steadily weaker until it is submerged by outside enemies, and eventually disappears," Quigley wrote.

However, Quigley also wrote that Western Civilization has been able to reform and reorganize itself, allowing for expansion to begin anew. Quigley wrote that Western Civilization is in the Age of Universal Empire with the United States being the seat of power. Quigley saw two possibilities for the future of Western Civilization: reorganization, or decay followed by invasion and the end of our civilization.

The United States grew into a great power because of our favorable geography, our government that ensured our liberties and unlocked the great potential of the human spirit, and our free enterprise system which made us prosperous.

We were fortunate that such a brilliant collection of people came together and wrote the U.S. Constitution which organized our government in such an exceptional way—under a combination of pragmatism, realism and principle which allowed our nation to grow freer and wealthier with each new generation.

The republican system of government and our free enterprise system made us into a great nation—a nation that promised its citizens freedom and the opportunity to pursue their dreams however they saw fit.

But, unfortunately, the Founders were not as successful in organizing our monetary system, which has fallen into the hands of private bankers. These bankers have shaped our monetary system to favor usurers and speculators over people who perform the productive work of providing goods and services for the American people. The monetary system we have today is designed to enrich usurers and speculators at the expense of working Americans. This system was specifically designed to place the American people and the nation at large in debt to private bankers who have grown rich off the collection of interest that compounds and grows year after year, decade after decade. This monetary system has corrupted our government and the free enterprise system, where today more than two centuries after the Declaration of Independence, we are facing economic decay, invasion, and possibly the end of our American civilization for all time.

Our nation was born in rebellion when Americans decided enough was enough and declared their independence from a tyrannical king. In 1776, Tom Paine captured the spirit of the day when he released an incendiary pamphlet, entitled *Common Sense*, which pointed out the ridiculousness of being ruled by a hereditary monarchy.

"Men who look upon themselves born to reign, and others to obey, soon grow insolent; selected from the rest of mankind their minds are early poisoned by importance; and the world they act in differs so materially from the world at large, that they have but little opportunity of knowing its true interests, and when they succeed to the government are frequently the most ignorant and unfit of any throughout the dominions," Paine wrote.

If Paine were alive today, he would undoubtedly turn his pen against our current rulers who have grown every bit as corrupt and are every bit as unfit to rule as any monarch of the 18th century. Today, we are ruled by Wall Street bankers—usurers and speculators who have empowered themselves and enriched themselves through control of our monetary system. This system has enabled them to create money from nothing and charge interest for it. They have grown insolent and their minds are poisoned by importance as they siphon off the prosperity of the American people and lead us down the road to ruin.

America is a great nation with a great heritage and great traditions. America is a nation worth saving. To save her, we must reorganize and reform our monetary system so that it is not controlled by private bankers to serve their interests, but instead put under democratic controls and under American principles so that the system serves our interests.

Power in the United States today is concentrated in the Federal Reserve Bank. Today is the time for action to be taken against the bank—to fully audit it, arrest anyone involved in malfeasance, shut it down and put in place a new monetary system that is not controlled by a small clique of international financiers and shareholders of multinational corporations.

But before any action is taken, an understanding of our current predicament is necessary. To understand our misfortunes, first we must let the scales fall from our eyes and look back and understand how we got here.

Ben Franklin's Money

The American Colonial Era began on May 14, 1607, when English colonists founded Jamestown in Virginia. After the founding of Jamestown, more English settlers made the voyage to the Eastern seaboard of the North American continent where they built forts, farms, plantations and towns up and down the coast. These English settlers arrived seeking adventure, wealth, religious freedom, or just the chance to escape the crushing poverty of the Mother Country. Despite extreme hardships, their civilization took hold in the New World. The English settlements grew rapidly, forming into 13 American colonies under the rule of a distant English king and parliament.

The Colonial Era began with adversity and deprivation. Death always lurked; from starvation, disease, physical violence and massacre. Numerous wars against Indian tribes and rival European colonial powers occurred regularly. Raids on settlements and piracy also occurred with regularity. Slavery was widespread and a common fact of life, both in the form of European indentured servitude and race-based African slavery. Ignorance and superstition ruled the minds of many.

But the Colonial Era was also a time of great hope. Land was plentiful for the taking and resources were abundant. For those who were ambitious, intrepid enough to strike out into the wilderness in the face of danger, and willing to work, America was a land of great opportunity. America was far away from the oppressive class structure of England. A poor man in England could immigrate to the colonies, strike out on his own and become a landowner just like the gentry of Europe.

By the time Ben Franklin was born in Boston on January 17, 1706, the American Colonies were thriving. Tobacco, wheat, lumber, ships, horses, beef and pork were produced in large quantities. The towns, cities and the population were growing. Boston at the time was the biggest town in the colonies with around 9,000 inhabitants. The population of all the American colonies was about 330,000. The majority, like Franklin, had been born in the colonies. Many could trace their roots in America back at least two generations.

During the Colonial Era, gold and silver coins were used as money. But since the colonies produced no gold and silver, coins were scarce and hard to come by. American colonists traded with the Spanish and Portuguese colonies for the gold and silver coins that they then used as money back home. Americans used the coins to purchase imported manufactured goods from England and Europe. Since the colonists produced no manufactured goods themselves, the colonies ran a persistent trade deficit with England. Gold and silver coins were paid into the hands of English merchants and sent back to England. This caused a scarcity of gold and silver coins for use in commerce in the colonies.

Because coins were in short supply, the colonists often used other items as money, such as wampum, tobacco leaves and beaver pelts. Paper money was first used in 1690.

In a paper called *Creating Maryland's Paper Money Economy,* University of Delaware economics professor Farley Grubb reviewed the history of paper money in the colonies. Massachusetts was the first colony to issue paper money. The colony first issued paper money in 1690 as an emergency war measure during King William's War of 1688-1697.

This type of paper money issued by colonial assemblies became known as colonial scrip.

South Carolina began issuing colonial scrip in 1703. New York and New Jersey issued scrip in 1709, Rhode Island in 1710, North Carolina in 1712, Pennsylvania in 1723, Maryland in 1733, and Virginia and Georgia in 1755.

The paper currencies were issued in almost all cases as emergency wartime measures to pay for troops and materiel. Only Pennsylvania and Maryland issued their scrip in peacetime without the urgency of war as a primary motivator. The colonial governments issued paper money to pay debts. The colonists then used the money to pay taxes to the colonial governments.

The colonial period was a remarkable time of monetary experimentation. The different forms of currency in circulation at the time were used with varying degrees of success. Some of the paper currencies issued by the colonies facilitated commerce and economic growth, while others had disastrous effects. Massachusetts and Pennsylvania experienced economic benefits while the Carolinas and some of the New England colonies experienced inflation and depreciation of their currencies.

In 1723, Ben Franklin, as a young man, moved to Philadelphia to learn his trade as a printer. Upon arrival in Philadelphia, he observed that the city was experiencing economic stagnation and decline due to a lack of money. Gold and silver coins obtained through trade with the Spanish and Portuguese were the currency of the day, but the colonists had traded away all their gold and silver for European goods. The lack of currency meant that the colonists had to resort to barter, which was costly, inefficient and discouraged economic activity.

In the same year that Franklin moved to Philadelphia, the Pennsylvania legislature issued its first paper currency. Colonists borrowed the paper money from the government legislature using their land as collateral for the loans. The fact that the loans were backed by land and the scrip was needed to pay back the loans to the government gave the paper money real value. The colonists borrowed the money and spent it on improving their properties. Once the currency entered into circulation, it was used as a medium of exchange for internal commerce, replacing gold and silver coins. Franklin observed that with the printing of this money, the economic malaise ended and Philadelphia entered into a period of economic growth and prosperity.

Franklin had a deep understanding of paper money. After all, he was the printer who printed out much of it. Over the course of his life, he wrote several pamphlets, essays and letters extolling the benefits of paper money and analyzing its effects.

In 1729, he wrote the essay *A Modest Enquiry into the Nature and Necessity of Paper Currency*. The essay was written in support of

Pennsylvania's issuance of colonial scrip and advocated for additional issuances.

In the essay, Franklin stated that when money is scarce it raises the cost of borrowing and depresses economic activity. Because money is scarce, rich people can earn a greater gain on their money through usury and the charging of high interest rates. When money is plentiful, instead of usury, rich people earn greater returns by investing their money in trade and in improving the productivity of their lands, which causes an increase in economic growth and rising employment. The trick is finding the right balance between issuing too much money, which leads to price inflation, currency devaluation and economic ruin; and issuing too little, which leads to usurious interest rates, deflation and depression.

"There is a certain proportionate Quantity of Money requisite to carry on the Trade of a Country freely and currently; More than which would be of no Advantage in Trade, and Less, if much less, exceedingly detrimental to it," Franklin wrote.

In the second half of the 18th century, the British began to take measures to restrict the use of paper money in the colonies. British merchants wanted gold from the colonies and the British government wanted taxes to pay for the expenses accrued from defending the colonies during the Seven Years' War. The British Parliament passed the Currency Acts of 1751, 1764, and 1773, that regulated and restricted the use of colonial paper money. The acts forced the colonies into debt to London banks. Some historians believe that the Currency Acts, which contracted the money supply and resulted in a depressed economy in the colonies, were the primary cause of the discontent that led to the rebellion against the Crown.

In his essay *Scheme for Supplying the Colonies with a Paper Currency,* written in 1765, Franklin attempted to come up with a plan that would provide the British government with revenue from the colonies without sparking a rebellion. The British Parliament was about to enact the hated Stamp Act and Franklin hoped his plan would provide an alternative to the act that would appease both the British and their American subjects. His scheme was based on Pennsylvania's successful experiment with paper money. Franklin's plan was to set up loan offices throughout the colonies. The loan offices were to be run by elected officials. These offices would print paper currency that could be borrowed by the colonists using land and property as collateral. The loan offices would collect interest on the loans of 5 percent, which would replace taxes. The paper money would provide the Crown with revenue from the colonies while providing the colonists with a plentiful medium of exchange for the purpose of internal trade. This would free up gold and silver needed for internal commerce which instead could be used to pay British merchants for imported goods.

"It will operate as a general Tax on the Colonies," Franklin wrote, "and yet not an unpleasing one; as he who actually pays the Interest has an Equivalent or more in the use of the principal. But the tax, if it can be so called, will, in effect, spread itself more equally on all property, perhaps more so than any other tax that can be invented; since every one who has the money in his hands, does from the time he receives it, to the time he pays it away, virtually pay the interest of it, the first borrower having received the value of it (to use for his own profit) when he parted first with the original sum. Thus the rich who handle most money, would in reality pay most of the tax."

However, Franklin's paper money scheme was not adopted.

In 1766, an exchange between Franklin and members of the House of Commons was published in London and was reprinted back in the colonies. In the exchange, British parliamentarians questioned Franklin about the causes of the rising discontent in the colonies.

Franklin told the members of the House that prior to 1763, the American colonists looked at Great Britain with respect and affection and had been loyal subjects of the Crown. But the colonists had suffered great hardships, both in lives and money, during the Seven Years' War, which he said was not fought for the benefit of Americans but for the imperial ambitions of the

Crown.

Franklin was asked what had caused the affection and respect for Britain and Parliament to greatly lessen since 1763. "To a concurrence of causes," Franklin answered, "the restraints lately laid on their trade, by which the bringing of foreign gold and silver into the Colonies was prevented; the prohibition of making paper money among themselves, and then demanding a new and heavy tax by stamps; taking away, at the same time, trials by juries, and refusing to receive and hear their humble petitions."

Britain had borrowed heavily from bankers to pay for its expenditures during the Seven Years' War. Parliament was attempting to pay its debts from the war by levying internal taxes on the colonies. Franklin said the colonists agreed that external taxes, such as duties on imports, were lawful; but internal taxes had to be passed by the colonial assemblies. The levying of internal taxes in the colonies by Parliament amounted to taxation without representation. Franklin was asked about the Stamp Act, which was a tax on nearly all printed material in the colonies, everything from playing cards to mortgages to newspapers. The act caused nearly all economic activity in the colonies that required documentation to be taxed. Franklin told Parliament that the colonists would never submit to the Stamp Act.

Franklin's warnings to Parliament were ignored, especially about the hated Stamp Tax. The tax went into effect causing the American public to turn against the Mother Country. The tax caused the colonists to begin organizing against the Crown. Soon the Colonies were in open rebellion.

In April 1775, British redcoats marched on Lexington and Concord with the intent of disarming the American militias there. The American colonists refused to submit. The "shot heard round the world" was fired starting the long and arduous war for American independence.

The First Blow for Liberty. Battle of Lexington, April 1775. Copy of print by A. H. Ritchie

One hundred and sixty-nine years after the founding of Jamestown, the Colonial Era came to an end when the Continental Congress declared its independence from the Mother Country on July 4, 1776.

After eight years of war, against great odds, the American colonists emerged from the Revolutionary War victorious and free from the bonds that had tied them to the British Empire.

During the war, the Continental Congress issued its own currency, the Continental, to pay for the expenses of government. The Continental was a disaster, plunging in value and was soon not worth the paper it was printed on.

In 1784, Franklin analyzed the fall of the Continental in his essay *Of the Paper Money of America.*

Franklin wrote that when Great Britain and the colonies went to war, the colonies had neither arms nor ammunition, nor the money to purchase them or to pay soldiers. "The new Government had not immediately the Consistence necessary for collecting heavy Taxes; nor would Taxes that could be raised within the Year during Peace have been sufficient for a Year's Expence in time of War: they therefore printed a Quantity of

Paper Bills, each expressing to be of the Value of a certain Number of Spanish Dollars, from One to Thirty. With these they paid clothes and fed their Troops, fitted out Ships, and supported the War during Five Years against one of the most powerful Nations of Europe."

Franklin explained that the Continental was used for internal commerce replacing silver and gold, which were sent out of the colonies to purchase arms. Due to the expenses of the war, Continentals were issued in much greater volume than needed for the purposes of commerce, which was already diminished because of the war.

"It has been long and often observed, that when the current Money of a Country is augmented beyond the Occasions for Money, as a Medium of Commerce, its Value as Money diminishes, its Interest is reduced, and the Principal sinks if some Means are not found to take off the surplus Quantity," Franklin wrote.

He explained that this is true whether money is silver or paper.

The Continental rapidly depreciated in value as the war wore on. To make matters worse, the British flooded the colonies with counterfeit Continentals in an act of economic warfare with the intent of destroying its purchasing power.

The issuing of the Continental by the Continental Congress paid for the war, but due to overprinting and counterfeiting of the currency by the British, it depreciated badly and collapsed and was subsequently discredited as a currency.

In response to the collapse of the Continental, the Continental Congress chartered the Bank of North America in 1781. The bank was America's first central bank. It was run by a wealthy man named Robert Morris, who helped finance the war with his own money and who was serving as the superintendent of finance for the colonies at the time.

The Bank of North America issued a public offering of shares and borrowed gold and silver specie from France and the Netherlands. The gold and silver raised from the issuing of shares and foreign borrowing were used as reserves to back the paper currency printed by the bank. The Bank financed the final years of the Revolution.

On October 19, 1781, American and French forces won the Battle of Yorktown. More than 7,000 British troops surrendered at Yorktown, which ended the British will to continue the war. On September 3, 1783, American and British representatives signed the Treaty of Paris officially ending the war. The treaty also made official the United States as an independent country.

The newly independent country emerged from the war heavily in debt. The Continental Congress had acquired about $40 million in debt owed to France, the Netherlands and private individuals. The states owed another $115 million.

After the war, the Bank of North America continued to supply a national currency in the United States. However, the states were still printing their own currencies. The national currency competed with state currencies as mediums of exchange. Pennsylvania scrip was still in use and favored over Bank of North America notes in Pennsylvania.

The years after the end of the war were difficult ones. The national government was still Congress, which had limited powers. Congress attempted to pay its debts from the war with a duty on imports, but this required approval by all 13 states. Rhode Island, New Jersey and New York did not approve the plan. Congress could only raise revenue through voluntary requisitions from the states, which were not enough to pay the national debt.

To solve the problems of confederation, the Philadelphia Convention was held to draft a new constitution. After the convention, the U.S. Constitution was ratified by the state legislatures in 1788 and 1789.

The Preamble of the Constitution defined its purpose: "We the People of the United States, in Order to form a more perfect Union, establish Justice, insure domestic Tranquility, provide for the common defence, promote the general Welfare, and secure the Blessings of Liberty to ourselves and our Posterity, do ordain and establish this Constitution for the United States of America."

The Constitution united the states in perpetual union under a federal government with executive, legislative and judicial branches with the powers of each enumerated.

The Constitution addressed the monetary issue in the Coinage Clause, Article I, Section 8, Clause 5, which granted Congress the power to coin money and regulate its value. Article I, Section 10 grants the power to Congress exclusively by forbidding the states to coin money, emit bills of credit, or make anything but gold and silver coin a tender in payment of debts.

With the ratification of the Constitution, the states gave up their power to print scrip as they had been doing for nearly a century.

In *The Federalist Papers, Federalist No. 44,* James Madison explained the purpose of forbidding the states to coin money, emit bills of credit or make anything but gold and silver a legal tender in payment of debts.

Madison argued that if coining money was left to the states it would multiply expensive mints throughout the states and diversify the forms and weights of circulating coins, which would inconvenience commerce. In regard to states printing their own paper money, he said paper money had resulted in "pestilent effects on the confidence between man and man."

"Had every state a right to regulate the value of its coin, there might be as many different currencies as states, and thus the intercourse among them would be impeded; retrospective alterations in its value might be made, and animosities be kindled among the States themselves. The subjects of foreign powers might suffer from the same cause, and hence the Union be discredited and embroiled by the indiscretion of a single member. No one of these mischiefs is less incident to a power in the States to emit paper money, than to coin gold or silver. The power to make any thing but gold and silver a tender in payment of debts, is withdrawn from the States, on the same principle with that of issuing paper money."

With the ratification of the Constitution, the states

surrendered their power to coin money and to print paper money. A new single currency was created and a national currency union was formed. This increased and facilitated commerce between the states and unified the states economically into a single country.

However, the new monetary system that was put in place turned over money creation to private banks. The system was a rejection of the 100 years of monetary experimentation with paper money during the Colonial Era. The success of Pennsylvania scrip was forgotten while the failures of the Continental and of other state-issued colonial scrip were given as reasons for needing currency backed by specie.

Farley Grubb tells us in *Creating the U.S. Dollar Currency Union* that many of the Founders vehemently attacked colonial scrip during the Philadelphia Constitutional Convention. According to Grubb, at the time bank notes from the Bank of North America were in competition with the Pennsylvania pound. Pennsylvania's state-issued scrip was preferred by the public over notes issued by the Bank of North America. At the time of the convention, the Pennsylvania legislature was considering a new issuance of the Pennsylvania pound meant to ameliorate the deflation caused by the rapid retirement of wartime bills of credit. This issuance was opposed by the Bank of North America. The market preference for the Pennsylvania pound had caused a collapse of the Bank of North America's stock.

Grubb tells us what might have been the motivation for the attacks on colonial scrip at the convention. Of Pennsylvania's eight delegates at the convention, seven were stockholders in the Bank of North America: George Clymer, Thomas FitzSimons, Benjamin Franklin, Thomas Mifflin, Gouverneur Morris, Robert Morris, and James Wilson—and Robert Morris, FitzSimons, and Wilson were board members of the bank.

Ben Franklin, who had been one of the champions of colonial scrip for much of his life, was largely silent on the monetary question during the convention.

Grubb said that the arguments against paper money made during the convention were largely superficial. For example,

George Read from Delaware stated that the proposition to allow the government to emit bills of credit was "as alarming as the mark of the Beast in Revelations."

"The absolute, uncompromising, and argumentively-superficial position held by the anti-state-paper currency faction makes sense if their goal was something other than constitutionally establishing principles of sound monetary management," Grubb wrote. "The suggestion here is that these delegates sought the absolute elimination of state-issued paper money in order to increase the ability of the federal government's bank, the BNA and subsequently the FBUS, to provide and control the circulating medium of the nation and so empower and enrich themselves as stockholders of these banks."

The chain of events that unfolded in the early history of the United States resulted in our current monetary system that is dominated by privately owned fractional reserve banks. When the nation was founded, instead of having currency issued by the states or the national government, the issuance of currency was turned over to private bankers. It has been in their hands ever since.

Under the system of privately issued currency that was put in place in 1791, money evolved not as a medium of exchange to facilitate commerce, but instead as a debt instrument used by bankers to earn profits through usury.

Since the Philadelphia Constitutional Convention, the country has seen three central banks come and go followed by a fourth, the Fed, which dominates our economy today.

The arguments against state-issued currency led to the establishment of the First Bank of the United States. In March 1791, Congress chartered the First Bank of the United States, the FBUS, which became the successor to the Bank of North America. The FBUS was largely a creation of Alexander Hamilton. It was a privately owned central bank chartered for 20 years with 20 percent of its shares owned by the government and the remaining 80 percent owned by private individuals, which included American citizens and foreigners. The bank issued a national currency of paper bank notes backed by fractional reserves of specie, both silver and gold. The FBUS assumed the war debts of the states, which it paid through the imposition of a federal excise tax.

When Hamilton drew up plans for the bank, he had copied the charter of the Bank of England. The purpose of the FBUS was to issue a national currency, provide a place to keep public funds, offer banking facilities for commercial transactions, and act as the government's fiscal agent, including collecting the government's tax revenues.

The immediate effects of chartering the bank were the creation of a massive financial bubble, the Panic of 1792, and the nation's first government bailouts.

When the bank issued its first shares in the summer of 1791, people lined up to buy them, borrowing money to buy the shares and bidding up the prices. Down payments on the shares quickly doubled in price. A bubble also developed in U.S. debt securities, which were required to pay three-quarters of the price for FBUS shares. After the initial buying frenzy died down, the price of the bank's shares and U.S. securities collapsed, causing a tightening of credit across the economy and deflation. Hamilton, who was the Treasury Secretary, intervened by using the Treasury's sinking fund to purchase government securities to prop up their price. After the intervention, speculators rushed in again with borrowed money and drove the prices of the shares and securities back up. These speculators were so heavily indebted that when they began selling their shares and defaulting on their loans it caused the financial crisis known as the Panic of 1792. Credit dried up and the economy stalled. Hamilton jumped in again using the Treasury's sinking fund to prop up the price of securities.

Despite the financial turbulence, the FBUS became the largest corporation in the new nation, backed by millions from investors. It controlled substantial reserves made up of the deposits of the new federal government's monies. The bank used these reserves to issue commercial loans to private individuals and companies to earn profits through usury. Its bank notes entered into circulation when it issued commercial loans. The government's deposits allowed the bank to issue more loans than the nation's state banks. FBUS notes were also required for payment of federal taxes creating demand for the notes. These factors gave the FBUS a tremendous advantage over other banks that were just beginning to become established in the new nation.

The FBUS rapidly opened branches up and down the Eastern seaboard and in the west as the American people moved into the continent's interior. The FBUS soon came to be a dominant force in the national economy.

In 1793, the U.S. Mint began to coin silver dollars with a fixed weight and fineness, which standardized the nation's currency. The bank notes issued by the FBUS and by private state- and federal-chartered banks could be redeemed for silver dollars that were held in fractional reserves. These bank notes backed by silver dollars became the medium of exchange for the nation.

The FBUS was able to influence the money supply nationally by holding the bank notes of state banks in its vaults. If it wanted to expand the money supply, it would hold onto the notes. If it wanted to contract the money supply, it would redeem the bank notes from the state banks for specie.

The FBUS existed for 20 years before being shut down by Congress in 1811, due to allegations that it was constraining economic development and its ownership was dominated by British interests. In 1816, prompted by the debt incurred during the War of 1812, Congress chartered the Second Bank of the United States. It was nearly a carbon copy of the FBUS, only larger in scale. Its charter was revoked in 1836 and federal funds were removed from its vaults by Jackson.

America's current central bank, the Federal Reserve Bank, was chartered by Congress in 1913. While the First Bank of the United States and the Second Bank of the United States both operated for just 20 years, the Fed has been in operation for more than 100. Its power and the scope of its operations have increased over the decades and it has grown to dominate the American economy and the economy of the world.

The Fed stands like a colossus over us controlling our currency and our economy. Since 1913, the debt that it feeds on has grown to immense proportions. This debt siphons the wealth of the nation from the people and concentrates it into the hands of a small number of wealthy bankers.

The Tyranny of Debt

We have a debt-based monetary system. Most Americans today don't understand this concept. But the people who run the Federal Reserve Bank do.

No debt, no money.

Every dollar in existence is a debt that ultimately must be repaid to a bank, at interest.

On its face, this might seem absurd. After all, we use money to pay off debt. How can money itself be debt? We earn money through work and spend it to pay our bills. Money purchases our needs and wants. This seems to be a straightforward process.

But, make no mistake. Our money is debt. The dollar bills in your wallet and the digits in your bank account actually represent debts that must be repaid with interest, which are profits collected by banks.

Each dollar in your wallet and every digit in your savings account represents a debt that is gathering interest and must be repaid to banks. Those banks, in turn, must pay their debts to the Federal Reserve, minus the profits they earn through usury.

Most of us think of money as a measure of value and a medium of exchange. That is how most of us use money. Our employers pay us money for the work we do for them and we in turn exchange that money for the goods and services that we need to live our lives.

But for the banks, money is created as an instrument of debt that is used to collect interest for profit. Money is created by banks when they issue loans, either to people or to institutions.

Money enters the economy when a bank issues a loan. Once the loan is issued, the money is spent into the economy where, for most of us, it then serves as a measure of value and a medium of exchange. However, all the money that was issued as a loan must be paid back to the bank—and it must be paid at interest. This means that more money must be paid back to the banks than what entered into the economy when the loan was issued and used to make a purchase.

The volume of money in the economy is determined by the willingness of the banks to issue loans. If the banks are confident, they issue many loans and the money supply expands. If they are wary, they issue fewer loans and the money supply contracts.

Prior to the creation of the Federal Reserve, banks around the country competed with each other. Banks raised or lowered interest rates based on the demand for money in the economy. They competed with each other by attempting to offer higher rates for savings accounts to attract depositors and lower rates on loans to attract borrowers.

With the creation of the Federal Reserve, the process of setting interest rates was centralized.

Every five to eight weeks, the Federal Reserve's Federal Open Market Committee meets to determine interest rates and the level of reserves of the nation's banks.

The Federal Open Market Committee is made up of the seven members of the Fed's Board of Governors, plus the 12 presidents of the regional Federal Reserve Banks. The Board of Governors and five of the presidents of the regional banks have voting rights on the committee. The regional presidents rotate their voting rights, except for the president of the New York Federal Reserve Bank, who has permanent voting rights.

This committee determines the discount rate and the Fed funds rate. The discount rate is the interest rate the Fed charges its member institutions. The Fed funds rate is the rate member banks charge each other, mainly for overnight deposits with the Fed. By setting these rates, the Fed affects how much interest governments, banks, businesses and the public must pay to borrow money.

Remember, interest is a charge for the use of money. Since money enters the economy through loans issued through banks, money has interest attached—and interest collected by banks is profit for the banks. Furthermore, interest compounds and grows each time it is collected and lent back into the economy as new loans.

The Fed also sets the reserve requirements, which is the ratio of money a bank must keep in reserve versus how much it can issue in loans. Banks are required by the Fed to hold reserves in the form of vault cash or deposits with the regional Federal Reserve Banks. Currently, most banks are required to hold a 10 percent ratio of reserves versus loans. So when you deposit money into your bank, the bank can lend out 90 percent of it and hold 10 percent on hand at any given time.

By changing the reserve requirement, the Fed can expand or contract the money supply. If the reserve requirement goes down, the banks can lend more money into the economy. If the requirement goes up, the banks lend less and the money supply contracts.

The Fed also buys and sells U.S. Treasury securities. When it buys securities, it expands the money supply by trading cash for those securities. When it sells securities, it collects cash for the securities which contracts the money supply.

So the money supply is essentially determined by the amount of debt in the nation as a whole. The Fed controls the amount of debt that is issued by determining the amount of interest that banks charge, the level of reserves that banks must keep at the regional Federal Reserve Banks, and by buying and selling government securities.

The fact that our monetary system is based on debt is the most important issue of our time, yet most Americans have never given it much thought, or are completely oblivious to this fact. When the Federal Reserve Act was passed by Congress in 1913, privately issued debt-based currency was legally backstopped by the wealth, earnings and taxes of the American people. That was the way our current monetary system was intentionally designed by the men at Jekyll Island—to put you and the country at large into perpetual debt to interest-collecting bankers.

Money rules our lives. We spend our days trying to accumulate enough of it to provide ourselves with food and shelter. We spend our lives striving to earn enough of it to pay our obligations. When we have enough money, we live well. When we have too little, we struggle. Those who have none lead lives of want and desperation. While others have accumulated vast surpluses of it and live like modern day pharaohs. All the world is their playground.

People will toil under the hot sun for it. They will risk life and limb for it. They will sell their bodies for it. They will debase themselves. They will kill for it, die for it—all for scraps of colored paper made on a printing press, or digits on a computer screen that are effortlessly created by people who work in secret behind closed doors and who are accountable to no one.

Under our current monetary system, all the money that exists in the economy, either in the pockets of the poor or in the bank accounts of the rich, is debt that is owed to banks. This fact might seem counter-intuitive, but it is an important concept to keep in mind because of its incredibly negative ramifications for the vast majority of us, while making a few insiders fantastically wealthy and powerful and able to affect our lives to an incredible degree.

Each dollar we earn must be paid back to bankers at interest, which compounds and grows exponentially quarter after quarter, year after year.

If you were to ask the average American if he or she understands that we have a debt-based monetary system, you might get a blank stare. Go ahead and try it. See if your friends can explain our monetary system. If you were to ask even well-educated Americans—people who engage in complex thought regularly in their daily lives—doctors, lawyers, engineers, even bankers—ask them to explain our debt-based monetary system. Most would not have the slightest notion of where to begin.

Our debt-based monetary system is the source of many of the profound problems our nation faces today, from the economic upheavals that have thrown millions of Americans out of jobs and out of their homes, to the decline of our middle class, to the concentration of wealth into fewer and fewer hands, to the wars we seem to continually be drawn into, to the massive debt burden our government is placing on our shoulders and on the shoulders of our children and our grandchildren and their children and grandchildren.

This debt burden is making us and our descendants poorer and less free than the generations of Americans that came before us.

Our debt-based monetary system is undermining the independence the American revolutionaries fought for when our nation was founded more than two centuries ago. Our prosperity, our liberties and our future are being stripped from us and crushed beneath a growing mountain of debt that is compounding and expanding day after day, year after year, decade after decade.

On the hook

So what does it mean to have a debt-based monetary system?

The concept is simple. In our current system, money enters the economy as loans that must be repaid. All dollars in circulation originated as loans that must be repaid to banks, and ultimately to the Federal Reserve Bank.

Think of each dollar bill as bait on a hook attached to a line. A banker is holding the fishing pole. He casts the dollar bill out into the economy. Interest attracts other dollar bills to the bait. The banker reels in the original dollar with all the additional dollars attached to it by the hook of interest.

Every dollar in the economy is attached to a bank and in turn to the Federal Reserve.

The Fed has the power to create money, either as dollars printed by the Department of the Treasury or as digits typed into a computer. It can then disburse this money into the economy as loans to its member banks—banks such as Citibank, JPMorgan Chase, Bank of America, Wells Fargo, Goldman Sachs, and others. The Fed also lends money to foreign banks, such as Deutsche Bank, Sumitomo Corporation and Barclays. And it lends to foreign central banks, such as the Bank of England, the Bank of

Japan and the European Central Bank. The banks borrow money from the Fed at low interest and turn around and lend this money at higher interest to the public, small businesses, corporations and governments. The difference between the interest rate charged by the Fed and the interest rate charged by the banks is profit for the banks.

It's a racket.

Imagine you are allowed to borrow money in vast amounts from the Fed, say a billion dollars, at an interest rate of 0.25 percent, and then allowed to turn around and buy government securities at 3 percent. One year later, you will have earned a profit of $2.5 million from interest payments on those securities. Essentially, you have done nothing of value to anyone but you have still earned $2.5 million in profit. That profit was paid to you from the income taxes of the people. This is exactly what we have been allowing the big banks to do for the past several years. Nice work if you can get it.

When a borrower takes out a loan from a bank to buy, say, a car or a refrigerator, the borrower makes the purchase and his borrowed money then filters through the economy. It may even end up in your bank account if you earn a wage from a car dealership or an appliance store. This is how all money circulates through the economy—starting as loans made by banks. These loans must be paid back at interest.

In 2014, the Fed was lending money to its member banks at an interest rate of 0.25 percent. Banks, such as Citibank and JPMorgan Chase, borrow from the Fed and lend it out as credit card debt at rates as high as 15 percent and higher. Subtract 0.25 percent from the rate you pay on your credit card and that is the profit your bank is making from you. The banks borrow low from the Fed and lend high to you.

Goldman Sachs has borrowed vast sums of money from the Fed at 0.25 percent to purchase bonds from the federal government, which pay 3 percent. The federal government repays the principal and interest on the loans from Goldman Sachs with our federal income taxes. The difference between the interest the

Fed charges Goldman Sachs and the interest Goldman Sachs earns from the federal government is profit for Goldman Sachs, paid from the pockets of American taxpayers. This is profit with virtually no risk. The IRS ensures that taxpayers will pay back the bonds that Goldman Sachs has purchased. If you do not pay your taxes, your assets will be seized and you can be imprisoned.

In our debt-based monetary system, all the money the Fed creates and lends to the banks must be paid back to the Fed, plus interest. But the Fed only creates the principal when it lends money to its member banks—and the principal is the basis of the money supply. The Fed does not create the additional money needed to cover the interest on the principal.

If the Fed lends $1 million to a bank at 0.25 percent and the bank then lends that money into the economy, the money supply has just increased by $1 million. But the bank has to pay back the full $1 million to the Fed, plus interest. In one year the interest amounts to $2,500. And the people who borrowed the $1 million from the bank presumably are paying a higher rate than 0.25 percent that they must pay back to the bank before the bank pays back the Fed.

Only $1 million has been created. So where does the money to pay the interest come from?

The answer is: The money to cover the interest is never created. It does not exist.

In order to pay back the interest on debt, the Fed expands the money supply by creating money out of thin air and issuing new loans to the banks. New debt is created so there will be enough money in the economy to pay back old debt. The new debt, like the old debt, has interest attached, but the money to pay the interest is never created.

Under this system, debt must continue to grow so that old debt can be repaid in an ever growing pyramid of debt built upon debt. In our debt-based monetary system, the amount of debt in the economy must always exceed the money supply. It is a perpetually growing debt bubble that must continue to expand until the loans stop and the bubble pops. When this happens, as it inevitably must, the money supply quickly contracts and the economy slows and we fall into a recession or a depression.

Debt cycle

A debt-based monetary system causes a predictable debt cycle. This cycle begins when banks issue loans into the economy. Each loan issued causes the money supply to grow. This is because when a bank issues a loan, it does not subtract the money for that loan from the accounts of its depositors.

When a bank issues a loan for a home mortgage of $200,000, it merely creates the liability on its books without subtracting that amount from the accounts of its depositors. This is called double-entry bookkeeping.

If the bank doesn't have the $200,000 on hand in its reserves, it borrows the cash from other banks or from the Fed. The $200,000 is then used to pay for the house after which it is most likely deposited into another bank and the amount of money in the economy has increased by $200,000. This happens each time a loan is made.

When borrowing increases, more money becomes available to purchase goods. More people have money in their bank accounts. More people are making money and more people are employed producing goods and services. Optimism is in the air. As borrowing accelerates, the money supply begins to increase faster than the supply of goods available for purchase. Prices inflate as more money chases fewer goods. Loans grow larger as prices increase. People begin to borrow money to buy assets with hopes that prices will continue to rise and the appreciating assets can be sold at a profit.

This is when classic debt-fueled asset bubbles arise in the economy—in land, housing, stocks, bonds, student loans, tulips, or whatever asset the money spigot is pointed toward.

Meanwhile, the interest on existing debt continues to compound. The debt bubble inflates.

The Fed and its member banks build a pyramid of debt that must grow so that enough money exists in the economy to pay existing debt. And, like all pyramid schemes, the pyramid must inevitably collapse.

Eventually, high levels of debt become pervasive. Prices rise too high and the cash flow generated by debt-fueled assets no longer cover payments on the debts that were incurred to buy those assets. When the total debt burden reaches critical mass, consumers, companies and governments cannot earn enough income to pay back their loans. Their assets purchased with debt can no longer be sold at prices that can pay off their debts. Debt becomes so pervasive that fewer borrowers exist who can take out new loans from the banks. Less money begins to enter the economy. When no one is willing or able to take on enough debt to buy the inflated assets, overburdened borrowers begin to default.

The cycle, in short, begins when banks follow an easy credit policy and issue many loans which causes lots of money to enter the economy which stimulates economic activity. The money supply increases faster than production causing prices to rise. People borrow larger amounts to purchase inflating assets until the debt load grows too large to pay back. Then the bust begins. The banks stop lending. More people default. Money is extinguished from the economy with each default. Meanwhile, borrowers that still have income continue to pay back their loans to the banks, at interest, while no new money enters the economy. Money flows to the banks and grows scarce in the economy.

With less money available to purchase assets, prices deflate. The debt that was previously used to purchase assets has become greater than the price of the assets. Borrowers slip underwater. Defaults accelerate.

When a borrower defaults, the lender can legally seize his assets. During a bust, collection agencies working for the banks confiscate cars, houses, land, businesses, corporations, and even the assets of governments. The lenders become the owners.

The three stages of the debt cycle are: inflation, deflation and confiscation. Repeat this cycle of debt decade after decade, century after century, and over time, the bankers will own the

Earth.

An important distinction must be made between lending money at interest and investing money. When you invest money in a person or an organization, you give over your money so that it can be used in some enterprise that provides goods and services. You are hoping your money will be used wisely to increase the amount of goods and services in the economy. If your investment fails, you lose your money and that's that. If your investment is successful, you get to share the profits and society benefits from the increase in something that there is a demand for. The wealth not only of yourself but of the overall society has increased due to your investment. The more money that is invested, the more possibility there is for increased production and increased profits. However, when you lend money at interest, you are expecting to be paid back your principal plus interest whether there is an increase in production or not. Your borrower has agreed to turn over a portion of his income to you for a fixed term. The more money that you lend, the more interest you are hoping to rake in for yourself from the income of the borrower. If the borrower's income falls and he is unable to make payments on the loan, he will face the debt collector. You can seize his assets that he put up as collateral for the loan.

In our debt-based monetary system, the bankers have loaned out vast sums to the people, private enterprises and governments and they have accumulated enormous power and control. Through this power to create credit and the resulting cycle of inflation, deflation and confiscation, bankers have taken control of our media, our corporations, our land, our government and our national resources. The American public rides the debt cycle roller coaster seemingly oblivious to the fact that the ups and downs are designed into the system.

Economists and the media call it the business cycle. They talk about it as if it is some natural and inevitable thing, like the tides, the seasons or winter storms. Modern economists tell us that the business cycle hits a peak when we reach a period of full employment and output capacity has maxed out. Wage inflation occurs because businesses must compete for scarce labor. Meanwhile, rising wages mean more money is chasing the same amount of goods, causing inflation. Then we see a period of contraction when output, employment levels and income begin to fall. Output, employment and trade bottom out. Businesses then pull themselves out of the trough and the economy grows again. Under the traditional economic view of the business cycle, the problem is not rising levels of debt, but instead rising wages.

This traditional view of the business cycle completely ignores the role lending from banks has in driving expansionary periods which lead to booms and the role of banks in tightening lending which leads to contractionary periods. It's all the fault of rising wages, you see.

But it is the banks that cause the cycle, not businesses and workers. And it was the banks that created the Federal Reserve under the premise that the Fed would smooth out this so-called business cycle to reduce the pain, disruption and dislocation that occurs at the bottom of the cycle.

The cycle of debt caused by a debt-based monetary system is what causes the pain. The booms and busts are caused when money is created as loans owed to bankers and moneyed financiers.

Most people in this world must work for money to earn our daily bread. The banks create this money out of thin air using our own savings as collateral. The bankers use the people's money to feed off the productivity of the people.

John Adams wrote, "All the perplexities, confusion and distress in America arise, not from defects in their Constitution or Confederation, not from want of honor or virtue, so much as from the downright ignorance of the nature of coin, credit and circulation."

Henry Ford is alleged to have said, "It is well enough that people of the nation do not understand our banking and monetary system, for if they did, I believe there would be a revolution before tomorrow morning."

Our monetary system is not difficult to understand. It is a

system based on debt that has been designed to benefit the few at the expense of the many. It is high time Americans make the effort to understand our monetary system.

The current system needs to be reformed and reorganized. It is entirely possible to create a new system in which money is not debt owed to bankers who are enriching themselves off usury and the collection of interest that compounds year after year, decade after decade, generation after generation.

A new system can be designed in which money is not an instrument of debt but instead is merely a measure of value and a medium of exchange. It is entirely possible to create a new monetary system that is not designed to serve passive income seekers but instead rewards those who perform productive work that enriches society as a whole. It is possible to design a new system that does not serve the interests of plutocratic financiers but instead uses interest- and inflation-free money to serve the interests of the American people. We could design a new system that favors the interests of small business owners and workers over the interests of big banks, multinational corporations, usurers, speculators and rent seekers. We could design a system that serves the interest of free enterprise, commerce and work—a system that creates an economy of high production, full employment and high wages rather than our current economy of stagnant wages, high unemployment and corporate cartels. We could design a new system that is based on American principles of separation of powers, checks and balances and accountability to the people.

The purpose of our economy should be to serve the needs and wants of the American people. Unfortunately, the current purpose of our economy is to serve shareholders—passive income seekers. These passive income seekers are mostly made up of the richest segment of society—the 1 percent, and they are as likely to be foreigners as American citizens, without loyalty to our nation and our people.

It doesn't have to be this way. Our nation has produced some of the world's greatest scientists, inventors and thinkers in every field of endeavor. Monetary systems are not that complicated. We as a people are perfectly capable of designing a better system that can increase the prosperity and liberty of the American people and end the tyranny of the usurers who are now in control.

The Tyranny of Usury

The people of ancient civilizations understood early on that all manner of evil arises out of the practice of usury.

Aristotle called usury an unnatural mode of making money. He wrote in the fourth century B.C. in his book *Politics*, "The most hated sort, and with the greatest reason, is usury, which makes a gain out of money itself, and not from the natural object of it. For money was intended to be used in exchange, but not to increase at interest."

Usury was recognized as disruptive by the ancient Greeks. It was eventually condemned by Roman law, as well as in many other countries and civilizations. Judaism, Christianity and Islam all warned of the inequities that result from lending money at interest.

Shakespeare wrote, "Neither a borrower nor a lender be."

Benjamin Franklin wrote, "But ah, think what you do when you run in debt; you give to another power over your liberty."

The problem that arises with lending money at interest and then lending out your returns so they compound is a matter of simple mathematics.

An old legend about the origin of chess succinctly illustrates the power of compounding. The story goes that the inventor of chess showed his new game to a rich Indian king. The king was so impressed with the game that he granted the inventor a wish. The inventor asked for one grain of rice for the first square of his chessboard, two grains for the next square, four for the next, and so on for each of the 64 squares, with each square having twice as many grains of rice as the square before.

The king was amazed that the man had asked for such a small reward and ordered that a sack of rice be brought so that the rice could be apportioned for every square. One grain of rice was placed on the first square of the board, two on the second, four on the third, eight on the fourth, 16 on the fifth, 32 on the sixth, 64 on the seventh, 128 on the eighth, 256 on the ninth, 512 on the tenth, 1024 on the eleventh. On the 21st square, the amount was 1 million grains of rice, 2 million on the 22nd, 4 million on the 23rd, 8 million on the 24th with less than half of the squares apportioned. As the pile of rice began to overflow from the palace windows, the king realized that the reward added up to an astronomical sum, far greater than all the rice that could be harvested in a thousand years. The king had been duped because of his ignorance of the implications of exponential growth. He then executed the inventor of chess.

Mathematically, compound interest grows on a curve that rises modestly at first and then becomes ever steeper before going vertical and shooting to infinity. When you lend money at interest, you are attempting to climb this curve. The bigger the fortune you have to begin with, the faster your compound interest curve will rise.

However, the growth curve of actual economic production follows a different curve. Someone who farms for a living, owns a business or manufactures goods that are in demand will also see modest growth in the beginning, then often a strong rise in the curve of profits that he is making. But unlike with compound interest, once market saturation of capital is reached, the curve will flatten, and even perhaps decline as new competitors enter the field and existing machinery depreciates and needs to be replaced.

The lender of money has few capital costs to worry about. He does not produce goods that require factories and workers. He does not perform actual labor. All he does is lend out money to one person, charge interest for it, and then lend out his earnings to the next person. If he is conservative and only lends to people he is sure can pay him back, his money will grow and then outpace the profits of those who are producing goods and services in an economy—people who actually do work that allows society to function. The moneylender will see his fortune grow without the need to actually perform labor or spend his money on machinery, factories, warehouses, trucks, and salaries for large numbers of laborers. The moneylender feeds off the productive sector of the economy; he takes from it without contributing.

Like the Indian king in the legend of the chessboard, the American public has been duped into permitting our government to borrow at interest which compounds and is then paid back to bankers through taxes on our incomes. We taxpayers have been made responsible to pay for the rice that keeps piling up on the chessboard in greater and greater amounts due to the nature of exponential growth.

What the ancients recognized was that the rich have an advantage when it comes to moneylending. Since the rich have more money to lend, they can charge lower interest rates than the small lender and still make money faster. They can also weather defaults better than the small lender who has less money to fall back on. The large lender can quickly crowd out the small lender.

The rich by definition have a surplus of money so they will often lend out their extra money to others to gain a return. Since the poor have the greatest demand for money, they will by necessity borrow it from the rich. When the poor borrow money, they must pay back the principal plus interest, which means they will have to pay back a larger sum than they borrowed. The longer they take to pay back the loan, the more money they are shuffling from the earnings of their labor into the pockets of the rich. Charging interest on money is merely the shuffling of money from the pockets of the poor into the pockets of the rich. The higher the interest rate, the faster the rich are filling their pockets with the earnings of the poor.

In a society where usury has become commonplace, money will concentrate in the pockets of the rich and become ever scarcer in the pockets of the poor. People will become increasingly indebted to a plutocracy that will end up owning everything. The people will become bond slaves to the rich.

What the ancients realized from the bitter pill of experience was that a society in which usury is practiced will become unstable and injustices will become intolerable. The majority of the people will end up laboring under the heavy burden of debt in order to feed the greed of a small number of idle rich. The plight of the poor will eventually seek expression through violence and revolution.

For usury to be profitable, by necessity it must be backed by violence. The great danger of lending money is the possibility that the borrower will not pay back the loan, therefore there must be repercussions for defaulting or else the moneylender will quickly lose his principal.

We have heard stories of back alley loan sharks who will break the knees of deadbeats who do not make good on their loans. In the back alleys of Europe during the Middle Ages, medieval moneylenders would seek their pound of flesh from those who defaulted. Through the ages and in modern times, the use of force has been necessary to motivate the fickle borrower to pay back what he owes.

Moneylending was banned in Europe until the Late Middle Ages when the restrictions on usury were lifted. Borrowers signed legal contracts with moneylenders, which were enforced by the state. Borrowers who defaulted, by law, could have their property seized or could be thrown into debtors' prisons.

The restrictions on usury were lifted so that kings could borrow gold from rich usurers to build up their militaries. The kings of Europe paid back the moneylenders through taxes on their subjects.

Moneylenders are great students of human nature. Lending money to human beings quickly teaches the moneylender how to size up the character of a man. The moneylender has learned that a rich man can be a deadbeat and a poor man can never miss a payment, a man of sterling character can fall into bad luck and default after a lifetime of reliability; a borrower in need will swear on his mother's grave that he will make good on his loan, but after a year or two of living under the burden of loan payments he will find it to his advantage to shirk the moneylender. The moneylender knows that words and promises are ephemeral, and without the threat of force, even the most sincere borrower can become delinquent. Without the credible threat of force, the usurer will soon lose his shirt. The moneylender knows he must be willing to turn the screws on his borrower if need be.

Over the millennia, moneylenders grew wealthy by taking advantage of a defect in human character. People have needs and desires that they want fulfilled sooner rather than later. People have a tendency not to want to delay the gratification of their needs.

A king prefers to borrow from a moneylender because it is easier than facing the wrath of his subjects today if he raises their taxes, even knowing that to pay back the moneylender he will have to raise their taxes anyway not only for the original amount he needed but also for the interest that is compounding.

Instead of saving for months and months or even years to buy a flat-screen television or a car or to pay for a family vacation, people will borrow money to have what they want right now, even if it means paying usurious interest rates and paying much more money over time than the original amount needed. Someone who spends $5,000 on a family vacation using a credit card that charges 15 percent interest, and then only makes the minimum payment, will pay an additional $2,100 to the bank on top of what was originally spent on the vacation. So the bank gets $2,100 in profit for allowing the spender to avoid saving his money.

The borrower gets instant gratification at a steep price while the moneylender delays his own gratification and grows richer over time. The poor have the greatest need for money and their needs are often desperate and immediate. Moneylenders have always preyed on the poor with high interest rates causing them to fall into a cycle of debt that only further increases their poverty and need. Through much of history, falling into debt was the surest road to slavery.

In ancient times in societies where usury was allowed, the gap between the rich and the poor would often grow unbearable. The poor would fall into a web of debt and the fruits of their labor and toil would concentrate into the hands of an increasingly despotic plutocracy. The burden felt by the poor would grow to intolerable levels with mathematical certainty due to the singular effect of compound interest.

In a society where usury first begins to be practiced, in the beginning moneylenders are often viewed as beneficial. When interest rates are low and the debt burden is light, the moneylender is seen as offering a useful service in an economy by supplying money to facilitate production and commerce. But as the debt curve rises ever more quickly, the negative effects begin to be felt and the moneylender is seen in a different light. He does no labor and produces no goods. More and more of the goods produced by those who perform labor are claimed by him. His threat of force weighs heavily on those who are indebted to him.

John Turmel, an engineer and perennial candidate for public office in Canada, succinctly illustrated the relationship of the usurer to the working man in his poem *Thoughts of a Rich Man on Usury*:

> So I'll get down upon my knees and bless the Working Man,
> Who offers me a life of ease through all my mortal span;
> Whose loins are lean to make me fat, who slaves to keep me free,
> Who dies before his prime to get me round the century.
> Whose wife and children toil in turn until their strength is spent,
> That I may live in idleness upon my ten percent.
> And if at times they curse me, why should I feel any blame,
> For in my place, I know that they would do the very same.

Throughout the ages, the moneylender was often likened to a parasite—one who feeds off the labor of his host, the people, who must work for a living. He engorges himself like a blood-filled leach on the money of the people and grows increasingly fat and wealthy while the people toil under the heavy burden of debt. Because of the negative effects of lending money at interest, time and again, in place after place, the practice of usury was scorned and made illegal.

For millennia in Europe, usury was banned. But the

restrictions fell away as the demand for gold increased due to the needs of commerce and government. During the Late Middle Ages, usury became supercharged with the advent of fractional reserve banking. Through fractional reserve banking, bankers began practicing usury not with their own money, but with large pools of money held in their vaults—the savings of their depositors. Due to the practice of double-entry bookkeeping and because of the multiplier effect, bankers began lending out multiples of money that didn't actually exist.

Fractional reserve bankers quickly amassed great fortunes from the interest that accrued from multiples of money that they had created and issued out as loans. They became so rich that they were able to lend to kings and governments.

The bankers offered the kings, queens and emperors of Europe loans of gold which could be used to pay for armies, ships, castles and public works. The rulers of Europe saw these loans as advantageous to themselves. These rulers, who were in command over their lands and all their people and resources, who were the leaders of armies and navies, fell into the same web of debt as the poor man who borrows away his future savings from the moneylender. In their shortsightedness, the leaders of Europe fell into debt to wealthy bankers. The monarchs of Europe borrowed what they needed now without thinking that all the money they borrowed plus interest must be paid back by taxing the people.

By borrowing at 5 percent, in 20 years the king will pay a sum equal to the loan borrowed; in 40 years he will pay double; and in 60 triple; while the principal still remains an unpaid debt. For his short term advantage, the king has burdened the people with more taxes than he would have if he never borrowed to begin with and just taxed the people for the amount needed.

Just think of it. A king in need of money for some public work to benefit his people, such as a bridge or a dam, would borrow the amount from private bankers and get the entire sum now. The bridge is then built. But the entire cost of the bridge must be paid back to the bankers plus an additional amount in interest. The money to pay for the bridge and for the interest on the loan is paid through taxing the people. The bankers get back everything they lent plus a nice profit for doing nothing more than turning over the money of their depositors to the king while the people must pay back the entire cost of the bridge, plus profit for the bankers.

If the king had not borrowed the money from the bankers, he could have paid for the building of the bridge with the taxes of the people without having to pay the bankers and pay the additional interest. Instead of the cost for the bridge being extracted from the people and shuffled into the pockets of the bankers, it would have merely paid for the work and gone into the economy. The people would have gotten the benefit of the bridge without the extra cost.

Why not just place a temporary tax on the people now for the amount needed instead of having to continually raise taxes later to pay off even greater sums to wealthy bankers? The genius of the bankers was to present the borrowing of money as advantageous to kings when in fact it was advantageous to themselves and a disadvantage in the long run to both kings and their subjects.

This human weakness, this shortsightedness that allows both the common man and the king to fall into debt, has been a windfall for lenders. Lending money to governments is an incredibly profitable endeavor. When a banker lends to a private citizen or a business, the matter of debt collection is the banker's own concern. Collecting money from deadbeats is a messy and expensive affair. But when the banker lends to a government, debts are repaid through taxation. The state, with all its military, police and legal manpower, will pay the debts it owes by taxing a portion of the earnings of the population of the country. Lend to a government and your debts are collected with all the power and reach of the state.

But what if a king decides to default? After all, a king has armies at his disposal. What's to stop him from bilking his lenders? This is a concern to anyone who lends to a government.

The way to prevent a state from reneging on its debt is to

ensure that the right people are in office. The bankers must spend vast sums to put people they can trust into positions of power. If a king cannot be trusted to fulfill his obligations to his lenders, he must be replaced. Rivals and revolutionaries must be funded to topple the king from his throne. Foreign nations that present a threat must be lent large sums of money to build up their armies and navies so the king can never feel secure without money on hand from his wealthy creditors.

Of all the activities that a state undertakes, none is more profitable for the bankers than war. War is the great ally of the moneylender. A conservative king who is frugal with his finances and who carefully avoids debt will come to the bankers with outstretched hands during a time of war. The urgency of war will cause him to throw caution to the wind and he will borrow vast sums to cover the high expenses that come with building and fielding a military. Out of fear for national survival, the people will submit to a heavy burden of taxation to pay for their defense.

In 1690, the same year that Massachusetts issued its first colonial scrip, England was defeated by France in the Battle of Beachy Head. King William III needed to rebuild the English navy but did not have the money. In 1694, the Bank of England was founded to raise funds for King William to rebuild his navy.

The Bank of England became the first modern central bank. It was designed to lend money to the government yet remain privately owned and independent in its decision making.

King William borrowed from the Bank of England and built a powerful navy. His navy, built on debt, allowed England to expand its reach and grow into the mighty British Empire. The empire expanded around the world built on an ever-growing national debt owed to bankers, who were paid back through the slave trade and the slave economies of the New World, through the conquest of foreign lands where gold and diamond mines were exploited, through the sale of opium, and through the expansion of trade as the British economy produced every manner of goods after the onset of the Industrial Revolution. The Industrial Revolution allowed the United Kingdom to jump out in front of the nations of the world in technological, economic and military power.

The success of England's central bank was soon imitated and the central banking system of private, independently owned and operated central banks spread across Europe.

As the central banking system took hold, the debt burden of the people, private enterprise and governments grew exponentially. Europe lurched from one economic crisis to another and from war to war while the bankers grew increasingly wealthy and influential. Today, there is hardly a government nor a person in the world not indebted to banks that are members of a central bank.

In the time when gold was money, kings foolishly placed their nations in debt by borrowing gold from bankers and then taxing their people to pay back the amount borrowed, plus interest. But think of the ridiculousness of our present situation when gold is not money. Today, central banks print money with government printing presses, or merely create money as digits on computer screens. Money today is not backed by gold but by the power of governments to tax the people. Modern governments around the world have turned over the power to print money to privately owned, independent central banks. So when a modern government does not have enough money from taxation to cover its expenses, it borrows the money at interest from private banks by issuing bonds. The central bank then tells the government printing presses to print out the money for the bonds, then it lends that money at low interest to the private banks, which then lend the money at higher interest to the government! The government then pays back the banks the principal plus interest by taxing the people. This system enriches the banks while causing inflation of the money supply. Governments borrow money printed out of thin air and then pay back the principal plus interest to the banks from the pockets of the people! What could be simpler than just having the government print the money to pay for the materials and labor it needs and then taxing the people, rather than printing the money it needs, handing it over to bankers and then taxing the people to pay the principal plus additional interest for the profit of the bankers?

In an article in the *New York Times* on December 6, 1921, Thomas Edison was quoted as supporting Henry Ford's proposal for the government to complete a dam project in Muscle Shoals, Alabama, not by financing it with interest-bearing bonds, but instead with currency printed by the government for the purpose of paying for labor and materials. Edison pointed out the ridiculousness of having bankers purchase government bonds to fund public projects. "People who will not turn a shovelful of dirt nor contribute a pound of material will collect more money from the United States than will the people who supply the material and do the work. That is the terrible thing about interest. In all our great bond issues the interest is always greater than the principal. All of the great public works cost more than twice the actual cost, on that account. Under the present system of doing business we simply add 120 to 150 percent to the stated cost.

"But here is the point: If our nation can issue a dollar bond, it can issue a dollar bill. The element that makes the bond good makes the bill good, also. The difference between the bond and the bill is that the bond lets the money brokers collect twice the amount of the bond and an additional 20 percent, whereas the currency pays nobody but those who directly contribute to Muscle Shoals in some useful way."

"... It is absurd to say that our country can issue $30,000,000 in bonds and not $30,000,000 in currency. Both are promises to pay; but one promise fattens the usurer, and the other helps the people. If the currency issued by the Government were no good, then the bonds issued would be no good either. It is a terrible situation when the Government, to increase the national wealth, must go into debt and submit to ruinous interest charges at the hands of men who control the fictitious values of gold."

"... If the United States Government will adopt this policy of increasing its national wealth without contributing to the interest collector—for the whole national debt is made up of interest charges—then you will see an era of progress and prosperity in this country such as could never have come otherwise."

Article 1, Section 8, Clause 5 of the Constitution, known as the Coinage Clause, gives Congress the power, "To coin Money, regulate the Value thereof, and of foreign Coin."

There has been much controversy about this clause. As stated earlier, many of the Founders were wary of paper money because of their experience with colonial scrip prior to independence, and with the Continental during the Revolutionary War.

After the ratification of the Constitution, currency was issued by private banks backed by gold and silver coins held in their reserves.

Up until the Civil War, gold and silver backed the money supply. But with the outbreak of the Civil War, Congress, with President Lincoln's support, passed the Legal Tender Act of 1862, which allowed the printing of U.S. Notes, called greenbacks, which were not redeemable for gold. The greenback was declared legal tender for all debts, public or private. This was seen as an emergency war measure at the time. Because of the war, the banks had suspended redemption of their notes in gold and the cost of borrowing had skyrocketed. Congress authorized the printing of greenbacks to pay for war materiel and for the salaries of soldiers at a time when money was scarce and gold was unavailable. Many feared that by printing greenbacks and making them legal tender, Congress would continue to print them until they lost value due to inflation—just as had happened with the Continental. Devaluation of the greenback in fact happened. Congress printed several issues of the greenback and price inflation occurred. However, the greenback enabled the North to pay for the war without excessive borrowing from banks or drastically increasing taxes on the public for a war that became increasingly unpopular as the war years dragged on. Toward the latter years of the war, with each battle the North won, the greenback increased in value. As a result, some began to see the greenback as a viable alternative to gold—a non-debt-based currency free from the grasping hands of interest-collecting bankers.

A $20 Legal Tender Note from the Series 1862-1863 greenback issue. This issue featured the image of Lady Liberty.

After the war the bankers and the backers of gold pushed for the return of notes redeemable in gold and for the retirement of the greenback. The government began to retire the greenback from circulation, but due to poor economic conditions after the war and the contraction of the money supply, deflation set in. Supporters of the greenback were able to halt its retirement, allowing more than $300 million of the debt-free notes to remain in circulation alongside gold-backed notes.

After the war, controversy over whether the Constitution allowed Congress to print paper money led to a series of court cases. The issue was finally settled by the Supreme Court in 1884 in the case of *Julliard v. Greenman*. The Supreme Court upheld the validity of legal tender laws during peacetime, ruling that the federal government's monetary power was inherent in its sovereignty and did not need to be enumerated in the Constitution.

The greenback remained in circulation alongside gold-backed notes for the rest of the 19th century and for much of the 20th century. In 1913, the Federal Reserve Note came into circulation with the creation of the Federal Reserve Bank. The Federal Reserve Note was redeemable in gold until 1933 when the possession of gold was made illegal during the darkest and most deflationary days of the Great Depression. However, while gold had become illegal for Americans to possess, the Federal Reserve Notes remained redeemable in gold on international markets until

1971 when President Richard Nixon ended the currency's last link to gold. At that time, the Federal Reserve Note became a fiat currency like the U.S. Note. Both notes remained in circulation side by side with the difference being that the U.S. Note was free of interest whereas each Federal Reserve Note was backed by debt issued by the Federal Reserve Bank, generating interest for the Fed.

In 1993, the Treasury quietly destroyed the last of the greenbacks. Since then all notes in circulation have been debt-backed Federal Reserve Notes. Today, the national debt is exponentially higher than it was in 1913, and the value of the Federal Reserve Note is a fraction of what is was then. And with the Federal Reserve Note as their debt instrument, Wall Street banks have become bigger and more powerful than ever.

The monetary system we have today was purposefully designed to place our government in perpetual debt to bankers. But it didn't have to be this way. The American people, because of our lack of understanding of the monetary system, of the nature of money, of debt, and of the issuance of currency and credit, have allowed it to happen. There were other alternatives to a debt-backed currency controlled by an independent central bank that could have been put in place and would have led to different outcomes than what we are seeing today. Our current system benefits a certain clique of people to the detriment of the majority. That clique of moneylenders now dominates our country and our lives through controlling the issuance and volume of money while profiting from the collection of interest.

The Federal Reserve Bank is the center of this debt-based system. Its power is derived from the control of money and the willingness of the people and the government to fall into debt.

In his book *The Age of Turbulence*, former Fed Chair Alan Greenspan explained the importance of debt to the Federal Reserve Bank. In the book, Greenspan revealed that in early 2001 the Federal Reserve Board was disoriented and feared it was about to lose its grip on the economy. Greenspan discussed in detail a serious predicament for the Fed—government budget surpluses.

In January 2001 in the weeks before George W. Bush's inauguration, the dotcom bubble had already burst and the economy was in recession. The Fed's Federal Open Market Committee was discussing lowering interest rates. On January 3, the FOMC cut the Fed's fund rate by half a percent to 6 percent. Greenspan said at the time he thought it would be the first of many rapid cuts as the economic picture looked to be deteriorating. The FOMC cut the rate by another half a percentage point before January was over, and the same again in March, April, May and June, bringing it down to 3.75 percent.

However, at the same time, the Congressional Budget Office was predicting huge budget surpluses and the Fed was worried about this prospect. The issue looming large for the FOMC was the disappearance of the national debt. The CBO was predicting surpluses as far as the eye could see. Even allowing for the recession that was setting in, the CBO was getting ready to raise its projection of the surplus to a stunning $5.6 trillion over 10 years.

Imagine that—a $5.6 trillion federal government surplus was being predicted! In today's fiscal climate, it seems like an outrageous fantasy.

The consensus of economists and statisticians at the time was that the surpluses would continue to build because of a surge in productivity growth caused by the new technology of the Internet age.

The federal debt in January 2001 stood at $3.4 trillion. More than $2.5 trillion was considered reducible, or readily paid off. The rest was irreducible debt, which is considered savings bonds and other securities that investors would decline to sell.

The projected surpluses were so large that debt repayment was expected to be completed within a few years, with the surpluses continuing on after that. The CBO statisticians envisioned the surpluses at $281 billion in 2001, $313 billion in 2002, $359 billion in 2003, and so on. The CBO expected the reducible debt to be fully paid off by 2006. Any surpluses thereafter would have to be held not in federal debt but in some form of non-federal assets. In 2006, the surplus was predicted to break $500 billion. Thereafter, more than a half trillion in excess dollars would flow into Uncle Sam's coffers each year!

The money would pile up year after year. Greenspan asked in his book what would the Treasury do with that much money? Where would it invest? Our government would become the world's biggest investor, pouring money into the stock market, real estate, corporate bonds, etc., which Greenspan found to be a "truly scary" prospect.

"As the evidence for this ongoing surplus mounted, I felt an odd sense of loss," Greenspan wrote. He explained that he had a theory that human nature, being what it is, would always lead governments into budget deficits. "Had human nature changed?" he asked.

"In our late January meeting we spent hours trying to imagine how the Fed would operate in a brave new world of minimal federal debt," Greenspan wrote. "Of course, shedding the debt burden would be a happy development for our country, but it would nevertheless pose a big dilemma for the Fed.

"Our primary lever of monetary policy was buying and selling Treasury securities—Uncle Sam's IOUs. But as the debt was paid down those securities would grow scarce, leaving the Fed in need of a new set of assets to affect monetary policy.

"For nearly a year, senior Fed economists and traders had been exploring the issue of what other assets we might buy and sell. A result was a dense 380-page study that plopped on our desks in January.

"The good news was that we weren't going out of business. The bad news was that nothing could really match the Treasury's market in size, liquidity and freedom from risk. To conduct monetary policy, the report concluded, the Fed would have to learn to manage a complex portfolio of municipal bonds, bonds issued by foreign governments, mortgage-backed securities, auctioned discount window credits and other debt instruments. It was a daunting prospect."

Greenspan said he came to the conclusion that chronic

surpluses were almost as destabilizing as chronic deficits. He came up with a plan to phase out the surpluses through tax cuts and by funding Social Security to "work down the surpluses before they became dangerous," with triggers to stop the tax cuts if deficits returned.

Greenspan came out in support of President George W. Bush's tax cuts in 2001, to the dismay of Democrats. On June 7, 2001, Bush signed a $1.35 trillion tax cut without the triggers Greenspan wanted. The surpluses were still going strong at that time.

But within weeks, before the tax cuts went into effect, it became apparent that the CBO forecasts were wrong. Suddenly, federal revenues plunged. The flow of personal income tax payments to the Treasury were coming up short billions of dollars. The surplus was effectively wiped out overnight, and starting that July, red ink was back to stay.

The CBO's predictions of budget surpluses as far as the eye could see turned out to be in actuality an outrageous fantasy.

The revenue shortfall was a reflection of the stock market's broad decline, Greenspan explained in his book. Taxes on capital gains and on the exercise of stock options had plunged. It was the tech bubble that had generated the surpluses, not productivity, and the bear market had taken the surpluses away. The booming economy was nothing more than a debt-fueled asset bubble inflated by irrational investment in companies like Pets.com and Webvan and facilitated by money from the Fed and from Wall Street banks.

In January 2001, the CBO had estimated total government receipts at $2.236 trillion for 2002. By August of 2002, the figure had shrunk to $1.86 trillion, a $376 billion downward revision in 18 months. Greenspan said $75 billion of the shortfall was attributable to the Bush tax cut, with $125 billion from weakening economic activity, while $176 billion was unexplained.

Of course, only a few months after the Bush tax cuts were signed, came 9/11, followed by two expensive wars and massive budget deficits as far as the eye could see. The chronic surpluses faded into memory and so too the Fed's fears of managing a complex portfolio and having a reduced influence over our lives. The low rates the Fed put in place in 2001 resulted in a housing bubble, which burst in 2007, followed by massive government spending during the nation's most severe economic crisis since the Great Depression. Government debt exploded as budget deficits topped $1 trillion year after year. Only a few years after Greenspan lamented the possibility of the Fed losing influence over the economy due to budget surpluses, the Obama administration granted the Fed broad new powers to deal with the recession, making the Fed more powerful than ever.

And the prospect of the Fed ever having to face chronic surpluses again seems less and less likely, nearly mathematically impossible.

We, as a people, are buried in debt. This debt must be paid off through the income taxes of not only the people alive today, but of future generations. The unborn must pay off the debts of those alive today.

In 1864, President Abraham Lincoln in his Gettysburg Address reiterated the principles of the Declaration of Independence. He asked for a new birth of freedom in the country so "that government of the people, by the people, for the people, shall not perish from the earth."

Now 150 years after he gave his address, as we look at our country today, do we have a government of the people, by the people and for the people?

The *Bible* tells us, "The rich man rules over the poor, and the borrower is servant to the lender."

Debt has often been referred to as the money of slaves. When we go into debt, we are promising to pay the lender more of our future earnings than we are borrowing today. The lender gives us momentary financial relief in return for our future financial freedom.

For a clear example of how our government is not looking out for the interests of the American people, one need only look at the rapid rise in student loan debt in our country. In 2014, total student loan debt reached $1.1 trillion—almost equal to the gross domestic product of South Korea at the time. All that student loan debt is being paid back to banks at the cost of the future earnings of our college graduates.

American students are told their whole lives about the importance of a college education. They learn how those without college degrees have lower earning power over their working lives and are more likely to be unemployed. After all, our factories have been shipped overseas and those old blue collar jobs that once provided a middle class standard of living are mostly gone. And because of our high immigration rate, competition for the remaining working class jobs is high and the jobs don't pay what they used to. Young people today are told that more education is the answer. Yet in school they are not taught how to keep a family budget, about the importance of saving for retirement, or about the dangers of going into debt.

When young students leave home for the first time, they arrive at college and find that banks are offering them money to pay for their tuition and for the other expenses that come with getting a degree. The credit card companies often have desks set up in university centers offering credit cards to 18-year-old students who have not even started taking classes yet.

To the young student, student loans sound like a great deal. The student is offered money up front without payments until graduation. The student can pay the loans once he has his degree and gets that great job that a college education is supposed to bring. For an impressionable young person away from home for the first time, with little life experience, it sounds reasonable, even advantageous. The student can take out a student loan now, pay his tuition, pay for a car note, pay for rent on an apartment, take trips and enjoy the college experience without having to scrimp and work at lowly minimum wage jobs to make ends meet. The student is given the impression that he is being offered student loans because he is getting educated for a high-paying career.

College costs have been soaring over the past decade, outpacing the rate of inflation. Since there are fewer well-paying blue collar jobs around, more young people are going to college, driving up the demand for a university education while also driving up the supply of college educated people. Since banks and the government have made student loans easy to get, young people are able to pay for tuition by going into debt. And prices always rise when more money is available to pay for a particular good or a service, such as a college education in this case. College tuition shows all the signs of being a classic debt-fueled asset bubble—a bubble that inflated from $550 million in 2007 to over $1 trillion by 2011.

When the student leaves college, carrying his burden of debt, he enters the job market and his payments on his student loans begin. One of the first things he finds is that those high paying jobs that college graduates are supposed to be able to find are not easy to come by. They don't pay as well as he thought and there are millions of people just like him competing for the jobs that are available. Not only are there millions of college-educated Americans to compete against, there are millions of highly educated immigrants applying for the same jobs. When the American college graduate applies for a job in his hometown, he is competing with people from China, India, Russia, Latin America, Europe and everywhere else. These days, it is not only blue collar jobs that immigrants are filling, but also jobs that require a college education—from management positions to science, technology, engineering and mathematics fields. And these immigrants are often from countries where salaries are far lower than in the U.S. so they are willing to work for less because it is more than they are used to having back home. Not only does the American college graduate have to compete for employment with a million new immigrants each year, he has to compete with them in purchasing such things as housing, a car, food and everything else that costs money. When the college graduate decides to take out a mortgage and put a bid on a house in his hometown, he is just as likely to be bidding against someone from Guangzhou or Mumbai as from Dallas or Cleveland.

It's tough out there in America for recent college graduates, especially if they have large student loans hanging over their heads. For debtors carrying too much debt, they have the option of declaring bankruptcy, allowing for relief from their debt by liquidating or restructuring it. But bankruptcy is not an option for those carrying student loan debt. If they are unable to find work that pays enough for them to pay off their debt and their bills are piling up and they are facing substantial hardship, their student loan debt, whether owed to the federal government or to private banks, remains with them. Student loan debt is not dischargeable in bankruptcy. These loans usually have 10-year terms, so the young person who took on student loan debt in the inexperience and shortsightedness of youth enters an increasingly competitive job market shackled with an average of $20,000 in debt.

The student loan debt load is now over $1 trillion, most of it owed to private banks. Just imagine. Interest is being collected on over a trillion dollars from people who went to universities to try to better themselves, and in most cases those universities are public. So the same students that borrowed money at interest to pay their college expenses are also paying taxes to pay the expenses of public universities long after they graduated.

So the government is putting in place policies that encourage young people to go into debt to get an education at public schools. Meanwhile, it has put in place immigration and trade policies that drive down wages and reduce the number of jobs available. And when the banks get into trouble by risky lending, the government bails out the banks to the tune of hundreds of billions of dollars. Yet student loan debt cannot be discharged in bankruptcy by law. When a person gets in over his head with student loan debt, the government will ensure that the debt is repaid, through garnishment of wages and seizure of assets. Does this sound like a government of the people, by the people and for the people?

The example of student loans should cause you to question whether our government is one by the people, for the people and of the people, or instead, a system designed to siphon off the prosperity of the people through interest payments and taxation.

The borrower is servant to the lender. If you are in debt, you are a servant of your lender.

There is no bigger debtor in the world today than the U.S. government. It has amassed the greatest amount of debt in human history. If you are wondering why our government does not seem to be looking out for the interests of the American people, look no further than our national debt. Make no mistake, our government is a servant of its lenders, and its biggest lender is the Federal Reserve.

Thomas Jefferson wrote: "Merchants have no country. The mere spot they stand on does not constitute so strong an attachment as that from which they draw their gains."

The usurer is worse than the merchant. Like the merchant, he has no country, but unlike the merchant, he does not provide goods and services that people want, only money that he has amassed through a mathematical phenomenon that he took advantage of because of a willingness to prey on human weakness and dispense violence if need be.

The usurers are loyal to no country and have been actively subverting our country since its founding.

The Tyranny of Fractional Reserve Banking

Most banks in the world today engage in fractional reserve banking. This practice has had profound effects on the world. It is a powerful aggregator of wealth.

Its practice creates a monetary vortex that sucks in money in ever growing quantities. The modern fractional reserve system is a money machine that enriches and empowers bankers while periodically throwing thousands, even millions, of people out of work. It is a debt-based system that is inherently unstable and which regularly, like clockwork, causes extreme economic upheavals.

If you have a checking or savings account, you are participating in the fractional reserve banking system. Most Americans are in the dark when it comes to understanding how this system operates and what its ramifications are.

Nearly all of us keep our money in banks. The convenience of having our money stored while being readily available is undeniable.

In this day and age of direct deposits, credit cards, debit cards and e-commerce, it just doesn't make sense to hold onto significant amounts of cash for any length of time. Modern banking is unquestionably convenient.

For most of us, we keep our money in banks because it feels safer and is more convenient than carrying around a lot of cash, or keeping cash under our mattresses or locked up in safes in our homes.

But there are significant and destructive consequences of keeping our money in fractional reserve banks.

The concept of fractional reserve banking is simple to understand. Banks only hold a fraction of their deposits on hand while lending out the rest. You put your money in the bank, the bank lends out most of your money to other people but allows you to pull out all that you deposited on demand. The bank can do this because everyone usually doesn't pull out all their money at the same time.

Under our current system, the Federal Reserve determines the fraction of your deposit that your bank must keep on hand, called the fractional reserve requirement. The Fed can inflate or contract the money supply by changing the fraction that banks are required to hold in reserve at their regional Federal Reserve Banks. At the time of this writing, the fraction is set at 10 percent. This means that banks are required to keep in reserve 10 percent of the amount they have out in loans.

The business of banking is lending. Since the advent of fractional reserve banking during the medieval period, customers were promised ready access to the money they deposited into a bank. But when the customer deposited, say $1,000 worth of gold coins into his bank account, the coins were not stored in the bank's vault but were issued out into the economy as loans collecting interest. Those $1,000 in gold coins had just increased the amount of money the bank could lend. At a 10 percent reserve ratio, the bank would keep $100 worth of gold coins on hand in reserve while lending out $900 of gold coins into the economy.

The bank was in possession of only $100 in gold coins of the original deposit, but it still allowed the customer to withdraw all of his $1,000 in gold coins on demand, even though $900 of it had been given to someone else as a loan. As long as depositors didn't withdraw more than 10 percent of the total deposits in the bank, the system worked fine for both the bankers and depositors. The bankers were able to profit off the use of other people's money—essentially practicing usury not with their own money but with the money of their depositors—while the depositors were usually offered up some of the interest.

However, under this system every so often bank runs occurred when depositors demanded more than what the banks had in their vaults. Depositors would learn that they could not get their money back because their money was not in the bank. A run on the bank or a spate of defaults on loans could easily cause a bank to fail. Bank runs were disastrous, both for the bankers and the depositors, and have been a fairly common occurrence in the history of fractionally reserve banking.

It was the Panic of 1907, a nationwide run on banks which wiped out families, banks and businesses that was offered as the impetus for the creation of the Federal Reserve.

If depositors happen to demand more than 10 percent of what is in their bank, the bankers can cover the amount not in their vaults by borrowing from other banks. And today, they have something else to protect them from bank runs, their lender of last resort—the Fed. The Fed can create money out of thin air and lend it to a bank that does not have enough money on hand to cover its obligations.

Fractional reserve banking has characteristics which have profound effects on the economy. The constant threat of bank runs is one of those characteristics. Another is the expansion of the money supply every time a loan is made due to the practice of double-entry bookkeeping in which a bank does not subtract the amount of a loan from its depositors' accounts, but instead just adds the amount of the loan to the borrower's account. Another characteristic is the multiplier effect, which allows banks to collect interest and compound it on money that does not actually exist. These characteristics create a systemic instability that has caused economic turmoil and upheaval ever since the practice of fractional reserve banking began.

Compound interest

Most Americans learn about the magic of compound interest when they begin saving for retirement. We invest our savings to earn a return. If we earn a return and reinvest it, our nest egg grows, slowly at first, but faster over time as the interest compounds. Quarter after quarter, year upon year, our initial investment can grow significantly—just as the rice piled onto the chessboard in the fable about chess and the Indian king.

An initial investment of $10,000 that earns a return of 5 percent, which is reinvested and compounded annually, more than doubles to $26,500 in 20 years' time. In 40 years it has grown to more than $70,000. In 60 years, it is more than $186,000. This growth comes only from reinvesting the interest and not adding to the principal.

The more you add to your principal, the more you can earn in interest and the faster your investment will grow. If you are disciplined enough to make sound investments that do not carry too much risk of default, the magic of compound interest can enable you to earn money without doing actual labor. Your money works for you.

The true rich live off the earnings of their money. They do not earn wages from working for others, but invest so that they can earn a return on the money they already have. But most Americans spend a lifetime working for wages and attempt to save enough so that they can live comfortably off their savings in retirement.

To earn money, most of us must produce goods and services that other people are willing to pay money for. But banks are different. They don't produce goods. But they do provide a service—holding your money for you and giving you access to it. But providing you that service is not their main moneymaker. For a bank, its lifeblood is compound interest. Banks reap the profits of compound interest by using money from their depositors to make loans. They make their profits by lending out your money and collecting interest on it.

The multiplier effect

The multiplier effect is a more obscure concept for most people. Yet, its effect is even more profound than that of compound interest.

The multiplier effect is a powerful phenomenon that can result in the rise of fantastic fortunes and a booming economy, or else, in the blink of an eye, cause an economic crisis and a collapse into bankruptcy.

As mentioned previously, in a fractional reserve banking system, the concept is that when you deposit $1,000 into a bank, that bank keeps $100 in its reserves and turns around and lends

$900 of your money to someone else. But it doesn't subtract the $900 from your account when it lends out the amount to someone else. Your bank account still says $1,000 and you are still told you have access to the full amount. The bank uses double-entry bookkeeping in which your account is still credited with $1,000 while the $900 is recorded as a loan on the bank's books.

Let's say the $900 was lent to a borrower who wants to buy his neighbor's tractor. The borrower uses the money from the loan to purchase the tractor, and then he begins to pay back the $900 to the bank, paying off the principal plus interest in monthly installments.

But what happened to the original $900 in cash used to buy the tractor?

The seller of the tractor deposited the $900 into his bank account. His bank then kept 10 percent of the $900 in reserve and lent out the rest, which is $810.

The $810 was lent to someone else, perhaps as a loan to buy a horse. The money is used to make the purchase and eventually winds up back in a bank and becomes the basis for another loan. Ten percent of the $810 is kept in reserve and $729 re-enters the economy to make another purchase.

That $729 is spent and finds its way back into another bank where it becomes the basis for another loan of $629.

A loan is made. The money lent ends up back in a bank account and becomes the basis for a new loan, which ends up back in a bank, which becomes another loan. And on and on it goes.

This continues multiplying down the line with the same money being recycled and used again and again for new loans.

For simplicity's sake, let's say the smallest loan the banks will issue is about $100. In this example, the multiplier effect turns a $1,000 deposit into about $8,000 in loans.

Deposit	Reserve
$1000	$100
$900	$90
$810	$81
$729	$72.9
$656.1	$65.61
$590.49	$59.05
$531.44	$53.14
$478.30	$47.83
$430.47	$43.05
$387.42	$38.74
$348.68	$34.87
$313.81	$31.38
$282.43	$28.24
$254.19	$25.42
$228.78	$22.88
$205.89	$20.59
$185.30	$18.53
$166.71	$16.67
$150.09	$15.01
$135.09	$13.51
$121.58	$12.16
$109.42	$10.94
$98.48	$9.85
---------	---------
$8113.67	911.37

An initial cash deposit of $1,000 has been lent out again and again creating $8,000 in loans that the banks are collecting interest on.

Meanwhile, the initial depositor believes his $1,000 is safe in a vault. But that is not the case. Only $100 of his original deposit remains in the bank.

Of the $8,000 in loans that was multiplied into existence from the initial deposit, all the depositors who received cash from these loans believe their money is safe in a bank. Yet, there is only $1,000 in actual cash backing $8,000 in deposits! The money has been recycled into the economy each time it has been lent out and re-deposited into a bank.

The banks are collecting interest on $8,000 in deposits, when actually there is only $1,000 in real money from all those deposits. An upside down pyramid of $8,000 in debt has been built on a base of $1,000 in cash. The banks are collecting interest on money that doesn't actually exist simply by promising the initial depositor that his money is safe and sound in a vault. This is the magic money machine of fractional reserve banking. The banks collect interest on multiples of money that don't actually exist.

So, $8,000 in credit has just been spent into the economy to purchase real goods and services. Yet, only $1,000 of that $8,000 actually exists as money. So the actual buying and selling of $8,000 of goods and services has occurred with only $1,000 in cash.

While only $1,000 in cash exists, the borrowers have to pay back $8,000 in actual cash to the banks, plus interest. The banks collect interest off of debt that has been conjured into existence through the magic of the multiplier effect. The interest compounds and grows and becomes a growing profit for the banks. This profit can then become the basis for new loans.

The fractional reserve bankers construct an upside down pyramid of debt upon a foundation of deposits placed into their hands by the people.

The above example is an oversimplification. The way it works today is that each deposit made into the banking system and each loan issued by banks become part of the reserves that member banks hold in their accounts with their regional Federal Reserve Banks. Each withdrawal and each loan payment subtracts from the reserves. Economists have generally agreed that the multiplier effect increases the amount of debt in the economy by 10 times what is deposited into the banks.

Bank runs

The magic of the multiplier effect and compound interest quickly creates fantastic fortunes for the fractional reserve bankers. These bankers do not create wealth through the work of their hands or minds. Instead, they use other people's money to build debt pyramids which allow them to lay claim to the wealth created by the hands and minds of the people.

When this system took root in Europe in the late Middle Ages, its practice resulted in the rise of great banking dynasties, such as the House of Medici, which grew enormously powerful and influential. Giovanni di Bicci de' Medici founded the Bank of Medici in 1397. The Medici lent money to the kings and royals of Europe and grew fantastically wealthy. Medici became heads of state, popes of the Catholic Church and royalty.

While fractional reserve banking can create vast fortunes, it has a fatal weakness. The system rapidly accumulates wealth, but it can collapse just as quickly. Depositors put their money in a bank because they believe it is safe there and they will have access to it on demand. Yet their money is not in the bank. If enough loans default, or if more than 10 percent of depositors demand their money at the same time, then the game is up and the bank fails. The bank does not have the money to cover its obligations.

When people believe their bank is not sound, they tend to panic and run to the bank to pull out what they can so they are not the last person standing in line with empty hands. These panics have been a regular feature of banking through American history. Banks have periodically collapsed, depositors have lost their savings and the bankers have run for the hills.

The Panic of 1907 was particularly catastrophic. A banker had tried to corner the copper market using borrowed money from the Knickerbocker Trust Company. The bid failed and depositors questioned the solvency of Knickerbocker and demanded their money back, leading to a run on the trust. This panic spread to other banks. As more people pulled money from their accounts, banks in New York stopped lending. Liquidity dried up leading to the bankruptcy of other banks and businesses. The lack of cash and confidence in the economy caused the stock market to collapse by 50 percent. As news of what was happening in New York spread, people across the country started pulling their money out of their bank accounts leading to a nationwide run on the banks. With banks and businesses collapsing due to a lack of liquidity, the nation fell into a severe recession.

The Panic of 1907 was nothing new for the nation. Prior to 1907, the U.S. experienced panics in 1792, 1819, 1837, 1857, 1873, 1884 and 1893. Of course, panics were not unique to America. They occurred around the world wherever fractional reserve banking was practiced.

As the Panic of 1907 deepened and people became increasingly desperate, J.P. Morgan, one of the richest bankers in the world at the time, stepped in. He led the way with other bankers, including John D. Rockefeller, and lent money to prop up banks that were experiencing runs. Morgan restored confidence in the banking system.

Morgan was widely believed to have prevented the crisis from deepening. He was credited by the press with saving the day.

But not everyone believed Morgan had acted heroically. In 1908, Upton Sinclair released a novel, called *The Moneychangers,* in which the villain was a rich New York banker who purposefully caused a devastating economic crash only to take credit for rescuing the economy. Sinclair's villainous banker bore a striking resemblance to J.P. Morgan. In the story, Sinclair's banker was also a sexual predator.

The international banker J.P. Morgan was a leading figure in the creation of the Federal Reserve.

The bankers' solution

In the years leading up to 1907, bankers had been calling for the establishment of a European-style central bank in the U.S. The crash of the economy in 1907 was an opportunity for them. The bankers were determined not to let the crisis go to waste. They demanded reform and set in motion their plan to bring into creation another American central bank.

The House and Senate passed the Federal Reserve Act in late December 1913. On December 23, 1913, President Woodrow Wilson signed the act into law and once again a central bank came into existence in the United States.

The stated purpose of the Federal Reserve Act was to provide us with a safer, more flexible, and more stable monetary and financial system. On its surface, the act appeared to have created a decentralized monetary system under American principles and under public control, but in reality international bankers had seized control and centralized the issuance and volume of the American money supply. They had seized the reins of power and were now in control.

Looking back from our present vantage point one hundred years later, did the passage of the act provide us with a safer, more flexible, and more stable monetary and financial system? Were financial disasters like the Panic of 1907 eliminated or mitigated?

Or instead, have we become the soulless corporate republic that Alfred Owen Crozier warned us of—ruled by a government of the corporations, by the corporations and for the corporations?

Looking back, there is no doubt that the currency is now more flexible as far as the bankers are concerned. The bankers have all the flexibility they need to churn out dollars for themselves by the boatload. The Fed can print out trillions of dollars and wire it around the world to wherever it pleases without oversight and without any of us the wiser. But safer and more stable it definitely is not. It should be obvious to all that the Fed has not provided us with a stable and safer monetary and financial system. Every year, the value of the dollar goes down and the price of everything else goes up. According to the Bureau of Labor Statistics Consumer Price Index Inflation Calculator, it took $23.53 in 2013 to purchase the same amount of goods and services that cost $1.00 in 1913. That is why your grandfather remembers paying a nickel for a Coke and you pay $1.50 for one today. That is why a house that sold for $30,000 in 1970 in California sells for $400,000 or more today. It is why the stock market goes up year after year. It is why people earning wages have a harder time paying the bills with each passing year and why those on fixed incomes always seem to be falling behind.

The Fed today has a stated goal of 2 percent inflation per year. That means year after year the price of nearly everything you must pay for goes up by around 2 percent, if that low inflation number is to be believed. If your salary doesn't go up in any given year, then you just took a 2 percent pay cut. This is a great way for corporations to keep labor costs down. By holding off on raises for a year or two while raising prices they can cut pay with most of their employees none the wiser.

Prices will continue to rise year after year and debt to banks will continue to grow exponentially as long as the Federal Reserve is in control. The banks must continually issue more and more debt and continue to inflate the money supply to keep its debt-based monetary system going.

And what of the problem of booms and busts?

The Federal Reserve Act was passed to bring stability to the monetary and financial system after the catastrophic bust of 1907. Was it successful?

History gives us the answer. It was absolutely and without question not successful. We have been in an age of financial turbulence for the past 100 years. Former Fed Chairman Alan Greenspan even acknowledged this fact in the title of his memoirs, *The Age of Turbulence*.

Since 1913, we have lurched from one economic crisis to another. There have been 18 recessions in varying degrees of severity since the passage of the Federal Reserve Act.

The bankers promised us the Federal Reserve Act would

mitigate these economic crises, yet just four years after the passage of the act the country fell into the severe Recession of 1918 at the close of World War I. That recession was every bit as bad as the Panic of 1907. In 1920, that recession became a painful and devastating depression. Following the Depression of 1920-21, the economy boomed for eight years. Then, just 16 years after the founding of the Fed, the country experienced the greatest panic, the biggest financial collapse, the longest and most severe depression in American history—the Great Depression. Millions of Americans lost their life savings, their jobs, their farms and businesses, their homes. Fortunes across the land were wiped out, bank failures spread across the country wiping out the savings of millions. A contraction of credit made money hard to come by. People lined up at soup kitchens to avoid starvation.

The Federal Reserve Act was passed in 1913 in response to the Panic of 1907, yet just 16 years later the country experienced an economic crisis that made the Panic of 1907 seem like a minor economic footnote in comparison. The Great Depression lasted 12 years and ended in a cataclysmic global war in which nearly 100 million people were killed around the world.

And what was the cause of the Great Depression? At Milton Friedman's birthday on November 8, 2002, Ben Bernanke, a student of the Great Depression who was soon to become the Federal Reserve Chairman, gave us a clue. "I would like to say to Milton and Anna: Regarding the Great Depression. You're right, we did it. We're very sorry. But thanks to you, we won't do it again."

Today, eight years later our country is still struggling with the aftermath of the 2007 housing crash and the devastating recession that followed. One hundred years after the passage of the Federal Reserve Act, we can look back and say without a doubt that the Federal Reserve has totally and utterly failed in its stated objectives. It did not give us a safer and more stable monetary and financial system. Yet the Federal Reserve Bank remains in operation. It has grown to become the nexus of power not only in the United States but in all the world.

What is the legacy of the Fed's 100-year reign?

Our once mighty industrial base has been exported overseas. Our nation, which was once the world's greatest creditor, is now buried under the largest debt burden in history. Fewer and fewer Americans as a percentage of the population are working and more Americans have become reliant on food stamps and government handouts. The big banks that own the Federal Reserve have grown larger, more influential and more powerful than ever. They have become too big to fail. Our once mighty middle class is on the ropes. More and more of the wealth of the American nation is being concentrated into fewer and fewer hands while the ranks of the poor are growing. The once prosperous American people have fallen under the domination of a grasping international plutocracy. Our military is pulled into wars in distant countries where our youth are killed and our nation is pushed further into debt. A handful of obscenely rich people now dominate our country as the masses descend into poverty and government dependence. Our shameless politicians grovel before a few billionaires and promise them more wars in return for campaign financing. For more and more Americans, the once attainable American dream now seems like a bitter joke. These are the fruits of the Federal Reserve Act.

Back in 1907, the solution to the booms and busts caused by fractional reserve banking was not to form a new central bank. The obvious solution was to take fractional reserve banking head on.

In a fractional reserve banking system the amount of debt will always grow to exceed the money supply until the debt burden becomes so large that it can never be paid back. Then the inevitable defaults will occur and the banks will seize assets. That is the natural outcome of fractional reserve banking—the natural outcome of promising people that they can receive the money they deposited in a bank on demand when in fact the money has been lent out to others.

The solution given by the bankers to get around the weaknesses of fractional reserve banking is the central banking system. This solution is an admission by the bankers that their system is inherently unstable and needs the backing of a government-sponsored monopolistic bank in order to reduce the inherent risk of lending out multiples of money that do not actually exist. A central bank is a fractional reserve banker's lender of last resort to provide liquidity by printing money out of thin air when the inevitable bust occurs. When a bank run occurs the central bank merely prints out enough money to satisfy the depositors so that the bank can stay afloat. The bankers use a central bank to create money from nothing to prop up their unstable money-making machines.

However, even with central banks acting as lenders of last resort, by its very nature fractional reserve banking remains unstable, whether a central bank backstops the system or not. The central banking system has done nothing to increase the stability of the fractional reserve banking system. Banks continue to create debt upon debt upon debt until the bubble pops and the inevitable contraction occurs. The system always and inevitably creates booms and busts, like the Panic of 1907. Central banks have only served to save the bankers by keeping them afloat during crises by printing money out of thin air when bank runs occur. The Fed did not stop the booms and busts and panics, it just made sure that the big banks that control the Fed wouldn't go under when the busts occurred.

The obvious solution back in 1907 was to outlaw fractional reserve banking altogether. If the people of the day had recognized the inherent instability of fractional reserve banking and that the practice is based entirely on fraud—based on bankers making promises that they are unable to fulfill under certain conditions—then perhaps today we would have a safer and more stable financial and monetary system. But that didn't happen.

Reformers of the day could have required banks to keep all their depositors' money on hand that they were promising to give on demand. They should have made it illegal for a bank to lend out 90 percent of your money and tell you that 100 percent of it is available to you. This would have eliminated the need for a lender of last resort when the inevitable bust came because banks would not be lending out more than their depositors could withdraw.

How simple is that?

If you wish to allow the banks to lend your money to others and for the bank to collect interest on it, then your money should have been lent out on a fixed term, like a certificate of deposit where you cannot pull your money out of the bank on demand while it is being used by someone else. You then receive it back in fixed installments with added interest. If the borrower defaults, you lose your money. If you do not want to put your money at risk, then you put into an account where it is not lent out by the bank to other people.

This is called full-reserve banking. While it would not solve the inequities caused by usury, bank runs cannot occur under full-reserve banking and thus there is no need for a central bank.

However, the bankers had grown rich and powerful from fractional reserve banking and they didn't want the people to enact reforms that would end the gravy train, no matter if the train is always on the brink of derailing into catastrophe. After all, it was the booms and the busts that were the source of the bankers' great wealth. When the booms came, they could ride the upward trend. And when the inevitable busts occurred, these were times of great opportunity for those with access to credit. Those with money could buy up businesses, farms, houses and other banks for pennies on the dollar. The big banks with access to money and credit could buy up real assets on the cheap when everyone else was bankrupt from the bust. The busts were opportunities to seize and control the real wealth of a nation. The last thing the bankers really wanted was to end the boom and bust cycle. That's why this destructive cycle is still around 100 years after the creation of the Fed. The Fed made it easier for the big banks to get the money they needed to buy up assets when the busts came and that's exactly what they have done.

Money exists to be circulated. Money is the lubricant that keeps the wheels of the economy turning. Economic crises have occurred time and again by no other means than the withdrawal of money from circulation. When money dries up, the wheels of the economy grind to a halt and economies stagnate. When money becomes scarce, governments, businesses and the people must take out loans at whatever interest rates usurers demand. The loans then burden the finances of the nation with the payment of interest. Nations become bond slaves to the banks.

Before the existence of the Federal Reserve, banks determined the amount of money that circulated in the economy. After the creation of the Federal Reserve, the ability to withdraw money from circulation became centralized. The Fed became the one institution that determined how much or little lubricant the wheels of the economy would receive.

Simply by raising interest rates or increasing the required bank reserves, the Fed can withdraw money from circulation and an economic crisis can be created. Businesses will stop hiring and start firing. People will be thrown out of work. Elected officials will receive the blame and be thrown out of office. New politicians will be elected to take their place.

Simply by lowering interest rates, lowering the required reserves, or buying government securities, money will flood into the economy and an economic boom can be engineered. The stock market will rise. Assets will increase in price. Businesses will hire. Wages will go up. Politicians in office will be popular and get reelected.

A central bank centralizes the process of creating booms and busts and puts a handful of people in control of the economic well-being of a nation.

The Fed was not created to end booms and busts like the Panic of 1907. It was created to keep the unstable fractional reserve banking system in place and consolidate the power of the biggest bankers in the land.

What the bankers got in 1913 was a central bank that could provide them with all the credit they needed. Instead of having J.P. Morgan use his own money to rescue the fractional reserve banking system during the inevitable collapses, the bankers would use the full faith and credit the United States government to bail them out during the crises that they create. The people of the United States were made responsible for bailing out the banks. The banks keep their profits when times are good and the people shoulder the losses when times are bad.

Since the passage of the Federal Reserve Act, the Fed has grown into the most powerful institution in the country. It has the power to make or break presidents, to enrich those its favors and destroy those it does not.

Congress delegated this enormous power to the Fed, and, when it gave the president the power to appoint the Board of Governors, it gave the executive branch a degree of influence over monetary policy, which under the Constitution is the responsibility of Congress.

The Congress can strip that power away from the Fed at any time by repealing the Federal Reserve Act. But unfortunately, the Fed's influence over our elected politicians and our media is a formidable obstacle to any monetary reform.

In 2012, the House of Representatives passed the Federal Reserve Transparency Act of 2009. The act was meant to allow the Government Accountability Office the power to fully audit the activities of the Fed, including its discount window, its funding facilities, its open market operations and its agreements with foreign bankers. The bill had the support of both Democrats and Republicans in the House and passed 327 to 98.

However, Senate Majority Leader Harry Reid refused to allow the Senate's version of the bill to come to a vote.

One of the arguments for the existence of the Fed is that Congress is a political body and is influenced by election cycles and public opinion whereas the Fed is independent from partisan politics. But this is not the case.

Ben Bernanke, the Fed Chairman at the time, was outspoken in his opposition to the audit bill and politically interfered with the Congress regarding the vote on the bill. The Fed had previously resisted a partial audit in 2011 which revealed that between 2008 and 2009 the Fed had provided $16 trillion in secret low-interest loans to American and foreign banks and businesses during the downturn caused by the housing the bust. This $16 trillion was on top of the $700 billion Troubled Asset Relief Program (TARP) bailout of the banks that Congress authorized in 2008.

The 2011 partial audit revealed that the Fed had doled out more money to banks than the gross domestic product of the United States—an amount nearly five times the size of the U.S. government's annual budget. This money not only went to America's biggest banks, but to foreign banks in Europe and Asia, and Congress had no knowledge of it. The mainstream media largely ignored the results of the audit.

The partial audit also revealed that William C. Dudley, who was a senior official at the Federal Reserve Bank of New York at the time, owned stock in the insurance firm American International Group (AIG) when the Fed had bailed it out.

Ben Bernanke lobbied against the Federal Reserve Transparency Act, even writing letters of praise to Congress members who opposed the bill.

"While the outcome of the vote was not in doubt, your willingness to stand up for the independence of the Federal Reserve is greatly appreciated," Bernanke wrote in the letters. "Independence in monetary policy operations is now the norm for central banks around the world—and it would be a grave mistake were Congress to reverse the protection it provided to the Federal Reserve more than 30 years ago."

Obviously, the Fed is a political body that engages in politics. Public opinion is important to Fed bankers and they manipulate it constantly. Right now, we live in an upside down world where it is not our elected representatives in Congress that are interfering with the operations of the Fed, but the unelected Fed members who are interfering with the operations of our Congress. And it's the Fed that is in control of the purse strings. No doubt the Fed would consider it a grave mistake if Congress and the public were to know what the Fed was doing behind closed doors.

Where is all the money going? Is the Fed secretly wiring money to favored banks and corporations? What business people and politicians are favored by the Fed? Why is the Fed making the decisions that it does?

Do you honestly think the Fed is making its decisions for the good of the American people? Is that why some of the richest bankers in the world, Paul Warburg, J.P Morgan and John D. Rockefeller, set up the Fed—out of the goodness of their hearts?

Money is power. The Fed has the power to create $16 trillion out of thin air, more money than the entire yearly economic output of any nation on Earth, and far more than the yearly budget of any government. It has the power to wire enormous sums of money in secret to the banks and corporations of its choosing.

Power corrupts and absolute power corrupts absolutely.

Does anyone believe that any institution should be granted absolute power over money without checks and balances or oversight? If a partial audit revealed that the Fed created $16 trillion and sent it to banks and corporations around the world, what would a full audit reveal?

The Federal Reserve and its beneficiaries do not want you to know.

The Tyranny of Gold

On September 24, 1572, Tupac Amaru, the last Inca emperor, ascended a scaffold in the main square in Cuzco. In the book *The Last Days of the Inca*, Kim MacQuarrie vividly described the scene. Tupac Amaru, flanked by a Spanish priest and an Indian executioner, looked out at the multitude of Indians, African slaves and Spaniards that had crowded into the square to see him.

The multitude had packed tightly into the square, filled the balconies and windows, lined the rooftops and stood on hilltops in the distance, everyone straining to see the man known as the Royal Serpent. When the Indians caught sight of their emperor atop the scaffold, they deafened the skies with their sobs and moans.

Tupac Amaru slowly raised his hand and then let it fall and the multitude fell deathly silent. The emperor then addressed them.

"Let it be known that I am a Christian and they have baptized me and I wish to die under the law of God—and I have to die. And that everything that my ancestors the Incas and I have told you up till now—that you should worship the sun god, Punchao, and the shrines, idols, stones, rivers, mountains, and sacred things—is a lie and completely false."

Tupac Amaru told the people that when he would enter the temple to speak to the sun god, it was just a trick. The sun god was an idol of gold and merely an inanimate object. Tupac Amaru told them that the words he had attributed to the sun god were his own because gold cannot speak. He told them that he had learned from his brother that whenever he wished to tell the Indians to do something that he should enter the sun temple alone and then come out and tell them that the sun god had spoken to him. Then he could tell the people whatever he wanted to tell them because they venerated the sun god, and they would obey.

Tupac Amaru then asked the people to forgive him for deceiving them.

The emperor laid his head on the block like a lamb. His head was then severed with one blow from the executioner's knife. The executioner held the head up high by the hair for all the crowd to see. So ended the life of the last Inca emperor.

The Incas did not have a monetary system that used money as a medium of exchange. All property in the Inca Empire belonged to the emperor. The people paid their taxes to the state with their labor. For two to three months a year, the males of the empire gave their labor to the emperor or served as soldiers. That meant that up to two million Indians were working for the emperor at any given time. They provided the labor to build irrigation canals, temples and palaces. Their surplus food and goods supported the Inca nobility. The peasant Indians were allowed to own their own plots of land on which they worked for the remainder of the year. In return for their labor, the emperor guaranteed them food, clothing, shelter and protection from invasion.

According to MacQuarrie, the revenues of the Inca Empire were enormous. The surplus created by the Inca peasantry was kept in storehouses located throughout the empire. These storehouses were full of blankets, wool, clothes, sandals, knives, shields, armor and various metal objects. The Spaniards were astonished at the quantity of goods whenever they encountered these repositories. The gross domestic product of the empire was so great that periodically the storehouses had to be emptied and their contents given away to the people in order to make room for new goods.

This empire of 10 million people existed without money. The Inca had no shops or markets and engaged in no commerce among themselves. The necessities of life were issued to the people from state storehouses. Goods were not purchased and thus there was no need for a monetary system.

Although the Incas had no money, they valued gold and silver. For the Inca, gold was symbolic of the sun and silver symbolic of the moon. These metals were worked into decorative and religious objects, but not used as any form of money or medium of exchange.

The Inca had so much gold and silver that when Francisco Pizarro and his conquistadors captured the Inca emperor Atahualpa in 1532, the emperor offered Pizarro a ransom for his freedom of a roomful of gold and two roomfuls of silver. Pizarro took the gold and silver but killed Atahualpa anyway.

The old Inca economy and way of life collapsed after the Spanish conquest. The Spanish took all Inca gold and silver objects, melted them down and minted them into coins. Merchants from New England traded with the Spanish for these coins which became the medium of exchange for the North American colonists.

Gold and silver have long fascinated the human species. There is something about these precious metals that excites a corner of our primate brains. Although gold and silver have less utility than other metals, their shininess and luster give them value to us.

Gold is durable yet malleable. Its scarcity when compared to other metals has served to drive up its value. Gold has long been a symbol of the wealth and riches of kings. Women are flattered by it and adorn themselves with it. Men will travel to the far ends of the Earth, toil, and even kill to attain it. Yet, unlike copper or iron, gold has little practical utility except for use as coins and jewelry. Unlike copper and iron, the demand for gold is driven by human vanity and a perception that gold equates with wealth.

Gold coins were used as money for thousands of years. The faces of gods and emperors were stamped on golden coins which were used as a medium of exchange. Gold bullion was used by states as reserves to back up their money supplies. Gold was the currency of international trade and was seen as the measure of a nation's wealth.

In today's era of fiat currencies where money is backed by nothing but the faith and credit of governments, many people hold gold as a means to store value, even though gold earns no income, unlike assets such as real estate or business enterprises which can earn rents or profits. Gains on gold can only be made by selling it at a greater price than you paid for it—in short, speculating. People who purchase gold today are betting that its value will go up in relation to paper money. They purchase gold to protect their savings from inflation and currency devaluation caused by central banks expanding the money supply. Their purchase of gold as a hedge against currency depreciation makes perfect sense if past history is anything to go by. Paper currencies come and go—they depreciate, decay and turn to dust. Yet, through fire, shipwrecks, wars and revolutions, gold endures. As governments fall into debt and more and more money is printed, the value of gold rises with the increase in the money supply. Decade after decade, century after century, as populations increase and economies expand, the value of gold increases. The stock of gold remains relatively stable as populations increase and economies grow, resulting in more people demanding it for more and more paper money. People will willingly pay more of a depreciating currency to purchase gold. Today, people who do not have faith in the credit of governments or in the central banking system see gold as the answer to their inflationary fears.

The gold standard became common in the Western world in the late 1800s. Governments pegged the value of their currencies to gold, which eased international trade and gave people confidence in the money they used for commerce. In the United States in the decades after the Civil War, two of the leading advocates for the gold standard were J.P. Morgan and John D. Rockefeller, two of the richest men in the world.

Under a gold standard, paper money could be redeemed for a fixed amount of gold. Currency backed by gold was called hard money or sound money, and was unlike the fiat money we use today, which is backed only by perception and the necessity to use it to pay taxes.

When the Federal Reserve came into being in the early 20th century, hard money advocates were common, especially in the banking, financial and business communities. Even Alfred Crozier, a harsh critic of financiers and bankers, wanted government money backed by gold reserves with every dollar redeemable in gold, which he said would satisfy the demands of hard money advocates and give the people confidence in a new government currency. Today, the call for a return to the gold standard is often given as a solution to our current monetary woes of inflation and government deficit spending.

Money backed by gold is said to be sound money. But has this ever really been the case?

When money was backed by gold, we still had booms and busts. We still had inflation, deflation, terrible depressions, bank runs and bank collapses, and massive government borrowing and indebtedness. We still had wars. In fact, some of the biggest wars in world history began when nations were following the gold standard.

Back in 1921 when the United States was still on the gold standard, Thomas Edison criticized gold in a December 6, 1921 article in the *New York Times,* stating that gold is a tool of moneylenders and a way to enrich bankers at the expense of the people whenever the government issues bonds to pay for public works. "It is the money broker, the money profiteer, the private banker, that I oppose," Edison said in the article. "They gain their power through a fictitious and false value given to gold. ... Gold is a relic of Julius Caesar and interest is an invention of Satan. ... Gold is intrinsical of less utility than most metals. The probable reason why it is retained as the basis of money is that it is easy to control. And it is the control of money that constitutes the money question. It is the control of money that is the root of all evil. ... Gold and money are separate things, you see. Gold is the trick mechanism by which you can control money."

The gold standard is believed by many to keep inflation in check, increase the value of savings and stabilize the economy by keeping prices stable. Its advocates claim that the gold standard is advantageous and creates prosperity—that it is superior to the fiat system we have today. Yet, no country today uses the gold standard. The gold standard has been abandoned by every country that ever adopted it. Today, all countries use fiat currencies. Not a one uses the gold standard. If the gold standard is advantageous, why is there not a single country in the world that uses it? Why did the gold standard fail so completely and so universally that not a single nation in the world today uses gold as money?

The fact is that the gold standard has been the ruin of any nation that has adopted it. Gold simply cannot satisfy the demands for money when an economy or a population is growing. Because gold is scarce and exists in a relatively fixed amount, when an economy grows or a nation's population increases, the demand for gold increases, which drives up its cost and causes deflation in the prices of the goods and services being exchanged in the economy. When prices are falling and the value of gold is rising, people tend to hoard gold, especially the rich who own most of it, which means the medium of exchange that serves as the grease that keeps an economy running will dry up and economic activity will grind to a stop. The scarcity of money results in increased borrowing at high interest rates. This causes the indebtedness of the people to increase along with unemployment and poverty.

In his pamphlet *A Modest Enquiry into the Nature and Necessity of a Paper Currency*, Benjamin Franklin pointed out that when money is scarce interest rates will be high and the holders of money will find more profit in usury than in commerce. Money will not be invested in improving land and in commerce because it will be lent out at high interest. The result is that fewer laborers are employed and economic activity falls. Franklin said that the rich opposed the issuance of colonial scrip because they preferred lending money on security at exorbitant interest over trade which was riskier. When money was scarce, the rich got richer from collecting interest while the common people were driven into poverty from the lack of trade and work. This drove down the cost of land which the rich could buy up with an appreciating currency. In his pamphlet which was an argument for the issuance of Pennsylvania scrip, Franklin said opposition to Pennsylvania issuing paper money would come from the rich, from lawyers who make their living off people falling into debt and suing one another, and from office holders, tenants and debtors who are dependent on the rich.

In the modern era, Carroll Quigley has given us great insights into the rich and powerful and of the importance they have long given to gold. Quigley, an establishment intellectual, studied the power elite's papers, wrote about them extensively, and even taught them as a professor at Georgetown.

Quigley was tied into the power elite in our country and knew them on a personal level. He lectured at the Brookings Institution and at the Industrial College of the Armed Forces. He gave talks at the State Department, wrote for the *Washington Post*, the *Washington Star* and the magazine *Current History* where he served on the editorial board. He was a consultant to the House Committee on Astronautics and Space Exploration and played a minor role in the creation of NASA. Quigley was famously Bill Clinton's history teacher when Clinton attended Georgetown in the 1960s. Clinton sometimes mentioned Quigley in speeches, including in his first inaugural speech as governor of Arkansas, again in 1991 at Georgetown when he launched his presidential bid, and again when he accepted the presidential nomination at the Democratic National Convention in 1992.

As an aside, in the December 1996 issue of *George Magazine*, Scott McLemee wrote about Clinton and Quigley in an article titled *The Quigley Cult*. McLemee tells us that in the fall semester of 1964, Clinton received a B in Quigley's Western Civilization class, while nearly half the class scored D's. "Bill Clinton, it seems, mastered the basic Quigleyism in rapid order," McLemee wrote. "Friends recall that he would stay behind after class with a clutch of students who threw questions at the professor."

In 1966, just a decade before his death, Quigley released his epic historical work *Tragedy and Hope*, which examined the history of Western Civilization, the technological, intellectual and economic developments that have led us to where we are today, and the people who influenced the direction and course that our history has taken. What made Quigley's interpretation of history remarkable was his acknowledgment, deep understanding and candidness regarding the importance of finance and banking to Western history.

In *Tragedy and Hope,* Quigley wrote that in the 19th century the richest international banking families were advocates and promoters of the gold standard. According to Quigley, these families "were, accordingly, fanatical devotees of deflation (which they called 'sound' money from its close associations with high interest rates and a high value of money) and of the gold standard, which, in their eyes, symbolized and ensured these values..."

Quigley continued: "The influence of financial capitalism and of the international bankers who created it was exercised both on business and on governments, but could have done neither if it had not been able to persuade both these to accept two 'axioms' of its own ideology. Both of these were based on the assumption that politicians were too weak and too subject to temporary popular pressures to be trusted with control of the money system; accordingly, the sanctity of all values and the soundness of money must be protected in two ways: by basing the value of money on gold and by allowing bankers to control the supply of money. To do this it was necessary to conceal, or even to mislead, both governments and people about the nature of money and its methods of operation."

Quigley described the gold standard as an upside down pyramid balanced on its point. According to Quigley, "in the point was a supply of gold and its equivalent certificates; on the intermediate levels was a much larger supply of notes; and at the top, with an open and expandable upper surface, was an even greater supply of deposits. Each level used the levels below it as its reserves, and, since these lower levels had smaller quantities of money, they were 'sounder.'"

"In all countries," Quigley wrote, "the demand for and volume of such credit was larger in time of a boom and less in time of a depression. This to a considerable extent explains the inflationary aspect of a depression, the combination helping to form the so-called 'business cycle.'"

In an economy under the gold standard where fractional reserve banking is practiced, gold accumulates in banks where it is then lent out at interest into the economy. The multiplier effect and the mathematics of compound interest apply to gold just as they do to the fiat money we use today. In an economy where gold is money and people keep their gold in banks, the banks retain a fraction of the gold in their vaults while issuing loans that exceed the supply of gold by at least 10 times.

The bank lends an amount of gold at interest to a borrower and the borrower spends the gold into the economy. The gold then ends up back in a bank, which then lends the gold again, and the cycle of lending and the multiplier effect run their course. Because of the multiplier effect, the amount of debt issued by the banks will eventually exceed the amount of actual gold that exists in an economy. The banks will collect interest that compounds on multiples of the amount of gold that they hold in their vaults. Since paper notes are more convenient than gold coins or bullion, the banks will issue notes that circulate through the economy, with each note representing gold that can be redeemed. As the interest owed to the banks compounds and grows, far more gold-backed paper currency will circulate than there is gold in an economy. All these paper notes are not actually backed by gold at all because there is not enough gold held in reserves in the banks to be redeemed if everyone were to exchange their notes for gold.

In an economy where fractional reserve banking is practiced, hard money backed by gold is an illusion. The gold-backed paper notes are not backed by gold, but only by the confidence in the holders of the notes that they can redeem the notes for gold. However, if enough of them were to redeem their notes at once, they would find that their confidence was misplaced. Once that confidence is lost by the public and a bank run occurs, the people learn the hard way that the gold they thought was in the bank vault is not there at all. Not enough gold exists to be redeemed.

Gold-backed money is not sound money after all, but is just paper, much like the fiat currencies of today. The bankers have deceived the holders of their notes with an illusion, with the glitter of gold. Under a gold standard, the banks collect interest on gold that doesn't actually exist.

The major difference between fiat money and gold-backed money is that the creation of gold-backed money is restrained by the gold supply, which tends to cause deflation over time; however, fiat money is not backed by gold and has no such restraint, which causes inflation over time.

As Ellen Brown explained in her book *Web of Debt*, the mathematics of compound interest mean that in an economy where gold is money, if banks were to lend just 10 percent of the money supply at 6 percent interest compounded annually, in 40 years all of the gold in the economy would be vacuumed up by the banks. Where gold is money, it only takes a generation for the bankers to own all the gold!

That is exactly what happened. In Europe, fractional reserve bankers vacuumed up all the gold and became the masters of the continent. The bankers had so much gold that governments borrowed it from them and paid it back by taxing the people. Imagine that. A government with sovereignty over millions of people with the ability to tax land, businesses, luxuries and commerce of every sort, would turn to a private bank, owned by private citizens, in order to finance itself. The governments of Europe came hat in hand to bankers and voluntarily turned over their financial freedom for want of a shiny inert metal. Since banks controlled the world's gold, and because gold was money, the bankers used it to buy up the world, including the world's governments.

Gold was needed to conduct commerce, especially international commerce. So in order to conduct commercial activities, producers and merchants borrowed gold from banks. Actually, what they borrowed were gold notes that were printed out in numbers beyond the actual gold that existed. The bankers then controlled economies by raising or lowering interest rates.

When they lowered interest rates, commerce increased; when they raised interest rates, commerce contracted. Since governments needed gold for their operations, they also borrowed from banks. Banks controlled governments in the same manner, by raising or lowering interest rates. To finance their activities, governments became dependent on banks purchasing government bonds.

The source of a banker's wealth and power simply comes from the effortless multiplication of money and compounding of that money with interest. But for most people in the world, wealth comes from the ability to work—to produce tangible goods and useful services in demand from others.

A nation's wealth is not determined by the amount of gold in the treasury, but by the capacity of its people to work, produce goods and perform services.

If one nation has an abundance of gold and the other an equal abundance of iron, which nation is wealthier? The gold can be made into coins and jewelry. The iron can be forged into steel and made into weapons, plows, engines, ships, tanks, airplanes, railways, trains, automobiles, bridges, skyscrapers, and every manner of machinery, weaponry and useful devices.

The nation with iron could produce armor, shields and swords and quickly overrun the other nation and seize the gold of its bejeweled neighbors. But if the people with iron believe that gold is wealth, they will sell their iron for gold coins and their neighbors will end up making the swords and plows.

It is not the gold that is the source of wealth but the ability to produce goods through work. Seashells and wampum could just as easily be used to purchase the iron if human perception made it so. And if human perception caused seashells to be seen as money, the people with the most seashells could buy up all the wealth of the people who work to produce tangible goods, simply because people believed that seashells were money.

During the depths of the Great Depression when the United States was on the gold standard, President Franklin Delano Roosevelt made private gold ownership illegal. In 1933, in our supposedly free country, Americans were banned from owning gold by executive order. Americans were told to turn in their gold or face a $10,000 fine or 10 years in jail.

The people were paid $20 per ounce for their gold, which was delivered to Federal Reserve Banks and their branches around the country. Once the Federal Reserve Banks had all the gold, the government arbitrarily changed its value from $20 to $35 an ounce. Americans were no longer allowed to redeem their dollars for gold and gold could no longer be exported by law. The United States was taken off the gold standard, or rather, the American people were taken off the gold standard.

While Americans could not own gold or redeem dollars for it, the metal could be sold on international markets for foreign currency. Gold was used to back the dollar internationally but Americans could not own it themselves. In fact, the government began arresting anyone in the country who held gold coins or bullion or sold it to others.

The rationale behind the seizure was that hoarding gold had caused money to stop circulating during the Great Depression. By seizing gold from hoarders, money would begin flowing again and the economy would recover. The seized gold would then back the dollar and strengthen it.

The government did not let the crisis atmosphere of the Great Depression go to waste and seized the moment to confiscate the people's gold and turn it over to the Federal Reserve. The gold seizure did in fact strengthen the dollar, but this was no consolation to the average American down on Main Street. After the seizure, the Great Depression continued to grind on. Despite the gold seizure, Americans suffered through eight more years of poverty, bread lines and the longest stretch of high unemployment in our history. Then came World War II.

When World War II came to a close, exchange rates were fixed at $35 for an ounce of gold. Every U.S. dollar held by foreign governments could be redeemed for gold under the terms of the Bretton Woods agreement of 1944. The American dollar became the world's reserve currency.

After the war, the American economy boomed. But by the

late 1960s, Japan, Germany and Western Europe had been rebuilt from the destruction of World War II and the United States began running a trade deficit. Tariffs had been removed and foreign goods flowed in. More dollars began to accumulate overseas as more dollars were used to pay for more and more foreign-made goods. The Federal Reserve also began to print more dollars as the government ran larger and larger budget deficits to pay for the Vietnam War and increased spending on the welfare programs of President Lyndon Johnson's Great Society initiatives. Foreign nations began losing confidence in the dollar and began redeeming their dollars for gold. Gold began to rapidly drain out of the United States. On August 15, 1971, President Richard Nixon issued Executive Order 11615. To stop the drain of gold, he ended the convertibility of dollars to gold. This effectively killed the gold standard in the United States and in the rest of the world.

With the end of Bretton Woods, the last link to gold was severed and we entered a new monetary era. Gold was no longer a restraint on money creation. Every note in the world printed out as money by a national mint was not redeemable for a fixed amount of gold. Money could now be created without limitation.

Gold is no longer money, but it is still held by those who want to protect themselves from inflation. And it is still held by governments who are the largest holders of gold in the world. If the International Monetary Fund is to be believed, as of 2015 the U.S. Treasury holds the single largest amount of gold. Germany has the second largest holdings while the International Monetary Fund is third. The Bank for International Settlements in Basel, Switzerland, has the 32nd largest holdings.

Gold is not money, but governments and central banks hold on to it, just in case.

The history of gold has been an unending tale of greed, war, environmental destruction and economic ruin. It has been worshiped, like the golden calf of the *Bible;* it has caused the downfall of kings who coveted it, as epitomized in the fable of King Midas. Like the American Indians who sold Manhattan

Island for a handful of beads and trinkets, the people of the Earth have traded away the true wealth of their nations for a shiny, inert metal. Even worse, today they trade it away to banks for nothing more than slips of paper and numbers on computer screens.

The Tyranny of Central Banks

Today, the vast majority of money in the modern economy is not made up of printed notes. Most of the money supply is nothing more than numbers on bank computer screens.

In the Bank of England's *Quarterly Bulletin 2014 Q1*, Michael McLeay, Amar Radia and Ryland Thomas of the Bank's Monetary Analysis Directorate, explain how money is created and controlled in the modern world.

In their article, titled *Money creation in the modern economy,* the writers explain how the majority of money today is created by commercial banks making loans. The money we get when we receive our paychecks and the money we spend in order to live our daily lives is not actually printed out at the national mint or by a central bank but is actually just bank credit—numbers created on computers and credited or debited in bank accounts. Banks create the money, or numbers, whenever they make new loans. When the loans are repaid, money is extinguished.

According to the writers, whenever a bank makes a loan, it simultaneously creates a matching deposit in the borrower's bank account, thereby creating new money. Each new loan creates a new deposit in a bank thereby expanding the money supply. The borrower can then spend the deposit into the economy whenever he makes a purchase with his debit card, checkbook or with cash. The new money then circulates through the economy, much of the time without cash exchanging hands, but merely numbers debited and credited in bank accounts.

According to the article, "When a bank makes a loan, for example to someone taking out a mortgage to buy a house, it does not typically do so by giving them thousands of pounds worth of banknotes. Instead, it credits their bank account with a bank deposit of the size of the mortgage. At that moment, new money is created. For this reason, some economists have referred to bank deposits as 'fountain pen money', created at the stroke of bankers' pens when they approve loans."

If the property owner does not have an account in the same bank as the borrower purchasing the house, the bank uses money from its depositors so that the borrower can use the money to make the purchase. If the bank does not have enough money on hand in deposits, it borrows the amount from another bank, or it simply borrows the money from the central bank which creates the money out of nothing. Deposits held by a bank do not limit the amount of loans that the bank can issue. A bank will make a loan first and then find the money to cover the loan as long as the bank's loan officers believe they can profit off the interest received from the borrower.

When loans are repaid, the banks debit from the accounts of the borrowers and money is extinguished.

The creation of new money in this manner is limited by the number of borrowers in the economy that the banks can lend to and still remain profitable. As long as the banks believe they will be paid back, they will continue to make loans. Risk and profit margin are taken into consideration with each loan issued. The amount of profit the banks make from collecting interest on their loans is determined by the interest rate set by the central bank.

When a central bank raises interest rates, borrowing becomes expensive and fewer people take out loans thereby reducing the money supply. When the central bank lowers rates, money becomes cheaper and more people take out loans and the money supply expands.

According to the article, "The ultimate constraint on money creation is monetary policy. By influencing the level of interest rates in the economy, the Bank of England's monetary policy affects how much households and companies want to borrow. This occurs both directly, through influencing the loan rates charged by banks, but also indirectly through the overall effect of monetary policy on economic activity in the economy. As a result, the Bank of England is able to ensure that money growth is consistent with its objective of low and stable inflation."

This process works the same in the United States and

around the world. Commercial banks issue money into the economy when they make loans and central banks control the supply of money through monetary policy.

The buying and selling of government bonds are a key tool in conducting monetary policy. When the U.S. federal government runs a budget deficit, it borrows money from banks by issuing U.S. Treasury bonds. The budget deficit is the amount of money the government spends over the amount it takes in from taxation. Each Treasury bond is debt that the government promises to pay back through taxation.

The interest rate that the government, and ultimately the American people, must pay on the bonds is determined by the Fed's 12-member Federal Open Market Committee. The government sells the bonds in what is called open market operations when banks purchase the Treasury bonds from the government. Banks that are designated as primary dealers by the Fed are allowed to purchase the bonds. The money from the sale of the bonds is used by the government to pay for its deficit spending.

In 2014, the primary dealers were:

Bank of Nova Scotia, New York Agency
BMO Capital Markets Corp.
BNP Paribas Securities Corp.
Barclays Capital Inc.
Cantor Fitzgerald & Co.
Citigroup Global Markets Inc.
Credit Suisse Securities (USA) LLC
Daiwa Capital Markets America Inc.
Deutsche Bank Securities Inc.
Goldman, Sachs & Co.
HSBC Securities (USA) Inc.
Jefferies LLC
J.P. Morgan Securities LLC
Merrill Lynch, Pierce, Fenner & Smith Incorporated
Mizuho Securities USA Inc.

Morgan Stanley & Co. LLC
Nomura Securities International, Inc.
RBC Capital Markets, LLC
RBS Securities Inc.
SG Americas Securities, LLC
TD Securities (USA) LLC
UBS Securities LLC.

As you can see, many of these banks are foreign. Our debt is owned by international banks.

The banks hold onto the government bonds. The Fed then controls the money supply by buying and selling these bonds in mandatory transactions. When the Fed wants to increase the money supply, it buys bonds from banks in exchange for dollars that it creates on a computer screen. The banks hand over the bonds to the Fed for dollars, which increases the amount of money the banks have on hand for loans. When the Fed wants to decrease the money supply, it sells bonds to the banks for dollars, removing those dollars from circulation.

So by changing interest rates and buying and selling government debt, the Fed controls the amount of money in the economy. Virtually, the entire money supply is debt, both public and private, that is collecting interest and must be paid back to banks either directly as bank loans are repaid, or indirectly through taxation that pays back bonds issued by the government and purchased by banks.

This system came to a head in the first decade of the 21st century. Unrestrained by the need to hold gold reserves, commercial and investment banks issued more and more loans and created more and more debt. Consumers, companies and governments took on so much debt that they were buried under it. It became too much debt that could ever be paid off, especially in the housing sector. Around 2007, defaults on loans began to occur in increasing numbers and money was rapidly being extinguished from the economy. Because of the heavy debt load that already existed, few borrowers existed to take out new loans to replenish the money supply. Money was not circulating. The American economy and the global economy at large tanked. Millions of people lost their homes, their jobs and their savings.

In reaction, central banks slashed interest rates to historic lows. In the United States, the Fed lowered the federal funds rate to between zero and 0.25 percent. Banks could borrow from the Fed essentially for free. But this had little to no effect in stimulating the economy, at least for Main Street. Wages remained stagnant and the labor force participation rate hit historic lows.

Fewer loans were being made by commercial banks resulting in less money entering the economy, depressing economic activity. Central banks needed to get more money into the economy but their traditional tool of lowering interest rates was no longer working. They had lowered rates as far as they could go but the borrowers just weren't there. Banks were sitting on piles of cash from government bailouts but were not lending it out into the economy because the debt market was saturated.

According to the writers at the Bank of England, once short-term interest rates reached the effective lower bound, it was not possible for the central bank to provide further stimulus to the economy by lowering the rate at which reserves are remunerated. The solution was to provide further monetary stimulus to the economy through a program of asset purchases, called Quantitative Easing, or QE for short.

According to the writers at the Bank of England, "QE involves a shift in the focus of monetary policy to the quantity of money: the central bank purchases a quantity of assets, financed by the creation of broad money and a corresponding increase in the amount of central bank reserves. The sellers of the assets will be left holding the newly created deposits in place of government bonds. They will be likely to be holding more money than they would like, relative to other assets that they wish to hold. They will therefore want to rebalance their portfolios, for example by using the new deposits to buy higher-yielding assets such as bonds and shares issued by companies—leading to the 'hot potato' effect discussed earlier. This will raise the value of those assets and lower the cost to companies of raising funds in these markets. That, in turn, should lead to higher spending in the economy."

Essentially, what central banks have done was create trillions in new money out of thin air which was used to purchase securities from over-leveraged banks, pension funds and insurance companies under the assumption that this new money would then be used by these banks, pension funds and insurance companies to purchase assets. The purchasing of assets would cause the new money to enter the economy and stimulate economic activity.

Of course, these institutions that offloaded their bad debts to central banks for cash under QE poured all this new money into speculation in the stock market (shares issued by companies) causing stocks to soar. The stock market in the U.S. hit record highs during a period of low wages, high unemployment and economic stagnation for the public at large. Main Street was struggling while Wall Street enriched itself like never before with money printed out of thin air that was used to buy stocks at ever inflating values.

Since the richest minority of our country holds far and away most of the stocks, under QE the rich have become unseemly rich through no other reason than the policies of the Federal Reserve—the same institution whose policies crashed the economy in 2007 and threw millions of Americans out of their jobs and out of their homes. Americans who work for wages and who do not have the majority of their net worth tied up in stocks have scratched and scrambled to make a living in a dog-eat-dog economy. Meanwhile, the richest percentage among us live high on the hog as the Fed fills their slop trough higher and higher.

Just think for a second about the insanity of this system. It is a system where a small minority of people become exorbitantly rich through the collection of passive incomes—the collection of interest, dividends, rents and capital gains. The vast majority of people who work for a living producing the goods and services of the economy are doing so to make the passive income collectors richer and richer.

In 2014, the federal government paid $430.8 billion in interest on the federal debt. This is at a time when interest rates are at historic lows. The government taxed the people to pay this amount to holders of the debt in just one year. The holders of this debt include the Federal Reserve, foreign governments, banks, mutual funds, insurance companies and government agencies, such as the Social Security Administration.

American taxpayers are now shelling out more than $430 billion a year to pay interest to bond holders. People who hold bonds tend to be the richest among us. And a large percentage of them are foreigners.

And think for a moment of the insanity of the Social Security Administration holding government bonds. You pay a Social Security FICA tax of 6.2 percent if you are employed, 12.4 percent if you are self-employed. The Social Security Administration has been using excess revenues from this tax to purchase government bonds. The interest on these bonds is paid by your income taxes. So first you pay the Social Security tax out of your wages and then you pay your income tax to pay the interest on bonds held by the Social Security Administration. The first tax purchases the debt and the second tax pays the interest! You are paying taxes to pay interest that is accruing on debt purchased with your taxes. And the principal on this debt still needs to be paid off with more of your taxes. And after paying all these taxes your entire working life, when you are finally old enough to collect Social Security, they tax you again on your Social Security income!

Due to the large number of retirees compared to the number of people working and paying the Social Security tax, the government is saying that the revenue to pay out Social Security benefits will be exhausted by 2033. So young people working today and paying the Social Security tax and their income taxes can expect to receive less money than those who started collecting before 2033.

Think of the insanity of our government. Congress delegated the power to create money to private bankers who use this power to grow rich through usury and speculation. The government prints money and then hands it over to the Fed which in turn gives it to private banks. The government then borrows this same money that it printed itself from private banks in order to pay its operating expenses. Then the government pays back the banks with interest by taxing you. It's insanity.

Actually, it's a racket.

Why not just have the government print the money itself and cut the bankers out of the action? That would save $430 billion a year in interest payments paid on the debt. Many people say that this would be inflationary because the government would just print out all the money it wanted.

But the government already prints out all the money it wants. The current system does not restrain the government at all. The government runs massive budget deficits every year unrestrained by tax revenue and then just issues bonds to cover the deficits. The Fed ensures that however high the deficit goes, the money will always be there to spend. There is no restraint on money creation at all under this system.

In 2014, the government had record revenues from all taxes of $3.02 trillion. But it spent $3.5 trillion with a budget deficit of $483 billion.

The government has no shortage of money. It taxes and taxes and spends and spends and if it spends too much the banks just create more money and lend it to the government, fully expecting the taxpayers to pay them back.

Under the current system, we get the inflation plus the debt with no restraints whatsoever on the creation of money. If the government just printed the money itself to cover the deficit, the main difference is we wouldn't have to pay $430 billion a year in interest payments to banks, foreign governments and rich people through taxes.

This current system is insanity. It is a system that has created mountains of debt owed to bankers and foreigners—mountains of debt so high that all of it can never be paid back. In 2014, the federal debt grew to more than $17.8 trillion. That's more than 100 percent of our gross national product and larger than the entire American money supply. All the money in America is not enough to pay it back.

According to the Federal Reserve's website, in 2014 the U.S. monetary base, which is the amount of bank reserves held at the Fed plus the total amount of money circulating in the public, amounted to about $3 trillion. The total amount of cash and coins outside of the private banking system plus the amount of demand deposits, travelers checks and other checkable deposits plus most savings accounts, money market accounts, retail money market mutual funds, and small denomination time deposits, came to about $11.5 trillion.

So the amount of money that exists in the economy is less than the federal debt. More money has to be created to pay the debt. And money is created when more debt is issued.

And here we're just talking about federal debt, not municipal debt, state debt, corporate debt, mortgage debt, consumer debt, student loan debt, and on and on.

It's madness. Of course, the beneficiaries of this system are quite happy with it. They put a lot of time, effort and money into setting up this system and keeping it going. Why wouldn't they? We let them do it and it's made them extremely rich and powerful. Remember, the borrower is a servant of the lender. The lenders are in control. They are in control now more than ever before.

This system has placed the lenders at the top of the global power structure. Once you figure out the system, then the reasons events happen in the world cease to appear seemingly random and mysterious and begin to make sense.

Damon Vrabel explained the global power structure in his online documentary *Renaissance 2.0 – Financial Empire*.

Vrabel described the structure as a pyramid with we the people at the bottom as the foundation. We produce the goods and services that keep the economy going. We take out debt and pay interest to have homes to live in, cars to drive and products that are produced in the economy. We pay taxes to the government. Like in the movie the *Matrix,* we are the batteries that keep the system going through our work and through the payment of debt and taxes. We are the human energy that the rich feed off through the collection of interest.

The next level in the power structure consists of small businesses—the Main Street businesses in our local communities. These businesses provide us with employment, goods and services. They also pay taxes and interest to banks on their loans. It is here where innovation resides. The higher levels are in constant fear that some entrepreneur will arise with some new innovation that will threaten corporate profits. Money is used to control, buy out or outcompete any competition from this level.

The next level includes our federal, state and local governments, which are run for the interests of the higher levels. Politicians and bureaucrats pretend to serve we the people but are selected by the higher rungs of the power structure that provide campaign funds, media coverage and purchase the bonds that keep the government from collapsing from overspending and lack of funds.

Above the government are the multinational corporations. These giant corporations operate internationally. They provide the money that politicians need to get elected and the advertising dollars that keep mainstream media operating. These giant corporations are wholly dependent on big banks for financing their operations.

The highest rung of power consists of the big international banks. These banks create money as debt which they use to finance the multinational corporations and the government. The money the banks create as debt trickles down to us at the lowest rungs as wages and loans. We must scramble, scrape and struggle to earn every penny of what the banks create as debt out of thin air. Much of what we earn through work is sent back up the system through our taxes, debt payments and consumption. The banks create money and we the people work to earn it. The output from our work is funneled up the pyramid.

The largest U.S.-based commercial banks are JPMorgan Chase, Bank of America, Citigroup, Wells Fargo and the Bank of

New York Mellon. The largest U.S.-based investment banks are Goldman Sachs, Morgan Stanley, JP Morgan Chase, Bank of America Merrill Lynch and Citigroup.

In 1999 with the passage of the Gramm-Leach-Bliley Act which repealed the 1933 Glass-Steagall Act, the lines between commercial and investment banks were blurred and commercial banks were allowed to engage in investment banking—the issuing of securities, trading of derivatives, issuing of equities, and so on. The act allowed banks, such as Citigroup, to use depositors' money to engage in speculation on Wall Street. The act also allowed commercial banks, investment banks and insurance companies to consolidate and become far larger and more powerful.

Combined, these banks have more assets than the annual budget of the U.S. federal government. The Federal Reserve serves to back the banks by providing them with all the liquidity they could ever need to issue new debt and to speculate. The government is entirely dependent on these banks, both foreign and domestic, to purchase the bonds that allow it to operate.

The bankers created the Fed to consolidate their power over the government, over the economy and over the people. The Fed ensures that the banks will never run out of money. It ensures that all the banks are on the same page. Interest rates are controlled so no wayward bank can undercut the others.

The Federal Reserve is wholly owned by the banks. The biggest banks control the shares in each of the 12 regional Federal Reserve Banks. The banks choose the members of these regional Fed banks, the most powerful being the Federal Reserve Bank of New York.

Quigley described the relationship between central banks and private banks in *Tragedy and Hope*. "It must not be felt that these heads of the world's central banks were themselves substantive powers in world finance," Quigley wrote. "They were not. Rather, they were the technicians and agents of the dominant investment bankers of their own countries, who had raised them up and were perfectly capable of throwing them down. The substantive financial powers of the world were in the hands of these investment bankers (also called 'international' or 'merchant' bankers) who remained largely behind the scenes in their own unincorporated private banks. These formed a system of international cooperation and national dominance which was more private, more powerful, and more secret than that of their agents in the central banks. This dominance of investment bankers was based on their control over the flows of credit and investment funds in their own countries and throughout the world. They could dominate the financial and industrial systems of their own countries and throughout the world. They could dominate the financial and industrial systems of their own countries by their influence over the flow of current funds through bank loans, the discount rate, and the rediscounting of commercial debts; they could dominate governments by their control over current government loans and the play of international exchanges. Almost all of this power was exercised by the personal influence and prestige of men who had demonstrated their ability in the past to bring off successful financial coups, to keep their word, to remain cool in a crisis, and to share their winning opportunities with their associates."

At the apex of the power pyramid are the international bankers who are the owners of the shares of the Federal Reserve Banks.

Who are these owners? The Federal Reserve's website gives us a vague answer.

According to the Fed's website: "The 12 regional Federal Reserve Banks, which were established by the Congress as the operating arms of the nation's central banking system, are organized similarly to private corporations—possibly leading to some confusion about 'ownership.' For example, the Reserve Banks issue shares of stock to member banks. However, owning Reserve Bank stock is quite different from owning stock in a private company. The Reserve Banks are not operated for profit, and ownership of a certain amount of stock is, by law, a condition of membership in the System. The stock may not be sold, traded, or pledged as security for a loan; dividends are, by law, 6 percent per year."

Does that clear everything up?

It almost seems written to give the impression that the Federal Reserve Banks are not owned by human beings. Member banks own shares of stock. They get a dividend. Move along. Nothing to see here.

But make no mistake. These shares are owned by actual human beings. They are owned by people who own stock in the largest banks in the world which control trillions in assets. The names of these owners are hidden behind a complex array of financial LLCs, capital firms, equity partnerships and so on.

In *Tragedy and Hope,* Quigley tells us how these owners rose to power. "The merchant bankers of London had already at hand in 1810-1850 the Stock Exchange, the Bank of England, and the London money market when the needs of advancing industrialism called all of these into the industrial world which they had hitherto ignored. In time they brought into their financial network the provincial banking centers, organized as commercial banks and savings banks, as well as insurance companies, to form all of these into a single financial system on an international scale which manipulated the quantity and flow of money so that they were able to influence, if not control, governments on one side and industries on the other. The men who did this, looking backward toward the period of dynastic monarchy in which they had their own roots, aspired to establish dynasties of international bankers and were at least as successful at this as were many of the dynastic political rulers. The greatest of these dynasties, of course, were the descendants of Meyer Amschel Rothschild (1743-1812) of Frankfort, whose male descendants, for at least two generations, generally married first cousins or even nieces. Rothschild's five sons, established at branches in Vienna, London, Naples, and Paris, as well as Frankfort, cooperated together in ways which other international banking dynasties copied but rarely excelled."

Quigley tells us about the financial activities and

characteristics of these bankers. "In concentrating, as we must, on the financial or economic activities of international bankers, we must not totally ignore their other attributes. They were, especially in later generations, cosmopolitan rather than nationalistic... They were usually highly civilized, cultured gentlemen, patrons of education and of the arts, so that today colleges, professorships, opera companies, symphonies, libraries, and museum collections still reflect their munificence. For these purposes they set a pattern of endowed foundations which still surround us today."

Quigley named the families that set up the system that rules us today. "The names of some of these banking families are familiar to all of us and should be more so. They include Raring, Lazard, Erlanger, Warburg, Schroder, Seligman, the Speyers, Mirabaud, Mallet, Fould, and above all Rothschild and Morgan. Even after these banking families became fully involved in domestic industry by the emergence of financial capitalism, they remained different from ordinary bankers in distinctive ways: (1) they were cosmopolitan and international; (2) they were close to governments and were particularly concerned with questions of government debts, including foreign government debts, even in areas which seemed, at first glance, poor risks, like Egypt, Persia, Ottoman Turkey, Imperial China, and Latin America; (3) their interests were almost exclusively in bonds and very rarely in goods, since they admired 'liquidity' and regarded commitments in commodities or even real estate as the first step toward bankruptcy; (4) they were, accordingly, fanatical devotees of deflation (which they called 'sound' money from its close associations with high interest rates and a high value of money) and of the gold standard, which, in their eyes, symbolized and ensured these values; and (5) they were almost equally devoted to secrecy and the secret use of financial influence in political life. These bankers came to be called 'international bankers' and, more particularly, were known as 'merchant bankers' in England, 'private bankers' in France, and 'investment bankers' in the United States. In all countries they carried on various kinds of banking and exchange activities, but everywhere they were sharply distinguishable from other, more obvious, kinds of banks, such as savings banks or commercial banks."

The international bankers that Quigley described set up the monetary system that we have today, not just in the United States but around the world. They used the power to create money and debt to buy up industry, the media and our politicians. They influenced the direction of academia and built the institutions that direct our lives today.

The ruling elite in the world today are direct inheritors of the system set up by the international bankers of the 19th century. This elite is transnational and transgenerational. They are following a path that was paved for them two centuries ago.

This system has given this elite immense wealth and power. According to Quigley, these international bankers had an ultimate goal and were using their wealth and power to achieve it. So, what was their goal?

Quigley tells us: "The powers of financial capitalism had another far-reaching aim, nothing less than to create a world system of financial control in private hands able to dominate the political system of each country and the economy of the world as a whole. This system was to be controlled in a feudalist fashion by the central banks of the world acting in concert, by secret agreements arrived at in frequent meetings and conferences. The apex of the system was to be the Bank for International Settlements in Basel, Switzerland; a private bank owned and controlled by the world's central banks which were themselves private corporations. Each central bank... sought to dominate its government by its ability to control Treasury loans, to manipulate foreign exchanges, to influence the level of economic activity in the country, and to influence cooperative politicians by subsequent economic rewards in the business world."

So there you have it in a nutshell.

The international bankers rose to prominence around the world through fractional reserve banking. They used their influence to set up independent central banks that dominate the economies and governments of each country. The Bank for International Settlements in Basel, Switzerland, is the central bank for all the world's central banks. This bank is a private corporation not under the jurisdiction of any country. It operates above the laws of any nation. Its officials are unelected and unaccountable to governments. In Basel, the central bankers of the world act in concert, by secret agreements arrived at in meetings and conferences. At their meetings, the bankers have been constructing their global control system of debt using the American dollar as their tool for achieving global dominance. Through this control system, all the wealth of the world is funneled upward into the grasping hands of the international bankers.

Incidentally, if you ever wondered where Fed Chairman Alan Greenspan was on 9/11, according to his memoirs, he was on an airplane over the Atlantic returning to the United States after a meeting at the Bank for International Settlements. His plane turned around mid-flight and returned to Switzerland after the planes hit the World Trade Center and the Pentagon. Fed chairmen are often at the BIS, but what happens at meetings there are not reported to the public or subject to Freedom of Information Act requests.

The central banking system is still evolving and consolidating as its inheritors continue down a path that was laid down for them generations ago. Their path is leading us to the end of the American nation, the end of our sovereignty and our independence, the eradication of our heritage and culture, the destruction of our Constitution, the loss of our rights and freedoms as American citizens and the theft of our prosperity. The monetary system that rules us today is leading us down a path that ends in global tyranny—a world system of financial control in private hands able to dominate the political system of each country and the economy of the world as a whole, controlled in feudalist fashion by the central banks of the world acting in concert, by secret agreements arrived at in frequent meetings and conferences.

It doesn't have to be this way.

Money created as a debt instrument to enrich bankers through usury is an abomination. This system is un-American and anti-American. We need to end it and set up a new monetary system that does not serve the interests of usurers and speculators, but instead rids us of them and all the evils they bring.

We can reform and reorganize the monetary system so that it conforms to our values and principles as Americans. We can design a new monetary system that serves Main Street and not Wall Street— one that serves the needs of the American people and facilitates commerce in a free enterprise system. We can set up a new system that guarantees all Americans the rights to life, liberty and the pursuit of happiness.

What would such a system look like?

The ideas and writings of Alfred Owen Crozier and Benjamin Franklin shine a guiding light down a path that leads to a brighter future.

A (not so modest) Proposal for a New American Monetary System

Alfred Crozier and Ben Franklin both wrote about alternative monetary systems which they proposed to serve the interests of the American people rather than the interests of the rich. Using their ideas and applying them to today, a new system can be designed that is not under the power and at the service of Wall Street banks.

Liberally stealing from their writings, a new monetary system is here proposed. This system is designed based on their ideas with the purpose of serving Main Street and not Wall Street. This new monetary system seeks to secure our inalienable rights to life, liberty and the pursuit of happiness—rights that have been passed down to us by the Founders and are part of our birthright as American citizens.

First, the financial practices that gave rise to our current monetary system must be addressed.

Recognizing that usury results in the concentration of money in the hands of a small number of unproductive rich people while impoverishing nations and crushing the poor under a grindstone of poverty, the practice of collecting interest for private profit must be made illegal. As observed over the millennia by a collection of humanity's greatest thinkers and moralists, usury is an unnatural and corruptive method for earning profit out of money itself, the practice of which should be recognized as a crime against modern civilization in the same vein as slavery and piracy.

Recognizing that fractional reserve banking is a particularly noxious form of usury which results in a destructive and destabilizing boom and bust cycle, it must be made illegal. Fractional reserve banking should be seen as a fraud that has been perpetrated on the American people—a fraud by which banks promise depositors access to money that is not kept in bank vaults but is actually collecting interest as loans and is multiplied by many times the amount of money that actually exists. This fraudulent practice causes instability in an economy and has become dependent on the backing of governments and taxpayers to keep the whole pyramid scheme going. This practice of lending more money than is kept in banks—more money than actually exists in the economy—has distorted economic production, played havoc with employment, devalued money and has concentrated economic and political power into the hands of a few usurers and speculators who have corrupted our government, our economy and our culture. Through a process of inflation, deflation and confiscation, international bankers have seized the wealth of the American people and now threaten our very liberty and independence. This system, which pyramids debt upon debt, has allowed bankers to create money out of nothing and rise to global power and prominence. Fractional reserve banking has been destructive to the prosperity and liberty of the American people and it should be seen for what it is: fraud. The lending of money at interest from private banks should be banned in the United States.

Recognizing that the Federal Reserve System is a creation of international bankers for their own aggrandizement to the detriment of the American people, the Federal Reserve Act must be repealed by Congress. The Federal Reserve Bank should be audited, any fraud and corruption prosecuted, and the Fed must be forever abolished.

Federal Reserve Notes should be removed from circulation and burned. The Federal Reserve Note should be replaced by U.S. Notes not backed by debt nor under the issuance and control of private banks.

With usury, fractional reserve banking and the Fed out of the picture, the U.S. Note would not be a debt instrument, but instead could serve as a measure of value and a medium of exchange for the use of the American people in commerce in a free enterprise system. With usury outlawed, investors would no longer be able to purchase government bonds that collect interest paid through income taxes collected from the American people, or purchase corporate bonds that cause prices to increase and result in financial dependency on lenders; but instead investors would direct their savings toward productive investments that add to the wealth, wages and economic growth of the country rather than extract and detract from it. Usurers must be completely removed from the picture.

As the Continental proved during the Revolutionary War, there is a danger in allowing the government to directly issue currency. That danger is inflation caused by the overprinting of the currency. Should the government issue too much money, the currency will depreciate and lose its value.

Governments tend to lack discipline and spend more than they should. If the power to create money is taken away from private bankers and returned to Congress, what is to prevent the government from hyperinflating us to disaster as was experienced with the Continental?

Monetary systems collapse when money is issued into an economy above the amount needed by the demands of commerce and the needs of the population. As Ben Franklin told us, issuing too much money leads to mischief by those who control it and hardship for everyone else. The inverse is also true. Issuing too little money leads to depression and poverty for the people. The difficulty is finding the happy medium in which enough money exists to facilitate commerce and serve the needs of the people without causing mischief and hardship and without resulting in depression.

To keep governments from getting into mischief and causing hardship on the people, restraints on the issuance of money need to be put in place. Those restraints should be based on the American principles of checks and balances, representative government, transparency and accountability. Whether you believe such a system could work depends on whether you believe in the American experiment of self-government. The current ruling class does not believe in the American experiment and prefers to have unaccountable private bankers in charge of the money supply instead of Congress as specified in the Constitution.

Since rule by the international bankers has been a disaster of global proportions, giving self-government and the Constitution another chance is at least worth a shot. If we continue with the current system, we are going to lose our country, our independence, our prosperity and our freedom. If we are going to save the country, a new monetary system is the answer.

Under a new system, how would the issuance and volume of money be determined and how would money be brought into circulation?

A United States Monetary Council

In place of the Federal Reserve, Congress should create a United States Monetary Council mandated to regulate the issuance and volume of the American money supply.

Understanding that the value of a currency is not governed by legal tender laws nor fixed exchange rates between gold and silver, but instead by the quantity of money relative to the volume of internal trade and the population, the Council should be tasked with regulating the quantity of money so that the currency provides a stable measure of value, facilitates commerce and exists in sufficiency to serve the needs of the American people. The creation of too much money relative to the population and the volume of internal trade will cause inflation; the creation of too little will cause deflation. Understanding this principle, the Council should determine the proper volume of money based on the population of the country and the productivity of the economy so that the value of the currency remains stable over time.

The Council should be organized under the U.S. Constitution following the American principles of transparency and accountability to the American people. The Council should consist of 103 members, a majority being a quorum. The Chief Justice of the Supreme Court, Vice-President and the Speaker of the House should be ex-officio members of the Council, each having power to appoint an alternate to act in his stead at any meeting. Fifty Monetary Council members should be selected by the governor of each state and confirmed by each state legislature. Thirty-five members should be appointed by the House of Representatives and 15 by the Senate. The term for each Monetary Council member should be four years, appointed so that one-half of those appointed by the states and one-half appointed by Congress will go out of office every two years. Impeachment for cause by the Council shall lie against any officer of the Council. Any state may recall its representative and substitute another at any time.

The council should appoint from its membership an executive committee of 13 members. The executive committee should be tasked to manage and oversee the Monetary Council's routine affairs, supervise its committees and ensure that its rules, regulations and by-laws are being followed. The 13 members of the executive committee should include the Chief Justice of the Supreme Court, the Vice-President and the Speaker of the House as ex-officio members. Five members should be appointed by Monetary Council members who were appointed by Congress—three representing the House and two the Senate. Five members should be appointed by Monetary Council members who were appointed by the states.

What is important here is that the Monetary Council represent both the interests of the people and the states through its membership. It should not represent the interests of banks or be under undue influence from the executive branch as it is today due to the fact that the Federal Reserve Bank governors are appointed by private banks and the Fed's Board of Governors is appointed by the President. The elimination of the Fed and the creation of a Monetary Council with members appointed by Congress and the states will bring the issuance of money back into compliance with the Coinage Clause in Article 1, Section 8, of the Constitution.

Under our current system, money is put into circulation by bank lending and government spending.

Under the new system, the Monetary Council would be

responsible for putting currency into circulation by two methods: federal government spending and through 435 public loan offices, with the public loan offices distributed across the country in each congressional district.

Currently, our elected officials are subservient to the banks and corporations that fund their campaigns. By placing the power to appoint Monetary Council members with Congress and the states, congressional representatives and state legislators will be highly interested in the volume of money entering circulation through government spending and through the public loan offices. How this effects the economic well-being of the voters who put them in office will be of utmost concern to our elected officials.

Taxing and spending

Currently, the federal government collects taxes to pay its bills and then borrows from banks and foreign governments to pay for excess spending not covered by tax revenues. Under the new system, the federal government would fund its operations not through taxation and the issuing of bonds sold to banks and foreign governments, but through the issuance of debt-free U.S. Notes. Eliminating the Federal Reserve Note and issuing U.S. Notes would immediately end the government's subservience to the bond market, banks and foreign governments and eliminate the need to collect federal income taxes to pay more than $400 billion a year in interest to bond holders—not to mention the $17 trillion in national debt principal that is continually compounding and growing.

Taxation under this system would not be for the purpose of funding government operations and paying debt to bond holders. Instead, the purpose of taxation would be to remove excess currency from circulation to prevent inflation.

With the bond market and the need to pay interest to bond holders eliminated, taxes could be much lower than they are today. The federal income tax and the IRS could be eliminated altogether, and federal taxes could be confined to duties, imposts and excise taxes as stated in the Constitution's Taxing and Spending Clause.

Since taxes are no longer needed to fund the government but instead are used to regulate inflation, the electoral process will serve as the check and balance that regulates inflation, taxation and government spending.

The middle class majority is most sensitive to inflation and taxes. Inflation serves to undercut middle class wages as prices rise. Taxes are felt heaviest by people earning middle class incomes. Unlike the middle class, the majority of the assets of the rich are in real estate, stocks and other assets that rise in price with inflation. The rich have enough money to pay their tax bill without scrimping and scraping up spare change.

Under our current system, when inflation accelerates or the economy crashes and people are laid off and struggling, we go to the polls to kick out the bums in Congress and kick out the bum in the White House. But the members of the Federal Reserve Board, who are most often the cause of the economic hardship, remain safely in their positions.

Under the new system, Monetary Council members will serve four-year terms and will be accountable to our elected representatives who are accountable to us. Today, we kick our representatives out of office as soon as inflation becomes too steep or the economy becomes too sluggish—even though our representatives have no control over monetary policy. As it is today, our economic well-being is the major focus of nearly every election. Yet, under our current system, un-elected and un-accountable private bankers have the most influence when it comes to our economic well-being.

Under the new system, our elected representatives will actually have the power to affect monetary policy so booting them out when their policies are detrimental to our well-being will actually have an effect. We will then have the power to replace our representatives with people who will appoint new members to the Monetary Council who the voters feel will best serve their interests. This is the whole point of elections which the bankers craftily found a workaround under the Federal Reserve Act.

When the middle class is comfortable and has sufficient income, the majority of voters are more likely to favor small government, less spending and lower taxes. Big government is a product of the poor, who want handouts, and the rich, who want control. The middle class tends to vote for governments that are less intrusive in the lives of citizens. Since the middle class has the most voting power, making monetary policy accountable to the electorate should serve to regulate government spending and inflation.

Public loan offices

Benjamin Franklin told us how in colonial Pennsylvania, farmers borrowed scrip from public loan offices with their lands as collateral. The scrip was used to pay for improvements to their lands which increased the productivity in the economy. In this manner, the scrip circulated through the economy as a medium of exchange that facilitated commerce. The farmers paid back their loans with scrip at interest. The interest replaced taxation and was used by the Pennsylvania government for public improvements, such as building roads and improving ports, which further boosted the economy. The issuance of scrip backed by land caused an increase in prosperity in Pennsylvania.

Under our current monetary system, money enters the economy as debt created by banks. The money filters down from the banks to the government, corporations, businesses and then finally to the people. Wall Street gets the money first and then filters it down to Main Street. It increases in cost as it moves downward through the economy. Interest is collected as profits for banks. Taxes are collected to pay interest to banks for loans made to the federal, state and local governments.

The current monetary system must be changed so that like in colonial Pennsylvania, money serves the interests of the people and not the banks. Under our new monetary system, money would first enter circulation through public loan offices that issue home mortgages and small business loans at the local level. The people and small businesses would get first access to money which would then circulate locally and filter upward and outward from Main Street rather than the other way around.

Under this proposed system, each congressional district should have a public loan office. Public loan offices would oversee the circulation of money in each respective congressional district. These offices should be managed by a board of five trustees elected by the voters of each district. Each public loan office should oversee branch offices that are distributed throughout the district based on population, with voters electing the boards of trustees for the branch offices in their respective communities, just as they elect their city councils and school boards. Each congressional district encompasses approximately 700,000 people. Each district could have 14 branches serving about 50,000 people per branch.

The district and branch loan offices will be non-profit government institutions with employees paid fixed government salaries that are public information.

The branch offices would circulate money in their respective communities through home mortgages and business loans. These loans should be collateralized by real property.

Home buyers would be able to take out home mortgages from their branch office in their community where the property is located. The property backs the loan so that if the borrower defaults the home and land become the property of the branch office to be resold to the public.

Entrepreneurs would take out business loans or lines of credit from their branch office with the loans and credit backed by a sound business plan, property, other collateral, and the productive capacity of the business.

Interest rates should be fixed by the district loan office with oversight by the Monetary Council. Interest collected from loans should be paid to the branch office where the loans are issued. The interest collected is not profit, but instead should be used to pay for the operation of the loan offices, with the surplus used to replace taxes in the local community.

Currently, interest is extracted from communities as profit that goes to bankers who use it to pay for skyscraper banking headquarter buildings, bonuses, large salaries, mansions, yachts, Learjets and so on.

Instead of being extracted from communities by banks which are as likely to be in New York City as in the local community, interest should remain in the community where it is collected and should be spent in the public interest. Instead of enriching bankers and bond holders, interest should remain in the community and be used to pay for schools, police and fire departments, roads, parks, the reduction of blight, infrastructure improvements that enhance commerce, and for whatever purpose the voters of that community deem important.

Because public loan offices issue loans and then re-spend the interest back into the community where the interest is collected, money will circulate at the local level. The fact that borrowers must repay their loans at interest prevents money from stagnating and keeps it circulating through the economy as the money is issued, repaid, and issued again, with the interest re-entering the economy when it is spent on public improvements.

Under our current monetary system, men like the billionaire real estate mogul Donald Sterling are able to borrow money to purchase rental properties, such as apartment buildings. They then charge rent on these properties that are higher than their loan payments. The rents must be higher than the loan payments to pay off the loans and provide profits to the borrower. In this manner, Sterling became a billionaire landlord in Los Angeles, merely by having access to large amounts of credit which he used to buy property to collect rents. His profits allowed him to live a lavish lifestyle. Sterling used his profits to buy mansions in Beverly Hills, Malibu and elsewhere; purchase an NBA team; and attract young mistresses a fraction his age. Under our current system, the poor are given Section 8 rental housing assistance from our taxes to pay rents to private landlords. Our taxes pay rent for the poor to profit absentee landlords.

Under our new system, collecting interest for profit would be illegal. Instead of paying rent to absentee landlords, the poor would take out mortgages from their local public loan office to purchase apartments, condos or single-family homes in their communities. The loans would be backed by the properties. Instead of paying rent to men like Donald Sterling, the borrowers would pay their mortgages to their local public loan office. As the mortgages are paid down, the borrowers gain equity in their homes, giving them a sense of ownership in their communities. The goal is that by the time they are elderly their mortgages will be paid off and they can retire without a mortgage payment or the need to pay rent. In the case of a default, the public loan office takes possession of the home and puts it back on the market. Defaults are an indication that prices are too high in that community and must come down to an affordable level. As homeowners pay their mortgages, the interest on the loans would not go to profit absentee landlords but instead would fund public improvements, such as school renovations, reduction of blight, graffiti abatement, neighborhood beautification, the building of parks, enhancements for public safety and general community improvements to boost quality of life and improve infrastructure to enhance commerce. Interest spent on public improvements would increase employment in the community.

In addition, the public loan offices would provide credit for businesses in communities, so that local entrepreneurs could open such establishments as grocery stores, shops, restaurants, and whatever other enterprise entrepreneurs in the community wish to open provided they have a solid business plan and collateral to back their business loans.

Under this system, the currency is backed by real property and by the requirement for the repayment of loans taken out from the branch offices. The currency is also backed by the need to use it for payment of taxes. This gives the currency real value.

Under this system, private banks will no longer be allowed to profit from usury and the creation of money through the issuing of debt. The public will no longer be forced to backstop the profits of banks through the Federal Reserve System. Instead, banks will serve merely as warehouses for money, as well as check clearing houses. Banks will profit by charging fees for their services and not from the collection of interest. Banks will become regular businesses and not the driving force behind our economy and government.

Investing will no longer include the buying and selling of securities, but instead will consist of investing money into productive enterprises with gains determined by dividend payments from profits and from increases in equity.

The public can keep its money in accounts at the public loan office branches which will not charge fees for transactions due to the fact that associated expenses will be paid through the collection of interest from loans issued by the branches.

Digital currencies, such as Bitcoin, have proven that money in digital form does not have to be kept in banks but instead can be kept on personal computers in encrypted digital wallets. New digital currencies have proven that buying from merchants does not have to come with fees to banks and credit card companies, but can be conducted without fees. U.S. Notes issued digitally by public loans offices can share these qualities with digital currencies which would eliminate the need for private banks altogether and reduce costs to merchants and consumers by cutting out the fee-collecting middlemen.

Under this system, the economy would shift from being dominated by Wall Street banks and multinational corporations to a vibrant and diverse free enterprise system made up of Main Street small businesses. This system would provide capital to our local communities and free the American entrepreneurial spirit that has been suppressed in recent years by expensive financing, corporate predation and a heavy tax and regulatory burden.

Under this system, power will be shifted from Wall Street to Main Street. Money would be made a servant of the people rather than our master.

Monetary policy

Under this new system, monetary policy will not be made in secret behind the closed doors of the Federal Reserve. Instead, it will be made transparently by the U.S. Monetary Council.

The council should be made responsible for determining the volume of the money supply based on the gross domestic product and the population. It would be responsible for reporting to Congress and the people the balance between federal spending, taxation and the issuing of loans at public loan offices. The council would be mandated to determine the best level of federal spending, taxation and lending at public loan offices to maintain a stable currency that retains its value, promotes commerce and serves the needs of the American people.

The council should also be made responsible for conducting regular audits of each public loan office.

Today, small businesses employ the majority of the work force. They are the drivers of the economy and of innovation and the employers of the majority of the American people. However, capital is monopolized by large corporations that have cartelized our economy and sapped our entrepreneurial spirit. Our cities and towns are filled with the same big box stores, franchise businesses and chain restaurants all organized to extract profits from our communities and funnel them up the corporate structure to the richest and smallest segment of the population.

We have become a nation of employees dependent on corporations to provide us with our livelihoods, our wants and our needs. We compete with each other not as business owners, inventors, skilled tradesmen, professionals and entrepreneurs, but as employees jockeying for scarce job openings at corporations. These corporations periodically purge their workforces with layoffs leaving the dependent employee adrift in the economy with work skills that can quickly become obsolete. The current system, which was created in 1913, has transformed our country into a soulless corporate republic under the power and control of grasping international bankers.

By scrapping the old system and replacing it with a new one that serves the people and not banks and corporations, our republic could be reborn under a free enterprise system. The old American entrepreneurial spirit could be revived. Under our new system, capital would first be made available to entrepreneurs at the local level rather than to banks and multinational corporations.

Multinational corporations have been offshoring their American workforce and replacing us with lower wage foreigners. These corporations entangle us in the affairs of foreign nations and seek to involve us in overseas wars. They have corrupted our government and debased our culture. They have no loyalty to our nation and our people. We must stop viewing these multinational corporations as economic units and see them for what they are: traitors that are systematically undermining our sovereignty, stealing our livelihoods and extracting our prosperity for the benefit of international bankers.

Under our new system which gives first access to capital to small businesses and homeowners, full employment could be achievable. By making capital available to small businesses, these businesses could have the money to compete for domestic workers which would drive up wages. We could have a vibrant and diversified economy based on the free enterprise system that our Founders valued. Our inner cities and downtowns could be revived, our standard of living lifted again to the highest in the world and the promise of the American dream could be reborn.

The purpose of the economy should not be to provide passive incomes to shareholders but instead to provide high wages to workers who produce the goods and services of the nation. Our new system could achieve that.

Much debate has been made over the past few decades regarding the Social Security System. The system was designed to tax current workers to pay benefits to retirees in their old age. This system is dependent on young workers paying FICA taxes to provide benefits for the elderly. But changing demographics have undermined the stability of this system. The baby boom resulted in a demographic bubble so that now we have fewer workers supporting more retirees who live longer. These retirees have paid into the system their whole lives and expect to get what was promised them. The solution the government has seized upon to solve this dilemma is to make younger workers pay more for longer and receive less in benefits than the current generation of retirees. Also, inflation is being used to undercut the value of the benefits that are being paid. This is inherently unfair and creates ill will and resentment between the young and old.

Under our new system, there would be no need for working people to pay FICA taxes that pay benefits to retirees. Benefits paid to retirees would merely be factored by the Monetary Council as money entered into circulation that must be balanced with federal spending, taxation and loans issued by public loan offices. The correct balance of the money supply would ensure a stable value for the currency.

Under our new system, the Social Security System could be scrapped altogether and instead replaced with a national pension. All American citizens could receive a pension paid by the federal government when they reach retirement age, say 67 years old. The amount of the pension could be set at the national median salary with the same amount paid to all Americans regardless of whether they are rich or poor. Since the pension would not be dependent on FICA taxes, there would be no resentment from those who feel they paid more into the system than others. Everyone would get the same amount. The goal of the pension would be to provide a sufficient income to Americans in retirement so that they could enjoy their golden years with dignity, regardless of how economically successful they were during their working years. This would remove the burden of the old from the young and allow grandparents to enjoy their old age and their grandchildren without financial worry, while also allowing them to provide support to their working children if they so choose.

A national pension would not be inflationary if the Monetary Council balanced the amount paid to retirees each year to the level of the money supply that corresponded with the population and the productivity of the economy.

Of course, implementing any new monetary system that shifts power away from big banks and corporations and toward Main Street will be fiercely opposed by those who benefit from the collection of interest, taxes, and the private control of the money supply. The bankers and their lackeys in government, the media, academia and the corporate world will wail and gnash their teeth at the very thought of a new system that curtails profits from moneylending. That is to be expected. But, we the American people, have the numbers and the power to tear off the leaches that feed off our labor. We are the sleeping giant they fear. This is why they spend so much money and energy on the relentless production of propaganda in an attempt to keep us asleep and confused.

In 1921, Edison said in the *New York Times* regarding financing public works with government currency rather than interest-bearing bonds, "There is a complete set of misleading slogans kept on hand for just such outbreaks of common sense among the people. The people are so ignorant of what they think are the intricacies of the money system that they are easily impressed by big words. There would be new shrieks of 'fiat money,' and 'paper money' and 'greenbackism,' and all the rest of it—the same old cries with which the people have been shouted down from the beginning. ... Now, as to paper money, so called, everyone knows that paper money is the money of civilized people. The higher you go in civilization the less actual money you see. It is all bills and checks. What are bills and checks? Mere promises and orders. What are they based on? Principally on two sources—human energy and the productive earth. Humanity and the soil—they are the only real basis of money. ... Don't allow them to confuse you with the cry of 'paper money.' The danger of paper money is precisely the danger of gold—if you get too much it is no good. They say we have all the gold of the world now. Well, what good does it do us? When America gets all the chips in a game the game stops. We would be better off if we had less gold. Indeed, we are trying to get rid of our gold to start something going. But the trade machine is at present jammed. Too much paper money operates the same way. There is just one rule for money, and that is, to have enough to carry all the legitimate trade that is waiting to move. Too little or too much are both bad. But enough to move trade, enough to prevent stagnation on the one hand and not enough to permit speculation on the other hand, is the proper ratio."

Americans didn't listen to Edison back then. As a result, today we are carrying a heavy burden of interest-bearing bonds that siphon the wealth of the American people into the hands of bond holders, many of them foreigners. But it doesn't have to be this way.

Edison said, "If the United States Government will adopt this policy of increasing its national wealth without contributing to the interest collector—for the whole national debt is made up of interest charges—then you will see an era of progress and prosperity in this country such as could never have come otherwise."

We need a new monetary system that eliminates the interest collector from the picture. Implementing a new system will take organization, leadership, purpose and a popular movement of the American people that has reached critical mass. In short, creating a new system will take a revolution.

It has been a long and winding road that we have followed to arrive at this point in the history of our nation. And the interpretation of our history has been distorted by those who are now in control. They use a complete set of misleading slogans kept on hand to prevent outbreaks of common sense among the people.

In *1984*, George Orwell wrote, "Who controls the past controls the future; who controls the present controls the past."

Those in power today have seized control of the past. They are in control of the present. And they have definite designs on our future.

To understand what they have in store for us, it is necessary to re-examine the past to understand how we arrived at our current sorry state of affairs.

The Road to the Great Depression

The Great Depression was a traumatic event in the history of our nation. It scarred a generation and shaped the way that generation thought about money, debt, work, banks, government and just about everything else.

The Great Depression in the United States lasted from 1929 to 1941—the longest stretch of economic hardship in the history of our nation. It began with an economic slowdown then the sudden Wall Street Crash of 1929.

Following the crash, thousands of banks collapsed, businesses went bankrupt, the unemployment rate soared to 25 percent, families lost their savings and were made destitute, thousands of homes and farms were foreclosed on, and the gross domestic product of the nation went into steep decline. Overnight, the United States went from a rich and prosperous nation with a 3 percent unemployment rate to a nation of hungry people standing in breadlines without means to support themselves or their families.

The Great Depression made the Panic of 1907 look minor in comparison. Yet, the Federal Reserve had been created after the Panic of 1907 to ensure that just this sort of crash and all the economic fallout that came with it would not occur again. But it was after the creation of the Fed that our nation experienced the worst and most traumatic economic crash in American history.

How did it happen?

If you were educated in American schools, you might think it was caused by the Smoot-Hawley Tariff. Or by the excesses and income inequality of the Roaring Twenties. Or perhaps by the unrestricted capitalism and laissez-faire economic policies of presidents Calvin Coolidge and Herbert Hoover.

But the blame for the Great Depression falls squarely on the shoulders of the Federal Reserve. This has been admitted by no less than Great Depression scholar and former Fed Chair Ben

Bernanke. As stated earlier, economist Milton Friedman and his wife had written a book that argued that the Fed had caused the Depression when it contracted the money supply and caused economic activity to grind to a halt. In a speech given on Friedman's 90th birthday, Bernanke said, "Regarding the Great Depression. You're right, we did it. We're very sorry. But thanks to you, we won't do it again."

The Fed did it. But to understand how it happened, we must go back to 1912 and the election of President Woodrow Wilson.

Wilson was somewhat of an anomaly as president. He would never have been elected if former President Teddy Roosevelt hadn't turned on his former vice president and friend President Howard Taft, who was running for re-election. Roosevelt ran as an independent in the election of 1912 and split the Republican vote, allowing Wilson to win the White House.

The election of Wilson brought profound changes to the United States that still affect us today. During Wilson's tenure, many American political traditions that had been long established were reversed.

Wilson was an intellectual who had been the president of Princeton University. He was a man of the Progressive Era and is regarded highly by academics and media today as one of our greatest presidents—a social reformer and visionary internationalist. In 1919, he was awarded the Nobel Peace Prize for his Fourteen Points that called for a new diplomacy, free trade in Europe and for his advocacy for the League of Nations.

Today, high schools across the country are named after him as is the Woodrow Wilson School of Public and International Affairs at Princeton.

Before his election, Wilson wrote a short book called *Congressional Government*, which was a critique of the U.S. Constitution. In the book, he wrote that he was not an admirer of our constitutional form of government and its checks and balances, but instead favored the British parliamentary system.

Wilson was a president who would rather have been a

prime minister. He was a social reformer but also a segregationist who wrote racist statements about blacks and was sympathetic to the Ku Klux Klan. He was a man who promised to help the American worker but surrounded himself with millionaire bankers. He was a man who spoke loftily of democracy and freedom but curtailed freedom of the press and freedom of speech at home, shutting down newspapers and jailing critics of his administration and war dissenters critical of American entry into World War I. He was a Nobel Peace Prize winner who promised to keep us out of war but also a military interventionist who invaded Mexico and Haiti and drafted more than two million Americans into the military and sent them to Europe where more than 100,000 were killed on foreign soil fighting a foreign war.

One of the most significant changes during Wilson's presidency that still affects us today was the passage of the 16th Amendment on February 13, 1913. Prior to the amendment, the United States had no income tax, except a temporary one that funded the Civil War but expired soon after and another short-lived income tax during the Cleveland administration that was declared unconstitutional by the Supreme Court and scrapped.

The main source of government revenue before 1913 was the tariff. Foreign goods imported into the United States were heavily taxed and bore the burden of funding the government. During Wilson's presidency, the tariff was slashed and lost government revenues were replaced by taxing the wages of the American people.

Later in that same year, Wilson signed the Federal Reserve Act into law on December 23, 1913. With the passage of the act, Congress delegated its power to coin and regulate money to an independent central bank owned by private shareholders with a board of governors appointed by the executive branch.

Only a year after the passage of the Federal Reserve Act in 1913, the world plunged into the worst war in history up to that time—the Great War, now called World War I. The imperial powers of Europe clashed and millions were killed in cataclysmic battles that raged across the European continent. The British were the superpower of the day. British foreign policy was to play one country off the other in a balance of power strategy that attempted to keep any nation from dominating Europe and becoming a rival. As Germany rose in economic and military strength at the end of the 19th century, Britain allied itself with France, which had been Britain's bitter rival for centuries. Britain also allied itself with Russia, which had also been a rival. These three nations formed the Triple Entente against Germany, which allied itself with Austria-Hungary, who together were called the Central Powers. Europe, in the years before 1914, had become entangled in a series of alliances between nations with each power attempting to balance the alliances of others. The assassination of Archduke Franz Ferdinand of Austria by a Serbian nationalist caused Austria-Hungary to declare war on Serbia, which, due to the entangling alliances of each power, set off a series of declarations of war with the end result being one of the deadliest cataclysms in human history.

The United States kept an arm's length from the war during its first three years. The American people wanted no part of it. The foreign policy tradition articulated by President George Washington of avoiding foreign entanglements and staying out of the quarrels and wars of Europe was still deeply ingrained in the American psyche. But American banks and manufacturers were growing fat off lending money and selling arms to the Entente. And British intelligence agents had been busily conducting a propaganda campaign in the United States to convince Americans that the Central Powers, and the Germans in particular, were committing atrocities in Europe and were a threat to the American people. The newspapers began to fill with atrocity stories of Germans bayoneting babies and mutilating women. The sinking of the British ocean liner RMS Lusitania on May 7, 1915, was used by British propagandists and their allies in the American newspaper industry to rile up the American public against Germany.

In *Tragedy and Hope,* Carroll Quigley tells us of the extent of the propaganda campaign and how the sinking of the Lusitania was used in an attempt to pull America into the war. "The propaganda agencies of the Entente Powers made full use of the occasion. The *Times of London* announced that 'four-fifths;' of her passengers were citizens of the United States' (the actual proportion was 15.6 percent); the British manufactured and distributed a medal which they pretended had been awarded to the submarine crew by the German government; a French paper published a picture of the crowds in Berlin at the outbreak of war in 1914 as a picture of Germans 'rejoicing' at news of the sinking of the Lusitania."

Quigley continues: "A great deal was made, especially by the British, of 'atrocity' propaganda; stories of German mutilation of bodies, violation of women, cutting off of children's hands, desecration of churches and shrines, and crucifixions of Belgians were widely believed in the West by 1916. Lord Bryce headed a committee which produced a volume of such stories in 1915, and it is quite evident that this well-educated man, 'the greatest English authority on the United States,' was completely taken in by his own stories. Here, again, outright manufacture of falsehoods was infrequent, although General Henry Charteris in 1917 created a story that the Germans were cooking human bodies to extract glycerine, and produced pictures to prove it. Again, photographs of mutilated bodies in a Russian anti-Semitic outrage in 1905 were circulated as pictures of Belgians in 1915."

In 1916, President Woodrow Wilson was re-elected as a peace president under the campaign slogan, "He kept us out of war."

The following year, a British naval intelligence officer presented the U.S. government with a slip of paper today known as the Zimmerman Telegram. The telegram was either the greatest diplomatic blunder in German history or else Britain's greatest propaganda victory. The contents of the telegram consisted of a short message from Germany to the Mexican government stating that Germany would assist Mexico in reconquering Texas, New Mexico and Arizona, and join forces with Japan against the United States, should German unrestricted submarine warfare cause the United States to enter the war on the side of the Entente.

Antiwar sentiment was still high in the United States, but the Zimmerman Telegram served to rile American emotions at a time when Pancho Villa had recently made raids on the southern border and a rising Japan was seen as a rival in the Pacific. The telegram pushed all the right buttons when it came to convincing Americans that Germany was in fact an enemy of the United States.

Wilson asked Congress for a declaration of war, citing German unrestricted submarine warfare as the reason and the telegram as evidence of the German government's hostile intent toward the United States. On April 6, 1917, Congress declared war on the Central Powers.

The telegram couldn't have come at a more desperate time for the Entente. By late 1917, Germany was starving under a British naval blockade, but it had defeated Italy to the south and Russia to the east. In the west, the French army was in open rebellion and the British army was exhausted and demoralized. German troops from the Eastern Front poured onto the Western Front and massed for an offensive toward Paris and a last ditch effort to win the war.

But entry of the United States into the war gave the Entente renewed hope. Millions of fresh American troops arrived in Europe and were thrown into the meat grinder.

In 1918, the German army burst through the Western Front and advanced relentlessly toward Paris. By May of 1918, the German army was within artillery range of Paris. But in June, fresh American troops halted the German advance at Chateau-Thierry. The Entente Powers, supplemented by nine American divisions, were then able to counterattack and turn back the German onslaught.

The German offensive had stalled with Paris in its sights. Back in Germany, the effects of the British naval blockade and of a communist uprising caused the German people to turn against the war. The failure of the German offensive and the renewed Entente counteroffensive resulted in the collapse of the German military, capitulation and a German offer of surrender.

Defeat brought more starvation and national humiliation to Germany. Under the terms of the Versailles Treaty, Germany was stripped of territory and forced to pay burdensome reparations.

Wilson pushed for the formation of the League of Nations—the forerunner of the United Nations—and in 1919 that international organization was formed. The stated purpose of the League was to maintain world peace through international cooperation. However, the U.S. Senate voted not to join. Americans had become weary of the internationalism and idealism of the Wilson administration and wanted nothing to do with the League and the intrigues and hypocrisies of Europe.

In just one year of war, the U.S. lost 116,000 men. The country and its principles had been turned upside down. For the first time since the Civil War, and only the second time in our history up until then, Americans had been drafted into the military against their will. They had been thrown in jail for speaking their minds—and even lynched by angry mobs. Newspapers had been closed for criticizing the war. The price of goods had skyrocketed as agricultural and industrial production were shifted to support a wartime economy. The American economy had been centralized as the federal government took control of industry and shifted production to the manufacture of munitions. The newly implemented income tax jumped from 7 percent on the highest incomes in 1913 to 77 percent with the passage of the War Revenue Act of 1917.

Looking toward Europe and its empires, Americans questioned the reasons given them for the war. They questioned what American interests were at stake to justify so many American dead abroad and so much hardship at home. The idealism of Wilson began to look more and more like lies. People began to realize that the atrocity stories that were used to pull them into the war had been false.

Quigley wrote, "On the whole, the relative innocence and credulity of the average person, who was not yet immunized to propaganda assaults through mediums of mass communication in 1914, made the use of such stories relatively effective. But the discovery, in the period after 1919, that they had been hoaxed gave rise to a skepticism toward all government communications which was especially noticeable in the Second Word War."

In the 1930s, the Nye Committee chaired by Senator Gerald Nye began hearings on the reasons America had entered World War I. The committee determined that the banking and munitions industries had influenced U.S. entry into the war. The munitions industry had made huge war profits by selling arms to the Entente. The committee found that American banks had bet on the Entente and had lent the Entente Powers more than $2 billion, while lending Germany only $27 million. The committee found that bankers had pressured Wilson to enter the war to ensure their loans were repaid.

In the period after World War I, American opinion shifted. A common belief arose that the war had not been fought for freedom and democracy, but instead for the interests of the "merchants of death."

World War I ended on November 11, 1918. American troops began coming home and the economy began to shift from wartime to peacetime production. The young Federal Reserve began to raise interest rates as prices began to rise. In 1920, the United States entered into a severe depression that lasted 18 months. Deflation, a declining gross domestic product and high unemployment only served to heighten the public's disillusionment with the Wilson administration.

In 1921, President Warren Harding, who is much maligned today, was swept into office in the largest popular vote landslide in American history. Harding, a former newspaper editor from Ohio, promised a "return to normalcy" from the radical changes and turmoil of the Wilson years. Harding's election was seen as a rejection by the American people of the Progressive movement.

Under Harding, many of the advances made by the Progressives were reversed. Income taxes were slashed, tariffs were raised, immigration was restricted and the interventionist foreign policy of Wilson was rejected in favor of a traditional foreign policy of avoiding foreign entanglements. The size of government, which had greatly expanded due to the war, was reduced and government spending was slashed. Harding freed political prisoners who had been jailed for speaking out against the draft, the war and the Wilson administration during the war years. Most famously, in 1921 Harding freed the socialist antiwar firebrand Eugene Debs, who had been sentenced to 10 years in 1918 for urging resistance to the draft.

The depression ended in 1921 and the United States entered into one of its longest and greatest expansions. The Roaring Twenties had begun. The 1920s were an era of rising prosperity and advancing modernity. It was the age that saw the rise of jazz music, the flapper, the automobile, the skyscraper, aviation, radio and Hollywood movies.

However, it is the excesses of the decade that are often what remain in the popular memory today. The 18th Amendment was passed at the tail end of the Wilson years and drinking alcohol had been made illegal in 1920. Due to Prohibition, the 1920s saw rising crime, corruption and law enforcement excesses. The 1920s also saw a wave of terrorist bombings by radical European anarchists. Racism and bigotry were common and out in the open. Jim Crow laws and segregation were still very much in effect. During the 1920s, America continued the imperialistic policies that had resulted from victory in the Spanish American War of 1898. Like the empires of Europe, we had become a colonial power with an empire that included Puerto Rico and the Philippines. American troops intervened in Latin America and continued the occupations of Haiti and Nicaragua.

Probably what comes to mind for most Americans when they think about the 1920s was the rampant speculation and stock market manipulation on Wall Street. Great fortunes were made through the stock market and a great gulf of inequality widened between the rich and the rest of the population.

But with Europe destroyed by the war and tariffs enacted on imports, American industry had little competition from abroad and went through a period of high growth and technological innovation. The United States enjoyed a large trade surplus during the decade and was paying off its debt. And since the European powers had borrowed heavily from American banks during the war years, European gold flowed across the Atlantic and into America as payments on loans were made. The American dollar strengthened as a result and young Americans flooded across the Atlantic to the bars and cafes of Paris where they threw dollars around taking advantage of their purchasing power.

In the black community, the Great Migration from the South to the North gave rise to black neighborhoods in northern cities filled with black businesses, theaters and schools. The 1920s was the time of the Harlem Renaissance when black musicians and artists made an indelible mark on American culture.

From 1890 to 1914, the U.S. had undergone a huge wave of immigration from Eastern and Southern Europe with about 1 million impoverished immigrants flooding onto American shores a year. Many Americans at the time saw the influx as depressing wages for American workers and threatening American identity as the number of "hyphenated" Americans grew. Immigration fell during the war years, and in 1924 Congress restricted immigration to a trickle.

With an expanding economy and the flood of immigration staunched, American labor found it had bargaining power. Wages began to rise and the nation entered a period of full employment. The unemployment rate during the 1920s averaged 3 percent.

In his book about the 1920s, called *One Summer*, Bill Bryson described the decade's economic optimism and rising prosperity: "To a foreign visitor arriving in America for the first time in 1927, the most striking thing was how staggeringly well-off it was. Americans were the most comfortable people in the world. American homes shone with sleek appliances and consumer durables—refrigerators, radios, telephones, electric fans, electric razors—that would not become standard in other countries for a generation or more. Of the nation's 26.8 million households, 11 million had a phonograph, 10 million had a car, 17.5 million had a telephone. Every year America added more new phones (781,000 in 1926) than Britain possessed in total.

"Forty-two percent of all that was produced in the world was produced in the United States. America made 80 percent of the world's movies and 85 percent of its cars. Kansas alone had more cars than France. At a time when gold reserves were the basic marker of national wealth, America held half the world's supply, or as much as all the rest of the world put together. No other country in history had ever been this affluent, and it was getting wealthier daily at a pace that was positively dizzying. The stock market, already booming, would rise by a third in 1927 in what Herbert Hoover would later call 'an orgy of mad speculation,' but in the spring of 1927 neither he nor anyone else was worried yet."

In the 1920s, America was a country that made things. We had the world's highest standard of living and were getting richer day by day.

For the United States, the 1920s were an era of high tariffs and protectionism, trade surpluses, low immigration, rising wages, full employment, low taxes, low military spending and no wars. We were a creditor nation with low government debt that was rapidly being paid down. Compare this to our current era. In 2014, tariffs were low to non-existent. We have free trade agreements with nations around the world, massive trade deficits, high immigration, stagnant wages with an official unemployment rate in 2014 of 6.7 percent. That rate climbs to 12.6 percent when you include total unemployed, plus all marginally attached workers plus total employed part-time for economic reasons, and all marginally attached workers. In our current era, taxes are far higher and more pervasive than in the 1920s, military spending is greater than the next 10 biggest military spending countries combined, and we are currently engaged in wars in the Middle East while acting as the world's police force and intervening in the affairs of nations around the world.

And what of the wealth inequality of the 1920s? In 2013, the richest 1 percent of Americans controlled more of the nation's wealth than they did at the greatest point of wealth inequality in the 1920s, which hit a high point in 1928 when the stock market reached a peak. Like then, today's wealthy are benefiting from a soaring stock market. But unlike then, unemployment in 2014 was more than double the rate at any point in the 1920s. In the 1920s, wages were rising while today wages have been stagnant for more than 30 years.

Like the British Empire at the turn of the 20th century, the United States today is a nation buried under a burdensome and growing government debt. Like the British a century ago, we are entangled in military conflicts around the world—in such places as Iraq and Afghanistan where British bones were left in the sand more than a century ago. We watch as our industries leave our shores for protectionist nations that run trade surpluses with us due to our free trade policies. We are a nation with a powerful military funded by debt while our citizens have more and more trouble making ends meet.

Yet, back in the 1920s, we had emerged from the turmoil of the war years to become the wealthiest nation in the world with its highest standard of living. This was done under government policies of protectionism, immigration restrictionism and an international foreign policy of neutrality and avoiding foreign entanglements.

Immediately after President Harding took office in 1921, he began to reverse many of the changes made during the tumultuous Wilson administration and set the conditions for a decade of peace and prosperity. He supported women's suffrage, the eight-hour work day, he signed the first federal child welfare program, he negotiated international disarmament treaties, he fought for an anti-lynching bill that was unfortunately defeated by Congress, and advocated for civil rights for blacks. Interestingly, Harding is often mocked or disregarded today by American academia, historians and media while Wilson is often ranked as one of our greatest presidents. If the average American knows anything about Harding, it is likely to be about the Teapot Dome Scandal or about his affair with his young mistress rather than about the economic and social advances made by the American people during his presidency.

Newspapers like the *New York Times* still today produce negative articles about Harding. On July 7, 2014, the *Times* ran a salacious article about Harding's letters to his mistress, complete with a photo of Harding with illustrated lipstick kisses on his face. The article stated that Harding is widely regarded as the worst president in American history while depicting him as an adulterer and even a traitor with sympathies for Germany in World War I. It should not come as a surprise that the owners of the *Times* despise Harding as the paper has long been the country's leading voice for an internationalist and interventionist foreign policy, free trade, mass immigration into the United States, while constantly propagandizing for the U.S. government to take on more debt.

After only two and a half years in office, Harding dropped dead in California while touring the West. He died of an apparent heart attack; however, rumors immediately circulated that he had been poisoned. Much mystery about the circumstances surrounding his death remains today.

Regardless, Harding had set the stage for a remarkable decade of economic growth and general prosperity that continued unabated through the presidency of Calvin Coolidge.

The international bankers, who had made so many advances under Wilson, viewed the Harding years with alarm. The great financiers of the time had pushed hard for more immigration, free trade and more international engagement. But the American people looked on them with suspicion as being behind America's entry into World War I.

In 1919, the Senate rejected joining the League of Nations—a stinging rebuke to Wilson, who had suffered a debilitating stroke during the national debate over joining his League. Wilson finished out his presidency as an invalid.

In a reversal of Wilson's policies, tariffs were raised with the Emergency Tariff of 1921 and the Fordney-McCumber Tariff of 1922. Congress then drastically restricted immigration with the

Immigration Act of 1924.

The great international banker Paul Warburg was particularly concerned with these reversals. Warburg was one of the principal planners of the Federal Reserve System at Jekyll Island and is widely considered the father of the Federal Reserve. He was its principal architect and was the leading advocate in Washington and in the press for the passage of the Federal Reserve Act.

Warburg was born in Germany into a financial dynasty that was tied by blood and marriage to the great banking families of Europe. In 1895, he married Nina Loeb, daughter of Solomon Loeb, the founder of the powerful Wall Street investment firm Kuhn, Loeb & Co. In 1902, he moved from Germany to New York permanently, becoming an American citizen in 1911.

Warburg served as vice chairman on the first Federal Reserve Board from 1914 to 1918 and was a member of the Federal Reserve's advisory council from 1921 to 1926. Interestingly, Warburg's brother, Max, was an influential banker in Germany with ties to the German government during World War I when Paul was serving on the Federal Reserve Board in the United States.

In response to the reversals that came with the end of the Wilson presidency, Warburg, with leaders of American business, government and the press, founded the Council on Foreign Relations in 1921. Warburg served as the Council's first director. The mission of the Council on Foreign Relations was, and remains today, the promotion of globalization, free trade, the creation of trade blocs, such as NAFTA, the EU and the Trans-Pacific Partnership, financial de-regulation, immigration, the interests of Wall Street banks and multinational corporations and the aggressive promotion of American interventionism abroad. Its founding members were opposed to protectionism and the American tendency in foreign policy of avoiding entangling alliances and staying out of European wars—a tendency they called "isolationism." They took it upon themselves to change entrenched American attitudes toward trade, immigration and interventionism through an intense propaganda campaign that has worked relentlessly to discredit isolationism, protectionism and immigration restrictionism in favor of interventionism and internationalism abroad, mass immigration into the United States and free trade.

The Council was funded by very deep pockets in the financial and corporate world, to include the Ford Foundation, the Rockefeller Foundation and the Carnegie Foundation. It became one of America's first "think tanks."

The think tank is a curious institution in which corporations and multimillionaires pay salaries to intellectuals who promote the interests of these corporations and multimillionaires full time in the press and academia. Think tanks proliferated in the 20th century and have become influential in the political life of our country. Our best and brightest are pulled into think tanks from elite universities and groomed and promoted for leadership in the media, the corporate world and in government.

The Council on Foreign Relations has far and away been the most influential think tank in the United States. It has been so successful that old traditional American attitudes toward immigration, foreign policy and trade have been completely reversed since the 1920s. In fact, the old attitudes have been made taboo and practically cannot even be discussed in polite society. To even mention that mass immigration might have negative impacts on the wages and living standards of working Americans could open oneself up to charges of bigotry. Make mention that America should take a less active role in the defense of Europe or Asia and you are labeled an isolationist. Doubt the benefits of the North American Free Trade Agreement and you are a protectionist and an economic illiterate. The Council has been so successful that today the leadership in both the Republican and Democratic parties have adopted its attitudes toward immigration, trade and foreign policy. These attitudes are considered mainstream by the media and academia and dissenters are not taken seriously. Dissenters are aggressively excluded from the public conversation and ridiculed with name calling.

But in the Roaring Twenties, a non-interventionist foreign policy and a protectionist trade policy were once again America's policies. Tariffs were raised, taxes were slashed and immigration was severely restricted. The American economy boomed and the future looked bright for both the rich, the middle class and the working class. However, one development of the Wilson years was left undisturbed. Behind the scenes, the Fed was consolidating its power and coming of age. More banks across the country were being pulled into the Federal Reserve System.

During the 1920s, the Fed followed an easy money policy of low interest rates that made borrowing cheap. The Fed had expanded the money supply through the decade. The easy money led to a real estate bubble in Florida. People were borrowing money to buy land in Florida and were flipping the properties for a quick profit. The boom went bust in 1925 leaving behind half-built development projects and ruining thousands of people. But the easy money kept coming. Speculators borrowed to buy stocks on margin on Wall Street causing the stock market to soar. Millionaires were being made overnight as stocks zoomed upward. The decade saw stocks rise by 400 percent. A spirit of irrational exuberance was in the air.

By 1927, the federal government was running a record budget surplus of $630 million and had paid $1 billion off the national debt. The economy was continuing its growth streak, unemployment was low and wages were rising. But things were not so great in Europe. Germany had only recently recovered from its disastrous experience with hyperinflation. France and Britain were still recovering from the war. The nations of Europe remained in deep debt to the United States and were struggling to pay off their war loans. Half of the world's gold was now in the United States, which was a problem because at the time most countries were on the gold standard. More and more of the world's gold was accumulating in the United States meaning that it was becoming scarce everywhere else.

In the summer of 1927, Benjamin Strong, governor of the Federal Reserve Bank of New York; Montagu Norman, governor of the Bank of England; Hjalmar Schacht, head of the Reichsbank in Germany; and Charles Rist, deputy governor of the Banque de France, held a secret meeting in Long Island on the estate of a wealthy businessman. They decided to lower the Fed's discount rate so that holders of gold in the United States would move it to Europe for better returns. Strong cut the discount rate from 4 percent to 3.5 percent, which caused a spike in borrowing in the United States. All that borrowed money plowed right into the stock market, causing it to double over the next year.

According to an article by Timothy Cogley on the Federal Reserve Bank of San Francisco website, starting in 1928 the Fed shifted to a tight monetary policy, motivated in large part by a concern about speculation in the stock market. Motivated by this concern, the Fed responded aggressively. Between January and July 1928 the Fed raised the discount rate from 3.5 percent to 5 percent. Cogley said tight monetary policy probably did contribute to a fall in share prices in 1929. He continued that the depth of the contraction in economic activity probably had less to do with the magnitude of the stock market crash and more to do with the fact that the Fed continued a tight money policy after the crash. Furthermore, monetary policy was tight not only in the U.S. but also throughout much of the rest of the world.

The central banks of the world, acting in concert, contracted the global money supply.

The Great Confiscation

On October 29, 1929, known as Black Tuesday, the stock market plunged, losing $14 billion in value in a single day. The Roaring Twenties came to a sudden end and the United States entered its deepest, darkest depression which lasted 12 years.

Money, which had been plentiful for a decade, suddenly became scarce. In 1929, the unemployment rate was 3 percent. It climbed to 8 percent in 1930; 16 percent in 1931; and 24 percent in 1932. It reached a high of 25 percent in 1933. The unemployment rate began to slowly decline after its peak in 1933, but remained at historically high levels for the next seven years, declining to 14 percent in 1940. It was the single longest period of sustained high unemployment in American history. It only dropped below 10 percent in 1941 when millions of American men were being taken out of the labor pool and drafted into the military before the start of World War II.

During the Depression, the gross domestic product of the U.S. dropped by 30 percent. Thirteen million Americans were unemployed at a time when the American population was about 122 million. Homes and farms were foreclosed on in record numbers. The birthrate dropped by 20 percent. The suicide rate went up. The crime rate spiked. Americans began emigrating in large numbers for the first time.

Back in the 1920s, the national debt was being paid down at a rapid rate. But after 1929, government spending exploded and so did the national debt. Meanwhile, taxes were raised to their highest level since World War I.

In response to the terrible unemployment that plagued the nation, President Herbert Hoover began massive public works projects, such as the building of the Hoover Dam and the San Francisco-Oakland Bay Bridge. President Franklin Roosevelt began his New Deal program in 1933, which entailed a massive expansion of the role of government. Government spending was increased and government took a more interventionist approach in the economy. The promise of the 1920s that the national debt would be paid off by rising productivity and prosperity vanished with the Depression as the government piled debt atop debt.

Unlike the Depression of 1920-21, which began just as severe as the Great Depression but was soon over without a massive increase in government spending, the Great Depression continued on even as the New Deal increased in scope and spending. In 1937, eight years after the crash of 1929, the unemployment rate had fallen to 14 percent. While this was an improvement from the nearly 25 percent rate of 1933, it was still far higher than the average of 3 percent during the 1920s. In 1937, the Federal Reserve further tightened the money supply leading to the Recession of 1937. In 1938, nine years after Black Tuesday, the unemployment rate was back up to nearly 19 percent!

As far as reducing unemployment was concerned, the New Deal was a failure. Unemployment remained far higher in the 1930s than at any point in the 1920s, or during any other time in our history, even as government spending soared to levels never seen before.

In the 1920s, government debt fell from $24 billion to $17 billion as government surpluses paid off the massive debts incurred during World War I. The debt more than doubled during the 1930s to $49 billion by the end of the decade. All that borrowed money was paid back at interest to lenders by extracting it from the pockets of wage earners who paid the income tax.

Interestingly, while the New Deal was going on in America, Germany, under Hitler's National Socialist German Workers Party (the Nazis), was undertaking a similar program of government spending and massive public works projects. During the mid-1930s, Germany went from being one of the most destitute and debt-ravaged nations in Europe, to an industrial powerhouse experiencing full employment while overnight building one of the most fearsome war machines the world had ever seen. The German currency was not backed by gold and all its spending was not done by borrowing. Instead, the Germans printed something called MEFO bills, which were promissory notes that served as bills of exchange that could be converted into Reichsmarks. The MEFOs were not borrowed at interest, but merely printed and paid out for productive work. People were put to work without incurring debt that had to be paid at interest to lenders. In the mid-1930s, the German economy flipped from chaos, impoverishment and hyperinflation, to full employment and industrial might. Germany's newfound prosperity resulted in Hitler earning popularity with the German people who later adoringly followed him into military disaster and national ruin.

Why did the New Deal fail to return America to the full employment of the 1920s? A large part of the problem was that the federal government, unlike in Germany, was funding its work programs with debt at a time when the banks were not lending money into the economy. The government was borrowing massive amounts of money to pay for workers and materials to build bridges, roads, dams and other projects. At the same time, the banks were not lending to businesses or the people. The government increased taxes on wage earners to pay back the borrowed money owed to lenders. Since money is borrowed at interest, the principal plus the interest must be paid back to the lenders, who are mainly made up of banks and the wealthiest members of our society. The money is paid back from income taxes on the wages of workers. So to pay for a New Deal dam, rich people would provide the principal, the government would pay for materials and labor and then tax the wage earners of the nation to pay back the wealthy lenders their principal plus profits for the lenders in the form of interest. The New Deal shuffled money out of the pockets of wage earners and into the pockets of wealthy lenders while putting a small fraction of the labor force to work in highly publicized public works projects. The more the government borrowed and went deeper into debt, the more money had to be extracted from the pockets of wage earners to pay principal and interest to usurers.

Why didn't the government just tax the people outright to pay for labor and materials without going into debt? Then the money spent would have ended up in the economy without additional taxation on the people to pay interest to the wealthy. What could be easier than that? But that is not the way our monetary system works. Our monetary system has been designed under the belief that the government must borrow at interest the very money it prints at the Bureau of Engraving and Printing. It prints the money, hands it over to the Fed, which hands it over to the banks, which then lend it to the government at interest, which then pays the banks back by taxing the income of wage earners. Many today even believe that borrowing is good for the economy and that taxing wage earners better off than themselves will benefit them somehow—but history shows that during the Great Depression this policy never got the unemployment rate under 14 percent, even over a decade span.

To recap, the Federal Reserve Act was passed in 1913 in response to the Panic of 1907 under the rationale that a central bank was needed to prevent such panics from ever happening again. Yet, only 16 years after the creation of the Fed, a panic far more devastating and lasting than the Panic of 1907 occurred.

If you are to measure the success of the Federal Reserve Act by its stated purpose of providing the nation with a safer, more flexible and more stable monetary and financial system, the Great Depression proves that the act was a failure of epic proportions. Not only did it not provide us with a safer, more flexible and more stable monetary and financial system, but the greatest panic and longest depression in our history happened under the Fed's watch—in large part due to the actions of the Fed itself. By any objective standard, the Fed is a failure, and it remains a failure today as repeated financial crises and the instability of our monetary system prove without a doubt.

But do its beneficiaries consider it a failure?

The American people suffered greatly during the Depression, and thousands of businesses and small community banks went bust, but the big Wall Street banks survived and grew even bigger and stronger. Those banks are still with us today. And in our present day following the traumatic economic crisis of 2007, they have emerged even bigger than ever. The bankers and the media tell us they are too big to fail.

Obviously, the Fed is a failure as an institution if you compare its performance in the 20th and 21st centuries with its stated objectives when it was founded. But what if you look at it from a different perspective? What if the Fed's stated objectives are a smokescreen for the institution's true purpose? If the bankers actually set up the Federal Reserve not for the benefit of the American people, but to protect themselves during the inevitable busts caused by the fractional reserve banking system, and to increase their own wealth and power; to siphon off the wealth of the American people and seize control of our government and our nation's productive assets; then the Federal Reserve has been a smashing success.

During the Great Depression, the old fractional reserve cycle of inflation, deflation and confiscation was magnified beyond anything that had occurred before. With the passage of the Federal Reserve Act, the power to issue money and control its volume was monopolized and concentrated into the hands of a few Fed governors who served the biggest banks in the world. The act had effectively centralized the monetary system.

Through much of the 1920s, the Fed had followed an easy money policy. Money was cheap to borrow, which resulted in a land speculation boom in Florida followed by a massive stock market bubble. People borrowed from banks at low interest rates to speculate on land and stocks. The value of stocks and land soared. In 1928, the Fed shifted to a tight money policy and began raising the discount rate. Lending slowed, borrowed money stopped pouring into the stock market and the bubble popped spectacularly. Bank runs swept across the nation. Thousands of banks collapsed and the savings of American families were wiped out. Banks were no longer lending to people to buy cars and homes. They were not lending to businesses and farms. Money became scarce. Businesses closed their doors in record numbers and workers were laid off in the millions. A great deflation was underway. The confiscation stage of the fractional reserve cycle then began.

During the Great Depression, the assets of the American nation changed hands. Millions of families that had owned businesses, real estate and stock in corporations went bankrupt. A new breed of owner then swooped in and scooped up assets for pennies on the dollar. This new breed had a new set of values that was very different from the values of those who had owned a good portion of the nation's assets since the Civil War. This new breed was made up of insiders who were connected to the Federal Reserve System, which had been founded only two decades before. This new breed had ready access to money at a time when money was scarce and prices for assets were low.

An obvious example of this new breed was a man named Eugene Meyer. Meyer was an investor and speculator who had worked in the Woodrow Wilson administration during World War I as the head of the War Finance Corporation. President Herbert Hoover later appointed Meyer to the Federal Reserve Board, where he served as chairman from 1930 to 1933. In 1933 during the darkest year of the Depression, Meyer left the Fed and purchased the *Washington Post* from its owner Ned McLean who had gone bankrupt.

As owner and publisher of the *Washington Post*, Meyer transformed the newspaper into one of the most influential papers in the world. It was the newspaper read by congressmen, senators, presidents and policy makers in the nation's capital. The paper became so prominent that it could influence events, drive policy and even bring down a president. The paper remained in the Meyer family for 80 years. Today, it continues to promote the policies and beliefs of the new breed that rose to prominence during the Depression years. Those policies and beliefs include: support for an interventionist American foreign policy abroad, mass immigration, and an unwavering, ardent support for free trade. This new breed was made up of men like Meyer who were fervent globalists who wanted America to lead the world into a new era of internationalism—an era of global institutions that regulated the world economy and international affairs.

When Meyer was 70 years old, President Harry Truman appointed him to be the first head of the World Bank. After serving with the World Bank, he returned to the *Post* where he served as its chairman until his death in 1959.

This new breed of elites moved seamlessly from Wall Street to positions at the Fed, to positions in government, especially positions in intelligence agencies, to positions in the new international institutions that were founded after World War II, such as the World Bank and the International Monetary Fund.

During the Great Depression when this new breed was rising to power, the old American policies and values that dated back to the American Revolution still remained strong in the minds and attitudes of the American people. A large majority of the American public still believed in the foreign policy tradition of George Washington—of avoiding entangling alliances. They wanted no part in European wars. The experience of World War I had only hammered home the wisdom of this attitude. Also, the alienation, ethnic friction and wage suppression caused by the great wave of immigration that occurred from 1880 to 1920 had turned Americans sour on immigration. The Immigration Act of 1924 had sharply reduced the immigration flood to a trickle.

With the onset of the Great Depression, the new breed began buying up newspapers, book publishers, banks, railways and shipping companies. They bought corporations that dominated American resources and production in every sector. They used their privileged access to money to start new companies, such as the national radio stations that began to have a profoundly influential effect on American thinking and culture.

This new breed began to relentlessly push for free trade, mass immigration and an interventionist foreign policy abroad.

The Tyranny of World War II

The Great Depression ended in the United States when we entered World War II. Millions of American men were drafted into the military and sent overseas to fight Germany, Italy and Japan. Production ramped up at home to build the American war machine. This war effort was funded by ever higher levels of debt.

Most of us have grown up hearing certain things about World War II. It was a war of good against evil and we were the good guys. It was a war for democracy versus dictatorship, freedom versus slavery, darkness versus light. It was not a war of choice but a war that was forced upon us by genocidal maniacs bent on world domination. If it wasn't for the USA, you'd all be speaking German.

World War II was a good war.

Think about that euphemism for a moment. This was a war that killed off 400,000 Americans and millions of others. It was carnage on an unprecedented scale. It destroyed bodies, shattered minds and caused untold suffering around the world. And some people call it a good war.

Was this war fought for American interests? Or were we pulled into this war for other interests that were not our own?

It is often said that history is written by the victors. It is the victors of this war that have called it a good war. Today, they use the myths they created about World War II to rally us to fight wars all around the globe—to send our young men and women to fight all the Hitlers hiding under every rock and behind every tree from Moscow to Baghdad to Saigon. New Hitlers seem to rise up every few years and once again we are at war.

There is no doubt that American soldiers, sailors, airmen and Marines made great sacrifices during World War II. They were killed in the hundreds of thousands and their victories against two of the most formidable military powers in world history is a feat that will never be forgotten.

But was this a good war? It almost seems like heresy to think otherwise, but the myths about the war are just that—myths and slogans meant to cloud our minds and appeal to our emotions so that more wars can be fought with our money and the blood of our children.

World War II began in Europe on September 1, 1939, when the Germans invaded Poland. France and Great Britain then declared war on Germany. The Germans, of course, felt that they were justified in taking back German territory that had been taken from them and given to Poland under the Treaty of Versailles. The Germans believed that German people were being abused in German territory that had been confiscated from them after they had surrendered in World War I. The historically German city of Danzig had been separated from the German nation by the Treaty of Versailles and Hitler was determined to resolve the disputes over the Polish Corridor to the city by either diplomacy or force.

When the attack came, the French and British were obligated to defend Poland due to treaties signed with that nation. The myth goes that the war began with Hitler's invasion of Poland and that the British and French were determined to draw a line in the sand and defend that nation from Nazi aggression.

However, it wasn't only the Germans who attacked Poland in September of 1939. At the time, the Germans were allied with the Soviet Union. On September 17, 1939, the Soviet Union invaded Poland from the east. Adolph Hitler and Josef Stalin had agreed to attack Poland together and divide it up among themselves, and they did just that.

While the Germans were ravaging Poland from the west, the Soviets were brutalizing the Poles from the east, murdering its officers and NCOs and massacring the civilian population.

Following the Soviet invasion of Poland, Stalin's Red Army then attacked and overran the Baltic states of Estonia, Latvia and Lithuania. In November, two months after attacking Poland, the Soviet Union attacked Finland in what is called the Winter War—a viciously fought war of aggression and territorial acquisition initiated by the Soviet Union against the Finns.

So France and Britain declared war on Germany for attacking Poland. Yet, both countries did not declare war on the Soviet Union when it also attacked Poland, as well as Estonia, Latvia, Lithuania and Finland.

Think about this for a moment. The most destructive war in human history began under the pretext of defending Poland from German aggression. But when Germany was defeated in 1945, Poland was not freed or allowed its independence. The Allies handed over Poland to the Soviet Union which ruled it with an iron hand for the next 44 years. The Allies turned over Poland to a dictator who had colluded with Hitler to attack it in 1939.

Obviously, the Allies were not fighting to defend Poland. This was just pretense. In fact, when news reached the West of the Katyn Forest massacre—the systematic Soviet mass murder of 22,000 Poles in 1940 that was officially authorized by Josef Stalin—the information was suppressed by the media and the British and American governments, despite pleas from Polish expatriates.

So, Poland was the pretext for war for the West, yet one of Poland's attackers later allied with the West after systematically mass murdering Poles. So, what were the true reasons for the war?

The true reasons involved nothing more than an age old balance of power strategy, and of course, the desire of Western bankers to defeat Germany and Japan, which both had withdrawn from the international financial system.

Britain, the master of the balance of power game, had for centuries been the mortal enemy of France when France was the dominant power on the European continent. When Russian power grew in the 19th century and threatened British interests in central Asia and the Mediterranean, the British allied themselves with the French and the Turks to take on the Russians—even invading Russia and fighting a brutal war in Crimea. When Germany unified in the second half of the 19th century and rose to become the dominant power in Europe, the British allied with the French and the Russians against the Germans.

In the Napoleonic Wars against France, or the Crimean War against Russia, or World War I and World War II, the British government and British press told the same story—that Britain was on the side of righteousness and was defending liberty and freedom against aggression, barbarism and evil. In the Napoleonic Wars, the British were defending the countries attacked by Napoleon. In the Crimean War, they were defending the Turks from Russian aggression; in World War I, they were defending Belgians from German rapists; in World War II, they were defending the innocent Poles against those same Germans (but not the Russians). Meanwhile, the British were running the biggest and most exploitative empire the world had ever seen.

During the 19th century, anti-British sentiment was high in the United States. Since the Revolutionary War, many Americans saw the British Empire as an enemy and the main threat to American sovereignty. British and American interests were often in conflict during the 1800s. But as the 19th century drew to a close, British diplomats began courting Americans. British policy had changed toward viewing the United States as a valuable ally in their balance of power global chess game.

At the start of World War I, the British government conducted a massive propaganda effort in the United States in our press and government to win over the American people who had long been suspicious of British intentions. That propaganda effort had been successful in demonizing the German people and presenting the British as on the side of good. But after the war, Americans realized that no American interests had been at stake other than those of the "merchants of death" and that American lives had been squandered to save the British and French empires from a rival. Americans had been hoaxed and paid with their lives and their economic well-being.

In the 1920s and 1930s, Americans still remembered the words of President George Washington who urged us in his Farewell Address of 1796 to observe good faith and justice toward all nations and to cultivate peace and harmony with all. Washington had warned us that republican government was susceptible to foreign influence and that we must remain vigilant in defending American interests against the wiles of foreign agents.

Washington had warned us: "So likewise, a passionate attachment of one nation for another produces a variety of evils. Sympathy for the favorite nation, facilitating the illusion of an imaginary common interest in cases where no real common interest exists and infusing into one the enmities of the other, betrays the former into a participation in the quarrels and wars of the latter, without adequate inducement or justification. It leads also to concessions to the favorite nation of privileges denied to others, which is apt doubly to injure the nation making the concessions, by unnecessarily parting with what ought to have been retained and by exciting jealousy, ill will, and a disposition to retaliate in the parties from whom equal privileges are withheld. And it gives to ambitious, corrupted, or deluded citizens (who devote themselves to the favorite nation) facility to betray or sacrifice the interests of their own country without odium, sometimes even with popularity, gilding with the appearances of a virtuous sense of obligation, a commendable deference for public opinion, or a laudable zeal for public good, the base or foolish compliances of ambition, corruption, or infatuation.

"As avenues to foreign influence in innumerable ways, such attachments are particularly alarming to the truly enlightened and independent patriot. How many opportunities do they afford to tamper with domestic factions, to practice the arts of seduction, to mislead public opinion, to influence or awe the public councils! Such an attachment of a small or weak towards a great and powerful nation dooms the former to be the satellite of the latter. Against the insidious wiles of foreign influence (I conjure you to believe me, fellow citizens) the jealousy of a free people ought to be constantly awake, since history and experience prove that foreign influence is one of the most baneful foes of republican government. But that jealousy to be useful must be impartial; else it becomes the instrument of the very influence to be avoided, instead of a defense against it. Excessive partiality for one foreign nation and excessive dislike of another cause those whom they actuate to see danger only on one side, and serve to veil and even second the arts of influence on the other. Real patriots, who may resist the intrigues of the favorite, are liable to become suspected and odious, while its tools and dupes usurp the applause and confidence of the people to surrender their interests.

"The great rule of conduct for us in regard to foreign nations is, in extending our commercial relations, to have with them as little political connection as possible. So far as we have already formed engagements, let them be fulfilled with perfect good faith. Here let us stop."

In the lead up to World War I, the wiles of foreign influence went to work on getting us to surrender our own interests while attacking patriots who were true to Washington's words. But after the war, many Americans had figured out the treachery that had led us into that horrific war.

When President Franklin Roosevelt took office in 1933, one of his first priorities was to establish ties with the Soviet Union. Before the end of his first year in office, Roosevelt established diplomatic relations with the Soviet Union, and communication channels between Stalin and Roosevelt were opened.

The Soviet Union at the time was one of the most totalitarian and murderous nations in the world. In 1933, a government-induced famine, called the Holomodor, was occurring in Ukraine with deaths estimated as high as 7.5 million people.

Yet, this atrocity was basically ignored in the Western press. Many in the West were sympathetic to the goals of communism and saw the Soviet Union as a working man's paradise.

In the 1930s, Soviet and British agents were at work in the American government, in our newspapers and radio, and in Hollywood, attempting to create sympathy for their own nations and antipathy for their enemies. Their American tools and dupes attacked real patriots who resisted and who spoke out against their intrigues.

During the 1930s, Hitler had built up the German military.

He then set about annexing German populations in areas that bordered Germany. He annexed Austria in 1938, and in March 1939 annexed the Germans of the Sudetenland, who had been separated from Germany by the Treaty of Versailles.

When the Germans and Soviets invaded Poland in 1939 and France and Britain declared war, Roosevelt, like Wilson before him, made public statements promising to keep the United States out of wars abroad.

After the attack on Poland, nearly a year of quiet passed on the Western Front with no significant military action by France and Britain to assist Poland. This period is known as the Phoney War. Then in May 1940, the German blitzkrieg steamrolled across France. The rapid German advance trapped the British army in the city of Dunkirk on the French coast. The Germans had the opportunity to destroy British forces, but halted their advance and allowed 300,000 British, French and Belgian soldiers to escape across the English Channel to England.

Why didn't the Germans destroy the British army when they had the chance?

The answer lies in Adolph Hitler's book, *Mein Kampf*. Hitler had stated openly in his book what his ends were.

If you read *Mein Kampf*, you will find that Hitler had very little to say about the United States, mainly a comparison of the organization of American states versus German ones, and a concern that without economic opportunity in Germany the best and brightest Germans would emigrate to America. However, he had plenty to say about Great Britain. Hitler wrote that Germany's great mistake prior to World War I was to challenge the hegemony of the British Empire. Because of German commercial competition, the building of a German navy and the expansion of the German overseas empire, British leaders began to see Germany as their enemy and allied themselves with their centuries-old enemy, France, to counterbalance the rise of German power. Hitler wrote that during World War I, Germany had underestimated both the tenacity and skill of the British soldier and the effectiveness of British propaganda. He said it should have been German policy to pursue an alliance with Britain rather than challenging it. "No sacrifice should have been considered too great if it was a necessary means of gaining England's friendship," Hitler wrote. "Colonial and naval ambitions should have been abandoned and attempts should not have been made to compete against British industries."

Germany is situated in the center of Europe with France on its western border and the vastness of Russia to its east. Germany's great weakness was that it was a densely populated, medium-sized nation surrounded by rivals. It did not possess enough farmland to feed its people, making it dependent on food imports from abroad. Germany's narrow and confined coastline made it vulnerable to blockade. Hitler pointed out that the British blockade of Germany during World War I resulted in a famine which led to loss of support for the war on the German home front. While German armies were advancing on the Western Front, communists used discontent caused by the deprivations of war to foment rebellion and labor strikes back in Germany, which Hitler bitterly attributed as a major contributor to Germany's defeat.

Hitler saw Germany's great strength in being a land power. He saw France and the Soviet Union as Germany's enemies while its natural allies were Italy and Great Britain. In Hitler's estimate, France viewed Germany as its great rival on the European continent. Hitler stated that after World War I France had been pursuing a foreign policy of subversion in an attempt to break up Germany into small states that could be divided against themselves. Meanwhile, the Soviet Union was pursuing the goals of international communism and was infiltrating Germany and supporting communists who were fomenting violent revolution in an attempt to seize control of the German state.

Hitler stated in *Mein Kampf* that his strategy in the next war would be first to defeat France in the west before turning his attention to the east and attacking the Soviet Union with the goal of seizing control of the vast expanses of agricultural land on the eastern plains. Hitler believed that once in control of this agricultural land, Germany would be self-sufficient in food and resistant to blockades. Thus, Germany would be able to stand as an equal with the other world powers rather than in the weakened, subservient and humiliated position it was in at the time of Hitler's writing.

In 1940, with France defeated, Hitler attempted to negotiate a peace with Britain. However, Prime Minister Winston Churchill rejected a negotiated peace and urged the British people to fight on.

In the summer of 1940, the Battle of Britain began. The Luftwaffe and the Royal Air Force clashed in the skies above England in one of the greatest air battles in history. London was reduced to rubble in what became known as the Blitz.

Many Americans like to think that if the USA had not entered the war, the British would be speaking German today. However, the Battle of Britain was won by the British a full year and a half before the bombing of Pearl Harbor which brought America into the war. While the Battle of Britain was raging in the summer and fall of 1940, the American public remained decisively against entering the war, despite Roosevelt's determination to assist the British.

In October of 1940, the Battle of Britain ended with a decisive British victory. Without air superiority and with no chance of defeating the Royal Navy, Hitler abandoned all plans to invade Britain. The threat of a German invasion had passed. The Germans did not have the capability to invade Great Britain, and in fact, this had never been Hitler's intention as he had made clear in his book. His sights were set on the east.

A claim you can hear people make nowadays about World War II is that Germany was a threat to the United States. Just think about this claim for a moment. Germany did not have the ability to invade Britain so how would it ever cross the Atlantic to attack America? Germany is a small nation compared to the US—about the size of Montana—and it had a population about half ours. During the war, it had virtually no navy except U-boats. How was Germany ever going to be capable of mounting any kind of threat to the United States, especially since Hitler never voiced any such intention? In fact, his national interest was in keeping us neutral and out of the war.

In September of 1940 while the Battle of Britain was still raging, Roosevelt signed the Selective Training and Service Act and the draft began. The draft and the American military buildup began a full year and three months before the bombing of Pearl Harbor. The draft was sold to the American people not as preparation for entering the war overseas, but as a defensive measure—to build up our strength to deter and ward off any attack on the United States.

In the election campaign of 1940, Roosevelt gave a speech in October in Boston while the outcome of the Battle of Britain was still in question. The speech was about the American military buildup that was ongoing. "I have said this before, but I shall say it again and again and again," Roosevelt said. "Your boys are not going to be sent into any foreign wars."

In 1940, the antiwar movement in the United States was beginning to organize and become more vocal as war propaganda on the radio, in the newspapers and in Hollywood movies bombarded the American people with pro-British and anti-German themes.

The same month that the draft began, the America First Committee was founded to counter the prowar propagandists who were trying to convince the American people to join the war. The Communist Party USA (CPUSA) had been aggressively anti-fascist and anti-German, but after the Soviet Union invaded Poland with Germany, it changed its tune and became a leading antiwar voice alongside the America First Committee.

A majority of the American people wanted no part of the war in Europe; however, Roosevelt and the British were working behind the scenes to bring the USA into the war. Congress had blocked Roosevelt from entangling the U.S. in the wars in Europe and Asia through passage of the Neutrality Acts, which were heavily influenced by the Nye Committee's report on "the merchants of death." These acts had limited Roosevelt's ability to provide wartime assistance to the nations at war with Germany, Italy and Japan.

To counter American antiwar sentiment, British Prime Minister Winston Churchill set up a British intelligence operation in the United States called British Security Coordination (BSC). The BSC was run by a Canadian man named William Stephenson—later known as "the man called Intrepid." Stephenson's mission was to covertly combat American antiwar advocates and bring the U.S. into the war by any means necessary. Stephenson ran his propaganda operation out of the Rockefeller Center in New York City.

According to an August 2006 article in the British newspaper *The Guardian*, "BSC became a huge secret agency of nationwide news manipulation and black propaganda."

The article said the BSC represented one of the largest covert operations in British spying history and that as many as 3,000 British agents were "spreading propaganda and mayhem in a staunchly anti-war America."

The BSC planted pro-British and anti-German stories, many of them outright false, in American newspapers and radio broadcasts, which were reported as fact. Rigged polls were run that falsely showed a higher percentage of Americans supporting involvement in the war. The polls were used to pressure antiwar congressmen from continuing their opposition to assisting the British war effort. Antiwar congressmen were harassed and smeared by British agents. The America First Committee was targeted for harassment and its rallies were disrupted by British agent provocateurs. Labor unions were infiltrated. British money was used in congressional elections to defeat antiwar politicians. The BSC pulled out all the stops using the black arts of espionage to subvert democratic dissent and fan the flames of war against Germany.

In his book about the BSC, called *Desperate Deception*, Thomas Mahl quotes Ernest Cuneo, an American who worked with the BSC, as saying, "Given the time, the situation, and the mood, it is not surprising however, that BSC also went beyond the legal, the ethical, and the proper. Throughout the neutral Americas, and especially in the U.S., it ran espionage agents, tampered with the mails, tapped telephones, smuggled propaganda into the country, disrupted public gatherings, covertly subsidized newspapers, radios, and organizations, perpetrated forgeries—even palming one off on the President of the United States—violated the aliens registration act, shanghaied sailors numerous times, and possibly murdered one or more persons in this country."

In March 1941, the Lend-Lease Act was passed allowing the United States to supply Great Britain and the Soviet Union with war materiel. By April, Roosevelt had increased U.S. involvement in the Battle of the Atlantic in violation of the Neutrality Acts.

These actions raised the suspicions of antiwar advocates who were convinced that Roosevelt was deliberately trying to create the conditions that would bring the U.S. into the war. More people began to speak out about the administration and Roosevelt's war ambitions.

In June 1941, Germany invaded the Soviet Union. The CPUSA, which had been a leading antiwar voice, suddenly did an about face and became one of the nation's loudest pro-war advocates. However, at the same time the America First Committee was reaching its greatest point of influence. The committee attracted some of the most prominent Americans from both the Republican and Democratic parties who spoke out against America getting involved in a war that they believed was not ours to fight.

After the German invasion of the Soviet Union, the communists joined the British in the covert campaign to bring America into the war.

But at the time, Americans still remembered the propaganda that pulled them into World War I, and they resisted the calls to war.

By the fall of 1941, the Soviet Union was in danger of being overrun and disappearing altogether under the German blitzkrieg.

Meanwhile, the British were on the ropes in North Africa.

On October 27, 1941, in a scene reminiscent of President Wilson's indignation over the Zimmerman Telegram, Roosevelt gave a speech on Navy Day in Washington, D.C. The speech began with outrage over the Nazi sinking of an American destroyer in the North Atlantic.

"We have wished to avoid shooting," Roosevelt said. "But the shooting has started. And history has recorded who fired the first shot. In the long run, however, all that will matter is who fired the last shot. America has been attacked."

Roosevelt held up a map that portrayed a plan for the Nazi takeover of the Western hemisphere. "I have in my possession a secret map made in Germany by Hitler's government—by the planners of the new world order. It is a map of South America and a part of Central America, as Hitler proposes to reorganize it. Today in this area there are fourteen separate countries. But the geographical experts of Berlin have ruthlessly obliterated all existing boundary lines; they have divided South America into five vassal states, bringing the whole continent under their domination. And they have also so arranged it that the territory of one of these new puppet states includes the Republic of Panama and our great lifeline—the Panama Canal. That is his plan. It will never go into effect. This map makes clear the Nazi design not only against South America but against the United States itself."

Roosevelt continued: "Your government has in its possession another document made in Germany by Hitler's government. It is a detailed plan, which, for obvious reasons, the Nazis did not wish and do not wish to publicize just yet, but which they are ready to impose, a little later on a dominated world—if Hitler wins. It is a plan to abolish all existing religions—Protestant, Catholic, Mohammedan, Hindu, Buddhist and Jewish alike. The property of all churches will be seized by the Reich and its puppets. The cross and all other symbols of religion are to be forbidden. The clergy are to be forever silenced under penalty of the concentration camps, where even now so many fearless men are being tortured because they have placed God above Hitler. In the place of the churches of our civilization, there is to be set up an International Nazi Church—a church which will be served by orators sent out by the Nazi Government. In the place of the *Bible*, the words of *Mein Kampf* will be imposed and enforced as Holy Writ. And in place of the cross of Christ will be put two symbols—the swastika and the naked sword. A God of Blood and Iron will take the place of the God of Love and Mercy. Let us well ponder that statement which I have made tonight."

These were alarming claims. Roosevelt's map was evidence that Hitler intended to invade South and Central America and seize the Panama Canal. Roosevelt was claiming that Hitler planned to abolish all religions and replace them with an international Nazi church. The only problem was that there never was a plan by the Nazis to abolish all existing religions. Roosevelt's speech was nothing more than made up propaganda that was an attempt to frighten and enrage the American people. And we now know that the map Roosevelt was holding was made by the BSC as a propaganda tool that was designed to trick Americans into believing that Hitler had plans to attack the Western Hemisphere. The map was a propaganda trick provided by British intelligence agents to Roosevelt to bring us into the war, just as the Zimmerman Telegram had been a pretext for war 24 years before.

Imagine that. An American president making a case for war using a phony document provided by a foreign intelligence agency in an attempt to incite fear and anger in the American people.

But the trick didn't work. American public opinion remained solidly against joining the war despite the propaganda. It was going to take something bigger to convince the American people that war was necessary—a catalyzing event that would change public opinion—a backdoor into the war with Germany.

Japan was America's great rival in the Pacific. Japan had been embroiled in a grueling war since 1937 when it attacked and invaded China.

A year before his Navy Day Speech when the Battle of Britain was coming to a close and Roosevelt was making campaign promises to keep American boys out of foreign wars, U.S. Navy Lieutenant Commander Arthur McCollum, an intelligence officer in the Pentagon who oversaw intercepts of Japanese military and diplomatic messages, produced a document called the Eight Action Memo, known today as the McCollum memo.

The memo stated that Britain was unable to defeat Germany and Italy alone. According to the memo, the British Empire served as a buffer against any attack by Germany and Italy against the United States; however, the survival of the British Empire was in doubt. McCollum continued that it was in the interest of Germany and Italy for America to remain a disinterested spectator of the war in Europe. While McCollum noted that Germany and Italy did not have the means to provide any material aid to Japan, they had allied with Japan to keep American attention focused on the threat in the Pacific.

The memo stated that Japan had some advantages in a war with the United States, such as a strong army, skilled navy and the geographically strong position of the Japanese islands. However, McCollum also pointed out the considerable disadvantages the Japanese would have in such a conflict. Japan was already engaged in an exhausting war with China, its domestic economy and food supply were severely straightened, it had a serious lack of sources of raw materials for war, it was totally cut off from supplies from Europe, dependent upon distant overseas routes for essential supplies, incapable of increasing manufacture and supply of war materials without free access to U.S. or European markets and its major cities and industrial centers were extremely vulnerable to air attack.

"It is not believed that in the present state of political opinion the United States government is capable of declaring war against Japan without more ado; and it is barely possible that vigorous action on our part might lead the Japanese to modify their attitude," McCollum wrote. He then listed eight steps to bring America into the war, some of which included re-positioning American forces throughout Asia, increasing aid to the Chinese, keeping the main strength of the U.S. Pacific fleet in Hawaii and placing an embargo against Japan.

"If by these means Japan could be led to commit an overt act of war, so much the better," McCollum stated.

McCollum had produced a plan to provoke the Japanese into firing the first shot.

While Roosevelt was making campaign promises to keep American boys out of the war, his administration was putting McCollum's plan into effect.

In the summer of 1941 before the bombing of Pearl Harbor, Roosevelt was covertly sending Americans to fight the Japanese without informing Congress or the American people. The American Volunteer Group, popularly known as the Flying Tigers, was sent to Burma that summer. The Flying Tigers were a mercenary group of highly paid American fighter pilots flying American warplanes and led by an American commander in the service of China. The pilots were sent to fight the Japanese at a time when American officials were in negotiations with Japan to defuse tensions. The arrival of American warplanes and fighter pilots in Indochina sent a clear message to the Japanese that the Roosevelt administration was not negotiating in good faith.

On August 1, 1941, the United States began an oil embargo on Japan. At the time, Japan was dependent on the United States for oil. As 1941 was coming to a close, Japan was being painted into a corner. It was fighting a costly war in China but lacked the resources to continue.

In the fall of 1941, Japan made two proposals to the United States that included a partial withdrawal from China and a withdrawal from southern Indochina if the United States would resume oil shipments and cease assistance to the Chinese. On November 26, Secretary of State Cordell Hull presented the Japanese ambassador with a proposal, now known as the Hull note, which demanded that the Japanese withdraw from both China and French Indochina. The proposal was unacceptable to the Japanese and the negotiations ended. Japan was not going to walk away from its empire in humiliation at the demands of the

United States. But to maintain its empire it needed oil that the United States would no longer provide. The Dutch East Indies had oil but the U.S. Navy in the Philippines and Hawaii and the British navy in Singapore were obstacles to seizing it.

Three days before the bombing of Pearl Harbor, the *Chicago Tribune* printed a front page story blaring the headline, "F.D.R.'s WAR PLANS!" The article reported a leaked report, called the Rainbow Five Plan that outlined an American invasion of Europe by 1943.

"It is a blueprint for total war on an unprecedented scale in at least two oceans and three continents, Europe, Africa and Asia," wrote reporter Chesly Manly. Manly revealed Roosevelt's hidden plan for the "total defeat of Germany." The plan outlined a step by step process of encircling Germany, strangling it and demoralizing the German people "by subversive activities, propaganda, deprivation, and the destruction wrought." The plan called for a large scale invasion of the European continent by 1943 with a massive five million man American army, with total forces numbering 10 million men.

Manly quoted the plan: "It is mandatory that we reach an early appreciation of our stupendous task and gain the wholehearted support of the entire country in the production of trained men, ships, munitions, and ample reserves."

At the time, the *Chicago Tribune* was owned by Robert McCormick, who was an opponent and critic of the Roosevelt administration. McCormick was a member of the America First Committee and was strongly against the United States entering the war in Europe or Asia.

The Rainbow Five Plan confirmed what many in the America First Committee believed—that despite campaign promises the year before to keep American boys out of any foreign wars, Roosevelt was actively planning for another war in Europe. The leak of the Rainbow Five Plan proved that a plan for war on a grand scale was already in place.

The Rainbow Five Plan gave resonance to an antiwar song called "Plow Under" that had been released earlier that year by the Almanac Singers. The folk group sang about a New Deal policy in which the government killed a million hogs a day, plowing under every fourth hog, in an attempt to keep pork prices from falling. The lyrics went that just as the government plowed under every fourth hog, it also had plans to plow under every fourth American boy in wars overseas.

With the release of the Rainbow Five Plan, opponents of the war accused Roosevelt of plotting to plow under every fourth American boy in the war in Europe, even using lyrics from the song in Congress, to Roosevelt's indignation.

Incidentally, shortly after "Plow Under" was released, Germany attacked the Soviet Union. The Almanac Singers then changed their tune and ceased writing antiwar songs. The group, which had ties to the CPUSA, apparently felt that plowing under every fourth American boy was fine if done for the interests of the Soviet Union and international communism. After the bombing of Pearl Harbor, the group began writing pro-war songs.

The leak of the Rainbow Five plan caused a sensation both in the United States and Germany. A hunt for the leaker began immediately in Washington, D.C. Several people were questioned by the government but the leaker was never identified.

Three days after the story had been printed as the fallout from the leak was still being felt, the Japanese bombed Pearl Harbor, attacked the Philippines and swept across Southeast Asia.

More than 2,400 Americans were killed at Pearl Harbor, shocking the American people out of their war opposition and plunging the country headlong into the war. The old foreign policy of staying out of foreign wars that dates back to President George Washington was relabeled as isolationism and blamed for Pearl Harbor. The old principles of avoiding entangling alliances, minding our own business abroad and staying out of overseas wars were said to be discredited—an attitude that continues to this day.

On December 8, Roosevelt gave his "date which will live in infamy" speech. Roosevelt told Congress that America had been in peace negotiations with the Japanese but had been treacherously attacked in a premeditated onslaught.

"No matter how long it may take us to overcome this premeditated invasion, the American people in their righteous might will win through to absolute victory," he said to cheers from Congress.

He said a state of war already existed between the United States and the Japanese Empire and asked that Congress declare war due to the "unprovoked and dastardly attack by Japan."

Less than an hour after the speech, Congress declared war against Japan with only one dissenting vote, by Representative Jeannette Rankin, a pacifist and the first woman elected to Congress.

On December 9, Roosevelt gave one of his Fireside Chats over the radio. In the chat, he made it clear that not only was Japan an enemy of the United States, but so were Germany and Italy. He said the attack on Pearl Harbor was done "in the Nazi manner" and that Germany had urged Japan to attack the United States. He explained that the attack was part of a joint plan of the Axis Powers to give Japan all the Pacific islands and the west coasts of North and South America. The speech shifted from the treachery of Japan to that of Germany and Italy. Roosevelt argued that war against the Germans would strengthen America's hand.

"Remember always that Germany and Italy regardless of any formal declaration of war consider themselves at war with the United States at this moment just as much as they consider themselves at war with Britain or Russia," he said.

"We expect to eliminate the danger from Japan but it would serve us ill if we accomplish that and found that the rest of the world was dominated by Hitler and Mussolini," he said.

The leaking of the Rainbow Five plan and Roosevelt's Fireside Chat of December 9 made it clear to the Germans and Italians that the United States had now entered the war against them.

On December 11, Germany declared war on the United States, citing American attacks on German naval ships and merchant vessels. Italy also declared war that day. Hours later, the

U.S. Congress declared war on Germany and Italy.

The bombing of Pearl Harbor was seen across America as a contemptible act—a sneak attack by a villainous enemy. The lives of more than 2,400 American young men had been snuffed out in a few hours. The press fanned the flames of fear and anger in the American people and the country entered into a state of war hysteria. All opposition to war immediately ceased and young men lined up to fight the Japanese.

But was the attack really a surprise? An August 7, 2013 article in the *Wall Street Journal* provides some insight.

The article cited newly released documents about how the Roosevelt administration mounted a no-holds-barred legal attack against journalists suspected of leaking military secrets. Six months after the bombing of Pearl Harbor, a *Chicago Tribune* reporter wrote an article about the Battle of Midway and revealed that the U.S. had cracked Japanese codes and knew in advance the Japanese battle plans, Japanese strength and the exact locations of Japanese ships.

The Battle of Midway was a devastating loss for Japan. The U.S. Navy's foreknowledge of every Japanese move was a major factor in the destruction of the Japanese fleet and put the U.S. on the offensive after suffering a series of losses earlier in the year

In response to the article about the Battle of Midway, the government appointed a special prosecutor who sought indictments of the reporter and the *Tribune*'s managing editor before a federal grand jury in Chicago. A conviction of aiding the enemy carried a potential death penalty, but the grand jury dismissed all charges.

The *Wall Street Journal*'s angle in 2013 was to compare the *Tribune* case of World War II with that of Army leaker Bradley Manning who was convicted of releasing classified information about the Iraq War to Wikileaks.

But the *Wall Street Journal* did not raise a significant question that seemed to be missed or ignored by the reporter and by the online commenters below the story, but surely was on the mind of *Chicago Tribune* publisher Robert McCormick when the Battle of Midway article was printed in 1942. If the government knew the exact location of the Japanese fleet and was listening to the communications of Japanese military leaders before the Battle of Midway, what did it know about the plans and location of the Japanese fleet six months earlier before the bombing of Pearl Harbor?

We now know that Japanese codes had been broken before Pearl Harbor and that American intelligence agents were monitoring Japanese communications about peace negotiations. We also know that the British had a far more sophisticated intelligence effort that had been monitoring Japan.

We know that just prior to the bombing, American aircraft were lined up on the runway at Pearl Harbor like ducks in a row. We know that the American Pacific Fleet's aircraft carriers were pulled out of Pearl Harbor shortly before the arrival of the Japanese Fleet while the older battleships were left behind. We know that on December 7, radar operators in Hawaii spotted large numbers of incoming planes but their warnings were ignored. We know that Roosevelt wanted to join the war but that the American people and Congress were obstacles to him because public opinion was solidly antiwar. We also know today that the Roosevelt administration was chock full of British and Soviet agents who were working relentlessly to bring America into the war. We know that a plan a year before had been drawn up to corner the Japanese into firing the first shot.

We know that the bombing of Pearl Harbor was the catalyzing event that allowed Roosevelt to enter the war with the American people behind him.

The attack on Pearl Harbor was the biggest blunder in Japanese history, resulting in millions of Japanese dead in a horrific bombing campaign that targeted civilian population centers. The end result of the attack on Pearl Harbor was total defeat for Japan, national destruction and the occupation of the Japanese home islands by American troops which continues to this day.

But immediately after the bombing of Pearl Harbor,

Roosevelt allowed the war effort against Japan to wait and turned the attention of the American military to the Atlantic and onto the Germans and Italians. American soldiers, sailors, airmen and Marines in the Pacific were all but abandoned in the first years of the war and left to their fates. American troops on Wake Island and Guam held up valiantly against the Japanese onslaught but received no support from the American government. On the Philippines, hundreds of Americans and thousands of Filipinos were marched to their deaths at Bataan. Meanwhile, plans were being drawn up for an American invasion of North Africa.

Pearl Harbor gave Roosevelt and Churchill what they wanted—a backdoor for American entry into the war against Germany.

In North Africa, the British, Italians and Germans had been fighting for dominance since 1940. The French and British Empires had long had imperial interests in North Africa and in 1940 the Italians decided to get into the game. When the Italians were routed by the British, the Germans sent in reinforcements.

The main goal for the British was to maintain control over Egypt and the Suez Canal. The canal was Britain's lifeline to India—the jewel of its empire. Exploiting India and its other colonies in Asia and Eastern Africa was an important part of the British economy. The loss of the Suez Canal would have made that exploitation more difficult.

The British needed American support in North Africa to prevent defeat and the loss of the canal. Josef Stalin also pressured Roosevelt to open a second front against Germany to take the heat off the Red Army on the Eastern Front.

To assist the British and appease Stalin, American soldiers landed in French North Africa in November 1942 and were met with resistance by Vichy Frenchmen. While Americans were being killed in the Pacific without support from their government, American soldiers began the war in the Atlantic by killing and being killed by Frenchmen.

The Germans and Italians were soon chased out of North Africa. Stalin continued to pressure Roosevelt to do more to defeat the Germans, so Roosevelt turned America's attention not to the Pacific and the country that had attacked us, but to Italy—a country that had barely been able to defeat Ethiopia a few years before. Of course, no rational person could believe that Italy was a threat to the United States. The sole reason for the attack on Italy was to keep the Germans from throwing all their might at the Soviet Union on the Eastern Front.

To placate Stalin, a man who hated the United States, and to assist Stalin in his fight against the Germans, nearly 20,000 Americans died in a bloody fight in Italy. The defeat of Japan—the nation that had attacked us—had to wait for Italy to be defeated. To Roosevelt, British and Soviet interests were more important than the lives of American troops in the Pacific.

Churchill wanted to follow up on Allied victories in Italy by pressing the fight in Southern Europe, which he called "the soft underbelly of Europe."

But Stalin and Roosevelt thought differently. In late November 1943, Stalin, Churchill and Roosevelt held the Tehran Conference in Iran. At the conference, they decided that Britain and the U.S. would invade France in 1944.

The invasion of Poland by Germany had started World War II. France and Britain had been allied with the Poles and had declared war on Germany under the pretext of an alliance with Poland. But the Soviet Union had also invaded Poland with Germany. At Tehran, Roosevelt and Churchill agreed to the Soviet Union's annexation of Polish territory—which was seen by the Poles as a betrayal. The cause of the war was the defense of Poland, but at the Tehran Conference, Poland was handed over to one of its attackers.

Prior to the Tehran Conference, the British and Americans disagreed on what strategy to pursue after the invasion of the Italy. The British favored a Mediterranean strategy of pushing up into Eastern Europe through Greece and the Balkans. The Americans, led by Gen. George Marshall and Roosevelt, favored a much riskier and costlier invasion of western France. Due to Stalin's insistence in Tehran, the French strategy was chosen.

Instead of attacking the soft underbelly of Europe, we attacked the hard shell.

On D-Day, June 6, 1944, the Allies invaded Normandy on the western coast of France. The accepted narrative today is that D-Day was a turning point in the war against fascism and led to the liberation of France and the defeat of the Nazis. This narrative has been reinforced over the past 70 years in Hollywood movies, books and in our schools.

The exact figure will never be known due to the violence and chaos, but as many as 2,500 Americans were killed that first day, with thousands more wounded. That's more killed in one day on the beaches of Normandy than in 13 years of war in Afghanistan.

Imagine being an American soldier on D-Day. You are standing on the deck of your landing craft that is being thrashed by the waves. The ramp drops down and you are yelled at to wade onto the beach while machine guns are firing down on you from hardened bunkers atop cliffs. Your leaders chose to land you on a heavily defended beach without cover under a cliff lined with machine guns. This choice led to up to 2,500 American deaths in a single day. More than 135,000 Americans were killed in France and Germany over the next year.

In books and movies, the German soldiers defending the beaches of Normandy are portrayed as formidable soldiers. But in reality, they were young boys, old men and invalids. They were the troops that didn't have the training, the experience or the ability to serve on the Eastern Front. Germany's best trained and best equipped troops were fighting the Red Army on the plains of Eastern Europe. And by 1944, the Red Army had killed off or captured a great portion of the Germany army. By the time the Allies landed at Normandy, the German army had already been broken and was in retreat in the east.

We have been told our whole lives that D-Day and all of the American deaths that resulted were necessary to defeat Germany. But was this the case?

U.S. Air Force Lt. Col. William Moore wrote an Air War

College research report that concluded that the Normandy Landings were unnecessary for the defeat of Germany and were done at the behest of Stalin who wanted to improve the Soviet strategic situation at the conclusion of the war. Moore also concluded that other better and less costly options were rejected because American commanders, especially Gen. George Marshall and Gen. Dwight Eisenhower, had long been committed to the invasion of France.

Plans for the invasion of France had been made and were committed to prior to the bombing of Pearl Harbor.

When Churchill, Roosevelt and Stalin met in Tehran in late 1943, Stalin knew that the Germans were already finished. In January 1942, the Soviets had won the Battle of Moscow. The Germans had failed to seize the Russian capital city, the ultimate objective of Operation Barbarossa. In early 1943, the Soviets won the Battle of Stalingrad, a turning point in the war. The Soviets then won the Battle of Kursk in the summer of 1943, effectively breaking the already depleted German army. At that point, the German military was destroyed as an offensive force and it was clear to all who were paying attention that the German invasion of the Soviet Union had failed.

The battles between the Germans and Soviets on the Eastern Front were massive with horrific casualties on both sides. Infantry, artillery, armor and aircraft had clashed on a scale never before seen in history. The Battle of Kursk alone involved nearly 3 million men, 8,000 tanks, and 5,000 airplanes. In comparison, the battles on the Western Front were minor sideshows. By the time the Allies landed in France in 1944, the major battles of the war had already been fought with the Soviets and the Germans suffering casualties in the millions.

Hitler had repeated Napoleon's mistake of 1812. The results were the same—the collapse and destruction of a great invading army and the occupation of the invader's capital by Russian troops.

At the Tehran Conference, Stalin knew the Germans were finished. The Soviets were churning out tanks, artillery and warplanes and had millions of trained soldiers while the Germans were at the end of the line as far as troops and equipment. The Soviets had numerical superiority across the board. In 1943, the Soviet Union had seized the initiative and had begun the march toward Berlin. But Stalin knew it was going to be a long, bloody road.

According to Lt. Col. William Moore, the invasion of Normandy was decided at Tehran not because it was the best course of action for the United States or Britain, but because it was best for Stalin. Stalin knew that if the Allies had followed Churchill's less risky plan of attacking "the soft underbelly of Europe" in the Mediterranean and up through the Balkans, Eastern Europe would have been liberated by the United States and Britain and not the Soviet Union.

Stalin knew that an Allied invasion of France would be costly for the United States, Britain and Germany and would confine the United States and Britain to Western Europe. The invasion of France would reduce the amount of casualties the Red Army would suffer on the Eastern Front as Germany shifted troops west in response. Stalin knew that the invasion of Normandy, while unnecessary to the defeat of Germany, would leave the Soviet Union in a stronger position at the end of the war.

Churchill's argument was that an invasion of France was unnecessary to the defeat of Germany, was risky and would result in high casualties. Instead, an invasion of the Balkans would be less risky and would result in the United States and Britain occupying Eastern Europe at the end of the war liberating those countries and leaving the West in a stronger position vis a vis the Soviet Union.

Roosevelt sided with Stalin and agreed to an invasion of France, deciding against the British position, and setting the stage for D-Day.

As predicted by the British, D-Day was a bloodbath. Allied troops were landed on beaches under cliffs lined with machine gun emplacements. They were mowed down in the thousands by German boys and invalids. The decision to invade France led to the deaths of 135,000 Americans in less than a year, while contributing little to the defeat of Germany other than trading Soviet deaths for American and British dead.

One argument for the Normandy landings was that they prevented our ally, the Soviet Union, from seizing Western Europe. Moore debunks this Machiavellian line of thinking. If the United States had not invaded France in 1944, Germany would have transferred its forces out of France and to the Eastern Front as the Red Army advanced on Germany. The German troops that had fought the Allies in the West would instead have fought the Soviets in the East. The United States and Britain could have waited until the bulk of the German force was spent in the East and then landed in France at a later date unopposed. The United States and Britain could have then seized Western Europe from a collapsing Germany allowing the Red Army to sustain higher casualties and leaving the Soviet Union in a weaker state at the end of the war. In fact, there was a plan for just this contingency, called Operation Rankin, which was designed to get the Allied armies into Germany as fast as possible in the event of a German collapse so that the Soviet advance would be stopped before reaching Western Europe. Moore stated that if the Allies had not invaded France on D-Day but had continued the offensive in the Mediterranean and had implemented Operation Rankin, most likely not only would this have prevented a Soviet occupation of Western Europe, but it would also have kept the Soviets out of much of Central and Eastern Europe and resulted in far fewer American dead.

Moore concluded that Germany could have been defeated without the high casualties of the Normandy landings by continuing the Western bombing campaign and the offensive in the Mediterranean while allowing the Germans and the Soviets to fight it out in the east. With the collapse of the German army in the east, Operation Rankin could have been implemented preventing the Soviets from seizing Western Europe without the 135,000 American dead on the Western Front.

According to Moore, the decision to go forward with the

Normandy landings interrupted the successes of the Allied bombing campaign which in 1943 was beginning to disrupt German war production. The bombing campaign was slowed to prepare for D-Day allowing the Germans to continue war production. The enormous amount of resources needed for the landings also diverted men and materiel from the Pacific, which was given second priority. It was the Japanese who had attacked us but Roosevelt was more concerned about the Germans, who had not attacked us. Japan could have been defeated a lot sooner if the Normandy invasion had never happened.

However, D-Day occurred not because it was our best course of action, but because Stalin wanted it, and Marshall and Roosevelt agreed. They were willing to trade Soviet dead for American dead to please Uncle Joe.

D-Day was nothing more than a blood sacrifice to Stalin, and that is how it should be viewed by honest historians. By the time the landings occurred it had become obvious to many in the German high command that the war was lost and that Hitler was leading Germany to ruin. German officers began reaching out to the West offering terms for surrender; however, Roosevelt rejected any offers for surrender due to his policy of unconditional surrender. Germans opposed to Hitler had no choice but to fight to the death. The policy of unconditional surrender resulted in a far higher body count for both sides than would have otherwise been the case.

In 1945, Germany was being destroyed by the Allied bombing campaign. Non-combatants were deliberately targeted, most notoriously in the bombing of Dresden in February 1945. British and American bombers committed the deliberate massacre of hundreds of thousands of civilians and the destruction of historic cities for no strategic military advantage. The bombing of Dresden came after the Battle of the Bulge when the Red Army was entering Germany and it was already evident that Germany was defeated.

The Roosevelt and Truman administrations had allowed for the deliberate targeting of non-combatants in the air war, both in Germany and Japan. This policy alone is enough to negate any claims that World War II was a "Good War" or that the West had the moral high ground in the war. In most wars, women, children and the elderly are killed as "collateral damage." But Roosevelt and Truman followed a policy of deliberately targeting women, children and the elderly, who were killed in the hundreds of thousands in both Germany and Japan. This policy was deliberate, conscious, calculated and entirely unnecessary. It was a war crime that should forever tarnish the names of these two presidents. Good guys in a "Good War" do not deliberately kill non-combatants, even if it could bring some kind of strategic advantage, which in World War II it did not. Let's face it, the carpet bombing of civilian population centers and the condemning of hundreds of thousands of innocent human beings to death in hellish firestorms cannot be justified if one is going to claim this war was fought for moral purposes.

The brief 12-year reign of the Third Reich ended with the total destruction of Germany. The German military was destroyed, German cities were bombed to ashes, German civilians were massacred in the millions and German women were raped on a massive scale by a rampaging Red Army. Eastern Europe was liberated from Nazi totalitarianism only to fall under the iron heel of Soviet totalitarianism. The war began with the German and Soviet invasion of Poland and ended with Poland under Soviet rule—the same Soviets who had massacred the entire Polish officer and NCO corps when the Red Army had invaded that country in 1939.

World War II finally came to an end under two mushroom clouds when atomic bombs obliterated Hiroshima and Nagasaki. The commonly accepted mythology today is that the atomic bombings of Hiroshima and Nagasaki were necessary to end the war quickly and avoid up to a million American casualties in an invasion of Japan.

However, this is merely rationalizing the mass murder of women, children, the elderly and other non-combatants. Japan was a defeated and destroyed nation by early 1945. Its leaders were willing to negotiate terms for surrender. When the Soviet Union began its offensive on Japan in Manchukuo on August 9, 1945, the Japanese knew they were finished and any delay in surrender could result in the loss of home islands to the Soviets. The only sticking point in the terms of surrender was that the Japanese wanted Emperor Hirohito retained. But instead of negotiating this point, President Truman decided to kill hundreds of thousands of non-combatants in the world's first and only atomic mass murders.

Gen. Dwight Eisenhower and Gen. Douglas MacArthur both thought dropping the bombs was unnecessary to achieve victory over Japan.

"... the Japanese were ready to surrender and it wasn't necessary to hit them with that awful thing," Eisenhower said in a 1963 interview with *Newsweek*.

In *The Pathology of Power*, Norman Cousins wrote, "When I asked Gen. MacArthur about the decision to drop the bomb, I was surprised to learn he had not even been consulted. What, I asked, would his advice have been? He replied that he saw no military justification for the dropping of the bomb. The war might have ended weeks earlier, he said, if the United States had agreed, as it later did anyway, to the retention of the institution of the emperor."

In *Tragedy and Hope,* Carroll Quigley quoted Director of Military Intelligence for the Pacific Theater of War Alfred McCormack, who Quigley thought was in as good a situation as anyone for judging the situation. McCormack believed that the Japanese surrender could have been obtained by blockade alone. "The Japanese had no longer enough food in stock, and their fuel reserves were practically exhausted," McCormack said. "We had begun a secret process of mining all their harbors, which was steadily isolating them from the rest of the world.

"If we had brought this operation to its logical conclusion, the destruction of Japan's cities with incendiary and other bombs would have been quite unnecessary. But General Norstad declared at Washington that this blockading action was a cowardly proceeding unworthy of the Air Force. It was therefore discontinued."

Quigley stated that it was clear in 1945 that the defeat of Japan did not require the A-bomb, just as it did not require Russian entry into the war or an American invasion of the Japanese home islands. Quigley even stated that if the bomb had not been dropped on Japan, the significance of this weapon of terror would not have become known to the Soviets, who did not understand the bomb and felt it was too costly and a strain on the Soviet system to produce. "Without the knowledge of the actual bomb which the Russian leaders obtained from our demonstrations of its power, they would almost certainly not have made the effort to get the bomb had we not used it on Japan," Quigley wrote.

But Quigley then justified its use because it restrained Soviet aggression after the war. Just think this over for a second. The United States helped the Soviet Union defeat Germany with billions of dollars from American taxpayers and hundreds of thousands of American lives only to face nuclear destruction from the Soviets after the war. Why were we aiding and ensuring the survival of a bloodthirsty totalitarian dictatorship in the first place?

On July 29, 1945, President Harry Truman made the decision to incinerate tens of thousands of human beings in Hiroshima in a conscious, deliberate, calculated and wholly unnecessary act of mass murder. He condemned thousands more to slow painful deaths from radiation poisoning.

If you believe in right and wrong, then there can be no doubt that the dropping of these bombs on Hiroshima and Nagasaki was wrong. These acts were not done for legitimate military reasons. They were not done to save American lives.

If you believe that women, children, the elderly and other noncombatants should not be purposefully and deliberately killed by the tens of thousands, whether there is a legitimate military reason or not, then obviously the bombings of Hiroshima, Nagasaki, as well as the fire bombings of Tokyo and Dresden, and the entire bombing campaign of the war which targeted enemy population centers, were war crimes of the highest order.

It is strange today that people still look back at Truman as being a good president. This was a man who in his 40s was a dues-paying member of the Ku Klux Klan. This was a man who gave away Eastern Europe to Stalin at the Potsdam Conference in 1945—a repudiation of democracy and freedom and an appeasement to dictatorship worse than Neville Chamberlain's Munich Agreement that turned over the Sudetenland to Hitler. In Korea, Truman set a precedent of going to war under United Nations auspices without a war declaration from Congress. He was a man who threatened to draft union workers into the military if they didn't settle the 1952 steel strike. Under his administration, the Central Intelligence Agency was founded and the military-industrial complex was made permanent.

Whatever good qualities Harry Truman had, his decision to commit the mass murder of civilians at Hiroshima and Nagasaki surely outweighs any of them.

If you are a religious person and you believe in heaven and hell; if you believe that it is an evil act to make a decision to deliberately kill innocent people when there are other options available; if you believe that we will be judged on the day we meet our maker, then there is no way around it. Harry Truman is burning in hell alongside Roosevelt, Churchill, Stalin and Hitler.

Many claim that World War II was fought to stop the aggression of a brutal dictator—that it was fought in the defense of freedom, democracy and Western Civilization. But the war ended with a brutal dictator in control of all of Eastern Europe. The war ended with more countries under the rule of a totalitarian dictator than when it began. Stalin, a butcher whose body count exceeded Hitler's, emerged from the war victorious. Stalin defeated Germany with the help of American money, materiel and lives.

With Germany destroyed, Stalin turned the focus of his aggression onto the United States. Americans were soon dying in the tens of thousands in Korea and Vietnam fighting against communists funded and supported by the Soviets and armed with

Soviet-made weapons.

No. World War II was not a "Good War," or even a necessary war. It was not fought for moral reasons, or for freedom or democracy, or to stop genocide. It was fought for other reasons that the victors of this war don't like to talk about.

History is written by the victors. Many like to think that America was a victor in this war. But what did the American people win?

Imagine for a moment that we have traveled back to 1942 in a time machine. We have landed on the beaches of Guadalcanal. The smell of rot, death and destruction is all around. We grab a U.S. Marine and pull him into our time machine and travel forward into the future. We drop our Marine in downtown Detroit in 2015.

Back in 1942, Detroit was a thriving city where the average American could find a job and make a good middle class living, buy a house and a car and raise children. But in 2015, that Marine would see a bankrupt city. He would see dilapidated buildings in various states of disrepair. Everything is covered in graffiti. The streets are crime-ridden and are not safe to walk alone even in the daytime. The people on the streets do not look healthy or prosperous. Panhandlers and the homeless are common sights. Many of the few businesses that are open are owned by foreigners. Foreign-born people make up a large portion of the population. Many of the signs for businesses are in languages other than English. A good percentage of the cars on the streets are made in Germany and Japan.

Now transport that same Marine to Hiroshima in 2015. He would find one of the most modern cities in the world with safe streets free of crime and vandalism. Most everyone is well-dressed, healthy, educated and prosperous. No poverty can be seen and no homelessness. All the cars on the streets are technological marvels and nearly all are made in Japan. Our Marine would learn that Hiroshima is no exception. Every city up and down the Japanese isles is similarly modern, safe and prosperous. Nowhere in Japan could our Marine find the blight, poverty and social breakdown that he saw in Detroit. Back home all across America, in our cities he would find homelessness, poverty, unemployment, underemployment, crime, vandalism and decay while a shrinking number of people live lives of opulence separated by class, money, lifestyle and outlook from their fellow Americans.

What would this Marine conclude from our little trip? Most likely, he would conclude that America lost the war.

America helped the Soviet Union survive in its war against Germany by supplying it with billions of dollars in war materiel, food, clothing, trucks and airplanes. America made its war plans not for what was best for the United States or for the lives of American soldiers, Marines, sailors and airmen, but for what was best for the Soviet Union.

America had assisted China in its fight with Japan and had totally defeated Japan only to end up fighting Chinese troops a few years later in Korea.

World War II saved communism in the Soviet Union and paved the way for a communist victory in China. Five years after the end of World War II, Americans were being killed in the tens of thousands in Korea by Chinese troops armed with Soviet-made weapons. More than 30,000 Americans died in that brutal war. In the 1960s, even more Americans were killed in Vietnam at the hands of soldiers supported by the Chinese and armed with Soviet-made weapons. About 60,000 Americans died in the war in Vietnam.

The Soviet Union and China were our allies against the Germans and the Japanese, but five years after the war ended, the Soviet Union and China were enemies and the Germans and Japanese were our allies.

What is the point of defeating one nation to help another if the nation you help is then going to turn around and fight you? Especially, if the one nation is smaller than the other?

This change of alliances and enemies after World War II is reminiscent of the scene in George Orwell's book *1984* when it was announced that Oceania was not at war with Eurasia after all. "Oceania was at war with Eastasia: Oceania had always been at war with Eastasia."

What was America fighting for in Vietnam and Korea? Why were we fighting to stop communism after losing so many lives fighting to save it in World War II?

We didn't stop communism in Vietnam. The communists won and what was the result? Today, Vietnam remains a poor country eager for American investment dollars while attempting to lure American tourists to come visit on vacation. In 2015, Vietnam is a country being threatened by China—which assisted Vietnam in its fight against us. China and Vietnam are still in conflict over territorial disputes that existed before the United States was even a country. Yet, we expended 60,000 American lives in Vietnam?

And were all those American deaths in the Korean War worth it? The Korean War was fought for almost identical reasons as the war in Vietnam, although the two conflicts had different outcomes. If America had stayed out of Korea, most likely North Korea would have won and today Korea would be a unified country. Like Vietnam today, it would probably be poorer than South Korea is today, but richer than North Korea, less militarized, not occupied by American troops, and probably not ruled by a tin-pot dictatorship. Like Vietnam, it would probably have abandoned its communist ideology while eagerly trying to develop its economy by wooing American investment capital.

If America had never joined the Korean and Vietnam wars, the 90,000 Americans who died in those countries would have lived out their lives here in America, working and raising children, and today they would be grandparents enjoying their retirement. They would have lived long lives here in the United States rather than dying violent deaths on frozen Korean hillsides or in the steamy jungles and rice paddies of Vietnam.

Without World War II, there would have been no Korean or Vietnam wars—at least not with American participation. Instead, the Koreans and Vietnamese would have fought anti-colonial wars against the Japanese and it would have been Japanese young men sent home in body bags in the tens of thousands.

Let's face it. World War II was not a fight between good and evil. It was a fight among fascists, communists and imperialists. It was an alliance of international finance capitalists and international communists to destroy nationalist governments that had formed in reaction and opposition to both.

We joined the war on the side of the communists and imperialists to further the goals of international finance capitalists and international communists. We helped the communists defeat the fascists only to spend the next 40 years losing lives, spending vast sums of money and facing nuclear annihilation from the communists.

Germany and Japan were two small nations lacking in natural resources. Combined, they were geographically only a fraction of the size of the United States, with smaller populations. Both nations were motivated by national interests and had regional ambitions. Neither had the capability or the desire to invade the United States. Both were already engaged in exhausting wars with nations far larger than themselves by the time the United States entered the war against them.

We joined the war on the side of Britain, the Soviet Union and China. While Japan and Germany had regional ambitions, the British and Soviets had global ones. The British were trying to save their global empire, which was being threatened by the rise of Germany and Japan. The Soviets were following an ideology that had an end goal of a global dictatorship of the proletariat. The United States helped defeat Germany and Japan saving Stalin from defeat and enabling the rise of Mao Zedong. Stalin and Mao were the worst butchers of the 20th century.

In the 1930s and 1940s, the propaganda efforts of the Japanese and Germans in the United States were minimal and ineffective. However, the British and Soviets were running pervasive propaganda operations in the United States and were engaged in large-scale subversive activities to serve the interests of their own elites. Agents from both countries infiltrated our media and our government for ends that resulted in the deaths of more than 400,000 Americans.

Think of the irony of the British strategy of bringing America into the war in Europe. The average British soldier believed he was fighting for crown and country, for the defense of his homeland from invasion and for the survival of the British Empire. The entry of America into the war gave him a fighting chance against the German war machine. But by allying with the United States and the Soviet Union, Britain was fighting alongside two nations that had always been indifferent at best and hostile at worst to the very concept of the British Empire. And Britain's enemy, Germany, was the one nation that was in favor of preserving that empire.

Hitler had written in *Mein Kampf* that he saw Britain as a natural ally of Germany. He stated in his book that it was folly for Germany to have challenged the British Empire by pursuing an overseas German empire before World War I and that it had been a mistake to have fought the British in that war. Going forward, he wanted to foster an alliance between Britain and Germany. "We Germans have had sufficient experience to know how hard it is to coerce England," he wrote. "And, apart from all this, I as a German would far rather see India under British domination than under that of any other nation."

If the British would have accepted the German peace offer after Dunkirk, Hitler would have left the British Empire alone and Britain wouldn't have lost another generation of men fighting the Germans. Instead, the war would have been between Germany and the Soviet Union—two dictatorships that had invaded Poland together in 1939.

Britain was one of the victors of World War II, but it lost its empire anyway. It plunged into the war as the world's preeminent power and emerged from it a bankrupted, second-tier nation. Today, Germany and Japan are economic powerhouses with economies far larger than Britain, which has become a shadow of its former self—with American troops stationed on its home island, its foreign policy subservient to America and its national union on the verge of break up.

The average British soldier, just like the average American soldier, made great sacrifices and died in great numbers in the war. From a military standpoint, the defeat of Germany and Japan were great victories.

But what was won? Did we fight to stop genocide?

If so, why did we side with the Soviet Union? Our government and media ignored and even tried to hide the Holomodor genocide that killed up to 7.5 million Ukrainians in 1932 and 1933. This genocide was intentionally committed by our ally Stalin. Lenin and Stalin inflicted millions of deaths on Russia and its satellites before Germany ever invaded it.

In 1943 when the Japanese took Burma, a preventable famine that resulted in anywhere from 1.3 million to 3 million deaths occurred in Bengal, India. When rice imports from Burma were stopped by the Japanese, the British government made a decision not to supply rice to Bengal, which resulted in mass starvation. Some Indian nationalists blame the famine directly on Churchill. Shiploads of grain from Australia passed by India and were not allowed to be diverted to the troublesome province and millions of Bengalis were condemned to death by starvation. American humanitarians and others pleaded with Churchill to allow relief to the starving Bengalis but were denied.

During British rule in India, famines causing millions of deaths were a regular occurrence and were much more severe than prior to British rule. Since the end of British rule, there has not been a single famine in India.

The average Englishman might look back on the British Empire with nostalgia—some in Britain think the purpose of the empire was to spread English common law, free trade and indoor plumbing around the world. Some still today see the empire as some kind of altruistic project to make the trains run on time. But Hitler rightly observed that the British did not conquer the world because they were affable gentlemen. They did it through ruthlessness, treachery, greed and a willingness to kill millions of human beings. The British Empire was one of the most exploitative and destructive in human history. It spread slavery, famine, war and oppression around the world for more than 200 years. Take a walk through the British Museum in London and it becomes obvious that the purpose of the empire was essentially to loot the planet. While the average Englishman may have positive feelings for this period in his history, he was not a beneficiary of his country's dominance. The empire served a plutocracy that sent the average Englishman, Scotsman, Welshman and Irishman around the world to plunder it. The British soldier and sailor fought in opium wars in China, diamond wars in Africa and oil wars in the Middle East. British soldiers left their bones around the world to enrich plutocrats in London while the average British person lived in grinding poverty. Writers such as Jack London in his *People of the Abyss* and George Orwell in *The Road to Wigan Pier* documented the depressed state of the average British person at a time when the British Empire was the most dominant power on the planet. Many of the worst conflicts in the world today are legacies of the British Empire. And it was that empire that was the main threat to American sovereignty and liberty for most of our history.

By the time Orwell was writing the *The Road to Wigan Pier*, the British Empire was exhausted. Generation after generation of British men had died abroad fighting to expand its reach. The plutocrats knew that Britain was too small to carry the weight of their global project. The transnational elite that controlled the Bank of England and the central banks of Europe had set up a central bank in the United States in 1913, seized control of our money supply and set to work on changing the course of American history.

World War II brought victory to Britain and the United States over the Axis powers. It also brought victory in the United States over the old guard of American leadership that for a century and a half had sought to follow George Washington's advice of avoiding foreign entanglements and the intrigues of Europe. With the end of World War II, America inherited the British Empire. Today, instead of the Royal Navy being the dominant power on the seas, it is the U.S. Navy. Instead of British men dying in the jungles of Southeast Asia, the deserts of the Middle East and the mountains of Central Asia, it is American men and women. The American plutocracy has grown richer than the British plutocracy could ever imagine, while American streets are filled with the homeless just like turn-of-the-century London.

No. It was not the American people who won World War II. Other than a brief period of middle class prosperity in the late 1950s and early 1960s when the American economy was the only game in town, the end of the war only brought more dead Americans in Korea and Vietnam, stagnating wages and unemployment. The war did not bring us peace, but a 40-year Cold War against our communist allies whom we had fought and died for in World War II. The war brought the rise of the military-industrial complex and of the intelligence agencies that today subvert and overthrow governments around the world and that watch our every move at home. The war did not bring lasting prosperity, but wage suppression and the loss of our jobs to free trade and to the largest influx of immigrants in our history. We emerged from the war not more prosperous, more free and at peace, but more taxed with a more overbearing government that has been eager to intervene in conflicts around the world and put the lives of our citizens at risk.

Make no mistake. When you get to the heart of the matter, all the sacrifices and deaths of British and American soldiers were not for the national interests of our countries or for the best interests of the majority of the British and American people, but for the international interests of a transnational elite that had hijacked both the British and American governments.

Quigley tells us in *Tragedy and Hope* that any war performs two contradictory services for the social context in which it occurs. "On the one hand," he wrote, "it changes the minds of men, especially the defeated, about the factual power relationship between the combatants. And on the other hand, it alters the factual situation itself, so that changes which might have occurred over decades are brought about in a few years."

To know who won the war, all one has to do is look at the

changes that the victors implemented at war's end. The victors of World War II immediately set about accomplishing the goals they had long coveted and had failed to achieve at the end of World War I. Unlike after World War I, when the doomed-to-fail League of Nations was established in Geneva, after World War II the victors established the United Nations on American soil to ensure American participation. They set up the Bretton Woods monetary system that established the U.S. dollar as the world's reserve currency backed by the American taxpayer. They implemented the General Agreement on Tariffs and Trade (GATT), which removed American tariffs on imported goods. They set up the World Bank to lend dollars to Third World nations and entrap them in a cycle of debt and poverty while siphoning off their wealth to international banks and multinational corporations. And they set up the International Monetary Fund to regulate international lending and enforce the collection of international debt.

This was what they wanted and what they had been unable to achieve until after the war—nothing less than a world system of financial control in private hands able to dominate the political system of each country and the economy of the world as a whole—controlled in feudalist fashion by the central banks of the world acting in concert, by secret agreements arrived at in frequent meetings and conferences.

The international bankers had learned their lessons from their failures to achieve their goals after World War I. Through the Federal Reserve, they had achieved dominance over the American economy, media and political system. By the end of World War II, their propaganda machine had grown more sophisticated. They were able to silence and ostracize "isolationists," "protectionists," and "nativists." They were able to use their power and influence to change the course of American history and transform our republic into the global enforcer of their empire of debt. They transformed us into a soulless corporate republic that was not of the people, by the people and for the people, but merely a vehicle to serve the ambitions of international bankers.

America emerged from the war a less sovereign nation indebted to international banks and entangled in alliances around the world. America emerged as the military enforcer and underwriter of a new international order that the victors of the war had established.

For the past 70 years, in our schools, in our media, in books and Hollywood movies, the victors of World War II have been propagandizing the world with a particular narrative about World War II. In this narrative, a great evil arose in Germany in the 1930s led by a fanatical racist dictator who wanted to conquer the world for the German master race. Due to the appeasement of the British and the isolationism of the Americans, this evil was allowed to build up its strength until it lashed out in hatred and ignited a world war. As a fascist storm of genocide and death engulfed the world, Americans remained deluded in the belief that they were safe across the ocean. Isolationists were either naïve or undercover Nazis who were thwarting the president's attempts to assist those fighting against the rising tide of evil abroad. On December 7, 1941, the sneak attack on Pearl Harbor shocked Americans into reality and proved once and for all the bloody consequences of isolationism. Shocked into reality, Americans heroically came together to fight and defeat the forces of evil that threatened our freedom and independence. Because of the sacrifices of the American people, good defeated evil. Never again must America fall into the death trap of isolationism that allowed evil to rise unchecked and create so much destruction and death in the world. World War II taught us that we are the good guys and we must always be ready to defend the world for freedom, democracy and the capitalistic system of free trade. World War II was a good war.

But there is an alternate narrative for World War II that is not taught in the schools or broadcast to the world through the megaphone of the media. This alternate version begins with the awful cataclysm of World War I. Americans were following the advice of our Founders to stay out of European wars that were none of our business and would bring no good to us if we were to get entangled in them. However, British intelligence agents were conducting a desperate covert propaganda campaign to bring America into the war on the side of the Entente. As a German victory appeared imminent, international bankers who had lent vast sums of money to the Entente Powers worried that their loans would not be repaid if the Germans won. The bankers began to work with British intelligence and used their influence with the media and the president to bring America into the war on the side of the Entente. The American entry into the war tipped the scales and resulted in the collapse of Germany. The Entente then imposed a vindictive peace on the German people. The bankers also used the end of the war to establish international institutions, such as the League of Nations, that they had long desired. The American people watched the imperialist powers selfishly carve up the world at war's end while shamelessly spouting idealistic nonsense about the noble purposes of the war. In America, a backlash occurred against the internationalism of the Woodrow Wilson administration. Warren Harding was elected president promising a "return to normalcy" after the economic upheavals and so many deaths of Americans abroad during the Wilson years. The gains made by the internationalists under Wilson were then rolled back as tariffs were raised, immigration was restricted and America pulled out of entangling alliances abroad. This resulted in a decade of peace and rising American prosperity. However, the most consequential act of the internationalists during the Wilson years was not addressed: the Federal Reserve Act and the founding of the Federal Reserve System. The Fed's loose lending policies of the 1920s resulted in a massive bubble of speculation that popped suddenly when the Fed tightened the money supply, causing the Great Depression. In the 1930s, the American middle class that had enjoyed prosperity in the 1920s, was wiped out and descended into poverty. America's ruling class fell into bankruptcy. The internationalists used the bankruptcies of the Depression years to buy up America's assets—our great companies and newspapers fell into the hands of a new class of people, a class that owed its rise to privileged access to credit that flowed from Federal Reserve Banks. President Franklin Delano Roosevelt, a hereditary multimillionaire, came to power due to the collapse of the American economy and the overwhelming support of newspapers and the new industry of radio. Roosevelt spoke like a populist, but his ties to Wall Street banks went back to the very beginning. His great-great-grandfather, Isaac Roosevelt, cofounded the Bank of New York with Alexander Hamilton in 1784. The Bank of New York was the first corporation listed on the New York Stock Exchange (NYSE). (In 2007, the Bank of New York merged with Mellon Financial Corporation and became the Bank of New York Mellon, which, as of 2015 is America's fifth largest bank.) Franklin Roosevelt's grandfather on his mother's side was Warren Delano, who made his fortune in the China opium trade. Franklin Roosevelt's time in the private sector had been spent as a Wall Street lawyer working for a firm that defended corporate interests. Under Roosevelt's leadership, Americans suffered as the Great Depression continued to grind on and the nation fell deeper and deeper into debt to Wall Street banks. Meanwhile, Germany and Japan pulled out of the international banking system and aggressively challenged the imperialist nations of Western Europe, resulting in the start of another great war. Americans had learned the lessons of World War I and refused to join World War II. As president, Roosevelt wanted to join the war on the side of the imperialists and communists but knew he would fall out of popularity with the American people if he voiced that desire openly. Roosevelt and British Security Coordination worked covertly to bring America into the war in the face of American antiwar sentiment. They knew that because of public suspicion for how America was hoaxed into World War I that jumping directly into the war against Germany would result in public outrage. They needed a backdoor into the war. A plan was devised to provoke Japan into firing the first shot. When Germany attacked the Soviet Union, Roosevelt and American leftists became desperate to get America into the war fearing a Soviet collapse. The Japanese were backed into a corner through an embargo and given an ultimatum during negotiations which they could not accept without losing face. Pearl Harbor and the Philippines were left undefended as bait for the Japanese navy. The Japanese took the bait with the hope of crippling the U.S. Navy so they could seize the oil of the Dutch East Indies unimpeded. American aircraft carriers were pulled out of Pearl Harbor prior to the attack yet our airplanes were lined up and left undefended and our sailors were not warned as the Japanese planes approached. The attack was bloody and murderous and served to ignite the outrage of the American people as the press fanned the flames of war. After the attack, a plan to attack Germany devised more than a year earlier was implemented. In less than four years, Germany and Japan were destroyed, occupied, and brought back into the international banking system. The victory enriched the fractional reserve bankers due to the massive amount of debt incurred by all the nations of the world. The end of World War II left the bankers at the pinnacle of world power. In the war's aftermath, they had a second chance to set up the international order that they coveted and which the world remains under today.

Prior to World War II, the old American establishment traced its heritage back to the Mayflower and Jamestown and the original Thirteen Colonies. They saw themselves as descendants of colonists from the British Isles who had settled America and had then broken away from the Mother Country to secure their rights to life, liberty and the pursuit of happiness which they had grown accustomed to in the New World. They saw Americans as a common people with a common culture, a common language and a common religion. They believed they had a Manifest Destiny to conquer the continent and populate it from sea to shining sea. They revered the U.S. Constitution and saw it as a protector of our liberties against the tyranny of unchecked power. They were wary of standing armies. They governed under the principle of avoiding foreign entanglements and wars abroad. They valued American sovereignty and independence—both political and economic independence. They were jealous of America's economic independence and protected it from foreign competition through tariffs. Their wealth and influence came through the ownership of property, land, productive enterprise and commerce.

At the close of World War II, the old American establishment had been swept from power. Its members lost control of the newspapers during the Great Depression while radio from the beginning was under the control of a new class of recent arrivals. The old fortunes of the American establishment had mostly been wiped out during the economic collapse of the 1930s. During the war, the press shouted down the old tendency to avoid foreign entanglements, which was now labeled with the epithet of isolationism, and economic independence was now called protectionism. A new establishment had come to power. It did not trace its heritage to the Mayflower and the Thirteen Colonies, but to the waves of immigrants that had come through Ellis Island in the late 1800s. This new ruling class did not see Americans as a common people with a common language, a common culture and a common religion, but as a multicultural nation—a nation of immigrants. This new elite pushed for immigration policies meant to overrun the dominant American majority and thus internationalize the American people through mass immigration from all corners of the Earth. This new establishment did not value independence but instead sought to increase interdependence with foreign governments and foreign economies. It sought to increase international trade through the abolition of tariffs and the signing of international trade agreements. Instead of avoiding foreign entanglements, this new ruling class actively courted them. This new class wanted U.S. military might to be the muscle of a new international world order based on international institutions that existed above the power of nation states. Instead of wariness of standing armies, the new establishment created a vast military-industrial complex and a massive permanent military that today occupies nations around the world. Our new ruling class does not value the checks and balances of the U.S. Constitution as the protector of American liberty, but instead sees the Constitution as an obstacle to be overcome. It sees the Constitution as a "living document" that can be interpreted in ways that are in line with internationalist goals. This new establishment does not care for the Constitution's restrictions on power but instead seeks positive powers for the government—expanded powers that reach deeply into all our lives. This new establishment's wealth and influence flow directly from the financial sector—from Wall Street fractional reserve banks and from control of the Federal Reserve System. This new elite controls the money supply and uses it to control our media, our politics and academia.

World War II is the central event of history for the international bankers. For the rest of the world, the war was an unmitigated disaster that brought untold misery and mass death. But for the bankers, it was a Good War, a Necessary War. It was their greatest victory. They emerged triumphant and in control of the governments, media, educational systems and economies of the world. Unlike after World War I, this time they used the American taxpayer to finance their international institutions. The United States military became their muscle that gave them power and authority on the international stage.

A relentless propaganda campaign has been underway since the war's end to constantly remind us in movies, books, the nightly news and in our schools about our glorious victory over the world's greatest evil. Year after year, decade after decade, Hollywood pumps out movies glorifying this war. Actors, most of whom never spent a day in the military, pretend to be soldiers up on the big screen. They pretend to suffer and sacrifice. They play the hero in unrealistic but heavily financed blockbuster films that attempt to convince the next generation of American youth to sacrifice themselves in more wars overseas against all the Hitlers out there. As a result, most Americans today have a cartoonish understanding of World War II. It was a war of good against evil. We are constantly reminded even 70 years later that our enemies were black leather wearing, racist, genocidal, sadomasochistic Nazis. The Nazis have become history's greatest villains. Today, to call someone a Nazi is to accuse them of being a vile racist with possibly murderous intent. Most people today don't even realize that the word Nazi itself was not used by the Germans but was a propaganda term of the Allies. America's great villains are people that never attacked us. We attacked them and assisted in their destruction at great cost in lives which resulted in Stalin ruling over Eastern Europe with an iron fist and threatening us with nuclear annihilation.

The reality of the war was that it was none of America's business. We should have heeded George Washington's advice and stayed out of it. Germany did not have the ability or the intention of crossing the English Channel, much less the Atlantic Ocean. If Germany had won the war, Hitler would have reestablished the Austro-Hungarian Empire in Central and Eastern Europe and would have spent the second half of the 20th century attempting to put down uprisings against German rule. Instead, it was the communists who ended up putting down the uprisings. In all likelihood, Germany would have been defeated by the Soviet Union without our involvement and France would have freed itself during the German collapse without American or British help. Without British or American intervention, the Soviet Union most likely would have won the war but would have exhausted itself in the process and emerged in a weaker position and unable to threaten us.

All those American boys who were plowed under would have lived out their lives here at home rather than dying young overseas.

If we had negotiated with the Japanese with the intention of avoiding war, Japan would have spent the second half of the 20th century attempting to maintain its control over China. The Chinese, being an ancient people with a proud culture, would never have submitted to Japanese rule and would have eventually organized an effective resistance. If the United States had stayed out of the war, instead of Americans fighting and dying in wars in Korea and Vietnam, it would have been the Japanese dying in those places.

But this is easily said in hindsight. It is easy to look back and say we should have stayed out of the war, or that we should have fought it differently. But we joined the war. All that we can do now is look back at history critically to understand why things happened the way they did. Now is the time to look back at the war honestly and not through the smoke and distorted lens of propaganda. We must clear away the smoke and look back and learn its lessons so that we do not get hoaxed into another such catastrophe again.

World War II has been for far too long the rallying cry that our current ruling class has used to plunge us into new destructive wars abroad that are killing off our youth, bankrupting us as a nation and stripping us of the freedoms the Founders handed down to us.

We joined the war and America emerged from it not a better country, but an empire under the control of a class of people who are attempting to systematically destroy our nation from within to achieve goals that are counter to the interests of the American people.

No, it was not a good war. Any person who refers to World War II in those terms has naively internalized the victor's narrative without a full understanding of the war. Either that or the person is a sociopath.

We were hoaxed into World War II. It is time we as a people accept this fact. We've been hoaxed about that awful war for the past 70 years.

What do the Bankers Want?

To summarize, the fractional reserve bankers became fabulously wealthy in Europe during the 19th century. Their wealth was not derived from work, production, invention, or anything else beneficial to the societies they lived in. Their wealth was derived through usury—a special form of usury called fractional reserve banking that allowed them to collect interest off other people's savings and multiply that amount in loans many times over the amount of money that actually existed in their vaults. This system of fractional reserve banking is based on parasitism on the people who actually work for a living—people who do the productive work of an economy. The fractional reserve system is inherently unstable and results in booms and busts that bring extreme hardship to the people who do the work of a society and an economy. The fractional reserve bankers used this systemic instability to confiscate property and have become an ownership class. They own the media, corporations, apartment buildings and houses, professional sports teams, politicians and nearly everything else.

The bankers used their great wealth to influence governments. They consolidated and centralized their power through the creation of central banks, which gave them control over national currencies and over governments. The first modern central bank was the Bank of England, established in 1694. The bankers used the model of the Bank of England to spread central banks across Europe. Three times they established a central bank in the United States but were thwarted and their banks were shut down. But in 1913, they were successful in creating the Federal Reserve Bank, which has risen to become the most powerful central bank in the world. In the early years of the 20th century, a web of interconnected central banks already stretched over much of the planet.

World War I was a time of extreme profiteering for the

fractional reserve bankers. Central banks printed the money which was supplied to banks which lent the money mainly to the Entente. When Germany was on the brink of winning the war, which would have caused France and England to default on their war loans, the bankers pulled in the United States to tip the balance against Germany.

In 1929, the Fed caused the Great Depression which ended the prosperity of the Roaring Twenties. The next 12 years of unprecedented economic hardship resulted in an overturning of the old order in the United States as the American establishment fell into bankruptcy and lost its assets to a new establishment which bought up American assets for pennies on the dollar with credit that flowed from Wall Street banks and ultimately from the Federal Reserve System. The new establishment bought up American newspapers and invested heavily in radio networks and Hollywood movie production.

The new establishment used its influence in media and the government to bring a reluctant America into another world war—World War II, the most destructive and deadliest war in human history.

World War II was an alliance of international finance capitalism with international communism against nationalistic governments in Germany, Italy and Japan. The international finance capitalists and the international communists emerged from the war victorious and divided the world up among themselves.

At the end of World War II, the international bankers found themselves in a position of unchallenged power over the world's money supply and unprecedented control over the media and academia. The old American establishment was impotent and its values were relentlessly discredited by the controlled media and academia. The war had transformed America from a republic into a global empire that replaced the British Empire as the dominant military and financial power on the globe. America had become what it had rebelled against a century and a half before. The bankers used the end of World War II to reshape the economies and governments of the world in an attempt to achieve their ultimate goal.

What is this ultimate goal?

As stated earlier by Carroll Quigley, "The powers of financial capitalism had (a) far-reaching aim, nothing less than to create a world system of financial control in private hands able to dominate the political system of each country and the economy of the world as a whole. This system was to be controlled in a feudalist fashion by the central banks of the world acting in concert, by secret agreements arrived at in frequent meetings and conferences. The apex of the system was to be the Bank for International Settlements in Basel, Switzerland; a private bank owned and controlled by the world's central banks which were themselves private corporations."

The international bankers dominate governments by their ability to control treasury loans, to manipulate foreign exchanges, to influence the level of economic activity in the country, and to influence cooperative politicians by subsequent economic rewards in the business world.

At the end of World War II when half the world was still a smoking pile of rubble, the bankers began to piece the world back together under the direction of the international institutions they had established at the war's end—the United Nations, the International Monetary Fund and the World Bank. Central to this new international system is the Bank for International Settlements—the central banker's central bank, founded in 1930 to collect reparations imposed on Germany after World War I. The Bank for International Settlements (BIS) was the key institution in the creation of the European Union.

In the years after the war, step by step, treaty by treaty, the creation of the EU was planned and implemented with agreements arrived at in frequent meetings and conferences behind the closed doors of the BIS.

In July of 1944 when the end of Germany was in sight, a new monetary order was established at the Bretton Woods Conference in Bretton Woods, New Hampshire. The lead negotiator for the United States at the conference was Harry Dexter White, who skillfully ushered in a new internationalist era in which the U.S. dollar was made the world's dominant international currency. The Federal Reserve supplied the dollars which were then distributed around the world through loans. The IMF and the International Bank for Reconstruction and Development, which today is part of the World Bank, were designed to oversee the new economic order and usher in an era of international trade with the purpose of ending nationalism around the world and ending the sovereignty of nation states.

Because of Bretton Woods, the American dollar became an international currency used by international banks for cross border purposes. The dollar, backed by the labor and taxes of the American people, which pays for the American military machine, substituted for gold and became a lending and investment tool of international banks, used not for the benefit of the American people but more often to our detriment. The dollar was used to invest overseas in countries and economies that were in direct competition with American workers and businesses.

Harry Dexter White was the principal architect of the international order that has existed since Bretton Woods. On the IMF website, White is described in heroic terms as being a founding father of the IMF and of the World Bank, both of which became pillars of the international financial system.

Interestingly, over the course of his career, Harry Dexter White was several times accused of being a communist and a Soviet agent, most famously by Joseph McCarthy in 1953. In a counterintelligence operation called the Venona project which occurred during the Harry Truman administration, the NSA and the FBI identified White as a double agent supplying national secrets to the Soviet Union, but no action was taken against him. After the fall of the Soviet Union, a KGB archivist revealed that White was in fact a Soviet agent.

White was one of the key players in the victory of the communists over the nationalists in China. White blocked a $200 million loan to China that would have helped to defeat Mao's forces.

How could the founder of an international bank that has been at the service of other international banks, such as Goldman Sachs and JPMorgan Chase which are at the heart of Western capitalism, be accused of being a communist?

The fact is that international communism and international finance capitalism have long been allies in attempting to usher in an age of globalism and the withering away of states to be replaced by international institutions.

In Harry Dexter White, we have the embodiment of the international finance capitalist and the international communist all rolled up into one.

Harry Dexter White, while possessing a WASP-ish name that rings of the American establishment, was the son of an immigrant named Weit, who like the communist leaders Lenin, Stalin and Trotsky, changed his name to appeal to the host population. Harry Dexter White was working not for the American people but for the globalists who saw the peoples of the world not as members of nation states with national interests, but as a global proletariat.

White, an international banker, was an agent of the communists because he shared their ultimate goal, and the institutions he founded were designed to work toward that goal.

Quigley described communist theory as nonsense. Essentially, communism is a utopian philosophy for tyrants and fools. Wherever communist leaders have come to power, the results have been predictable and consistent: oppressive dictatorship and poverty for the people. In the *Communist Manifesto*, published in 1848, Marx and Engels plainly stated the goals of communism:

"The Communists are distinguished from the other working-class parties by this only: (1) In the national struggles of the proletarians of the different countries, they point out and bring to the front the common interests of the entire proletariat, independently of all nationality. (2) In the various stages of development which the struggle of the working class against the bourgeoisie has to pass through, they always and everywhere represent the interests of the movement as a whole."

Essentially, what they were saying was that communism was an international political movement that sought to organize working class people into a force that could overthrow the existing power structure in each country—especially the bourgeoisie, or the middle class.

"The immediate aim of the Communists is the same as that of all the other proletarian parties: formation of the proletariat into a class, overthrow of the bourgeois supremacy, conquest of political power by the proletariat."

And of course, wherever this conquest was successful, the old order of a nation was overthrown, often murdered, and a new clique of leaders took over and established an oppressive dictatorship. In his book *Animal Farm*, George Orwell brilliantly illustrated in allegory how Stalin used ideology and violence to organize the working class and overthrow the bourgeoisie, not to improve the lives of the working class, but to drive away the bourgeoisie and install himself as a dictator with all the privileges of a king.

Marx and Engels succinctly described their ends in their *Manifesto*: "In this sense, the theory of the Communists may be summed up in the single sentence: Abolition of private property."

The communists had very little to say about fractional reserve banking, usury, the charging of interest and the negative effects these practices have on working people. Their goal was seizing the property of the ownership class of each nation—essentially, to monopolize all production and property for themselves. The leaders of the communists sought to inflame the envy and grievances of the working classes and organize them into a political force that could wrest private property from the bourgeoisie and centralize all instruments of production and credit into the hands of the state. If the seizure of property could not be done through despotic means, the *Communist Manifesto* spelled out a political plan to seize property by a series of measures—different measures in different countries but generally applicable in all. Those measures are:

1. Abolition of property in land and application of all rents of land to public purposes. (In the United States this measure is achieved through the property tax.)
2. A heavy progressive or graduated income tax. (This was achieved in 1913 with the ratification of the Sixteenth Amendment.)
3. Abolition of all right of inheritance. (The inheritance tax.)
4. Confiscation of the property of all emigrants and rebels.
5. Centralization of credit in the hands of the state, by means of a national bank with state capital and an exclusive monopoly. (This was implemented in 1913 with the passage of the Federal Reserve Act and the creation of the Federal Reserve System.)
6. Centralization of the means of communication and transport in the hands of the State. (In the United States, several media outlets and telecommunications companies seemingly compete with each other; however, centralization has occurred with consolidation into a few large, heavily capitalized communication companies dependent on credit from Wall Street banks. Recently, telecommunications companies have been cooperating with intelligence agencies to monitor the people with intrusive surveillance technologies. In transport, control of our railroads, airlines and even of many of our freeways has fallen into the hands of heavily financed multinational corporations.)
7. Extension of factories and instruments of production owned by the state; the bringing into cultivation of waste-lands, and the improvement of the soil generally in accordance with a common plan. (Corporatization of production of manufactured goods and food through heavily capitalized multinational corporations replacing privately owned small businesses for nearly all economic production.)
8. Equal liability of all to labour. Establishment of industrial armies, especially for agriculture. (This is being achieved in the United States through mass immigration and free trade

policies designed to flood the United States with pauperized labor and goods produced overseas in poor countries. The goals of immigration and free trade policies are to squeeze the American middle class and submerge the American people in the global proletariat.)

9. Combination of agriculture with manufacturing industries; gradual abolition of the distinction between town and country, by a more equitable distribution of the population over the country. (Zoning for high-density apartments clustered around public transportation hubs. High property taxes force family farmers to sell off farmland to highly capitalized corporate farmers and developers.)

10. Free education for all children in public schools. Abolition of children's factory labour in its present form and combination of education with industrial production. (Federalization of the American educational system and the reduction of local control. According to the *Manifesto*, the family is a bourgeois institution that will vanish with the abolition of private property. Control of education allows the state to replace parental influence on the child with social education by the state.)

The goals of international communism were to abolish countries, nationalities, religion and the family. The international communists wanted to see the state wither away. The ultimate goal was to see the governments of nation states replaced by international institutions that regulate economic production in a world without borders, nationalities and even ethnicities.

Harry Dexter White shared these same goals with the communists. This was why he served as an agent of the Soviet Union. He was an international banker and an international communist who set up international institutions that were designed to serve as international loan sharks for developing countries.

Nearly all the communist leaders were not from the working class but from the bourgeoisie. Many were the children of wealth. Karl Marx's father was a wealthy lawyer who owned several vineyards. Marx never performed any kind of manual labor in his life. He spent the second half of his life supported by wealthy benefactors while living in London, ground zero for international banking.

Marx's philosophy was used successfully to overthrow the ruling classes in less developed nations, such as Russia, China and Cuba. Eastern Europe was brought under communist control due to conquest after World War II with the approval of the Roosevelt and Truman administrations.

At the end of World War II, a new dialectic was created in the minds of world leaders—international capitalism versus international communism.

On February 17, 1950, James Warburg, who had been a financial adviser to Franklin Roosevelt and was the son of the father of the Federal Reserve Bank, addressed the U.S. Senate's Subcommittee on Revision of the United Nations Charter. "We shall have world government, whether or not we like it," Warburg told the subcommittee. "The question is only whether world government will be achieved by consent or by conquest."

Warburg outlined a program to establish a world federation, with the United States playing the lead role in implementing it. Warburg urged the United States to take an active role in creating the mechanisms to enforce international law around the world. He said the United States should play an active role in creating a world federation as a counterweight to the Soviet Union, which was also attempting to bring about a communist world government. Warburg said the United States should pursue a world federation for the interest of world peace.

Warburg's advice was followed and the United States transformed its military into a world police force. Warburg spoke of world peace, but since his speech to the Senate, our active role in international affairs has embroiled us in war after war around the globe. Only four months after he spoke to the Senate, Americans were being killed by the thousands trying to hold back the communists in Korea while leading an international force under the banner of the United Nations. The United Nations brought no world peace, but almost immediately entangled us in a brutal war. Our military members have been giving up their lives around the world not for the defense of the American republic, but for an unspoken utopian ideal of world government. The American military has become the enforcer and muscle that the globalists have been using to keep uncooperative nations in line with the international financial system.

It is ironic that James Warburg used the threat of communism as the reason why the United States should take an active role in establishing a world government. James Warburg's uncle, Max Warburg, helped finance the Bolshevik Revolution in Russia. Max was an influential banker in Germany who served as an adviser to the Kaiser during World War I and sat on the board of Germany's central bank, the Reichsbank, in the early 1930s.

International bankers helped finance the rise of the communists in Russia. They had long sought to bring down the tsar. The German-born American international banker Jacob Schiff financed the militarization of Japan and funded the Japanese in the Russo-Japanese War of 1904-05.

One of the leaders of the Bolsheviks, Leon Trotsky, was a frequent visitor of Schiff's in New York.

The international bankers provided the money that allowed the communists to take over in Russia. So why did James Warburg, whose uncle paid to put the communists in power in Russia, urge the U.S. Senate to counter the communist threat and pursue a world federation opposed to communism?

The threat of war between East and West was the organizing force that the internationalists used to impose international agreements in both the capitalist and communist worlds. The threat of the one against the other allowed both to suppress nationalistic impulses in both their spheres.

Without the Cold War, the United States would have demilitarized after World War II and returned to its traditional foreign policy of neutrality in conflicts outside the Western Hemisphere. The Cold War enabled the centralization and the massive expansion of the federal government, the rise of the intelligence agencies and the growth of the military-industrial complex. The Cold War and the threat of communist expansion was used to shout down isolationists and justify an aggressive American foreign policy of interventionism in the affairs of nearly every nation on Earth.

The capitalist West faced off with the communist East just like Oceania opposed Eurasia and then Eastasia in Orwell's *1984*.

In *1984*, Oceania, Eurasia and Eastasia were in perpetual war over disputed parts of the Earth. Perpetual war served the purposes of the ruling parties in these major powers by creating a state of fear and hatred in the people, which could be focused not on the exploitations of the ruling party, but on the foreign enemy. The state of war unifies the people against the enemy and justifies the overbearing actions of the government. The ruling party uses the state of war to justify declining living standards, government oppression and constant surveillance. For the ruling party, "war is peace."

For 45 years, the Cold War served its purpose for the international bankers. But by the late 1980s, it became evident that communism could not compete economically with the capitalist systems of the West. The communist world was falling further behind in terms of economic development and living standards for the average person.

As Quigley noted in *Tragedy and Hope*, communism, like any authoritarian system, fails to produce innovations, flexibility and freedom. Communism had failed to satisfy the growing popular demand in the East for the rising living standards that were being achieved in the West.

Overnight, communism was abandoned and the Cold War came to an end. The Soviet Union broke up and both Russia and China adopted capitalist economic systems. American dollars flowed into China and financed its incredible economic rise. China abandoned Marxism as an economic theory while retaining an authoritarian government that still clings to communist imagery and party structure.

When the Cold War ended, there was no longer a global

threat that could be used to keep America engaged in pursuing an internationalist agenda and continued military interventionism abroad. By the late 1990s, isolationist sentiment was again rising in the American public with louder and louder calls for a "peace dividend" after the end of the Cold War.

The communist facade had collapsed, but the 10 planks of communism were still being relentlessly implemented around the world. With the United States triumphant and Russia in a state of disorganization and weakness, the internationalists began to aggressively push for neoliberal economic policies in the former Soviet Bloc and in the developing world. Privatization, free trade, open markets, and deregulation were the economic policies the internationalists were pushing from Russia to China to the United States.

The North American Free Trade Agreement (NAFTA), which codified the regulatory and economic merger of the United States with Canada and Mexico came into effect in 1994. The treaty was bitterly opposed in the United States, requiring a united front from establishment Democrats, Republicans and the corporate media to push the treaty through. In 1995, the World Trade Organization was formed to manage and regulate trade around the globe. In 1999, protests against the WTO reached a climax in the Battle of Seattle—an anti-globalization rally of 40,000 people which erupted into violence. In Europe, the European Central Bank was established in 1998 and the Euro was officially adopted as an accounting currency in 1999, entering into widespread circulation in 2002.

With the fall of the Soviet Union, the international bankers began to piece together the world in larger and larger economic blocs. However, all was not well. A populist backlash against globalization and economic liberalization was growing. In the United States, the American demand for a peace dividend and an end to large-scale Cold War military spending and the occupation of nations around the world could not be ignored. To top it all off, at the end of the 1990s, the United States was experiencing an economic boom which resulted in a tax revenue surplus that was being used to pay down the national debt. The end of the Cold War earlier in the decade led to a growing feeling in the nation that interventionism abroad was no longer in the American interest. Government surpluses, rising incomes and low unemployment were resulting in a demand for lower taxes and less government intervention in the lives of Americans at home. In 2001, George W. Bush was elected president on promises to slash taxes and conduct a "humble foreign policy," shifting focus away from Europe and Asia and toward improving relations with Latin America.

After the internationalism of the Clinton years, Bush's indifference toward internationalism was met with scorn and disdain from establishment politicians and the media.

Unfortunately, the calls for a peace dividend were short-lived. The terrorist attacks of September 11, 2001, were the catalyzing event that returned the United States full throttle to aggressive interventionism abroad. The 9/11 attacks caused an immediate shift in the Bush administration's "humble" foreign policy to a belligerent one. The administration immediately became one of the most aggressively interventionist administrations in American history.

Prior to 9/11, the neoconservatives had wanted to use American military dominance to establish a Pax Americana similar to the Pax Britannica that existed at the height of the British Empire. They wanted to use American military leadership to promote economic liberalization, free trade and democratization around the world. Wayward regimes were to be brought into line by American military force—preemptive war if need be.

The neoconservatives wanted to increase military spending. They were concerned over a lack of focus on international strategy and a growing ambivalence toward their interests overseas by the American public. They wanted to increase military research and development on drones, stealth, missiles, surveillance and space warfare technologies to bring about a revolution in warfare and assure American military supremacy over the planet.

However, with the Soviet rival gone, American defense spending was on the decline. No global challenge existed that justified an increase in military spending. Defense spending was being squeezed by increased spending on entitlements, such as Social Security, while more Americans were demanding the peace dividend that would come from a decrease in defense spending due to a lack of any global threat.

The neoconservative think tank, Project for a New American Century, stated the goals and concerns of the neoconservatives in a 2000 document titled *Rebuilding America's Defenses: Strategies, Forces, and Resources For a New Century*. The document stated that the political climate at the time was not amenable to the United States increasing spending on the military and taking a more interventionist and aggressive role abroad. In an infamous sentence in the document, the writers stated: "Further, the process of transformation, even if it brings revolutionary change, is likely to be a long one, absent some catastrophic and catalyzing event—like a new Pearl Harbor."

A year after the document was released, a catastrophic and catalyzing event occurred with the 9/11 attacks. As with the attack on Pearl Harbor, 9/11 immediately shocked the American people out of isolationism.

Following 9/11, the neoconservatives ascended to power and influence in the American government and media. The neoconservatives seized the moment and became the leading proponents in the Bush administration for two overseas wars and aggressive American interventionism around the world.

The neoconservatives had used their influence in the government and media to argue strongly for the invasion of Iraq. Military spending was ramped up and the American intelligence agencies were unleashed and allowed to act nearly without constraint by the Constitution or the rule of law.

The neoconservatives became the drivers of American foreign policy and military affairs, and, just as in World War II, patriotism and the defense of American interests and values were the rallying cries.

The neoconservatives are rooted in the Council on Foreign Relations that was founded by Paul Warburg, the father of the Federal Reserve. The neoconservatives are globalists who reject and seek to discredit the American foreign policy tradition of George Washington.

Ironically, the Republican Party in the 20th century had opposed entry into both World War I and II and was the party of non-interventionism for much of its existence. The Republicans were also strong opponents of international communism. However, unbeknownst to most Republicans today, neo-conservatism began with leftists and former communists who had grown disillusioned with the Democratic Party and so infiltrated the Republican Party, seeking to use the party's reflexive patriotism and support for the military, and redirect the party toward globalist goals—essentially, to continue the work of Woodrow Wilson and Franklin Roosevelt, but under a Republican banner.

The attacks of 9/11 were the new Pearl Harbor that the neoconservatives used to bring about a transformation in American policy that would have been very difficult, if not impossible to achieve otherwise.

In short, the neoconservatives are pursuing the same internationalist goals that communists and international finance capitalists had been pursuing for more than a century. Those goals are to reduce the sovereignty of the nation-state—to bring about the withering of nation states—and replace them with international institutions reigning supreme over national governments in a world without borders.

The neoconservative Paul Wolfowitz was a leading advocate for the Iraq War when he served as Deputy Secretary of Defense in the Bush Administration. He was appointed president of the World Bank when his stint as Deputy Secretary of Defense ended. Remember, international institutions, such as the World Bank, were put in place after World War II with the understanding that they were going to integrate nations and bring a more peaceful world. Yet Wolfowitz was instrumental in plunging us into an unnecessary and destructive war and he was put in charge of the World Bank.

Political and economic theories come and go with the changing times but the goals of the international bankers who fund the creators and promoters of these theories remain the same. The goals are one world government and one world currency controlled by a supranational central bank—a central banker's central bank, which today is the Bank for International Settlements in Basel, Switzerland.

To understand what the bankers and their agents have in mind for the United States, one only need look to Europe, which has moved further down the bankers' timeline than we have. Europe has been ravaged by wars, economic crises and revolutions for more than 200 years. After World War II, the continent lay in ruins and was occupied by two superpowers. After the war, the international elite, in frequent meetings and conferences, began to piece together a new Europe. The new Europe began with treaties that formed innocuous sounding institutions, such as the European Coal and Steel Community (ECSC), formed in 1951. The ECSC formed a common market in Europe for coal and steel, but its signers had larger aims in mind, nothing less than encouraging world peace, making war impossible between its members, revitalizing the European economy and improving the economies of Africa and the world as a whole, as stated by French foreign minister Robert Schuman about the ECSC. The ECSC was a supranational institution that regulated trade between member states.

According to Adam LeBor's book *The Tower of Basel,* the CIA played a role in the creation of the ECSC and was heavily and covertly involved in the movement toward European unification. Bill Donovan, an American intelligence officer and head of the Office of Strategic Services, which was the forerunner to the CIA, was chairman of the American Committee for United Europe (ACUE). The ACUE was formed after World War II to use psychological warfare techniques to push for a united Europe.

American Director of Central Intelligence Allen Dulles and CIA director Walter Bedell were also on the board of the ACUE. The organization used propaganda and money to push for the creation of the ECSC, according to LeBor.

LeBor quotes Wall Street banker, World Bank president, chairman of the Council on Foreign Relations and Warren Commission adviser John McCloy, who stated in a speech in 1950 in London, "The fact is, we cannot solve the German problem without fitting it into the larger context of a United Europe. ... These economic factors lead directly to the political. To insure the freer flow of trade and the development of European markets will require effective political machinery. ... I say no permanent solution of the German problem seems possible without an effective European union."

The goal of American intelligence operatives and international bankers like McCloy was clear: piece together a single European economic market which would eventually lead to the political union of Europe.

"During the 1980s, the BIS hosted the Delors Committee, whose report in 1988 laid out the path to European Monetary Union and the adoption of a single currency," LeBor wrote in *Tower of Basel*.

By secret agreements arrived at in frequent meetings and conferences, in treaty after treaty, supranational institution after supranational institution was created culminating in the creation of the European Central Bank (ECB) in 1998.

In 2002, the ECB began to circulate Euro banknotes in Europe, replacing national currencies that had existed for centuries in some of the richest countries in the world. The ECB was the first supranational central bank that did not regulate the currency of any one country, but instead controlled a single currency used today by 18 European countries.

Today, the Eurozone is the largest and wealthiest economic bloc in the world. The nations in the Eurozone surrendered their economic sovereignty and the right to regulate their own national currencies to the ECB with the promise of increased prosperity and peace. The ECB is a privately owned corporation, like the Federal Reserve, which pays a dividend to its stockholders, which are international banks. The ECB is not under the jurisdiction of any government and is organized to operate independently from government interference.

By surrendering their economic sovereignty to a supranational central bank, relinquishing their national currencies and opening their borders to the free flow of goods and people, the people of Europe were told they were ushering in a new era of rising living standards, peace and stability.

But what has been the result? The unemployment rate in 2014 in Spain, just 12 years after the implementation of the Euro, was 25 percent, as bad as during the Great Depression. On November 15, 2013, the *New York Times* reported that youth unemployment in Spain was 57 percent with Great Depression levels of unemployment across the continent. Across Europe, the unemployment rate remained stubbornly high at 10 percent. Highly educated young people with master's degrees were leaving their countries to work low paid jobs as shelf stockers or in sandwich shops. Europe has a dearth of jobs for young people, the *Times* reported.

With borders opened, lower paid workers from Eastern and Southern Europe flooded into Northern Europe. They left their homes and families to work jobs as plumbers, construction workers and unskilled labor in Germany, France, the Netherlands and Great Britain, putting downward pressure on wages for the working class in the wealthier nations.

A working class English plumber paying a mortgage on a house and raising a family was now in competition with Polish plumbers who lived in groups in apartments and were willing to work for less while sending their money back to their families in Poland where the cost of living was lower.

To top it all off, for the past 60 years Europe has been experiencing a huge wave of mass immigration from Africa, Asia and the Middle East. Once homogenous countries, such as Sweden, the Netherlands and France, now have large ghettos full of unassimilated immigrants. Millions of immigrants and their descendants live in every country in Europe and now travel freely throughout the European Union. Immigrant riots, such as the 2013 riot in Stockholm, Sweden, periodically break out across Europe with immigrant youths burning cars and clashing with police.

The creators of the Euro promised stability, but the era of the Euro kicked off with speculatory bubbles in housing in Spain and Ireland and with spiking levels of government debt. In 2009, less than a decade after the Euro began to circulate, the bubbles popped resulting in massive bank bailouts across the continent and unemployment rates shooting through the roof. The Euro era has not been one of stability but one of constant economic crisis.

The creators of the European Union promised peace. But as the Eurozone expanded eastward it welcomed in countries that have traditionally been in the Russian sphere of influence. Through its history, Russia was often threatened and attacked by the great powers of Europe. Countries on the Russian border that were once part of the Russian Empire and the Soviet Union have been absorbed by the European Union. The European Union and the United States are promising to defend these countries from the military might of Russia. Russia is seeing itself encroached upon and boxed in by Europe and the United States. Rather than ensuring peace, the European Union is now finding itself in conflict with Russia—conflict that could easily erupt into a destructive war.

Under the Euro, wages are being suppressed, unemployment has been high, conflict with Russia looms, and all the while wealthy international bankers have gotten wealthier and more powerful. The European Union has not delivered on the promises that were made to the European people.

So what is the solution to the economic turmoil and the crises that the Euro has wrought? The internationalists are never ones to let a good crisis go to waste. For the international bankers who are the beneficiaries of this system, the solution is clear: a further reduction of sovereignty of the European nations and a political union with more political power and control ceded to the European Parliament, the Council of the European Union and the European Commission. In short, the internationalists want the end of independent nation states in Europe and the creation of a federal European government, which so happened to be the goal of the CIA after World War II.

The formation of the European Union was not done democratically and did not reflect the will of Europeans. It was an elitist project—a carefully designed plan by international bankers enacted step by step over a generation.

Here in the United States, the same agenda and processes are at work, although on a different timeline. By secret agreements arrived at in frequent meetings and conferences, the American economy has been subverted and made interdependent to the global economy. A watershed moment for the globalists was the signing of NAFTA in 1994.

The creators of NAFTA promised that by merging the economies of Mexico, Canada and the United States, the American economy would expand and wages and economic opportunities would increase for American workers. Detractors were ridiculed in the media for saying that jobs would flee south to Mexico where wages were lower.

Since NAFTA was enacted, wages in the United States did not rise, upwards of 50,000 factories in America were shuttered and moved across the border and no new jobs replaced the jobs that were lost. In fact, in 2014 the American labor force participation rate fell to 63 percent, lower than the 67 percent when NAFTA was signed, even as tens of millions more people were added to our country through immigration.

According to a January 25, 2014 article in the *New York Times*, the United States lost nearly six million manufacturing jobs from 2000 to 2009.

In the United States, the total compensation for an autoworker was $45.34 an hour in 2012. However, in Mexico an autoworker earned $7.80 per hour. Is it any wonder that American manufacturing is leaving our borders and fleeing to low wage countries? By paying a Mexican $7.80 an hour versus paying an American $45.34, the shareholders of manufacturing companies are slashing labor costs and pocketing the difference. The cost of a new car has not fallen yet labor costs have fallen dramatically. The end result of NAFTA has been a massive transfer of wealth from workers to passive income earners who own stocks and bonds. By moving production to low-wage nations, the passive-income earning class has widened the wealth gap between itself and the working and middle classes. In 2015, this gap has grown to its most extreme in all American history—worse than at any point during the Gilded Age or the Roaring Twenties. They promised us that NAFTA would make us all wealthier but in fact it impoverished the nation while making a small segment of society fabulously richer.

The average Mexican autoworker earns $7.80 an hour—less than the starting wage for an unskilled teenage fry line cook at McDonald's. Is it any wonder that our manufacturing jobs go to Mexico and their surplus labor floods across our border to compete for jobs that formerly went to unskilled American teenagers?

NAFTA has been a disaster for the average American and a great windfall for a small number of rich people. Those rich people use their money to exert a great deal of influence over our media, our government and our schools. This is why you hear very little criticism of NAFTA in the media or from academics. In fact, as of 2015, by secret agreements arrived at in frequent meetings and conferences, our government has been drawing up plans for a far larger trade deal, called the Trans-Pacific Partnership (TPP), which is a free trade agreement involving 12 nations on the Pacific Rim. This trade agreement, if passed, would put American workers under further wage competition with workers in Malaysia, Peru and Vietnam, and would create independent corporate tribunals that would allow investors to sue governments that are accused of breaching the treaty's rules. The treaty is less about trade since we already run trade deficits with these countries and our borders are wide open to their goods. The

TPP is more about creating the international institutions that will regulate our integrated economies. The TPP creates a new global authority called the Trans-Pacific Partnership Commission that has enforcement powers above the authority of national governments. This commission will have the authority to admit new members, such as China. These international institutions are being designed to be supranational and to override our Constitution and the ability of our elected representatives to enact laws that effect our economy. Instead, our economy will be regulated by a world system of financial control in private hands that will dominate our political system.

The TPP is nothing less than a direct attack on the American wage earner, small business owner and on the sovereignty of our nation. It is a treaty designed to set up a supranational regulatory system above the power of elected governments—a system of international corporate feudalism.

To make matters worse, our U.S. Trade Representative is also secretly negotiating and planning the Trans-Atlantic Trade and Investment Partnership (TTIP) that will put in place international commissions that will regulate and merge the United States economy with the EU. Also being secretly negotiated is the Trade in Services Agreement (TiSA), a 51-nation agreement to regulate and liberalize global trade in services, everything from e-commerce to health care to education and much more.

European nations signed away their sovereignty piece by piece and trade treaty by trade treaty over a 50 year timespan beginning with the European Coal and Steel Community in 1951. Each trade agreement brought the internationalists closer to their goal of eliminating the sovereignty of the nations of Europe.

That same process has been at work in the United States and our once prosperous middle class is being brought down to wage parity with low-wage, developing nations, such as Mexico and Malaysia, while the transnational elite pockets the difference.

Europe is clearly the furthest along in this process. In Europe, national currencies have been eliminated and replaced by the Euro, controlled by the supranational, privately owned ECB.

In America, the goal is the same—to merge the United States, Canada and Mexico in a North American economic union under a single currency controlled by a North American supranational central bank. The globalists do not feel confident to reveal this plan just yet due to the fierce backlash from American patriots that would surely result.

The goal has been to crush the economic well-being of the once prosperous American middle class through wage competition with foreign labor. By eliminating economic security, the elites are seeking to encourage dependency on government to sap the juices out of the once fiercely independent American people.

Further economic decline and financial crises are being used to attempt to convince Americans that more economic integration is necessary and that more sovereignty must be ceded to international institutions. It's for our own good, you see.

Fractional reserve banking made the international bankers fabulously wealthy through parasitism off the proceeds of the work of the people. The bankers used their wealth to create central banks in each nation of the world. This gave them great power over governments and economies. Acting in concert, they have been relentlessly chipping away at the sovereignty of nations year after year, decade after decade with the end goal of eliminating the nations of the world and replacing them with a world government. Nation by nation, piece by piece, the powers of international finance capitalism have been busy.

The prospect for world government might seem agreeable to many people in the world today. The elites are selling a dream of world peace—that by creating a world government conflict between nations will be eliminated and wars and chaos will be replaced with a new international order.

This is a utopian pipe dream. The reality is that our democratic republic will be replaced by a global tyranny controlled in feudalist fashion by unelected elites acting in concert and in secret. The American people will lose what little decision-making ability we have left to a far-off elite that makes decisions for us—much like the British government that our forefathers fought against to establish self-rule. We will lose our Constitution and our Bill of Rights, which today are being rendered subservient to international treaties and international law. World government means the loss of our sovereignty as an independent nation and the loss of our liberties and rights as a free people.

World government will not end wars in the world. Wars will merely be renamed and called rebellions or insurgencies. People will rise and fight for self-determination against tyranny as has always been the tendency of people the world over. World government means world tyranny and perpetual war.

What the international bankers do not realize is that the failure of their plan is inevitable. Too much wealth and power corrupt the human spirit, cause arrogance, and cloud the human mind with delusions of grandeur. Power corrupts and absolute power corrupts absolutely.

The transnational elites are small in number and we are many. They are a collection of usurers and speculators who have grown rich off the work of others. They are not fit to rule. Their power is dependent on lies and propaganda and the relentless suppression of truth. But it is human nature to seek truth, to resist tyranny and rebel against it. Every day the globalists remind us of their weakness by their fear of being found out. They hide in the shadows behind cooperative politicians whom they provide with subsequent economic rewards in the business world. The bankers are fearful of taking the blame for the pain and suffering they are bringing to millions of people around the world so they hang the blame on their lackeys while remaining in the shadows.

The transnational elites rely on lies and propaganda because they are afraid that the people will understand the object of their actions and resist them. We live in a time of great deception, but it is also a time of great revelation. No other time in history has there been this much information available to the average person.

As Americans, we must live up to the values of our nation's founding and resist the enemies of our liberty and sovereignty.

We have been deluded. We have been made confused by the corruption that runs through our media, our education system, our government and the corporate system. We have been lulled into complacency while the plan to end America moves forward year after year, decade after decade. But it is in our nature to resist tyranny. The hour is late but all is not yet lost. We Americans must never forget that the Spirit of 1776 runs in our veins. It is part of who we are.

They have their goal of world government that they see clearly and have been working toward deliberately decade after decade with all their ill-gotten wealth and resources. We the people have no unified goal and are easily led to destruction and oblivion because we are without direction or leadership. But we must remember that as Americans, we share common goals. As a people, we hold these truths to be self-evident, that all men are created equal, that they are endowed by their Creator with certain unalienable Rights, that among these are Life, Liberty and the pursuit of Happiness.

Thomas Edison said that the people have an instinct that is telling them that something is wrong, and that something centers on money. "They have an instinct also, which tells them when a proposal is made in their interests or against them," he said.

Edison estimated that only about 2 percent of the people think. He said the 2 percent are constantly shouted down by the powers that be when it comes to the money question, and he hoped for the day when the thinkers could be shouted down no longer.

"The only dynamite that works in this country is the dynamite of a sound idea," Edison said.

The population of the United States is about 320 million people. Two percent of 320 million is 6.4 million. If Edison is right, that means that there are more than 6 million people in the United States that are awake and thinking. That is a number greater than the size of any army on Earth. We have 6 million people in our country who can appeal to the people with a sound idea that is made in their interest. We have 6 million people who can lead the way to reform of our monetary system. That is a force once awakened that no international banker can suppress.

All we need to do to defeat the bankers is lay the dynamite of a sound idea.

Our Founders declared independence from a tyrannical government that was driven to global empire. The Founders mutually pledged to each other their lives, fortunes and sacred honor to break free from that tyranny. They succeeded and brought into the world the most prosperous, most free and most powerful nation the world has ever known.

But today, a tyranny driven to global empire has infiltrated the government that our Founders created, and corrupted the Republic that the Founders made free.

To stop the American decline into subservience to a transnational elite that seeks to end our sovereignty and independence, the first step is to understand the methods they are using against us.

The international bankers have three primary government policies that are being used in the United States to bring about their goals. These policies are crucial to their goals of ending our independence as a free nation and reducing us to subservience to a world government. These policies have been implemented over time through relentless effort and pervasive propaganda. This propaganda has been so successful that many Americans have been convinced that these policies are part of who we are as a people, even though the implementation of these policies has reversed the course of our history and is reducing us to poverty and dependence and is resulting in the deaths of hundreds of thousands of our citizens in overseas wars that are counter to American interests.

The three policies that are critical to the goals of the international bankers are free trade, mass immigration and American interventionism abroad.

The Tyranny of Free Trade

Income tax. Property tax. Sales tax. Utility tax. Gasoline tax. Capital gains tax. Estate tax. Air transportation tax. Luxury tax. Telephone tax. Gift tax. Dog license tax. Fishing license tax. The list goes on and on and has been growing year after year.

In 1913, the U.S. federal tax code was 400 pages long. By 2013, it had grown to 73,954 pages.

For a nation that was essentially founded because of a tax rebellion, we have become one of the most taxed peoples on Earth.

Taxes have become so onerous that at the time of this writing there has been a surge of individuals giving up American citizenship due to the American tax burden. American companies are leaving our shores for foreign ones to avoid paying taxes here.

The taxman loves to tax us. If you drive a car, he'll tax the street. If you try to sit, he'll tax your seat. If you get too cold, he'll tax the heat. If you take a walk, he'll tax your feet. So sang the Beatles.

But there is one tax that our current leaders actually hate. They recoil from it. If it is brought up in discussion, they will react with defensiveness and insults. They become indignant at the mere mention of it. The tax they hate is one that the Founders explicitly granted the federal government the power to collect to pay the government's debts and provide for the common defense and general welfare of the United States.

Article I, Section 8, Clause 1 of the Constitution states: The Congress shall have power to lay and collect taxes, duties, imposts and excises, to pay the debts and provide for the common defence and general welfare of the United States; but all duties, imposts and excises shall be uniform throughout the United States...

Excises are sales taxes while duties and imposts are tariffs. The Constitution does not list the income tax as one of the taxes the federal government is granted to collect as one of its enumerated powers. But the tariff was named as a tax that was to be used to generate government income.

Following American independence, tariffs were the main source of government revenue. Rancorous and divisive debate in Congress over tariffs raged for much of the first half of the 19th century. The industrializing North was largely pro-tariff while the slave-based plantation economy of the South was largely anti-tariff. With the election of President Abraham Lincoln, pro-tariff forces became dominant and the United States followed a protectionist trade policy for the second half of the 19th century. For half a century, American industry and the wages of American workers were protected from foreign competition behind a high tariff wall.

The stated purposes of the tariff were to promote American industry, protect the American high-wage structure versus the pauperized wage structure of Europe and generate government revenue.

In 1741, Benjamin Franklin wrote an essay called *Observations Concerning the Increase of Mankind, Peopling of Countries, etc.* The essay was about what causes the population of a nation to increase or decrease. Franklin wrote that the availability of land, the production of food and the exportation of manufactured goods increased a nation's population. Nations where all land is occupied, manufactured goods are imported and slavery is common will see their populations decrease. Being conquered by foreigners, losing territory, losing trade, losing the ability to produce food and being subject to bad government diminish a nation's population. Franklin wrote that high taxes were a cause for a nation's population to decline due to the fact that a heavily taxed people will not have the resources available to them to raise families.

Franklin wrote that America, unlike Europe, had an abundance of available land for the common man. This led to Americans being more prosperous and having a higher birth rate than in England and Europe at large. According to Franklin, the ability to own land and earn a living off of it encouraged

Americans to marry and have children while in Europe all the land was already claimed and owned. Laborers worked for landlords for low wages and thus married later and had fewer children. Franklin also noted that nations that export manufactured goods can support more families than nations that import goods. "If the nation be deprived of any branch of trade, and no new employment is found for the people occupy'd in that branch, it will also be soon deprived of so many People," he wrote.

According to Franklin, "Foreign luxuries and needless manufactures imported and used in a nation, do, by the same reasoning, increase the people of the nation that furnishes them, and diminish the people of the nation that uses them. Laws therefore that prevent such importations, and on the contrary promote the exportation of manufactures to be consumed in foreign countries, may be called (with respect to the people that make them) generative laws, as by increasing subsistence they encourage marriage. Such laws likewise strengthen a Country doubly, by increasing its own people and diminishing its neighbours.

"Some European Nations prudently refuse to consume the manufactures of East India. They should likewise forbid them to their colonies; for the gain to the merchant is not to be compar'd with the loss by this means of people to the Nation.

"Home Luxury in the great, increases the nation's manufacturers employ'd by it, who are many, and only tends to diminish the Families that indulge in it, who are few. The greater the common fashionable expence of any rank of people, the more cautious they are of marriage. Therefore luxury should never be suffer'd to become common."

Basically, Franklin was saying in 1741 that exporting manufactured goods allowed the people of a nation to have employment that enabled them to raise families. But by importing goods from Asia, a nation reduced the ability of its people to earn a living and raise families. According to Franklin, industry and frugality should be regarded as religious duties and educated into the minds of American children.

Thirty-six years after Franklin wrote this essay, the American colonies were at war with Mother England. The American colonists won the war and the right to formulate their own tax and trade policies.

After the American victory in the Revolutionary War, Alexander Hamilton, George Washington and many of the Founders concluded that their hard won political independence would not last without economic independence. There was no point in breaking away from the Mother Country if the newly independent United States remained economically dependent on her. At the time, the economies of Europe were more developed than the small, rural, newly independent 13 colonies in the New World. While the new American nation was already an agricultural powerhouse, it had little industry to speak of.

Hamilton observed that Britain had grown into prosperity by protecting its domestic manufacturers from foreign competition. He concluded that American industry would never develop if it had to compete directly with imports from the more advanced manufacturers already established in Europe. His proposal was to protect infant American industries behind tariffs and reward them with bounties, or subsidies, which would allow them to develop and catch up to their European competitors.

In 1791, Hamilton put down on paper his thoughts on economic and trade policy in his *Report on Manufactures.*

He proposed to use tariffs as a means to provide revenue for the government and protect American manufacturers from foreign competition to allow them to grow and develop domestically. Revenue from the tariff would be used to support the growth of industry through subsidies and to pay for "internal improvements," or infrastructure, such as canals, roads and ports that would further facilitate commerce.

His plan was controversial due to the fact that many thought subsidies were a form of corruption and because of disagreement on which parts of the country should receive internal improvements. He also proposed a central bank, which unfortunately was privately owned and designed to profit its owners through usury. Despite the controversy, Congress enacted the tariffs that Hamilton had proposed.

Hamilton's ideas were further developed into a school of economic thought, named the American System by Senator Henry Clay.

The American System had three main tenets:

1. Protect American industries with tariffs and support them with subsidies.
2. Spend on internal improvements, or infrastructure, to encourage commerce.
3. Create a national bank to provide credit to industry.

While the system did promote economic independence and development, it unfortunately resulted in the creation of two privately owned central banks: The First Bank of the United States and the Second Bank of the United States. These powerful institutions were the forerunners of the Fed, and, while they created credit for industry, they also created debt-based money. They were privately owned fractional reserve banks that profited their shareholders through usury. Both banks engendered opposition across the nation with charges of corruption and favoritism toward wealthy investors. Both banks were killed off, but the tariffs remained and the economy developed and grew by leaps and bounds.

The Northern economy was based on industry and small family farms. It favored the tariff. The tariff protected American manufacturers from cheaper foreign imports from the more developed manufacturers of Europe, and it protected laborers from competing with low-wage "pauperized" labor abroad.

The Southern economy was based on slavery and producing cotton, tobacco and other agricultural commodities. There was little industry in the South and fewer family farms. The South favored free trade. Southern slave owners could sell their goods at a higher price to the English market. Southerners also preferred to buy cheaper imports from Europe rather than the goods produced in the North. And competing with low-wage European paupers was not a concern in the South because slaves weren't paid wages.

The tariff was fiercely debated in Congress and was often a central issue in elections, with Northerners supporting the tariff and Southerners demanding free trade. The issue came to a head when the Tariff of 1828, known as the Tariff of Abominations, was enacted.

The Tariff of 1828 raised tariffs on imports to an average of 25 percent. Slave owners were outraged, especially in South Carolina where plantation owners had grown rich exporting the produce of their slave-based labor force to the English market. English imports became more expensive in the United States causing the Northern manufacturing base to grow. The British reduced their imports of American cotton, which hurt the Southern economy. The tariff caused a severe rift between the North and South that presaged the Civil War. South Carolina declared the tariff null and void and unconstitutional leading to the Nullification Crisis. Military preparation was made in South Carolina. Force was authorized by Congress to enforce the tariff. The crisis was resolved by a combination of threats from President Jackson and by reduction of tariffs by Congress.

During the period when the Tariff of Abominations was in effect, the slave-based economy of the South suffered but the American economy as a whole grew, especially in the North where the manufacturing base expanded. The tariff was detrimental to the system of slavery while benefiting free labor and manufacturing.

The divisive issue of slavery in the United States was resolved by our nation's worst war—a national bloodletting that killed off 600,000 Americans and left a large portion of the South in ruins.

With the slave owners defeated, the protectionists became dominant in Congress. The post-Civil War government followed a version of the American System of economics which resulted in the United States becoming one of the most protectionist nations in the world.

Tariffs were high. The government became heavily involved in infrastructure projects, especially the building of railroads.

The post-Civil War economy was marked by enormous gains in agricultural and industrial production. During this period of high tariffs, there was no income tax except for two brief interludes. An income tax was implemented in 1861 to pay for the costs of the Civil War. That tax expired in 1872. Government revenue then relied mainly on tariffs and excise taxes as stipulated in the Constitution. In 1894, the Wilson-Gorman Tariff was passed, which lowered the high tariffs of the day and implemented the first peacetime income tax in United States history. The tax was 2 percent on incomes over $4,000, which equates to incomes of about $88,000 today. However, in 1895 the Supreme Court declared that the income tax was unconstitutional and that tax was struck down.

During the protectionist years, the United States experienced the greatest economic expansion of our history and the American nation and its people became the richest in the world. By the 1880s, American economic production and the standard of living of the average American had eclipsed that of Great Britain, the dominant world power of the time.

New technologies, such as the railroad, steamship and telegraph were causing an economic transformation of the nation. During the second half of the 19th century, tariffs remained high and the American government ran a massive revenue surplus. The government budget surplus actually became a divisive issue of the time. Congress was divided on how to stop the surplus, whether the extra money should be spent by the government or returned to the people.

Wages were rising for American workers, but falling prices and deflation were major issues of the day. Gold was money and fractional reserve bankers were in control of the money supply. However, gold strikes in the 1800s in California, Canada, Australia and South Africa expanded the supply of gold and thus the money supply, somewhat mitigating the deflationary effects of the gold standard.

New technologies were resulting in massive productivity increases, both in agriculture and industry. The economy was producing a surplus of food and an expanding offering of consumer goods, but with fewer workers, causing prices to fall. This, coupled with the gold standard of the day, resulted in deflation that was occurring across the economy, making it difficult for farmers to pay off loans as prices for their crops fell and the value of the dollar climbed.

A growing economy and a growing population coupled with a gold standard monetary system meant that prices were falling due to the scarcity of money.

In our present era of inflation, stagnant wages, high taxes, deficits and massive government debt, it may seem incredible to imagine that there was once a time in American history when a massive government surplus was looked at as a problem and falling food prices were something people worried about. It might seem incredible to many to imagine a time when there was no IRS, no income tax and no central bank reigning supreme over monetary policy while the economy was growing like gangbusters.

During the protectionist era, one tenet of Hamilton's national economic plan was not revived—the creation of a national bank. President Andrew Jackson had killed the Second Bank of the United States in 1836, and no new central bank was created to replace it.

Money in the American economy was a creation of fractional reserve banks. Banks would lend out notes into the economy which were redeemable for specie. The paper was redeemable for gold and silver, but, of course, under the fractional reserve system more paper was lent out than the gold or silver in the vaults.

When the Civil War broke out, the banks suspended gold payments for their notes. The United States government followed suit and suspended gold payments for its bonds. The government needed money to pay the costs of the war but President Lincoln did not want to raise taxes or borrow excessively from the banks or from foreign governments. In 1862, Congress passed the Legal Tender Act, which authorized the issuance of United States Notes, which were colored green on the back and were not backed by gold or silver. The government used these greenbacks to pay Union soldiers and the costs of the war.

The Confederacy issued the greyback, which also was not backed by hard assets.

Like the Continental issued during the Revolutionary War, the greenback and the greyback fell in value as currencies. The price of gold surged in relation to both currencies as did the price of goods.

In the North, the purchasing power of the greenback fluctuated with every battle won and lost. The currency fell in value with every battle lost and rose when a battle was won.

For the South, the greyback remained a stable medium of exchange until it became clear that the South was going to lose the war. By 1864, the currency was worthless.

In the North, the printing of money to pay war expenses was considered by many an emergency wartime measure. The push to return to a currency backed by hard assets began before the war had ended.

The National Banking Acts of 1863 and 1864 established a system of national banks and encouraged the development of a national currency backed by bank holdings of U.S. Treasury securities.

While the greenback was backed by nothing, bank notes were backed by government debt and ultimately the ability to collect taxes to pay the principal and interest on that debt.

With the end of the war, the value of the greenback began to climb and stabilized in value when its issuance was set at a stable level. Because of the success of the greenback as a medium of exchange, it remained in circulation alongside silver and gold notes.

In 1873, the Coinage Act put the United States on a de facto gold standard. In the decades leading up to the 20th century, gold, silver and the greenback remained in circulation together while the monetary debate over gold, silver and the greenback raged. The American economy and population were growing but the gold supply was relatively fixed. This exacerbated deflation and caused falling prices, which increased the value of gold and increased the purchasing power of holders of gold but hurt farmers and manufacturers. Borrowing became more expensive.

Farmers and workers, who were often debtors, wanted silver, which was more plentiful, and the greenback to be used as money. They wanted inflation to halt the deflation in prices for agricultural goods, which would allow them to pay back their loans with a cheaper, more plentiful currency. Hard money proponents—often the rich and creditors—wanted a "sound" currency backed by gold.

Throughout the 19th century, severe booms and busts wracked the economy. Whether silver, gold or the greenback were being used as money, the inflation, deflation and confiscation game was being played by the fractional reserve bankers then as it is today. The busts followed by severe depressions happened regularly nearly every 20 years, in 1819, 1837, 1857, 1873 and 1893.

But American industry and technological development were growing at a breakneck pace and immigrants from around the world in their multitudes were drawn to our shores attracted by the opportunity and liberty that our nation offered. During this time of economic growth, the economy was protected behind a tariff wall that enabled American businesses to develop and thrive while bringing in enough revenue to the federal government to create a budget surplus. But during this period, just as today, Americans experienced spectacular speculatory bubbles in land and stocks followed by the inevitable and sudden busts that resulted in the bankruptcy of overextended investors and the contraction of the money supply, followed by business slowdowns and mass unemployment.

The booms and busts led to calls for monetary reform. Silver versus gold versus greenbacks.

Gold won. In the second half of the 19th century, the

nations of Europe, encouraged by the international bankers, began to adopt the gold standard and the United States followed suit.

On the gold standard, the booms and busts continued in the U.S. and in nations everywhere, for it was not gold, silver or greenbacks that could stop the cycle. The cycle of boom and bust—inflation, deflation and confiscation—was caused by fractional reserve banking. Fractional reserve banks always lend out more money than they can redeem until the debt pyramid they construct atop the economy becomes too massive to support and comes crashing down.

In the 1800s, the debate over monetary reform was intense, but the debate over the tariff had been resolved by the Civil War. The tariff won. The tariff protected American industry and wages from foreign competition. The tariff allowed American businesses to expand and become some of the greatest enterprises in the world. The wage structure in the United States differed from that in Europe with American wages being higher. Pro-tariff advocates during the 19th century liked to point out that the tariff protected the American worker from being "pauperized" like the wage earners of Europe.

In the United States, a version of the American System first explained by Alexander Hamilton had become dominant and the U.S. government pursued policies of protection to encourage industrial development and trade surpluses.

But in Britain, a different economic philosophy had taken hold. The free trade doctrine of Adam Smith, David Ricardo and Frederic Bastiat was directly opposed to tariffs, protectionism and mercantilism.

Smith told us of the "Invisible Hand," a godlike or supernatural force, seemingly worshiped by free trade economists, that if allowed to operate without interference would guide the economy to maximum prosperity.

Ricardo wrote of the theory of comparative advantage which posited that if two nations specialized in producing what they were best at, more goods would be made available at higher quality and lower prices increasing the prosperity of both nations. England would make shoes and Portugal would make wine and all of us would have the best wine and best shoes at the lowest prices making everyone better off.

Bastiat effectively attacked protectionism with parables, such as the *Candlemakers' Petition*. To increase the production of candles, Bastiat asked, why shouldn't the government outlaw sunshine? If the government blocked out the sun, the demand for candles would increase causing the production of more candles, which would enrich the candlemakers and provide more jobs for candle workers.

The free trade writers elegantly described how ending tariffs and implementing free trade would increase the wealth of all nations and the prosperity of all people and usher in a new utopian era of world peace. According to the free traders, nations that trade together do not go to war against each other.

By the second half of the 19th century, Great Britain was aggressively promoting free trade doctrine around the world.

The Industrial Revolution was sparked in the 1780s in England at a time when Britain was protectionist. New technology was developed at a startlingly fast rate and new manufactured goods poured out of Britain's factories. The country leaped out in front of the rest of the world in technological and economic development. Great Britain suddenly became the world's workshop. Shoes, textiles, ships, trains, guns and all types of machinery and consumer goods were being produced in Britain in amounts no other nation could rival.

At the start of the Industrial Revolution, Britain had high tariffs that protected its industries from foreign competition, especially its growing textile industry, which was protected by a high tariff wall from competition from superior Indian textiles. By the 1820s when Britain was far and away the most dominant economy in the world, it began to adopt free trade policies. Its industries were so productive and technologically advanced that they had little competition from the rest of the world. In 1846, the British Parliament repealed the Corn Laws. Cheap imported grain from the United States and Russia then poured into the country. British farmers and farm laborers couldn't compete and abandoned the countryside for the cities, providing British factories with a large and cheap labor force. By the 1850s, Britain had dropped most of its tariffs on imported goods and followed a free trade economic policy based on the writings of Smith and Ricardo. British economists and journalists relentlessly propagandized their countrymen that free trade would bring prosperity and peace to the world.

The United States since the time of President Washington had followed a protectionist trade policy that allowed infant American industry to develop behind tariffs. The Founders had sacrificed greatly to establish political independence from Great Britain. Their experience during the years that preceded the Revolution taught them that there could be no political independence without economic independence. Tariffs allowed America to develop domestic industry and economic independence from the more advanced European industries that sought to outcompete American ones and capture the American market.

Hamilton's industrial policy of protectionism influenced America's trade policies for 100 years, becoming dominant under President Lincoln. In Germany, a similar economic policy was in effect. The Germans were influenced by the economist Friedrich List.

List had immigrated to the United States from Germany in the 1820s where he became a successful farmer and editor of a German-language newspaper. He became friends with influential Americans of the day, including Henry Clay—proponent of the American System based on Hamilton's ideas. List began writing about the National System of economics, which was directly opposed to the free trade doctrine that was beginning to seduce economists in America and elsewhere. List called free trade a doctrine of cosmopolitanism—essentially, globalism. List moved back to Germany and published a book called *The National System of Political Economy*, which argued that if a nation is to develop it must protect its infant industries to allow them to grow. List said when a nation, such as Britain, develops its economy to such an extent that it can outcompete others, it will begin to promote free trade cosmopolitanism with utopian idealism to the protectionist nations in an attempt to get them to open their markets. List urged Germany not to follow the theories of Adam Smith, but instead follow the actual practices that had made England rich. England had grown rich during its protectionist period and had only followed a free trade policy after it had become the world's most dominant and productive economy. List's writings influenced the course of Germany's development in the 19th and 20th centuries.

But all the while the free traders were demanding that America, Germany and all other nations open their home market to imports, promising that this would bring prosperity to all. In America, slave owners, pro-British agents and free-trade utopian believers kept up a constant fight against the tariff.

But unlike today, the media, academia, politicians and policy makers were not united in the belief that free trade was good for the country.

Protectionists, such as Henry Charles Carey, pointed out the fallacies of free trade dogma that were plain as day to them at the time.

While Britain was following a free trade policy, it had become one of the most warlike nations in human history. Free trade did not bring peace to the British. Instead, the bones of British men littered the planet as Britain engaged in wars fighting for diamond and gold mines in Africa, for the right to sell opium in China and for oil in the Middle East. Meanwhile, the United States and Germany, which were following protectionist trade policies, had by the 1880s surpassed Britain in the size of their economies and in the living standards of their peoples.

As the 19th century was drawing to a close, Britain was at the height of its military might. But it had amassed a massive government debt owed mainly to American bankers. It was running large trade deficits. The shelves of British shops began to fill with goods that were no longer made in Britain but in the USA and Germany. In Britain, the gap between the rich and the poor had become a gaping chasm. The streets of London were filled with the homeless, as vividly chronicled by Charles Dickens, Jack London, and later by George Orwell, whose book *The Road to Wigan Pier* described the bleak lives of the English working class. Life was not good for the common man in the world's richest and most powerful empire.

At the start of the 20th century, free-trade Britain was the dominant military power in the world. Its navy kept the sea lanes open. Its soldiers were stationed around the world in an empire on which the sun never set. Yet its streets at home were filled with the poor while a small plutocracy grew ever richer and more influential in government. Britain was constantly engaged in faraway wars and its government was being buried under an enormous load of foreign debt.

Henry Charles Carey was an American economist in the 19th century who was a proponent of the American System and a harsh critic of the British (or English) System of free trade and imperialism.

Carey wrote a book in 1851 called *The Harmony of Interests: Agricultural, Manufacturing, and Commercial*, which compared the two systems.

Carey wrote that the American System raises the value of labor and increases wages while the British System tries to sink workers to the level of poverty found in India—a British colony at the time known for extreme poverty and periodic famines. Carey wrote that the British System increases the number of people engaged in trade and transportation while the American System increases the number of people engaged in work and production. Under the British System more people are trying to make money off the backs of workers while under the American System more people are engaged in actual production causing more goods to be produced and making everyone wealthier.

Carey compared the two systems: "One looks to pauperism, ignorance, depopulation, and barbarism; the other in increasing wealth, comfort, intelligence, combination of action, and civilization.

"One looks towards universal war; the other towards universal peace.

"One is the English system; the other we may be proud to call the American system, for it is the only one ever devised the tendency of which was that of elevating while equalizing the condition of man throughout the world.

"Such is the true mission of the people of these United States.... To raise the value of labour throughout the world, we need only to raise the value of our own.... To improve the political condition of man throughout the world, it is that we ourselves should remain at peace, avoid taxation for maintenance of fleets and armies, and become rich and prosperous. ... To diffuse intelligence and to promote the cause of morality throughout the world, we are required only to pursue the course that shall diffuse education throughout our own land, and shall enable every man more readily to acquire property, and with it respect for the rights of property."

Carey stated that free trade was the cause of the Civil War. The South had not industrialized because it traded cotton and other commodities produced by slave labor in exchange for British manufactured goods. Carey was a proponent of protectionism and he advocated for a continuation of the issuance of the debt-free greenback. Carey saw the greenback as a means to break free from British capitalists who used gold to control the wealth of the world.

Britain had jumped out in front of the world both economically and militarily under a system of protectionism. Once it had become dominant, it sought to kick the ladder away that it had used to climb up to wealth. Its leaders began propagandizing and coercing other nations to join them in free trade by using the elegant and easy-to-understand theories of Smith and Ricardo.

Ricardo stated that if Portugal was better at making wine and England was better at making cloth, then if both nations followed a policy of free trade, Portugal would stop making cloth and concentrate on making wine, and England would stop making wine and concentrate on cloth, and both nations would be better off. As a matter of fact, under this argument, Portugal did adopt a policy of free trade and opened its borders to British goods.

In her book *Aspects of Development and Underdevelopment,* Joan Robinson wrote, "In reality, the imposition of free trade on Portugal killed off a promising textile industry and left her with a slow-growing export market for wine, while for England, exports of cotton cloth led to accumulation, mechanisation and the whole spiraling growth of the industrial revolution."

So Ricardo's theory of comparative advantage, while elegant and convincing, when practiced did not work in reality. What happens in reality is that when one nation has an advantage over another—due to a higher level of economic development, better technology, cheaper labor or a number of other things—and both follow free trade policies, the advantaged nation will be enriched while the other will be impoverished and made dependent on the first. The advantaged nation will run trade surpluses with its trade partner and accumulate capital, which can then be used by its investor class as it sees fit. Under a gold standard, the disadvantaged nation that is running a trade deficit will quickly run out of money and fall into depression. It will borrow money from the nations running trade surpluses and be reduced to dependency on foreigners for the right to have any money at all.

Robinson noted that free trade benefits protectionist nations that refuse to follow free trade policy. Robinson wrote, "Free trade for *other* countries is obviously an advantage for an exporting nation. Ricardo's doctrine was very convenient for England at that time, but soon Germany, the United States and Japan began to develop industries (at first behind tariff walls) which demonstrated that static comparative advantage is a very poor guide to the possibilities of industrial development."

The United States, Germany and Japan kept tariffs high on imported goods while taking advantage of Britain's free trade policy. This resulted in the shelves of British shops filling with imported goods from the USA and Germany. By the 1880s, Britain's economic dominance had faded as the protectionist nations surpassed it in economic development, national wealth and the living standards of their peoples.

By the 1940s, Germany was bombing London, Japanese aircraft carriers were sinking British battleships and the British were begging the United States for money, equipment and men to save their empire from destruction.

While Smith, Ricardo and Bastiat claimed free trade would bring prosperity and peace, in reality it brings prosperity to international financiers who wish to deploy their capital where labor costs are lowest and returns are highest. The financiers sought to produce goods where costs were lowest and then import those goods wherever they could get the best price. In Britain, this led to the enrichment of a small plutocracy while crushing the working class.

Karl Marx supported free trade because of its negative effects on the working and middle classes.

In an 1848 speech about free trade, Marx stated: "Cheap food, high wages, for this alone the English Free Traders have spent millions, and their enthusiasm has already infected their Continental brethren. And, generally speaking, all those who advocate Free Trade do so in the interests of the working class."

But he saw clearly who the beneficiaries of free trade actually were. "To sum up," he said, "what is Free Trade under the present conditions of society? Freedom of Capital."

Free trade in actuality was freedom for international financiers to deploy their capital to places where wages are lowest. "It is really difficult to understand the presumption of the Free Traders who imagine that the more advantageous application of capital will abolish the antagonism between industrial capitalists and wage workers," Marx said. "On the contrary. The only result will be that the antagonism of these two classes will stand out more clearly."

While Marx noted the fallacies of free trade in his speech, he came out in favor of it. He stated that the protectionist system results in the development of manufacturing in a nation's economy which causes the expansion of the bourgeoisie, or middle class.

"But, generally speaking," Marx concluded, "the Protective system in these days is conservative, while the Free Trade system works destructively. It breaks up old nationalities and carries antagonism of proletariat and bourgeoisie to the uttermost point. In a word, the Free Trade system hastens the Social Revolution. In this revolutionary sense alone, gentlemen, I am in favor of Free Trade."

Basically, Marx supported free trade because he saw it as causing the breakup of nations. It turned the working class against the middle class, which he saw as beneficial to inciting a global communist revolution and to bring about the so-called dictatorship of the proletariat. It was destructive to the nation state so he was in favor of it.

Essentially, free trade was the favored economic policy of imperialists, slave owners, international financiers and those who wanted to see the end of nations and the creation of a world government.

The British situation at the turn of the 19th century looked remarkably like the American position today. Like Britain back then, the United States today is the premiere free trade nation on Earth and the dominant military power in the world. Our military spending outpaces the 10 next-largest militaries in the world. Our navy keeps the sea lanes open. The bones of Americans litter the jungles and deserts of faraway countries as we fight wars for so-called democracy and freedom. Instead of the trade surpluses and budget surpluses that we had at the turn of the 19th century, today we have massive trade and budget deficits, just as Britain did at the height of its empire. Our country carries a heavy debt load owed to China, Japan and other foreign nations. American stores are filled with goods produced by the protectionist economies of China, Japan and Korea. Our rich have become fabulously richer while our middle class shrinks and our streets are filled with panhandlers and the homeless.

If one looks at the free trade policies followed by the British Empire and the wars its military were involved in at the turn of the 19th century, and then looks at the American position today, the parallels become obvious—wars in Afghanistan and Iraq, an economic obsession with India and China, rivalry with Russia in Central Asia and ceaseless meddling in the affairs of every nation on the planet.

It's almost as if the imperialist decision makers in Britain in 1900 were transported through time to present-day Washington, D.C.

In a way, they were. By 1900, Britain was an exhausted nation. Its empire stretched around the globe, yet it was a small country carrying a heavy debt load. The USA and Germany were larger and had grown richer. The imperialists saw in America the manpower and resources they needed to continue the British Empire under an American flag. In Germany, they saw a rising threat to their hegemony.

In 1902, the Rhodes Scholarship was founded, funded by the estate of Cecil Rhodes who died that same year. With the death of Rhodes, his scholarships were administered by Nathan Rothschild of the international banking Rothschild family.

During his life, Cecil Rhodes was the British Empire's premiere imperialist and colonialist. He was a founder of the De Beers Mining Company, which was financed by N M Rothschild & Sons Limited. Rhodes grew wealthy from African diamonds and oil. He translated his wealth into political power and concentrated his efforts on the expansion of both the British Empire and his business interests in Africa.

Rhodes was driven by a belief that Britain should rule the world. The purpose of the Rhodes Scholarship was to select the best and brightest young students from America and other countries and bring them to England to study at the University of Oxford where they could be indoctrinated into supporting the goals of a global empire. Rhodes wanted to create an American elite that would bring the United States back under the direction of the British Empire. Bright and ambitious American students were brought to England under full scholarship and then returned home to advocate for free trade, mass immigration, the creation of a central bank, the establishment of a federal income tax and interventionism abroad in support of British interests. In short, they came home as ardent advocates for the British System and outspoken enemies of the American System.

In a nutshell, the Rhodes Scholarship was founded to create a bright and ambitious transnational elite that served the interests of international finance based out of the City of London.

In 1913, the Federal Reserve System and the progressive income tax were put into place. The Fed was set to supplant the Bank of England as the world's pre-eminent issuer of currency. With America's entry into World War I, the military alliance with Britain was formalized with the blood sacrifice of 115,000 American lives.

The election of Warren Harding to the presidency was a setback for the globalists, but Paul Warburg acted to create the Council on Foreign Relations, which went to work selecting and training a class of elites tasked to make the British System dominant in America.

The boom years of the Roaring Twenties ended with the Great Depression, which the propagandists for the British System blamed on the Smoot-Hawley Tariff. Globalist propaganda has been so effective that even today many Americans believe Smoot-Hawley played a role in bringing about the Depression, despite the fact that the tariff was enacted after the Crash of 1929, international trade was a minor percentage of the American economy at the time, tariffs were already in effect in the 1920s and we had high tariffs during times of economic growth in the past.

Smoot-Hawley was enacted after the Depression had already begun and was effectively repealed in 1934, yet the Depression continued on for seven more years. To blame the Great Depression on a tariff that went into effect after the Depression began and which was repealed seven years before the Depression ended is ridiculous and defies all logic and common sense. The tariff was in effect from 1930 to 1934, but the Depression lasted from 1929 to 1941. Obviously, the tariff was not the cause of the Depression.

The cause for the Depression lies squarely on the shoulders of the Federal Reserve, which caused a speculatory bubble in real estate and stocks with its easy money policy in the late 1920s, then rapidly raised rates in 1928 and then followed a tight money supply policy, which popped the stock market bubble and brought on the Depression.

The Depression was a period of massive confiscation of American assets by the transnational elite. By the end of the 1930s, this new elite was in place and in control of American corporations and the media.

The attack on Pearl Harbor then thrust America into another world war and another blood sacrifice of 400,000 American lives.

At the war's end, the American System had been defeated and the British System was firmly in place in the United States. Any calls for non-interventionism were met with shouts of, "Isolationism!" Any calls for tariffs to protect American industries and jobs from foreign competition were met with shouts of, "Smoot-Hawley!"

The globalists had taken over the United States government and media and ushered in an era of intense, British Empire-style free trade policy and violent interventionism abroad. Five years after the end of World War II, another generation of Americans was plowed under by the tens of thousands in Korea. A decade later, the next generation was plowed under by the tens of thousands in Vietnam. The 21st century began with wars in the Middle East that lasted more than a decade with thousands more Americans plowed under abroad. These wars are still ongoing.

Looking back to the period immediately following World War II, the world's leading industrial nations—Britain, Germany and Japan—were smoking ruins. But America emerged from the war relatively unscathed, our economy dominant in the world. Our leaders threw open the doors to the American economy to our former enemies and put a free trade policy into effect. Our economy was thrown wide open and left unprotected from lower cost, subsidized foreign goods produced with lower wage labor. Japanese and German goods began to flow in.

The Japanese know history. The Japanese government put into effect an export-oriented economic development policy that protected their home economy from foreign competition while aggressively seeking to expand exports, especially into the now-unprotected American economy. They did not follow the teachings of Adam Smith and David Ricardo, but those of Alexander Hamilton and Friedrich List. The Japanese government heavily subsidized its home industries and corporations, such as Toyota, while protecting the home market with tariffs, non-tariff barriers and currency manipulation.

The Japanese were following a version of Hamilton's American System and List's National System. The effects for Japan were similar to what had occurred in the 19th century when the protectionist economies of the United States and Germany experienced rapid industrialization and expanding exports into the free trade economy of Great Britain, which was borrowing heavily to finance imperialist wars abroad.

By the 1960s, the Japanese were running trade surpluses with the United States. By the 1980s, Japanese imports to the United States had become a flood and Americans were being laid off by the thousands as Japanese companies overran American industry after American industry. The Japanese government was subsidizing Japanese corporations, allowing them to sell at a loss in the American market to gain market share as American companies were pushed into bankruptcy. Industries that were founded in the United States, such as the television manufacturing industry, disappeared from our shores. Steel, shipbuilding, automobiles, electronics, textiles and nearly every other important industry were under attack in the United States by Japanese producers.

By the 1980s, Japan had become the second richest nation in the world and had a large and prosperous middle class—all while following a fiercely protectionist trade policy.

By the late 1980s, the Taiwanese and South Koreans had gotten into the act and were copying the Japanese success. South Korea and Taiwan followed the Japanese economic development model of protecting and subsidizing home industries while aggressively exporting to the United States. In the late 1990s, the Chinese began to play the game on a far larger scale—protect the home market, subsidize industries targeted for development and aggressively promote exports into the American economy.

American elites call this free trade, but it is nothing of the sort. Japan, Korea, Taiwan and China do not follow free trade policies. They are protectionist nations that are following nationalist economic development policies in an effort to run trade surpluses with foreign nations to maximize employment and income in their own countries at the expense of their foreign trade "partners." The Asian countries use a system of tariffs, non-tariff trade barriers and currency manipulation to protect their own home markets from imports while aggressively exporting to open economies.

If you visit Japan, you will see few American cars on the roads. In fact, there are few Korean cars on the roads either, despite the fact that Korea is only a short boat ride away. The overwhelming majority of the cars on the road are made in Japan. If you visit Korea, you will see few American and no Japanese cars on the roadways. The Korean market, like the Japanese market, is protected for domestic manufacturers.

These nations do not compete against one another in their home markets. They reserve their home markets for domestic manufacturers and businesses. But they vigorously compete against one another in the American market. The goal is to drive out American producers and foreign competition through price competition using government subsidies and currency manipulation to capture a segment of the American market. Once the market is captured, then they can raise prices.

The Japanese and the Koreans are justly proud of their automobile industries, which have brought them great wealth and high-wage employment for their peoples. In the United States, you are as likely to see Japanese, Korean or German cars on the roads as you are American cars. Each foreign car represents jobs and prosperity for the Japanese, Koreans and Germans, and the loss of prosperity for American workers. The state of the once-great city of Detroit is evidence of this. Each foreign car sold in the United States represents the loss of jobs in the United States and the loss of capital, which is sent abroad and then used to purchase American Treasury bonds which are paid back to foreigners by taxing the wages of the American people. The Chinese are building up their own automobile industry and due to the size of their economy, the industriousness of their people and the rapidly increasing ability of their engineers, China will most likely surpass Japan, Korea and Germany in automobile output in our lifetimes.

The free traders argue that foreign automobiles provide the American consumer with cheaper cars. Because we can purchase cheaper cars, we save money and are thus wealthier. However, we are awash with foreign cars and these cars are as expensive as ever. Young Americans today are less likely to own their own car than their parents or grandparents were back when American cars were the only game in town. Our trade policy has brought us blight and unemployment with the loss of automotive jobs without the cheap prices we were promised. The Koreans and Japanese are just as likely to own cars as Americans are, and they drive cars made by their own countrymen, and they get the high-paid middle class automotive jobs that have fled our shores.

The free traders tell us that if foreign nations protect their home markets, subsidize their companies and dump products on us below cost to drive American producers bankrupt—that this is good for us. The foreign nations are providing us with cheap goods, which benefit the American consumer. Does anyone actually believe this anymore? We get temporarily cheap goods but lose our middle class. And how is it that the homes of the Japanese and Koreans are filled with high-quality domestically made consumer goods while their nations are protectionist?

These nations experienced explosive economic growth under protectionist trade policies. In just a few decades of practicing a protectionist export-oriented trade policy, China has surpassed Japan in gross domestic product to become the second largest economy on Earth and is on pace to surpass the United States. China grew from a GDP smaller than Mexico into the second largest GDP in the world in just a few decades by rejecting Adam Smith's free trade dogma and practicing the same kind of protectionist policies advocated by Friedrich List and Alexander Hamilton.

Anyone who thinks about trade policy objectively will soon realize that free trade does not serve the interests of a nation. Instead, it serves the interests of international bankers who seek to maximize returns on their money by cutting labor costs. Why pay an American worker $45 an hour when you can pay a Mexican worker $7? That's $38 dollars an hour that goes from the pockets of the American worker into the pockets of the banker. These same international financiers are desirous of breaking down nation-states and replacing them with international institutions. Free trade is a win-win for them in more ways than one. It impoverishes the once mighty American middle class, enriches the transnational elite and breaks down the sovereignty of nations by making them subservient to international institutions. Free trade benefits financiers and middlemen while hurting domestic industries and labor. The beneficiaries of free trade convince Americans to go along with this nonsense by holding out the short-term carrot of cheap imported goods. Meanwhile, they plot to lay off American workers and shift production overseas where labor costs are cheaper.

These international bankers have succeeded in getting Americans and Europeans to accept policies that are impoverishing us and causing us to lose our sovereignty. But the Asians are not so blinded. The Asian countries have not been flooded with mass immigration that has diluted and divided their peoples under a barrage of corporate multicultural propaganda. The Asian nations have strong ethnic identities that allow them to clearly identify their national interests.

China, in particular, is emerging from a 200-year national humiliation inflicted on it by nations a fraction its size. China was a world power for nearly 2,000 years before it was carved up and exploited by imperial powers. China's leaders and people are determined to correct the historical anomaly of their recent history by reclaiming China's position as the most powerful and influential nation in Asia. They know to do this they must build up their industries and economy, which will lead to military dominance of their region.

The Asian nations are acting in their national self-interest. By building up production in their home countries, they are building national wealth and increasing the standard of living of their peoples.

However, they are acting in a world economic system that was created in 1945 and since then has been dominated by Western globalist elites. Those elites captured the American government and used American economic and military dominance to set up an international monetary system based on the U.S. dollar, which is printed and controlled by the Federal Reserve.

The system was formalized in July 1944 at the Bretton Woods Conference, which made the U.S. dollar the world's reserve currency. Other currencies were pegged to the dollar at fixed exchange rates. Foreign nations and central banks could exchange $35 for an ounce of gold. Because the United States was the world's foremost producing nation and had been running large trade surpluses, we had been a creditor nation with the bulk of the world's gold supply in American hands. Under the Bretton Woods System, the dollar was as good as gold, backed by the world's largest economy and its most powerful military. The American dollar was used to facilitate international trade. The dollar was made legitimate by the ability to exchange it for gold.

But by the 1960s, all was not well with Bretton Woods. The United States had reduced its protectionist tariffs and became a free trade nation while engaging in expensive welfare programs at home and costly wars overseas. Unlike during the protectionist years when the United States ran trade surpluses and government budget surpluses, the United States, like Britain before it, began running trade deficits and budget deficits and was falling deeper and deeper into debt. The Federal Reserve printed dollars hand over fist to keep up with government spending on the Vietnam War and Great Society programs, such as Medicare, Medicaid and the Older Americans Act, which were sold to the public as a means to end poverty in the United States.

Foreign nations, which were running up reserves of dollars due to trade surpluses with the United States, began to redeem their dollars for gold. However, far more dollars had been printed than gold existed in American vaults. The Bretton Woods System was a farce. The dollar could not be redeemed.

On August 15, 1971, President Richard Nixon announced that foreign nations could no longer redeem the dollar for gold. It was merely a statement of reality since there was not enough gold to redeem. The dollar was backed not by gold but by American power, which at the time was in doubt due to the Vietnam War and social turmoil at home.

The tyranny of the petro dollar

In the 1970s, the Nixon administration made a deal with Saudi Arabia to denominate all oil sales in dollars in exchange for American military weapons and protection. Oil sales had already been denominated in dollars out of convenience, but the deal made by the Nixon administration formalized the petro dollar. The U.S. dollar became the only currency used by OPEC to transact oil sales.

After the collapse of Bretton Woods, the dollar was no longer backed by gold. But it was backed by oil, and oil is of far greater value on the international stage than gold. In the modern world, all nations need oil. In order to purchase oil, all nations must have dollars. To attain dollars, nations must either borrow them from banks or run trade surpluses with the United States. But attain dollars they must or their economies will collapse from a lack of means to purchase oil.

When a nation runs a trade deficit with the United States, it falls into dangerous territory. Dollars flee that nation and are not available to purchase oil. The price of oil in that nation will skyrocket and its government will have to borrow dollars or else its economy will grind to a halt.

The Asian nations lack natural resources, especially oil. In order for these nations, and all nations, to have an economy, they must attain dollars. By the 1960s, Japan had perfected the export-oriented economic model. It imported raw materials from abroad, such as iron ore, timber and oil, and manufactured them into higher value goods for export. Tariff and non-tariff barriers, currency manipulation and subsidies were used to maintain trade surpluses so that more petro dollars flowed into Japan than flowed out.

The flow of high-value manufactured goods out of Japan and petro dollars in provided that nation with a growing economy and one of the world's highest standards of living. As Japanese manufacturers began to supply American consumers with goods that were formerly produced by American manufacturers, our factories shut down and American workers were laid off. The United States began to deindustrialize in the 1970s as economic production began moving offshore. Our wages became stagnant and our unemployment levels began to climb. Meanwhile, Japan reached full employment. Even in 2014, several years after a Japanese economic slowdown, its unemployment rate was 3.6 percent, lower than the stated American rate of 6.2 percent.

Japan is protectionist with zero immigration and a non-interventionist foreign policy. It has a lower unemployment rate than the United States, which is a free-trade, high immigration, interventionist nation.

Anyone who has visited Japan and walked its streets can attest that it is one of the most modern and developed nations in the world. Its people are prosperous and educated. Poverty and crime are virtually non-existent. Walk the streets of any American city and homelessness, poverty and vandalism are readily apparent.

Crime is a concern. Take the wrong turn into the wrong neighborhood and your life is in danger. There are millions of people in the United States who are desperate enough to assault you for the few dollars in your wallet. Yet, in Japan, this is not the case. Its streets are safe and clean. Japan is a place where people can leave their doors unlocked at night. America used to be a place like that.

But Japan's prosperity has come at a price. Its prosperity is dependent on exporting to the United States. With Korea, China and other nations copying its success, the American market has become saturated with exports as nations from around the world compete for petro dollars, making it harder for Japan to maintain the large trade surpluses with the United States that it used to run.

Japan's dependency on the United States has also reduced its sovereignty. It is a nation that has been occupied by the American military for 70 years.

Why do we occupy Japan? Is Japan not a democratic nation and an ally? Japan is a technologically advanced nation with nearly 130 million people. The United States is not protecting the Japanese from anyone. It is perfectly capable of defending itself. Yet, Japan remains an occupied nation. Why?

The Japanese government allows its nation to be militarily occupied in exchange for a trade surplus with the United States. The American government uses Japan's trade surplus as a tool to coerce its government to follow the geopolitical goals of our transnational elites. If a Japanese politician threatens to kick the U.S. military out of Japan, the American government will, for example, threaten a recall of Toyota cars, or use some other trade threat that would end the Japanese surplus. Since any loss of Japan's surplus would immediately throw thousands of Japanese people out of work, renegade Japanese politicians are quickly silenced or removed.

The American government has enabled foreign nations to run massive trade surpluses with us which it uses to coerce these nations to follow certain policies beneficial to our elites. American jobs and prosperity have been traded away for this purpose.

China began imitating the Japanese economic export model in 1978. At the time, China was one of the poorest nations on Earth, but it began a remarkable economic rise, and in less than 30 years became the world's leading industrial nation. In 2009, China surpassed Japan and now has the second largest gross domestic product on the planet.

The United States has had the largest gross domestic product in the world since 1871. But under a free trade policy, our domestic economic production has been rapidly dismantled and offshored to the protectionist nations of Asia.

The free traders tell us we can get rich by trading with China. However, unlike our leaders who are globalists, Chinese leaders are nationalists. The Chinese leadership views economic power and production as vital to national strength. They understand that China allowed itself to be economically surpassed in the 18th and 19th centuries by nations far smaller than itself. China then suffered through more than 200 years of national humiliation as its wealth was looted and its people murdered by foreigners. Chinese leaders see the world through this historical lens. They will never follow utopian free trade policies because they know history and see where these policies lead. Instead, they will continue to aggressively pursue trade surpluses with us and attempt to capture as much of the world's economic production as they can. This economic production is already being translated into Chinese military power.

In 2015, the Chinese began setting up their own international finance system with the founding of the Asian Infrastructure Investment Bank, designed to be a rival to the IMF. Eventually, the Chinese will attempt to break free from the international system that was set up by the international bankers after World War II. These international bankers have been using us for their own ends and will likely attempt to push us into war with China if the Chinese put up a credible challenge to their planned system of global control, just as the Germans and Japanese did in the mid-20th century.

The tyranny of the Trilateral Commission

How did America transform from the leading protectionist nation in the world to the leading free trade nation? Why is free trade such a dominant ideology in our country even though it is having such destructive effects on us as a people and nation? Why are we giving away our national productive capacity and surrendering our middle class after the generations before us put so much effort into building them up? How are we still following such destructive trade policies when their negative effects are all around us in the form of high unemployment, stagnant wages, economically devastated cities and regions, family breakdown and massive debt?

To understand how free trade became so dominant as policy in the United States, one needs to go back to the year 1972. That year, international banker David Rockefeller and Columbia University professor Zbigniew Brzezinski floated the idea for an international commission at a Bilderberg meeting in Belgium.

Brzezinski was the son of a Polish diplomat. He grew up in Canada, then attained a doctorate at Harvard specializing in the Soviet Union.

David Rockefeller is the last surviving grandson of the great robber baron plutocrat John D. Rockefeller, who amassed one of the world's great fortunes in the 19th century in oil and banking, and was one of the principal backers of the Federal Reserve Act. David Rockefeller's mother, Abigail, was the daughter of Senator Nelson Aldrich, the man who assembled the plutocrats at Jekyll Island to design the Federal Reserve.

David Rockefeller served as the chairman and chief executive officer of Chase Manhattan Bank, one of the world's largest banks. He started working for the bank in 1946, serving as chief executive officer from 1969 to 1980, and concurrently as chairman until 1981.

Every year, the world's leading bankers, industrialists, politicians, media owners, media personalities, military and intelligence officers and academics gather at a private meeting known as the Bilderberg Conference. At this meeting, which is not covered by the mainstream media, some of the world's wealthiest and most influential people discuss international issues. David Rockefeller has long been an attendee at these conferences.

At the 1972 Bilderberg Conference, Rockefeller and Brzezinski floated a plan for a new international commission, called the Trilateral Commission, which would be made up of leaders from Europe, North America and Asia. The purpose of the proposed commission was to foster a new international economic order, promote global economic interdependence and promote free trade by dismantling tariffs. The commission was to be made up of 289 hand-picked members from banks, corporations, universities, governments, media, law firms and NGOs located in North America, Europe and Japan. Ninety-seven of the members were to be from the U.S. from both the Democratic and Republican parties.

The Bilderberg Conference attendees liked the idea and thus the Trilateral Commission was born in 1973. Since the election of President Jimmy Carter in 1977, Trilateral Commission members have dominated the executive branch. Both Carter and Vice President Walter Mondale were Trilateral Commission members.

While President Reagan was not a Trilateral Commission member, his vice president, George H.W. Bush, was a member and later became president. President Bill Clinton and Vice President Al Gore were both Trilateral Commission members. President George W. Bush was not a member but his vice president, Dick Cheney was. President Barack Obama and Vice President Joe Biden are not members but they have surrounded themselves with members of the Trilateral Commission.

The National Security Advisor controls the information that reaches the president and is arguably the most important person on the president's staff. Ten out of 17 of the last National Security Advisors have been Trilateral Commission members, including Henry Kissinger, who served as the National Security Advisor from 1969 to 1975. Kissinger has been a perennial figure at the Bilderberg Conference for a generation. Brzezinski, who founded the Trilateral Commission with Rockefeller, served as Carter's National Security Advisor. All three National Security Advisors appointed by President Obama have been Trilateral Commission members: Gen. James Jones, who served in the position from 2009 to 2010; Tom Donilon, from 2010 to 2013; and Susan Rice, appointed in 2013. Rice's father, Emmett Rice, was appointed to the Federal Reserve Board by Carter in 1979. He served as a Federal Reserve Governor for seven years under Federal Reserve Chairman Paul Volcker.

As of 2015, Volcker is an active member of the Trilateral Commission. Along with Volcker, former Federal Reserve Chairman Alan Greenspan was a founding member of the commission. Federal Reserve Vice Chairman Stanley Fischer was also a Trilateral Commission member.

Stanley Fischer is an interesting character and emblematic of the transnational elite that rules over our country today. Fischer was born in Northern Rhodesia, which is now Zambia. He spent his childhood in Africa and Israel before earning degrees in economics from the London School of Economics. He then earned a Ph.D. in economics from the Massachusetts Institute of Technology. Over his career, he held high ranking positions at the World Bank, the IMF and Citigroup. In 2005, he was appointed chairman of the Bank of Israel—Israel's central bank. In 2014, President Obama appointed Fischer as the vice-chair of the Federal Reserve, which is the second most powerful position at the Fed, second only to the Fed chair. Because of Fischer's credentials, gravitas, extensive experience and international contacts, he is likely the true power behind the thrown on the Fed board, influencing and guiding the much less accomplished Chairwoman Janet Yellen. So, essentially, Fischer, an international banker who possesses foreign citizenship and who served as the chairman of a foreign central bank, was appointed to one of the most powerful and influential positions in the United States. And he was a card carrying member of the Trilateral Commission.

World Bank presidents are appointed by the president. Six out of eight of the last World Bank presidents have been Trilateral

Commission members, starting with Robert McNamara, who served as World Bank president from 1968 to 1981. Other notable commission members are Paul Wolfowitz, who served as World Bank president from 2005 to 2012, and Robert Zoellick from 2007 to 2012.

Nine out of 12 of the last U.S. Trade Representatives have been Trilateral Commission members, including Robert Zoellick, who was trade representative from 2001 to 2005, and Charlene Barshefsky from 1997 to 2001, as well as the current U.S. Trade Representative, Michael Froman.

U.S. Trade Representatives were crucial in negotiating, promoting and implementing NAFTA, which had profound effects on the U.S. economy. Over the last two decades, NAFTA and our other trade treaties have lowered trade barriers into the United States market and have resulted in offshoring of American production and the stagnation of American wages. These trade treaties have largely been the work of members of the Trilateral Commission. NAFTA was signed by President Bill Clinton after being aggressively promoted in the press by Vice-President Al Gore, who attacked unions that opposed NAFTA.

It is instructive to go back and watch the debates in the lead up to the passage of the NAFTA trade deal. On November 9, 1993, on CNN's Larry King Live show, Gore debated presidential candidate Ross Perot about NAFTA. Gore was well-polished and youthful and spoke in glowing terms about the treaty and patriotically about the ability of American workers to compete in an open economy. He said that NAFTA would increase cross-border trade which would increase manufacturing in the United States, increase employment and drive up wages. He even said that NAFTA would reduce illegal immigration into the United States because more trade would mean more good jobs in Mexico. Perot, on the other hand, said that because of the large wage differential between the United States and Mexico, and because Mexico had fewer environmental regulations, American manufactures would leave the United States to take advantage of Mexico's lower wages and lighter regulatory burden. Perot said this would even force American manufactures that wanted to stay in the United States to leave in order to survive when their Mexican-based competitors undercut American-based businesses with lower prices. Perot said NAFTA would result in falling wages in the United States and more unemployment. During the debate, Gore used personal attacks to get under Perot's skin, at one point even presenting Perot with a picture of Senator Reed Smoot and Representative Willis Hawley.

Gore estimated that the U.S. would create 200,000 new jobs in the years following the passage of NAFTA once tariffs were lowered. He said unions were wrong to oppose NAFTA. "The net change is positive with NAFTA," he said. "When you sell more products, you make more products. When you make more products, you hire more people. ... If I'm wrong and he's right, then you give six months' notice and you're out of it."

After the debate, mainstream media outlets, such as *Time Magazine,* praised Gore for winning, not on the strength of his arguments, but on his ability to get under Perot's skin and cause Perot to lose his temper.

Of course, in hindsight, we can look back and see that everything Gore said in the debate was wrong and everything Perot said was right. An American trade surplus with Mexico immediately became a growing trade deficit that grew to $60 billion per year. Manufacturers closed up their American factories and fled to Mexico along with our well-paying jobs. By 2013, more than a million American jobs had been lost due to NAFTA and the trade deficit with Canada and Mexico reached $181 billion. Cheap American corn poured into Mexico bankrupting Mexican small farmers who then crossed the border illegally in the millions in search of work in the United States, turning an illegal immigration crisis into a full-blown national catastrophe that is changing the character of our nation into a society that is becoming nearly unrecognizable from pre-NAFTA America. Wages did not rise and the good paying jobs Gore promised never arrived. Income inequality worsened as the middle and working classes saw their wages stagnate and their jobs disappear.

Meanwhile, the stock market soared and passive-income seekers raked in profits from corporations that were able to take advantage of lax Mexican environmental regulations and cut labor costs by replacing high-wage American workers with pauperized Mexican labor.

NAFTA was pushed on this nation by Trilateralists, such as George H.W. Bush, Bill Clinton and Al Gore. They promised us the moon, but instead gave us trade deficits and what is becoming a Mexican-style wage structure here in the United States.

The Trilateral Commission has worked relentlessly to integrate and merge the United States economy and our government with the economies and governments of Mexico and Canada, much in the same manner that the nations of Europe have been merged into the European Union. Commission members have been working to break down American sovereignty and economic independence to create a new international economic order and promote global economic interdependence. Free trade is the vehicle they are using to achieve their new economic order, one in which American workers are being submerged into the global proletariat and are increasingly being paid wages that are approaching par with Mexican, Chinese, Vietnamese and Peruvian workers.

Michael Froman, who was a Trilateral Commission member, was appointed U.S. Trade Representative by President Obama in 2013. Froman is the lead U.S. negotiator for the Trans-Pacific Partnership. This trade treaty, which has often been described as NAFTA on steroids, will create an international regulatory structure encompassing the Pacific Rim that will supersede the power of nation-states. Under the banner of free trade, Trilateral Commission members are creating a supranational system of international corporate feudalism in private hands.

Piece by piece, treaty by treaty, the sovereignty and prosperity of the American people are being stolen by the hand-selected agents of international bankers, agents such as Froman.

These agents, serving in organizations such as the Trilateral Commission, are working toward a far-reaching aim, nothing less than to create a world system of financial control in private hands able to dominate the political system of each country and the economy of the world as a whole. This system is being controlled in feudalist fashion by the central banks of the world acting in concert, by secret agreements arrived at in frequent meetings and conferences.

Today, the Trilateral Commission is the key organization that has been integrating the American economy and work force into the developing world, reducing the wages paid to American labor to Third World status.

In 2015, some notable members on the Trilateral Commission included former European Central Bank President Jean-Claude Trichet, former U.S. Secretary of State Madeleine Albright, *New York Times* columnist David Brooks, former Secretary of Homeland Security Michael Chertoff, former CIA Director John Deutch, *Time Magazine* executive editor Michael Duffy, Dallas Federal Reserve Bank President and CEO and former U.S. Deputy Trade Representative Richard Fisher, CNN Senior Political Analyst David Gergen, 9/11 Commission member and top legal counsel for British Petroleum during the 2010 Gulf oil spill Jamie Gorelick, former Congresswoman Jane Harman who was also wife of the owner of *Newsweek*, former governor of Utah and presidential candidate John Huntsman, *Washington Post* columnist David Ingatius, Instagram chief operating officer Marne Levine, former Chairman of the Joint Chiefs of Staff Admiral Michael Mullen, Google Executive Chairman Eric Schmidt, former U.S. Treasury Secretary Larry Summers and *U.S. News and World Report* Chairman and Editor-in-Chief Mortimer Zuckerman, among many more notables.

These people are given subsequent economic rewards in the business world for promoting the agenda of the international bankers and for selling out their fellow American citizens to further that agenda.

To understand the thinking of our globalist leaders one

only has to look at the globe. When the globalists look at the globe, they do not see a world made up of nation-states with distinct national interests. What they see are natural resources and labor. When they look at Asia they see a surplus of labor that is being underutilized. When they look at the United States they see abundant agricultural land and natural resources, but also a region where the cost of labor is too high relative to other parts of the world. Why should they pay an American factory worker $45 an hour plus benefits when they can pay a Chinese worker $2.50 an hour? From a globalist's perspective, you invest your dollars in industrial production outside of the United States to maximize your profits. And you push for more immigration into the United States from poor countries to drive down American wages, which are out of sync with the rest of the world where wages are low, poverty is the norm and there is a surplus of underutilized labor.

However, if you are not a globalist but instead an American patriot, you look at the globe and see the United States as a sovereign nation made up of a distinct people who share a common language and a common culture. You do not see the world as being made up natural resources and labor pools to be exploited at the lowest possible price for the highest profits. You see it as a collection of nations with unique cultures, heritages and interests.

For the American citizen, we have inherited certain political rights and economic prosperity that have been passed down to us because of the sacrifices made by our countrymen who lived before us. As an American citizen, we have been given certain rights and responsibilities that allow us to provide for the well-being of ourselves, our families, our communities and our nation. We have not been given rights and responsibilities in China, Japan, Mexico, Europe or any other nation or region. We cannot vote in those places and we do not have the same property rights as they do in their home countries. But American military dominance and the dominance of the dollar have given globalists the power to coerce other nations to bend to the globalist agenda. The globalists do this in our name.

As Americans, our common national interest is to defend this nation from enemies, both foreign and domestic; to protect the sovereignty and independence our forefathers fought and died for; and to increase the prosperity of the American people. It is not in our national interest to drive down American wages through free trade agreements and mass immigration, or to participate in overseas wars that kill off our youth and make us hated abroad. It is not in our interest to offshore economic production, which reduces our economic independence, reduces our national prosperity while enriching a transnational elite that is attempting to create a world government that usurps our Constitution and the rights of our people.

The globalists are seeking to strip us of our prosperity and rights as they put in place their world system of financial control. The solution to stop their project is simple. It is a constitutional solution. We must pull out of all free trade agreements and return to a trade policy of American protectionism. Tariffs should be raised to protect American industry, jobs and high wages.

During the age of tariffs between the Civil War and the Great Depression, the United States was still a great trading nation. The difference from today was that the tax burden that supported our government fell not on American wage earners and businesses but instead on foreigners trying to make a buck here. Foreigners paid the bulk of the taxes that funded the government. They did this for the right to make a profit in our country.

During the age of tariffs, our country ran trade surpluses and federal budget surpluses. Tariffs were used as negotiating tools to open up foreign markets to American goods by allowing lower tariffs on foreign goods that were not produced in quantity in our country. The era of tariffs was a time of price deflation, not inflation like today. Wages were rising and our economy went through its fastest growth in our history.

Raising tariffs on both foreign companies importing to the United States and on American companies that have offshored production would encourage production to return to the United States. This would cause a demand for American workers.

Companies would have to pay higher wages to attract workers. Higher wages would mean more purchasing power for working people but less profits for passive income earners who rely on wage suppression for their passive income streams. Tariffs would cause a change in the wage structure in the United States with more money going to the people who work for a living and less to the modern day Wall Street robber barons and international financiers. Poverty would lessen, the middle class would expand and become more prosperous and the passive income earners would find it harder to make a buck from imports produced in sweat shops in China, Guatemala or Bangladesh, and instead would spend their time in the media wailing and gnashing their teeth about overpaid American workers and the shortage of Americans willing to work for $7 an hour trimming their hedges and babysitting their kids.

The U.S. trade deficit for 2013 was $471.5 billion. The solution to this deficit is a simple policy change: raise taxes on imports. Then that deficit would be transformed into government revenue and spur domestic investment in production causing demand for American workers, which would cause wages to rise and unemployment to fall.

The U.S. should scrap free trade, raise tariffs and return to a policy of negotiated bilateral trade agreements. Instead of throwing open our borders to China, India, Bangladesh, Mexico, Japan, Germany and everyone else, we should raise tariffs while using the lure of profits in the American market to entice protectionist nations, such as China, Japan and Germany, to drop trade barriers and open their markets to American exports. We should negotiate for mutually beneficial trade agreements that protect American industries and jobs while providing us with foreign imports we truly need—but not imports that replace American production and destroy wages and employment.

The main obstacle to this course of action is the transnational elite, such as the aforementioned Trilateral Commission members, who dominate our media, government and academia. Any rise in tariffs would cause wailing and gnashing of teeth from the beneficiaries of free trade—the globalists, corporatists, bought-and-paid-for politicians, think tank propagandists, foreign lobbyists and their lackeys in the media and academia, who would bombard us with every argument under the sun for why the sky is falling and the world is ending if the U.S. returns to the trade policy that made us prosperous. Just as slave-owners wailed and gnashed their teeth when the Tariff of Abominations cut into the profits they made off their parasitical exploitation of slaves, our modern day slavers will use every argument and threat as to why rising wages and full-employment in the United States are bad for us. This is because it is bad for them. They will jabber incessantly about Smoot-Hawley, the Great Depression, candlemakers blocking out the sun and use every manner of sophistry, economic mumbo jumbo, pseudo-intellectualism, straw man arguments and reductio ad absurdum to fight for the system that feeds off our work.

When a host attempts to tear off a parasite, the parasite will dig in and fight and become fearful and angry. But the host should not concern itself with the well-being of the parasite and instead should take satisfaction with its own improving health once the parasite is gone.

When the media and pundits wail and gnash their teeth about protectionism, that is a sign that tariffs are a correct policy that benefits the American people and the nation at large.

When the pundits begin fear mongering about the prospects of a trade war, we should answer that we are already in a trade war and we are losing badly. It's time to fight back for the American worker and small business owner. Today, our trade partners use tariffs and trade barriers to run up massive trade surpluses with us that have strip-mined our economy of industries and jobs and have depressed American wages. The worst aspect of this trade war is that American corporations and our own government have allied themselves with foreign governments against the American people.

If tariffs are enacted and the Japanese become angry that their massive trade surplus with us is being threatened, our response should be that they should not complain about American protectionism when they themselves are protectionist against us. If they play the only card they have against us and demand that all American troops, ships and aircraft should be removed from Japan, we should answer, "Okay. It is time for the American occupation of Japan to end. We will bring our troops home." When they become concerned about no longer being able to purchase oil with surplus petro dollars earned from their trade surplus, we should answer that the petro dollar has been a tremendous burden on the American people and the people of the world. It has entangled us in destructive Middle Eastern wars and has enriched an international financial elite at the expense of working Americans. It is time to end the tyranny of the petro dollar and let each nation trade for the oil it needs in its own way without having to be dependent on profiteering international bankers as middle men.

When the Japanese and Chinese retaliate against tariffs by threatening to refuse to purchase American bonds, we should answer, "Why do we need you to purchase bonds with American dollars that have been printed by our own Treasury?"

How is it that we have become indebted to borrowing dollars from foreign nations—dollars that we have printed ourselves? Why are we taxing our own people to pay interest to foreigners? It is insanity and must stop.

We should tell foreign nations that the current debt-based dollar that is being used as an international currency has been foisted upon us by international bankers who are using the dollar to destroy the sovereignty and independence of all nations and that this has been bad for us and for them.

In the 19th century, free trade was the policy of imperialists and slave owners. Today, their descendants—the modern-day American imperialists, the globalists seeking a world government, and corporatist exploiters of cheap labor—would have us believe that free trade brings peace and prosperity to all. But we have been the leading free-trade nation for over half a century and we have not seen peace in that time. Our prosperity has been stolen from us and transferred upward to a small percentage of people to the detriment of the middle and working classes.

It is time we as Americans reject free trade philosophy, which is itself a foreign import, and instead return to our American roots. We should return to the American System that was a rejection of the British System that we have now. Henry C. Carey wrote so many years ago that the American System brings prosperity and economic independence while the British System brings war, dependence on foreign nations and poverty. Our current circumstances prove that Carey was right. We should rebuild our economy and the prosperity of our great middle class by returning to the American System that puts the interests of the American people above those of profiteering usurers, rent seekers and speculators, and the globalists who seek our ruin. But we can improve on the American System by revising it so that a central bank serving a fractional reserve banking system is not part of the equation. Instead, credit can be supplied to the nation through debt-free U.S. Notes issued by a U.S. Monetary Council under democratic controls. Credit can be supplied to Main Street businesses and American homeowners through public loan offices rather than through disruptive and unstable fractional reserve banks that siphon off the wealth of the people through usury.

The tyranny of Wall Street

Wall Street versus Main Street. We have heard that cliché time and again. But what does it mean?

The cliché actually acknowledges a very important conflict in our economy. It declares that there is a difference between the economy of Wall Street and the economy of us regular folks down here on Main Street.

The Starbucks Corporation gives us a window through which we can observe these two economies. In 1971, two teachers and a writer scraped up their personal savings, pooled their money together, and opened the first Starbucks coffee store in Seattle, which was a coffee bean retailer and not a cafe. Over the next decade, the store was operated essentially as a hobby by three friends. Back in the early days, Starbucks was a Main Street business. It was small, but successful and provided its owners with a nice profit.

Starbucks started out as the type of Main Street business that had been the foundation of the free enterprise system—the engine of our economy in the early days of the republic. The free enterprise system as envisioned by the Founders consisted of individually owned enterprises that competed freely among themselves. Citizens owned and operated their own businesses and farms and competed for customers which kept prices low, increased production and spurred innovation.

The free enterprise system allowed the common man to own property, make a living off the work of his own hands and be a free and financially independent citizen who could stand tall among his betters without feeling the need to bootlick. Common men like Thomas Paine, a corsetmaker, did not feel the need to bootlick the king and instead had the gumption to tell him that we weren't going to take his long train of abuses any longer.

In his autobiography, Benjamin Franklin described his experiences running a print shop in Philadelphia in the years before the Revolutionary War. He started out as an apprentice before owning his own shop. Due to a strong work ethic, his shop grew and became successful. With the printing of *Poor Richard's Almanack,* Franklin became prosperous. He brought in apprentices to his shop, trained them and provided them with capital to set up print shops in other cities in exchange for a percentage of their profits for a fixed number of years. Through his own efforts, industry and frugality, Franklin became a wealthy man. His hard work as a young man gave him the free time to experiment with electricity, invent the Franklin stove and enter public life, among many more accomplishments in his remarkable life.

The free enterprise system has always been part of America's allure. America has been seen as a land of opportunity where an industrious person could become prosperous through work and effort, by learning a trade, owning a piece of land and improving it, or opening a business that provides goods and services to the community.

But in America, there has always been a dark side to the drive for wealth. In the early days, a very different economic system operated alongside the free enterprise system. This system involved banks and financiers providing large amounts of capital through lending to men who used the capital to purchase large tracts of land and armies of slaves. Slave labor was used to grow commodities, such as cotton and tobacco, which were exported. The profits from the exportation of commodities were used to pay back the interest and principal owed to the banks and financiers.

In one system, the small farmer worked the land himself with his family and maybe a few hired hands. His industriousness and frugality brought prosperity. In the other system, the plantation owner used slaves to work huge tracts of land bought with money borrowed at interest from banks, often in London. The plantation owner's prosperity was produced through exploitation, speculation, greed and cruelty.

One system was motivated by the desire to become prosperous and financially independent, while the other promised riches through a willingness to enter debt bondage and to exploit human beings.

After the Civil War, the second half of the 19th century saw a new form of economic organization take shape in America. The American economy began to transform from one made up of individually owned enterprises to one dominated by corporations owned by shareholders.

The corporation was a legal creation with rights and liabilities separate from its shareholders. Investors purchased shares in the corporation, bringing their money together to create large pools of capital. The capital was used by the corporation to pay employees and purchase ships and goods for trade with a goal of earning profit and passive income for investors. Should a profit be made, it was distributed to the shareholders. If the corporation lost money, the shareholders were only liable for their own shares—a legalism called limited liability. The largest shareholders control the board of directors that governs the corporation.

Unlike an individually owned business or a partnership in which owners are liable for all debts and losses, corporate shareholders are protected from the actions of the corporation that result in loss, excessive debt or even criminal offenses. The shareholder is only liable for the shares he holds.

The corporation came of age during the Colonial Era. Corporations, such as the Dutch East India Company, Hudson's Bay Company and the British East India Company, were granted monopolies by their governments to conduct trade in different parts of the world. These corporations earned vast profits for their shareholders and even acted as quasi-governments in their territories, operating armies, large fleets and forts. They were drivers of Europe's colonial expansion. The British East India Company was the main driver of the British conquest of India.

Essentially, India was enslaved by British military power for the interests of wealthy corporate shareholders of the British East India Company.

In the early days of the United States, the corporation was viewed with suspicion and seen as a vehicle of imperialism, which the American colonists had fought against. Early American corporations were formed for specific purposes, such as building roads or bridges, and they had expirations on their charters and were only operated in particular locations.

The corporation developed over the 19th century through a series of court decisions that allowed them to grow bigger and more powerful. In the latter half of the 19th century, the Robber Baron Era was in full swing as international bankers, such as John D. Rockefeller, Jay Gould and J.P. Morgan, provided capital to men, such as Andrew Carnegie, Cornelius Vanderbilt and Edward Henry Harriman, to build and consolidate industries. Huge industrial concerns, from railroads to oil to shipping, began to dominate the economy.

The financiers provided vast sums of money to men

chosen for their organizational abilities and their ruthless competitiveness. Huge pools of capital were employed to create massive industrial concerns that exploited new technologies in manufacturing, communications and transportation. Great American fortunes were amassed and family dynasties were created during this era of breathtaking economic expansion.

The Robber Barons were hungry for resources, cheap labor and profits. American citizens were too expensive for them so they turned to immigrants. The Robber Barons were the engine behind mass immigration into America in the latter half of the 19th century. They brought in immigrants by the millions—starving Irishmen, Chinese coolies, pauperized Italians and Poles. They brought them over on ships and put them to work on the railroads, in the mines, in factories, foundries, meatpacking plants and sweatshops. The immigrants were low paid and worked long hours in dangerous conditions while the Robber Barons and their financiers made fortunes. The Robber Barons were hungry to bring more tired, poor, huddled masses—the wretched refuse from abroad—to our shores to push down wages and push up profits—to enrich themselves off the labor of others.

Toward the end of the 19th century, the states of Delaware and New Jersey loosened up restrictions on corporations and the modern American corporation took shape. Constraints on mergers and acquisitions were jettisoned and large corporations began forming, gobbling up smaller ones. Huge corporate concerns steamrolled over family-owned businesses, which were and remain today, employers of most of the nation.

By the end of the 19th century, the big corporations had become dominant not only in our economy but also in our government. Their profits financed political campaigns and turned legislation in their favor. But populism was also a force at the time, which worried the international bankers. To become the dominant power in the country, they needed to seize control of the monetary system itself—to centralize it and create a money trust just as they had with steel, railroads and oil.

The concern in Congress over the direction the country

was headed became so high that the Pujo Committee, chaired by Louisiana Congressman Arsene Pujo, was formed in 1912 to investigate the money trust. The committee found that a handful of financiers had formed a conspiracy to gain control of major manufacturing, transportation, mining, telecommunications and financial markets through at least 18 different major financial corporations under the control of a cartel led by J.P. Morgan, George F. Baker and James Stillman. These men held manipulative control of the New York Stock Exchange. The international bankers Paul Warburg, Jacob H. Schiff, Felix M. Warburg, Frank E. Peabody, William Rockefeller and Benjamin Strong, Jr., were all singled out in the committee's report as being part of the money trust that dominated the economy through 341 directorships held in 112 corporations.

The report instigated a drive for reforms. Ironically, the reforms enacted were the Federal Reserve Act, which gave us the Fed, and the passage of the Sixteenth Amendment, which gave us the progressive income tax on wage earners.

The people being investigated by the Pujo Committee were the very men who created the Federal Reserve Act and the income tax!

The Federal Reserve allowed the New York big banks to seize control of the American money supply, centralize its issuance and control its volume. No longer could interest rates be determined by the supply and demand of money in a free market. Instead, rates would be determined by a committee acting in secret under the control of bankers. By centralizing control of interest rates, booms and busts could be planned behind closed doors. The economic destiny of the nation could be shaped by a handful of people. The government could be brought down at will by tightening the volume of the money supply. Compliant politicians could be rewarded while independent ones could be starved of cash. The burden of taxation was offloaded from importers onto the backs of American wage earners, while passive incomes were taxed at lower rates. The income tax then became the main source of government revenue that paid interest to bond holders, who were men like J.P Morgan, Paul Warburg and Jacob Schiff.

Money flowed from the Fed to the investment banks to corporations that then used it to shape the economic, political and cultural life of the nation and world.

In the 20th century, the courts decided that corporations have one purpose: to earn profits for their shareholders. No more was the corporation chartered for a specific purpose in a specific location for a defined period of time. The 20th century corporation was a single-minded money machine. People purchased stock in the hopes of receiving some of that money that the corporation was organized to capture.

The trading of stock in corporations has always been a speculatory venture. Stock prices were bid up in bubbles and sold off in busts from the very beginning. Wall Street evolved through the 19th century to become a place where people made fortunes not only from owning stock in a company that earned a profit, but from the trading of stock. Large numbers of people were attempting to become rich not off investing in companies that provided goods and services, but off the practice of buying pieces of paper low and selling them high. A fortune could be made if someone who owned stock in some corporation could convince the public that the corporation was going to be the next big thing, even if that corporation produced nothing. If the public rushed to buy the stock, the price would rise and the owners who bought low and early could sell and reap the gains. Then, when everyone else realized that the company was not the next big thing, the selloff would begin and the last to sell would lose their shirts.

Many people believe that when they purchase stock they are investing. When they purchase the stock during the initial public offering, they are actually investing in the company. When the stock is initially purchased, the company takes the money that was raised and uses it to buy equipment, build facilities and hire employees—essentially, to grow the business. But after that, when you are buying stock, your money is not going to the company as an investment but instead to the holder of the stock. You are purchasing it with hopes that the company will pay a dividend from its profits or else that the value of the stock will rise and you will be able to sell it to the next guy for more money than you paid for it. You purchased the stock as a speculatory venture with the hope that some greater fool will come along and purchase it from you for a higher price.

Stock is also purchased to gain power in a company and control over how the company is run. Shareholders vote on who sits on the corporation's board of directors. The largest shareholders have the biggest say. Purchasing stock to control a company is a rich man's game and they and their institutions are the ones who control corporations. They buy up stock in huge volumes, often using borrowed money, to take over corporations, replace CEOs who are not performing to their liking, decide whether a company should be broken up and sold off piece by piece for profit, whether its employees should be laid off, outsourced and operations moved overseas to increase profits and stock prices by reducing expenses paid out in wages. The average American who purchases stock does not have a say in corporate governance. The system favors the rich and promises the rest of us a few crumbs during the booms, and then wipes us out in the busts. We ride the waves and read the tea leaves hoping to make some money and not lose our savings while the rich call all the shots.

Starbucks made the transition from a small enterprise to a multinational corporation when a New Yorker named Howard Schultz purchased the coffee retailer in 1989 for $3.8 million. Starbucks then began a rapid expansion. Its stores began opening at an incredible rate across the country and around the world. Seemingly overnight there was a Starbucks in every town and city. Today, in some cities there are multiple Starbucks cafes within a five-minute walk from each other.

Schultz did not take profits from his existing stores and reinvest them to build new stores. The money came first. He was provided with a bottomless pit of cash which he used to rapidly expand a coffee empire that is now global in scope. Starbucks cafes came into towns where Main Street cafes already existed and drove them out of business. With an endless supply of money, Starbucks used high-powered marketing, favorable media coverage, brand recognition and buzz to replace Main Street businesses with a Wall Street one.

Schultz had purchased a successful Main Street business and used unlimited access to money to turn it into a Wall Street corporation. Schultz was given access to Wall Street money because he is a talented leader and organizer who had a vision that he was able to act on and bring to fruition. Today, he is a billionaire—one of the richest men in the world. But he is a creation of Wall Street. He was not self-made but instead was chosen by Wall Street money men for his talents and because of his connections—not because he started a successful business from scratch. He purchased a successful business and globalized it by deploying vast amounts of money supplied to him by Wall Street.

Schultz was merely following the blueprint other Wall Street agents had implemented before him, such as Ray Kroc, who had purchased the McDonald's restaurant from the McDonald brothers, and turned it into a global corporation.

Of course, it is undeniable that people love Starbucks. When you enter a Starbucks cafe, whether you are in San Francisco or New York, London or New Delhi, you know you are going to find clean restrooms, a comfortable place to sit where you can read the *New York Times,* surf the net with free Wi-Fi, and get a decent cup of coffee. The convenience and familiarity of Starbucks has its appeal. Yet, when Starbucks comes into a town, something is lost. Family owned coffee shops that are rooted in the community are often put out of business, replaced by corporate franchises that extract profits from the community and send them away to Wall Street and to passive income seeking investors who are just as likely to be foreigners as Americans. When Walmart comes into town, people line up for their cheap foreign-made goods while our locally owned stores are driven out of our communities. Home Depot arrives and family owned hardware stores board up their windows. All our communities have the same restaurants, the same stores stocked with the same products. This corporatized economy is controlled by a handful of extremely rich people at the top who are connected to the big Wall Street banks that supply them with money that is deployed to dominate their industries. This money is created out of nothing, backed by the Fed, and turned over by Wall Street to men like Ray Kroc and Howard Schultz.

The small family business is replaced by a Wall Street corporation. The individuality of a community is replaced by standardized corporate franchises that are homogenizing the world. Instead of communities filled with small business owners working for themselves, we get franchise owners and store managers working for distant corporate headquarters. We have become a nation of employees, of corporate drones climbing corporate ladders. All money in our communities is funneled up to Wall Street while we work hard to keep our jobs by attempting to maximize profits for the corporation, which relentlessly tries to maximize shareholder value by holding down the cost of labor.

How does one become a Howard Schultz or a Ray Kroc, anyway?

That is not for us to decide. Wall Street decision makers choose the Howard Schultzes of the world. The money men choose insiders who are selected to deploy investment capital that is used to exploit new industries or take over existing ones and globalize them. To be a Howard Schultz you must have some kind of connection to Wall Street power players—family ties, friends, the right schools, a shared political agenda. Above all you must share the globalist vision. You must aggressively support mass immigration, free trade and American interventionism abroad.

Many people are under the impression that Wall Street practices free market capitalism. But this is not the case. If you create some new miracle invention or figure out some new way to run a business more efficiently or you write a great novel or a song or work harder and smarter than your competitors, that does not ensure your success in our modern economy. You can run the most efficient business in the world, but if your competitor has access to capital and you don't, even if his products are shoddier than yours and he runs his business less efficiently than you do, he is going to put you out of business. If he knows the right people, he can outcompete you without ever turning a profit until you are bankrupt.

In his book *One Summer: America, 1927*, Bill Bryson tells the sad story of Philo T. Farnsworth, the inventor of the television. Many people had been working on developing what today we call the television but it was Farnsworth who created a fully functional design. Farnsworth was a brilliant inventor, but he lacked financing.

Meanwhile, RCA president David Sarnoff was providing millions to the inventor Vladimir Zworykin to invent a television. However, they learned that Farnsworth had already figured out how to create a working model and that he had filed patents. Zworykin paid Farnsworth a visit. Farnsworth showed Zworykin how his television worked under the belief that RCA wished to license his patents.

RCA then went on to manufacture televisions using Farnsworth's technology. Farnsworth filed a lawsuit against RCA for patent infringement, which Farnsworth won. Despite Farnsworth's legal victory, RCA used its deep pockets to dominate the television industry while promoting Zworykin as the "Inventor of Television." According to Bryson, Farnsworth died drunk, depressed and forgotten at age 64 while Sarnoff and Zworykin lived long and prosperous lives.

Of course, the story doesn't end there. While the television was invented and popularized in America, by the 1970s, the Japanese began manufacturing TVs and exporting them into the United States. The Japanese government decided that its companies were going to dominate the industry that was pioneered in the United States. Through protectionism and subsidies, the Japanese began dumping televisions below cost into the American marketplace.

Japan's Ministry of International Trade and Industry (MITI)

formulated a plan to capture the American marketplace from American television manufacturers by protecting and subsidizing its own manufacturers while taking advantage of America's free trade policy.

The American government stood by while Japanese firms dumped low-cost televisions into the United States, which bankrupted American manufacturers. Other countries got in on the act until all American television manufacturing was driven abroad.

Wall Street and our free trade policy are not the free enterprise system that our Founders envisioned. In fact, they are the opposite of free enterprise. Wall Street and free trade are destroying the free enterprise system and replacing it with a globalized and centralized system run by insiders who control and direct the flow of money.

The Federal Reserve is the heart of this system. The Fed provides money to Wall Street investment banks which in turn provide credit to corporations which come into our communities and drive out Main Street businesses replacing them with franchises, big box stores or corporations with deep pockets which extract profits and send them back up to Wall Street.

The capitalist system we have today has nothing to do with the free enterprise system envisioned by our Founders. The system we have today is designed to steal ideas and bankrupt the Philo Farnsworths of the world and instead reward a small clique of insiders connected to Wall Street and the Fed.

Here's how it works. When a new technology is developed, usually several small companies will form to exploit it. Wall Street insiders will choose their wonder boy who will receive a bottomless pit of money. That wonder boy will then hire employees, buy facilities and buy up other companies. The press will then fill with stories about the new technology and the wonder boy entrepreneur who is changing the world. The wonder boy and his company will be in every newspaper, on the television news, books will be written and movies made until everyone knows about him and his company. The true inventors and pioneers of the new technology and industry are starved of capital and are ignored or written off by the media. The wonder boy and his lawyers tie them up in expensive lawsuits. Wall Street investors continue supplying the wonder boy with money—even if his company is not earning a dime of profit—until all his competitors are bankrupted and he dominates his industry. Then comes the IPO accompanied by endless media hype. The wonder boy and Wall Street investors get rich when the public buys the hype and purchases the stock. That's how they play the game. The money flows from the Fed to the Wall Street investment banks to the insiders selected to manage corporations.

Alfred Owen Crozier warned us over a hundred years ago not to allow a central bank to seize control of the money supply. "Then we shall have only corporate currency, and a government of the corporations, by the corporations and for the corporations—a 'soulless' corporate republic."

Isn't that what we've become? A nation run by corporations with a government of the corporations, by the corporations and for the corporations? A Starbucks and McDonalds on every corner. Walmarts in every town filled with foreign goods made by foreign pauperized labor. A people transformed from tradesmen, skilled craftsmen, artisans, freelancers, entrepreneurs, business owners and family farmers into corporate employees who punch the clock every weekday and backstab each other attempting to climb corporate ladders while always remaining one step away from the unemployment line.

Our government has been corrupted by lobbyists from multinational corporations whose shareholders and employees are just as likely to be foreigners as Americans. These corporations have no loyalty to the United States and to the American people but are loyal only to profit and to the globalist vision of free trade, mass immigration and interventionism abroad. These corporations lobby our government for overseas wars to protect their interests abroad. They lobby our government for more immigration to provide them with more cheap labor at home. These multinational corporations have become a direct threat to our sovereignty, our liberty and our Constitution. These corporations are financed by money that flows from the Fed.

There is a better way. Corporations owe their existence to their charters which are allowed by the states. These charters can be changed and reformed to redirect the purpose of corporations not just to the mindless pursuit of profits at all costs, but to the public good. Corporations could be chartered for specific purposes in limited areas for fixed periods of time. Corporate boards could be reorganized not only to represent the largest shareholders but also to represent labor, customers and the communities in which they do business.

Our current monetary system is designed to serve the banks and the corporations that have grown up around them. However, the monetary system can be reformed not to serve banks and corporations but instead to serve Main Street—to serve our communities and the free enterprise system.

Money could be stripped away from Wall Street passive income seekers and provided for investment to Main Street businesses. The flow of credit could be redirected away from Wall Street and onto home buyers and small businesses. Tariffs could be erected to protect production here at home from the predatory practices of foreign governments and their state-supported corporations, and from the exploitation of impoverished populations for cheap labor used to replace the middle class American worker. The tax system could be reshaped to favor small businesses over corporations and to encourage freelancing and self-employment over being an employee. A small business owner who provides goods and services to his community and who employs people should not be taxed at all and should keep all the profits that he earns. The tax burden should be removed from our productive citizens and placed onto the backs of importers of foreign goods and onto passive income seekers who earn their money through rents, dividends and speculation. We can re-create an economy based on work and production rather than on Wall Street manipulations.

We must abolish the Federal Reserve and replace it with a U.S. Monetary Council that is operated transparently, subject to checks and balances, accountable to the people and under the authority of Congress. We must retire the Federal Reserve Note and replace it with U.S. Notes that are not backed by debt but instead are issued and regulated by the Monetary Council. We must establish public loan offices in each congressional district that directly lend U.S. Notes to home buyers and small businesses. The interest from these loans must then be re-circulated into the communities from which it is collected and put to work for the public good.

We could re-create an economy of family-owned businesses and partnerships that are competing not against globalized, homogenized Wall Street corporations but instead against each other for customers in their own communities. We could re-create the free enterprise system that is under attack today by the Fed, by Wall Street, by foreign corporations and by our own government.

New technology already exists that could provide investment money to Main Street and cure us of the economic stagnation and unemployment that plague us. Through the Internet and crowdfunding, small investors have the means to pool their money to invest in businesses on Main Street. The Internet can allow communities to set up their own local stock exchanges where people can invest in businesses in their own communities by purchasing equity in enterprises they would like to see on Main Street. The technology exists to allow people in a town to pool their savings and purchase equity in local businesses—such as new restaurants, stores or local startups.

However, due to the Security and Exchange Commission, only accredited investors are allowed to invest in local businesses. According to the SEC, an accredited investor must have earned an income that exceeds $200,000 (or $300,000 together with a spouse) in each of the prior two years, and reasonably expects the same for the current year, or has a net worth over $1 million, either alone or together with a spouse (excluding the value of the person's primary residence).

There are about 9 million accredited investors in the United States. So the SEC limits investing in small businesses to a handful of well-off individuals and makes it illegal for the rest of us. The SEC believes we non-accredited investors are not sophisticated enough to invest in our communities; however, we are allowed to pour as much of our savings as we like into the stock market, penny stocks, lottery tickets and casinos.

In 2006, peer-to-peer lending websites began operating in the United States. People began pooling their money to fund personal loans over the Internet. Borrowers were able to take out loans on peer-to-peer sites to consolidate their debts. A borrower could take out a loan from a peer-to-peer site at a lower interest rate than he was paying on his credit card. The peer-to-peer loan could then be used to pay off credit card debt at a lower fixed rate with a fixed term. Instead of paying interest to a bank, the borrower could pay the lower rate to the peer-to-peer lenders, who often lent money in increments as low as $25. The borrower paid a lower rate on his debt while the lender earned a higher rate on his savings than he was receiving from his bank.

Peer-to-peer lending took off in a big way. The business model threatened banks in the same way peer-to-peer file sharing had threatened the music industry. In stepped the SEC, which shut down peer-to-peer lending in 2008 and required peer-to-peer lending companies to become compliant with the Securities Act of 1933.

In some states, small peer-to-peer lenders were restricted to investing a maximum of $2,500 in peer-to-peer loans while accredited investors were allowed to lend more. Some states banned peer-to-peer lending altogether. Prior to the SEC regulations, borrowers set their own interest rates and lenders competed for them in auctions, allowing for very low rates for borrowers with good credit. After the SEC stepped in, rates were set by the peer-to-peer companies in a centralized manner.

Today, big institutions dominate peer-to-peer lending while small lenders have been restrained by government regulations.

The SEC says the regulations are to protect the public. The rules have been tightened to restrict small lenders, yet borrowers are allowed to go into as much debt as they can take out. These borrowers get hassled by debt collectors if they miss a payment.

It seems the SEC regulations did more to restrict small investors from moving their cash into peer-to-peer investing and out of banks and the stock market.

This is the same old scam that the bankers have been pulling on us for over a century. Government regulators make rules that they claim are for protecting the public, but in actuality are written to favor the big banks and corporations and protect their profits. This was how they got the Federal Reserve Act passed and how they keep a lid on disruptive technologies that could put them out of business. If anyone thinks we live in a country that allows free enterprise, just take a look at how the SEC has regulated crowdfunding and peer-to-peer lending to protect the banks, Wall Street and favor wealthy accredited investors over the middle class.

The technology and knowhow exists today to decentralize credit and allow small investors to move their money out of Wall Street and earn returns investing on Main Street. The main obstacle, however, is government regulation, which favors Wall Street.

If anyone thinks the SEC is protecting them, all they have to do is look at the Bernie Madoff scandal. Madoff operated the largest Ponzi scheme in history, which made Charles Ponzi look like a bush-leaguer. Ponzi's victims lost $225 million while Madoff's lost $18 billion. Madoff was a Wall Street insider and a former chairman of NASDAQ. The SEC ignored informants who let them know about Madoff's scam. In fact, Madoff's niece, Shana, who worked for Madoff's firm, married Eric Swanson, a former Assistant Director of the Office of Compliance Investigations and Examinations at the SEC, whom she met when he was conducting an SEC examination of the Madoff firm. Eric Swanson began investigating Bernie Madoff in 2003. The investigation was closed in 2006. He married Shana in 2007. The Madoff scandal didn't break until 2008 when Bernie Madoff told his sons he was insolvent and they reported him to authorities.

Someone who has had a more lasting negative effect on the nation is former Treasury Secretary Robert Rubin. Rubin worked for 26 years as an investment banker for Goldman Sachs. He then served as the U.S. Treasury Secretary from 1995 to 1999. During that time, he was a leading advocate, along with Fed Chairman Alan Greenspan and Deputy Treasury Secretary Lawrence Summers, for massive deregulation of the financial sector. Most notably, Rubin advocated for the repeal of the 1933 Glass-Steagall Act, which separated commercial and investment banking. Essentially, before Glass-Steagall was repealed, a commercial bank, such as Citicorp, which held deposits from the public, could not trade in securities like investment banks do, such as Goldman Sachs, which does not hold deposits from the public.

The purpose of the Glass-Steagall Act was to insure that commercial banks didn't use deposits from the public for speculating, such as trading in stocks or purchasing and trading mortgage-backed securities, corporate bonds or bonds from developing countries.

With the passage of the Gramm-Leach-Bliley Bill in 1999, Glass-Steagall was repealed and the walls came down. Commercial banks and investment banks began merging and savings from the public flowed into securities. The deregulation allowed Citicorp to merge with the insurance giant Travelers Group and become Citigroup.

After his de-regulating was done, Rubin left the Treasury and joined Citigroup—the third largest bank in the U.S.—where he earned tens of millions of dollars serving as chairman of the executive committee and chairman of the board of directors. Think about that for a moment. The man whose actions in government resulted in the merger of two giant firms then leaves government and is employed at a huge salary with that firm.

With Glass-Steagall gone, Citigroup speculated heavily in mortgage backed securities (MBS) and collaterized debt obligations (CDO). The subprime mortgage crisis hit in 2007 and by November of 2008 Citigroup was insolvent.

But Citigroup was too big to fail. According to a 2012 *Bloomberg Business* article, while Rubin was at Citigroup, the federal government injected $45 billion in taxpayer money into the bank and guaranteed some $300 billion in illiquid assets.

Rubin left Citigroup in 2009. According to *Bloomberg*, Rubin was paid about $126 million during his tenure at the bank. After leaving Citigroup, he went on to become a co-chairman of the Council on Foreign Relations. He has also been a frequent attendee of the Bilderberg Conference and was on the list of attendees at the 2015 Bilderberg Conference at a luxury alpine resort in Austria. This man played a central role in causing the housing bubble which led to the crash of 2007 and one of the longest recessions in our history. He played a central role in bankrupting one of the world's largest banks which was then bailed out by the taxpayer to the tune of billions of dollars. And through all the destruction, he managed to personally enrich himself by $126 million.

International bankers like Rubin are our elites. They are the ruling class that became dominant in our country after the foundation of the Federal Reserve when they seized control of our money supply. They then proceeded to buy up our media, take over our economy and hijack our government. The agents of these international bankers are easy to spot. Just look for the personalities who move with ease from Wall Street banks, such as Goldman Sachs and JPMorgan Chase, to positions of power in our government, to international institutions, such as the World Bank and the IMF, to their globalist think tanks, such as the Council on Foreign Relations and the Trilateral Commission, and even to our intelligence agencies, such as the CIA and the NSA. These are the people who are transforming our nation from a prosperous and independent republic into a corporatized economic bloc populated by a global proletariat that is ruled in feudalist fashion by a clique of international bankers acting in concert and in secret.

Climate change and global governance

The American media has been telling us for years now that the Earth is getting hotter because of human activity and that something must be done. Media reports about climate change usually tell us that the evidence is clear that the burning of fossil fuels is the cause of global warming and that there is a scientific consensus about this. The media tells us that if current trends continue, global warming will have alarming effects on humanity and on the Earth. Our coasts will be flooded and billions of people will be displaced; crops will fail and famine will kill millions; tropical diseases will spread northward; deserts will expand; hurricanes, tornadoes and other extreme weather will increase; wars will rage due to competition for resources and the stresses caused by the changing climate, among many other negative effects.

In short, global warming will cause disasters to humanity of biblical proportions unless we come together and do something about it.

And what is to be done? The solutions being offered should make us skeptical because they will do little to stop climate change while doing much to bring about global governance.

Obviously, if one were serious about reducing carbon emissions into the atmosphere then our current economic system would be the focus for change. Our current system encourages the extraction of raw materials from around the world, loading them onto giant, carbon-spewing cargo ships and then shipping them to China where environmental regulations are few. Carbon-spewing factories in China turn these raw materials into finished goods which are then loaded back onto carbon-spewing cargo ships and shipped out as finished products around the planet. This is a wasteful and destructive state of affairs, especially if carbon emissions are a cause for concern.

If one were serious about reducing carbon emissions, then trade with China should be the first target for change. Local production should be encouraged and international trade should be subject to a carbon tariff. Instead of the wasteful process of shipping raw materials to China and other low-wage nations where environmental regulations are few, we should put a climate tariff on Chinese-made goods to encourage local production here in the United States where environmental regulations are strict. This would cut back on the wasteful practice of shipping raw materials to China and then shipping finished goods around the world on cargo ships that belch pollution into the air.

If tax incentives were made to encourage local production in the United States over international trade we could reduce a large portion of the pollutants that are spewed into the air during the transport of materials and goods over long distances. Instead of shipping goods from Asia and developing nations where environmental regulations are low compared to the United States, we should produce goods here in the United States and rail and truck them from state to state, which would reduce carbon emissions substantially.

What is the point of increasing environmental regulations in the United States if the result is to push American manufacturers to move to foreign countries where environmental regulations are lax, where they can pollute more into the atmosphere than if they were to stay put here in America? The end result of all of our environmental regulations is to increase pollution by encouraging manufacturers to leave regulated economics for less regulated ones.

What are the solutions to climate change that are being offered to us? The solutions that we are getting are carbon taxes and cap-and-trade schemes that are being pushed by the financial sector. These taxes punish economic production here at home and increase costs for the middle class.

In California, a cap-and-trade system was put into effect in 2012. The state of California has imposed carbon emission limits on businesses but allows businesses to purchase permits if they exceed the limits. Businesses can then buy and sell the permits. The limits on emissions are being lowered each year meaning that the cost of industry in the state is increasing, which either will force businesses to innovate to reduce emissions, drive up costs for consumers, or else force businesses to leave the state.

In California, gas prices are some of the highest in the country. The cost of housing is so high that middle and working class people often have long commutes from outlying suburbs where housing is cheaper to metro areas where the jobs are. The cap-and-trade scheme will directly hurt the middle and working classes by driving up the cost of gas and the cost of living while driving away more productive industries that provide high-paying jobs. California already has an extremely economically stratified population with a small number of very wealthy people, a shrinking middle class and one of the highest poverty rates in the nation. The middle class in California has been shrinking and is being replaced by immigrants who often work for low wages while living in subsidized housing while receiving a variety of government benefits.

Cap-and-trade in California will do nothing to stop global warming but will accelerate the destruction of California's middle class, which was once the envy of the world. In fact, cap-and-trade will most likely increase carbon emissions by driving more industry out of California where environmental regulations are high to places like Mexico and Asia where regulations are low. More pollution is allowed in Asia and Mexico while the transportation of finished goods back to California increases carbon emissions that would not have occurred if production had remained there.

What the cap-and-trade scheme has already accomplished has been to increase government revenues by the billions. From 2012 to 2014, cap-and-trade raised about $2.2 billion for the state government. That money is being funneled into everything from a multi-billion dollar bullet train proposal to affordable housing for immigrants to a variety of schemes to reduce pollution that usually come with an increase in bureaucracy or else crony capitalism where tax money is funneled to "green" companies.

These types of cap-and-trade schemes are being implemented around the developed world and are sold to the public with alarming claims about impending disasters if something is not done right now about global warming. In many cases, the alarmists are making demands that national sovereignty must be relinquished to international institutions in order to save the planet from global disaster.

In 2009, in a speech before the European Parliament, Belgian Prime Minister Herman von Rompuy accepted his appointment to the EU presidency. "We're living through exceptionally difficult times," von Rompuy said. "The financial crisis and its dramatic impact on employment and budgets, the climate crisis which threatens our very survival, a period of anxiety, uncertainty, and lack of confidence. Yet, these problems can be overcome by a joint effort in and between our countries. 2009 is also the first year of Global Governance with the establishment of the G20 in the middle of the financial crisis. The Climate Conference in Copenhagen is another step towards the global management of our planet."

Von Rompuy stated in so many words what the gist of global warming alarmism is all about—global governance and the global management of the planet by people like himself. But make no mistake, if people began to take meaningful action to stop carbon emissions by placing carbon tariffs on imported goods from Asia and started to encourage local production in local economies, the global warming hysteria would end overnight. If people began to point out that free trade and mass immigration is bad for the environment and is accelerating climate change, the internationalists and their media would immediately end the global warming alarmism they have been spreading for the past two decades.

And what is the primary source of all the alarmism about climate change? It is the United Nations International Panel on Climate Change (IPCC).

The IPCC produces study after study and report after report telling us that global warming is going to be a disaster of epic proportions unless something is done globally. Millions are spent by this organization to prove that global warming is occurring.

Don't you think an organization that was formed by

globalists to create a world government would produce reports that urge us to increase that organization's scope and power?

What are the solutions to global warming? Why, global governance, of course!

But let's face it. Even if the United States were to shut down all carbon emissions, this will do nothing to stop global warming. It will only make life more difficult for the American middle and working classes while doing nothing to stop climate change. The Chinese and the Indians and their billions of people are not going to give up their drive to increase their standards of living. Their economies will continue to grow and their production of carbon emissions will not stop, regardless of what we do as a nation. There is no stopping it. Carbon emissions will continue to increase as their economies grow and their people are lifted out of poverty and adopt middle class lifestyles. Our current trade and financial structure has been designed to assist them in their economic growth. While the global warming alarmists tell us that we must change our lifestyles, the financial elite are pouring investment dollars into China and India to help them develop. If these international elites were truly serious about stopping global warming, they would stop pouring American dollars into India and China and instead would enact a carbon tariff to prevent exports from those countries from entering our own country due to the wastefulness of producing consumer goods on one side of the planet for people who live on the other side.

Essentially, the global warming argument is that carbon dioxide levels in the atmosphere began to rise at the start of the industrial revolution in the 1800s. The argument goes that carbon dioxide is a greenhouse gas that retains heat. By increasing the level of carbon dioxide in the atmosphere the temperature of the Earth will rise, causing all manner of calamity.

The proof that increased levels of carbon dioxide will cause climate change is offered to us through computer models of the atmosphere. These models predict a future of rising temperatures, flooding, increased frequency of violent weather, droughts, famine, etc. But these computer models have been notoriously wrong in predicting the temperature over the past 20 years. These models cannot even predict the past. If you put the actual composition of the atmosphere from some past date into these computer models, they can't even predict what actually occurred in reality. Think about this for a second. What kind of real scientist believes a computer model can predict the future? What kind of scientist believes he can accurately forecast what is going to occur 30, 50 or 100 years from now? And we are supposed to increase our taxes and put in place global governance based on claims that computers can predict the future of the Earth's climate? We would be fools to fall for this nonsense. Does anyone actually believe that governments can stop the climate from changing?

Science does not predict the future. That is the realm of priests, prophets and fortune tellers. Scientists, by using the scientific method, make observations and form hypotheses, which can be tested. When the hypotheses are proven wrong, they are abandoned and new hypotheses are formed.

Pay attention to the climate change debate. When the models are wrong, they are not abandoned but are defended by the media. All observations about the climate, whether a summer is exceptionally hot or a winter is exceptionally cold, are used to bolster the argument for climate change. Data that supports global warming is promoted in the media while any observations and data that throw doubt on warming are attacked. Skeptics are called "deniers" and are treated like heretics. Global warming adherents discuss among themselves how to make doubters believe them. Their thinking is less science and more religion. This is because the promoters of global warming are not true scientists but instead are being used by people with deep pockets who are pushing a global agenda for global governance. Global warming fearmongering is merely a tool they are using in an attempt to achieve an agenda.

One thing that is not often said in this debate is that the history of life on this planet is the history of climate change. The climate of the Earth has always been changing. From about a billion to about 50 million years ago, the Earth had no regular ice ages. The Earth was much warmer than today for much of its history and had no ice caps. Snowy winters in the northern hemisphere and permanent glaciers are a relatively new phenomenon beginning 40 million years ago—more than 25 million years after the extinction of the dinosaurs.

The Antarctic ice sheet began to form around 45 million years ago. Due to plate tectonics and continental drift, the current position of Antarctica over the South Pole, and the fact that the Arctic Sea is boxed in by the North American and Siberian land masses—this favors the retention of ice at the poles.

The current ice age, called the Pliocene-Quaternary glaciation, started about 2.58 million years ago. Since then, the world has seen cycles of glaciation when ice sheets have advanced, followed by warmer interglacial periods when ice sheets have retreated. The advances of the ice sheets have lasted from about 40,000 to 100,000 years. Interglacials have lasted anywhere from about 8,000 to 20,000 years.

We are currently in an interglacial period called the Holocene that began about 11,700 years ago when the Earth began to warm again and the massive ice sheets that covered much of North America, Europe and Siberia began to recede. During the ice age before the onset of the Holocene, humans lived in small bands of hunter gatherers on a much colder and drier planet. Civilizations began to arise when the Holocene began as the Earth warmed and humans began to practice agriculture.

The ice age that preceded the Holocene was 120,000 years long. What is little discussed during the climate debate is the interglacial that preceded ours. That interglacial is called the Eemian. The Eemian began about 130,000 years ago and ended about 115,000 years ago.

About 130,000 years ago when the Eemian interglacial began, the ice receded and the Earth became warmer and wetter than our current interglacial. Forests extended well above the tundra line that exists today. Hippos lived in the Thames and Rhine rivers in Europe. Scandinavia was an island due to sea levels that were 13 to 20 feet higher than today.

Imagine Europe as a warm place with hippos, lions, hyenas, baboons and gazelles. That was Europe during the Eemian.

A warmer world is wetter, more humid with more vegetation. During ice ages when the Earth is colder, the planet is drier and dustier with larger deserts.

The Earth has been much colder than today, and it has been much warmer than our current interglacial. What is certain is that the climate is going to change again, either warmer or cooler, and there is nothing anyone can do about it. If the history of the planet is anything to go by, the only certainty is that the climate will change and it will change dramatically. It will change rapidly and it will change again and again and again. Some day the Earth will cool and the ice sheets will advance. Or the Earth might once again warm and ice sheets in Greenland and Antarctica will melt and sea levels will rise. The continents will continue to drift and effect the climate and the evolution of life on Earth. The Earth's orbit, the cycles of the sun and the composition of the atmosphere will all change, regardless of human activity.

Humans are not apart from nature. The same unbending natural laws that rule our universe rule us just as they do every other species. Humans are part of nature and not separate from it. We humans affect our environment just as beavers, elephants, termites and plankton do.

We all want a clean environment. We all want less pollution. But anyone who thinks global governance, cap-and-trade, green companies or any other scheme dreamed up in the global warming community will somehow stop climate change, that person is seriously deluded, or else lying to pursue a globalist agenda.

If the past is anything to go by, our current civilization will not end if the Earth warms. It will end when the planet cools and becomes much colder and drier. It will end when the snow continues to fall on the northern hemisphere until it buries it. Someday the snow pack will grow and thicken until Europe, North America and Siberia are once again buried under massive sheets of ice. This has happened before and it will happen again.

The survivors will be those who are most adaptable and best able to cope with a changing climate. But, make no mistake, no one can do anything to stop climate change, which happens to be a natural characteristic of planet Earth and which was the main driver of the evolutionary change that resulted in the advent of the Homo sapiens species.

The Tyranny of Mass Immigration

We are a nation of immigrants. How many times over your lifetime have you heard that the United States is a nation of immigrants? This notion is constantly drilled into our heads by our schools, the media and our government.

But it is a propaganda term used to support a specific government policy favored by moneyed people with an agenda.

In 1787 in the *Federalist Papers*, John Jay wrote: "With equal pleasure I have as often taken notice that Providence has been pleased to give this one connected country to one united people—a people descended from the same ancestors, speaking the same language, professing the same religion, attached to the same principles of government, very similar in their manners and customs, and who, by their joint counsels, arms, and efforts, fighting side by side throughout a long and bloody war, have nobly established general liberty and independence."

The Founders of this country did not consider themselves immigrants and did not consider the United States a nation of immigrants. They did not consider the black man, the Indian or the Spaniard, and often the Catholic, to be American citizens with the same rights in this country as themselves. They had created the United States of America for people like themselves and their posterity. Just as France was French and China was Chinese and England was English, they saw the United States as American populated by a distinct people with a common culture and a common heritage.

But in America, there has always been a demand by the investor class for labor. The investor class views human beings not as citizens or as free people with rights and dreams and aspirations of their own, but as labor—an expense, a commodity to be purchased as cheaply as possible. The problem in America for the moneyed classes was that labor was scarce and expensive and wages were too high. Due to the abundance of land and opportunity, the common laborer would sooner strike out on his own than toil for wages for an employer. This problem of expensive labor in America was first solved with indentured servitude, then with African chattel slavery, and later with mass immigration.

The "land of immigrants" propagandists would have us believe that America was settled by immigrants and that immigration to America is a necessity, and that immigration has always been constant and must continue in perpetuity. We are a land for all the world's huddled teeming masses yearning to be free. They would have us believe that we always have been and always will be a nation where a steady flood of immigrants is welcomed to our shores year after year, more than a million a year, for the rest of our history.

But this is not the story of immigration to America. The true story is that America was settled by a particular group of people who came here and took the continent by force of arms and numbers and then fought to break free from an oppressive empire that ruled over them. They attained their freedom and created a new nation for themselves that was free and prosperous. However, from the very beginning, wealthy investors wanted to exploit America's resources to earn passive income streams off the labor of others. To do this they needed cheap labor. Immigration became a source of cheap labor once slavery was abolished.

Throughout our history, plutocrats have always worked to increase immigration into the United States. They brought immigrants in waves to work at low wages in the fields, sweatshops, mines and factories. The results of these waves of immigration were declining wages for Americans, increased poverty, increased prices for the necessities of life, increased crime and the alienation of the people born here.

The native-born in America have always been tolerant of newcomers, but as the waves of foreigners arriving on our shores began to decrease the quality of American life, opposition to immigration would organize and the number of foreigners allowed to come in would be restricted. That is the story of immigration to America—investors flooding our shores with cheap labor for as long as they could until the limits of tolerance of the native born were reached and the flood was restricted. Once immigration was restricted and the flow of foreigners into the country slowed, the immigrants assimilated into the majority American population. The ties to the old country loosened and the immigrants set down roots here, both social and economic. They learned our language, absorbed our culture and inherited our values and lifestyle. They had children and within a generation or two their descendants were as American as those who could trace their roots back to the Mayflower. The ethnic solidarity, chauvinisms and ethnocentric interests of the immigrant gave way to American interests and values. Immigration restrictionism that resulted from native-born backlashes against the rising tide of foreigners in our country allowed those foreigners to assimilate and gain an economic foothold here in the United States.

Immigration into the United States was severely restricted from 1921 until 1965. But since 1965, we have been experiencing the largest, longest and most diverse wave of immigration in our nation's history. The results have been profound. Our nation is changing before our eyes under this latest wave. Our living standards are in decline while more wealth concentrates in fewer hands as the cheap labor floods in. You cannot have cheap labor without poverty. Poverty is being imported into our county to the tune of a million people a year. Our culture, our traditions and our freedoms are disappearing before our eyes. Ethnic interests lobby our government for participation in overseas wars that are against American interests and are killing off our youth and destroying our economy. They lobby for ethnic specific benefits and for privileges for their home countries. The process of assimilation has broken down as population growth by immigration exceeds that from births from our native born. Instead of immigrants being assimilated into American life, the American people are being assimilated by immigrants. Like the American Indian, we Americans are being demographically overwhelmed by new people coming to our shores who are changing the face of the continent with their numbers.

This national destruction is the result of a deliberate government policy promoted by the transnational elite that has hijacked our government and media for its own ends. Mass immigration is the policy of international bankers, as was slavery before it.

Their propaganda for more immigration is relentless, focused and financed by unlimited amounts of money. They would have us believe that all this immigration is a benefit to us. They would have us believe that we are not actually Americans, but we are immigrants ourselves—no matter how many generations back we can trace our ancestry in this country. They would have us believe that Americans are not a people, but just an idea, and that all people from around the world are Americans as soon as they set foot here.

The Americans who fought the Revolutionary War and the Founders who wrote our Constitution did not consider themselves immigrants. They were, for the most part, descendants of English colonists who had crossed the Atlantic to build a new life in a new world. They were Christians, they spoke English, they dressed in a certain way and had very specific customs and values. They were not a diverse bunch of people from every corner of the globe. By the time of the Revolutionary War, the majority of the people fighting on the American side could trace their heritage in the Thirteen Colonies back more than 100 years.

English colonists began arriving in what is now New England in the early 1600s. These colonists were adventurers, explorers, pioneers and religious pilgrims escaping persecution. They found a sparsely populated land that was rich in natural resources.

The first English colonists did not come as immigrants to a country with a government. They came as settlers who were attempting to establish their civilization in a wilderness. The American Indians who populated the land had been devastated by diseases from the Old World, some tribes losing half their populations. Much of the land the Indians had occupied as farmers and hunter-gatherers had been depopulated as epidemics spread through their communities.

The Indians were technologically behind the new arrivals from the Old World. They were small in number, divided by language and culture and often at war with each other.

The English colonists found New England to be ideal for their form of civilization. They began farming and exploiting the natural resources of the land. The New World was so favorable to them that they began to multiply in great numbers.

A poor, landless Englishman could come across the Atlantic to the colonies, strike out into the wilderness and claim his own land. He held on to it with knife and musket. By the work of his own hand he could build his own home and farm the land and become far more prosperous than he ever could back in England. With land, work to be done and plenty more open land to the west, the colonists married much earlier than their countrymen back in England and had more children.

Small English settlements quickly grew into towns which grew into cities.

The American Indians watched as the land they loved and called their own quickly became the property of others. The Indians did not view these newcomers as immigrants, but as invaders. The Indians and the English soon came into conflict, most notably in the Pequot War of 1634-1638. The Pequots fought for their land but lost. They were killed and sold into slavery and their land was stolen from them.

This was a theme for the American Indian that continued for the next 250 years.

The great Indian nations—the Iroquois, Cherokee, Sioux, Apache, Comanche, Navajo, Chumash, Chinook and countless others—they resisted the great human tide that was washing over them. They fought fiercely for their land and to preserve their cultures and their lifestyle. But they were divided by language and culture and often at war with themselves as they were being demographically overrun by Europeans who were politically united by language and culture and who had superior technology, weapons and tactics. The Indians were vastly outnumbered and unable to hold back the expansion of the United States as the American people moved westward across the continent.

Benjamin Franklin, in his essay *Observations Concerning the Increase of Mankind, Peopling of Countries, etc.* wrote that because land was plentiful and cheap in North America, the American colonist could easily support a large family. Franklin reckoned that each American family raised at least eight children compared to four back in Europe. In the year of his writing in 1751, Franklin stated that there were upwards of 1 million English souls in North America, yet only about 80,000 had come from over the sea. The American population was doubling every 25 years and was destined to overtake the population of the Mother Country and populate the continent.

The vast majority of people in the Thirteen Colonies at the time he was writing his essay had been born in North America and had parents that had also been born here. They were not immigrants but born of this land.

In 1885, more than 130 years after Franklin wrote his essay, the American general and president Ulysses S. Grant wrote in his autobiography that his family was American in all its branches and had been for generations. Grant traced his heritage in America back eight generations to 1630 when the first Grant in his line arrived in Massachusetts from Dorchester, England.

Today, we speak English because this land was conquered and settled by English colonists. We inherited our government and our culture from them and their descendants. They came here in small numbers and multiplied greatly because of the bounty and opportunity this land offered them.

Their experience coming here and surviving in a new world far away from the Mother Country shaped our culture and who we are today. Those first colonists survived in the New World due to their self-reliance, work ethic and the ability to organize and govern themselves far away from the central authority in England.

They had come from a country with a strict class structure and a government that considered them subjects to be exploited. Because the Mother Country was distant, social class became less important than the value each person brought to his or her community through talent and hard work. The colonists grew accustomed to the liberty they found in the New World as opposed to oppression from the overbearing government they had known back in England. They grew accustomed to retaining the fruits of their own labor and to the prosperity that their own efforts brought them. They became accustomed to the hope and opportunity that the New World offered them. Their experiences changed them and made them different from their fellow Englishmen back in the Mother Country. They became different in culture, in dialect, in outlook, in living standards and in social organization. They became a new people, the American people. By 1775, the differences between themselves and their cousins back in England had become great and the discord they had with the British government had become so intolerable that it led to war.

The Americans won the war and founded a new nation independent of English rule and organized under American principles. It was a nation where all men were considered equal under the law and where the rights to life, liberty and the pursuit of happiness were held dear.

The Founders lived in a small homogenous country that was surrounded by enemies. They did not consider themselves a multicultural nation open to all peoples. They considered themselves a distinct people surrounded by enemies. That was the whole reason they wrote the Constitution and unified into a single republic, so they could defend themselves as one against foreigners. They were a people who had almost always been at war; with the Indians, the Dutch, the French, the Spanish and the English. They broke away from England and founded the United States of America in order to free themselves from foreign rule and to unite the colonies so that they as a people would become strong enough to defend themselves from outsiders.

Benjamin Franklin thought of Americans as a distinct branch of the English people—the descendants of English settlers who had come to the New World in search of freedom and opportunity. In *Observations Concerning the Increase of Mankind, Peopling of Countries, etc.,* Franklin wrote that he did not consider German immigrants in Pennsylvania to be Americans like himself, calling them Palantine Boors after the province they had come from in Germany. Franklin did not even consider Germans to be white like himself.

Franklin wrote: "And since detachments of English born Britain sent to America, will have their places at home so soon supply'd and increase so largely here; why should the Palatine Boors be suffered to swarm into our settlements, and by herding together establish their languages and manners to the exclusion of ours? Why should Pennsylvania, founded by the English, become a colony of Aliens, who will shortly be so numerous as to Germanize us instead of our Anglifying them, and will never adopt our language or customs, any more than they can acquire our complexion?"

In short, the Founders of this country considered themselves a distinct people—descendants of English settlers who spoke a common language, had a common religion and a common culture.

They formed a government to correct the wrongs that had been committed by English rule and to protect the liberty that they had found and valued in the New World.

When Thomas Jefferson wrote in the Declaration of Independence that all men are created equal, he was not talking about black men that men like himself held in slavery. He was not talking about American Indians that were being conquered and driven off their land by men like himself. He was only talking about men who were like himself.

While the American people were willing to fight and die for their liberty and independence, they were also willing to hold other people in slavery. This contradiction has been a great stain on our history. Many of the men who spoke so eloquently about freedom were slave owners and were denying freedom to others.

Our early leaders and presidents took great pride in their humble beginnings and in being self-made men. For the young American man, the United States was a land of boundless opportunity. It was a land where anyone regardless of birth, could strike out on his own and through his own efforts build a fortune and even become president. Except for the black man or the American Indian.

For the black person, America was a land of bondage without opportunity or even free will.

How did this great contradiction arise?

Benjamin Franklin gives us insights: "... so vast is the Territory of North America, that it will require many ages to settle it fully; and till it is fully settled, labour will never be cheap here, where no man continues long a labourer for others, but gets a Plantation of his own, no man continues long a journeyman to a trade, but goes among those new settlers and sets up for himself, &c. Hence labour is no cheaper now in Pennsylvania, than it was thirty years ago, tho so many thousand labouring people have been imported."

In early America, labor was scarce and land was plentiful. This caused wages to be higher than back in Europe. If a laborer was unhappy with his wages or with working for someone, he could always strike out on his own and work for himself.

This caused a dilemma for the moneyed men back in London. They saw America as a land of great riches where enormous profits could be made. But labor was scarce and expensive. How do you get people to toil in the hot sun growing tobacco and cotton when there is opportunity for them to strike out on their own and farm land that they own themselves?

Chattel slavery ended in England in the 13th century. Much of the immigration to the American colonies in the 1600s was from indentured servants who paid their passage across the Atlantic by signing contracts to work for employers for a fixed number of years. The system of indentured servitude supplied labor to plantations; however, the indentured servants were set free after their terms were up. The system did not meet the demands for labor.

The demand was met through the African slave trade. By the end of the 1600s, African slaves began to rapidly replace European indentured servants in the South. Unlike their European counterparts, African slaves were enslaved for life. Because of their physical differences from the majority of the population, it was difficult for them to escape and assimilate without being noticed by bounty hunters.

Plantation owners borrowed money from London bankers to purchase slaves. They then paid off their debts by selling cash crops, such as tobacco and cotton, to England. This was known as the Atlantic triangular slave trade.

The demand for labor in the Americas was so high that millions of Africans were captured and enslaved and sent to the New World where they endured a lifetime of toil and bondage.

The barbarity and the corruption caused by this practice was known from the start. Franklin pointed out that African slaves were worked too hard, ill fed, their constitutions broken and their death rates high. He stated that African slavery depressed the wages of white laborers while corrupting white slave owners, causing them to be disgusted by labor, idle, proud and unfit to make a living through industry.

Thomas Jefferson, our most eloquent and revolutionary champion of liberty who wrote that all men are created equal, recognized his own hypocrisy in being a slave owner. He called slavery a "foul stain," yet he allowed himself to remain part of an economic system that permitted one group of people to oppress and profit off another. Jefferson wrote so knowledgeably and passionately about freedom because he understood slavery and he understood usury and debt. He owed his fortune and estate to moneylenders and slavery, and he died under a heavy burden of debt. His reputation will always be questioned because of the dark shadow cast by his ownership of slaves.

The debate over slavery raged in the United States for more than half a century. The abolitionists grew steadily more righteous while the slave owners became more indignant and rebellious. The Southern economy and way of life was dependent on this corruptive system of race-based chattel slavery. The plantation owners believed their world would end without this system of exploitation. After all, who would pick the cotton if slavery was abolished?

Our great national sin of slavery came to a head in 1861 when Abraham Lincoln was elected president. The punishment for this sin was the worst bloodletting in our history in which more than half a million Americans were killed in an internecine war that tore our nation apart.

But with the Union victory, slavery was abolished. In 1868, the Fourteenth Amendment was ratified giving black Americans what had previously been denied them—citizenship in the United States and the right to vote. The amendment made it illegal for any state to deprive them or any other citizen the right to life, liberty or property, without the due process of law.

The Fourteenth Amendment was a national recognition that black people were here from the start and had built this country and rightfully had the privilege of citizenship just the same as their white countrymen. That recognition was made legal and official, but of course, old prejudices rooted in race and history remained, and are still be worked out in our present day.

Slavery had been abolished but the need for cheap labor remained. However, the economy had changed radically since the nation's founding. The money men no longer needed armies of slaves to pick cotton and tobacco. They needed workers for Northern sweatshops and factories as the Industrial Age promised greater profits than the Atlantic triangular slave trade could ever produce.

But how do you induce a free American citizen to voluntarily toil for hours on end in a sweatshop for meager wages? This is a difficult proposition in a country where land is plentiful and opportunity is great.

George Orwell, in an essay called *Inside the Whale*, about the American writer Henry Miller, explained a change that came over

America as the demands of the Industrial Age took hold. Orwell described how Walt Whitman and early American writers were influenced by the freedom and prosperity they had experienced in the United States in our country's youth before the onset of the Industrial Age. Orwell wrote: "Whitman was writing in a time of unexampled prosperity, but more than that, he was writing in a country where freedom was something more than a word. The democracy, equality, and comradeship that he is always talking about are not remote ideals, but something that existed in front of his eyes. In mid-nineteenth-century America men felt themselves free and equal, were free and equal, so far as that is possible outside a society of pure communism. There was poverty and there were even class distinctions, but except for the Negroes there was no permanently submerged class. Everyone had inside him, like a kind of core, the knowledge that he could earn a decent living, and earn it without bootlicking. When you read about Mark Twain's Mississippi raftsmen and pilots, or Bret Harte's Western gold-miners, they seem more remote than the cannibals of the Stone Age. The reason is simply that they are free human beings. But it is the same even with the peaceful domesticated America of the Eastern states, the America of the *Little Women, Helen's Babies, and Riding Down from Bangor*. Life has a buoyant, carefree quality that you can feel as you read, like a physical sensation in your belly. It is this that Whitman is celebrating, though actually he does it very badly, because he is one of those writers who tell you what you ought to feel instead of making you feel it. Luckily for his beliefs, perhaps, he died too early to see the deterioration in American life that came with the rise of large-scale industry and the exploiting of cheap immigrant labour."

In America before cheap immigrant labor, life had a buoyant, carefree quality. We were a free people where democracy, equality and comradeship were the reality of the day—a reality given to us by those who had fought the Revolution and formed a new government based on American principles. For those Americans who were not slaves, they could earn a decent living without bootlicking.

Of course, for the wealthy investor class, this state of affairs could not stand. The members of the investor class want to earn returns on their investments. It was this class that gave us slavery. With the end of slavery, the investor class still needed cheap labor.

This class does not favor a society of free human beings who are safe in the knowledge that they can earn a decent living without bootlicking. The investor class seeks passive income. It does not work. To collect passive income, it needs labor and it needs it cheap. And labor is not cheap without poverty.

When the rich plutocrat back in London looked at America, he did not see a land of people with dreams and needs and a culture of their own. He saw a land rich in natural resources but scarce in labor. Labor was too expensive in America. This was a dilemma, a problem to be solved. If he invested his gold to exploit America's resources, too much of it would be wasted on wages for labor. With slavery abolished, the plutocrats needed a new source of cheap labor that did not require the high wages that American citizens demanded.

America was a land of prosperous, free people. Americans were a people that had other options than working as wage laborers in the sweatshops, factories and mines owned by wealthy men seeking passive income streams. If Americans wanted gold, like the miners in the stories by Bret Harte, they would sooner strike out into the wilderness and dig it up themselves than toil in a mine for a wage paid by some faraway investor.

But unlike America, the rest of the world was teeming with wretched refuse yearning to breathe free. The rest of the world had a surplus of tired, poor, huddled masses eager to work for subsistence wages. Moneyed investors desired to bring the world's homeless across the tempest-tossed sea to America to work in sweatshops, mines, forests and factories because the world's poor would work for less pay than Americans would.

When the plutocrats looked at Europe—especially at Eastern and Southern Europe—they saw a land of paupers where labor was cheap and abundant. Unlike Americans, these paupers were desperate and indigent enough to readily toil hours on end for the chance to earn just enough to feed themselves. The trick was to get the cheap labor across the ocean so that investments in America could be more profitable without wasting too much of the investment on paying wages.

The solution was simple. Bring a ship to Southern or Eastern Europe. Tell the paupers that they can borrow money to pay their passage to a land where the streets are paved in gold. The paupers could borrow money for passage and pay it back by working in sweatshops or mines until their debts were paid off. In this way, all the cheap labor needed is made available, and the paupers even pay their own passage, with interest, for the chance to toil in low-paid jobs across the sea.

This was an elegant solution for the investor class. Slavery was a barbaric and costly institution, but this new system of wage slavery was voluntary. The laborer was not kidnapped and whipped into submission, but had agreed to work for the chance to earn enough to survive. Unlike the slave, the wage earner was often grateful to have the chance to work to earn his daily bread. And unlike the slave, the wage laborer paid for his own food, shelter and for his own subsistence in his old age.

Immigrants were preferred by employers for multiple reasons. They would work longer hours for less pay than an American worker. They did not speak the language so they were outsiders here and had difficulty organizing to defend their interests or speak out against abuses. They did not understand our culture and our rights as citizens and could be exploited without standing up for themselves. In short, they would toil in poverty to enrich the investor class unlike American citizens.

To understand the purpose of mass immigration in this country and how the rich use immigrants for their own purposes, a look at the history of the Colorado mining town of Ludlow gives us some insights.

Coal mining was a lucrative business in Colorado at the turn of the 20th century. But it was deadly work. Miners of the day had a high mortality rate. In order to have enough miners to work at low wages, Colorado Fuel and Iron, a corporation owned by John D. Rockefeller and heirs of the financier Jay Gould, turned to immigrant labor.

The great fear of the owners of Colorado Fuel and Iron was that the miners would organize and demand higher wages and safer working conditions, which would cut into corporate profits. In response to a labor strike by the largely American miners, the company responded by bringing in immigrants from Mexico, Italy, Greece, Poland, Russia, and other European nations, to work the mines. The immigrant miners worked for less than $2 a day and were often paid in company scrip—pieces of paper printed by the company that could only be used to purchase goods at the company store.

The company mixed the immigrant work crews in the mines by ethnicity, which discouraged communication because of language barriers and cultural differences. This helped to prevent the immigrant miners from organizing to improve their work environment. The company also encouraged competition between the different ethnic groups to push them toward more productivity.

However, by late 1913, the immigrant miners had been pushed to their limits and went on strike. The Colorado National Guard was called in as tensions between the miners and mine operators reached a boiling point. Rockefeller paid the wages of the guardsmen who had been brought in to restore order. These guardsmen were Americans who looked at the miners as disruptive foreigners.

On April 20, 1914, a series of incidents escalated into a gunfight between the guardsmen and the immigrant miners. The guardsmen attacked a tent colony where the families of the miners were hiding. The attack and the ensuing fires resulting in the deaths of two women and 11 children. More were killed as they attempted to flee. Strike leader Louis Tikas, a Greek immigrant, was found dead shot in the back.

The ensuing rioting and violence resulted in the deaths of at least 66 men, women and children in what is now known as the

Ludlow Massacre.

The Ludlow Massacre is an extreme example, yet it illuminates the true nature of immigration and the relationship between our country's wealthy elite and immigrants.

Mass immigration propagandists have been selling us a story about America being a nation of immigrants—that our country is a beacon of freedom and opportunity for people around the world.

But the true nature of immigration involves a desire by corporate robber barons to flood the labor market with immigrants to undercut wages and weaken the organizing power of the American people. The employers of immigrant labor may talk about how wonderful immigration is and about how their immigrant workers are good, hard-working people doing jobs that Americans won't do, but when the immigrants get too uppity and make demands on their employers, watch out. Those employers are using them because of their vulnerability as outsiders and because of their willingness to take more abuse for less pay—not because of any special love for immigrants. These employers want bootlickers, not citizens with rights and better options.

Of course, the majority of immigrants are good, hard-working people who are trying to better themselves. They come here for opportunity and for freedom. But they are serving a purpose that is detrimental to the American people. They are being used for a purpose and are pitted against the native born for economic and political reasons that are detrimental to the country at large. Bringing in foreigners from every corner of the globe creates language and cultural barriers, alienation, and it breaks down solidarity and national cohesion. It lowers living standards for the average person while concentrating wealth into the hands of the few. It burdens our schools, hospitals and infrastructure. Mass immigration raises costs on such things as rents, housing and the necessities of life while putting downward pressure on wages.

If your aim is to lower wages, break down national identity and submerge a people into the global proletariat, which has no national identity or loyalty to the nation in which it resides, then mass immigration is a useful tool. If your aim is to create a North American Union, then you will want to demographically overwhelm the native-born population that identifies with the United States and values our Constitution and our heritage and is resistant to surrendering its sovereignty to supranational institutions. You will want to overwhelm our Southwestern border states with Spanish speaking immigrants so that when open borders are made official they won't resist but rather will welcome it.

Mass immigration is not a policy being pushed by the American majority, but is instead a policy of wealthy plutocrats. They spend hundreds of millions pushing for this policy.

Some of the richest men in the world are pushing this policy on us. Bill Gates, George Soros, Mark Zuckerberg, Sheldon Adelson, the Koch brothers, Michael Bloomberg, Larry Ellison, Rupert Murdoch and Carlos Slim—billionaires all—are all promoters and activists for more mass immigration into the United States. They bankroll ethnocentric activists and use the media to continually push for policies that bring more immigrants into the United States. This is not the 1 percent, but a tiny fraction of the 1 percent, the richest subsection of humanity. Do you think these extremely wealthy individuals are advocating for more immigration into the United States for our best interests? No. They are using foreign-born poor to bring down the American-born middle class for their own ends.

In a March 1, 2015 article in *Salon* titled, *The 1 percent's immigration con: How big business adds to income inequality, pits workers against each other*, Philip Cafaro explained that progressives are being conned into supporting an immigration policy that hurts labor and benefits the wealthiest sector of society.

"Consider that since 1965, changing policies have increased U.S. immigration numbers from 250,000 to approximately 1.3 million annually (legal and illegal). That is four times higher than any other country on Earth," Cafaro wrote.

"The upshot has been flooded labor markets for less-skilled workers in the United States, with predictable results. Wages have been driven down. Benefits have been slashed. Employers have been able to break unions, often helped by immigrant replacement workers. Long-term unemployment among poorer Americans has greatly increased. Mass immigration is not the only cause of these trends, but many economists believe it has played an important part in driving them," Cafaro wrote.

"In recent decades, mass immigration arguably has harmed poorer workers and increased economic inequality in the United States. But this should not surprise us. By importing millions of poor people into the United States and setting them in competition with other poor people for scarce jobs, we drive down wages and increase unemployment among those who can least afford it. Our current era of gross economic inequality, low wages and persistently high unemployment seems like precisely the wrong time to expand immigration.

"Arguably, today, progressives concerned about American workers should advocate reductions in legal immigration. After all, immigration can go up as well as down. Just as Congress increased immigration levels in the 1960s, 1980s and 1990s, it could decrease immigration levels today, at a time when tens of millions of Americans are unemployed and the majority suffers from stagnating wages. Perhaps a moratorium on non-essential immigration is in order, until the official unemployment rate declines below 5 percent and stays there for several years in a row, or until real wages for the bottom half of American workers increase by 25 percent or more," he wrote.

In short, mass immigration benefits wealthy corporatists while weakening the middle and working classes. Mass immigration is a tool of the globalists who want to end American independence and end the American people as a nationality and replace us with a continental economic trading bloc ruled by supranational institutions that are not beholden to the Constitution or the American electorate. If your far-reaching aim is to create a world system of financial control in private hands able to dominate the political system of each country and the economy of the world as a whole, controlled in feudalist fashion by the central banks of the world acting in concert, by secret agreements arrived at in frequent meetings and conferences, then mass immigration policy is a means to achieving that aim.

The rich are constantly lobbying for more immigration. Lobbying done by such organizations as Partnership for a New American Economy, formed by Michael Bloomberg, Rupert Murdoch, Bob Iger, Steve Ballmer and a handful of other globalist plutocrats, are pushing hard for more immigration into the United States. Billionaires are using their billions to push for amnesty for illegal immigrants, a streamlined process for filling jobs with immigrants and to increase opportunities for immigrants to enter the United States workforce "so that we can attract and keep the best, the brightest and the hardest-working, who will strengthen our economy," according to the Partnership for a New American Economy website.

The media is relentless in telling us about all the benefits of immigration and how our diversity is our strength. The *New York Times* tells us day in and day out about the hardships that immigrants endure and about their hopes and dreams and their love for this country. We are told about the honor graduates that fear deportation and about families being torn apart by our immigration policies. Meanwhile, the *Wall Street Journal* tells us about immigrant entrepreneurs who create jobs and wealth here, about economic growth caused by immigration and about a labor shortage in America that can only be filled by more than a million immigrants coming into our country year after year.

Anyone who questions the media's narrative is shouted down as a bigot or racist.

But when does the media tell us about the wage stagnation caused by immigration? When do they talk about the economic and social upheaval caused by the importation of more than a million people from overseas each year? When do they tell us about the crime and gangs in our neighborhoods, the decline in the quality of our schools, the closure of our hospitals and the reduction in our quality of life?

When do they tell us that not only does immigration have negative effects on America, but also on the home countries where these immigrants come from? If we must compete to bring in the best, the brightest and the hardest-working from abroad, aren't their home countries injured by so much talent leaving their shores? Wouldn't their best and brightest be serving their own countries by staying home? Or are they all supposed to come over here to increase profits for our billionaires?

In 2014, the population of the United States reached 316 million people. The majority of our population growth since 1965 has been from immigrants and their children. We are the third most populous nation in the world behind only China and India. With 316 million people living in our country, there can be no labor shortage. We have more labor than we know what to do with. We have a surplus of labor which is resulting in wage stagnation and a declining standard of living.

With productivity increasing due to technological development and as automation becomes more prevalent, the labor surplus in our country will only continue to grow. Do we really need to continue such high levels of immigration?

At what point do we finally say that America is full? At 350 million people? At 400 million? Or perhaps at a billion people, like in China and India?

Is that the goal of our current immigration policy? To reach 1 billion people here in the United States?

We are never told at what population immigration should stop.

We are told by the *New York Times*, the *Wall Street Journal* and all the corporate mainstream media outlets that immigration brings economic growth. More immigrants means more businesses, more workers, more houses, more apartment buildings, more strip malls, more freeways, more development all around as more people need food, shelter, transportation, consumer goods, entertainment and services.

In short, more immigration means filling up and paving over our remaining open spaces as more people come in. This type of economic development is a human Ponzi scheme that benefits developers and those who profit off cheap labor, but does it enhance the standard of living for the rest of us?

Like all Ponzi schemes, it will not end well.

Perhaps some may think that we are better off today with 316 million people than we were when we had 195 million back in 1965 before the current wave of mass immigration began. But was the economic growth brought on by mass immigration worth the crowding and environmental destruction that it wrought if we would have kept the low level of immigration that we had between 1924 and 1965?

Will we be better off in 2050 when our population reaches 440 million if current immigration levels continue?

Let's face it. The mass immigrationists won't ever talk about when our current immigration levels should end because they have an end goal in mind, and mass immigration is a key component to reaching that goal. They don't want to plant a seed in our head that immigration policy can return to restrictionism. They want high levels of immigration to continue until America can be dissolved as an independent nation and absorbed into a North American Union that is ruled by international institutions that are in private hands. That is key to their agenda of mass immigration.

Their agenda is to transform the United States from what it was into what they want it to be—a nation not of Americans with a common language, a common culture, and a common national identity; but a nation of immigrants from every corner of the globe. The agenda is to internationalize our population until we have no national identity left—to transform us into a nation of many peoples speaking many languages with many national identities—a multicultural nation without borders where the American people are no more.

This is not only a phenomenon occurring in the United States. It is occurring across the Western world. It would be occurring in Japan as well if the globalists had their way, except the Japanese national identity is too strong and the arguments in the media for more immigration there are rejected by both the public and Japanese leadership.

The agenda is clear—mass immigration to the Western nations. The international bankers are behind this policy. It is their money that pushes this agenda in the media, think tanks, immigrant activist organizations and government. The reasons for this policy are twofold: to break down the national identities of nation states and to drive down wages in the wealthy nations by creating a surplus of impoverished laborers. They want wage parity between the rich Western nations and the poor nations of the developing world. They want a single global proletariat, not a world of nations with independent peoples.

The Western nations were flooded with immigrants in the years after World War II due to changes in government immigration policies that were carefully planned, pushed and promoted. Nations that were once fairly homogenous, such as France, Britain, Germany, Sweden and Australia, now have large immigrant populations, and the media is trying to convince the populations in each of these countries that they are also "nations of immigrants."

France is being called a nation of immigrants by its media. So is Sweden, if you can believe that.

Periodically, immigrant populations in Europe rise up and riot against their hosts. In 2014, Sweden and France experienced immigrant riots. France, which has a very large immigrant population, suffered through massive immigrant riots in 2005 that resulted in the government declaring a state of emergency that lasted three months.

The media is key to the continuation of mass immigration policy. And our politicians are unified in their belief that mass immigration is a good thing and beneficial to our nation, because if they speak out against it their financial backers and the media will turn on them. In our media, whether it's the *New York Times* or the *Wall Street Journal*, MSNBC or Fox News, we hear about the benefits of immigration and the struggles of immigrants; that the hardships of immigrants are due to our own shortcomings as a people in not being welcoming enough to them. Whether it is the left or the right, the policy being pushed is the same—more immigration.

Immigration is always portrayed as positive, and any questioning of immigration policy or mention that there are negative effects as well as positive are met with name-calling and smears. Mass immigration advocates are always on guard for the rise of "restrictionism" and "nativism." Anyone who speaks out against letting more than a million people into our country every year without end is seen with alarm and met with derision, name-calling, sometimes even violence.

When the policy of mass immigration is questioned, the media, politicians and academia will circle the wagons and attack with ferocity. Their line is that mass immigration must continue at all costs and opponents of mass immigration must be silenced. More immigration and the breakdown of American sovereignty is constantly pushed in the media as something that will have positive effects on our lives as American citizens.

For example, on February 4, 2015, CNN posted an editorial online, called *Why we need a North American Passport*, by Andrés Martinez and Daniel Kurtz-Phelan, who argued that Americans, Mexicans and Canadians should all receive North American passports and the borders between the three countries should be opened. They argued that the solution to America's illegal immigration problem is to allow all Mexicans to freely travel into the USA and be allowed to work here. They presented NAFTA as having increased the standard of living of the American people, when in fact our wages have remained stagnant since NAFTA passed, and fewer Americans as a percentage of the population have jobs today than when NAFTA went into effect.

"In the North American context," the writers stated, "much like within the European Union, our economies and societies are far more integrated than our immigration system recognizes—and a North American passport, much like the E.U. passport, would align our laws with reality."

"Moreover," the writers continued, "Americans on this

side of the Rio Grande must acknowledge the 'Mexicanness' in the United States and treat Mexicans living here with the dignity and respect they deserve."

Do you see the game they are playing? Mexicans who have illegally crossed our borders must be given the dignity and respect they deserve by giving them passports and the right to work here. We must acknowledge our Mexicanness and open our borders, give up our sovereignty and merge with Mexico and Canada. This will make us richer and happier like in the EU where immigrants riot and burn cars, where Spain has a 25 percent unemployment rate and where Greece faces national insolvency. Does anyone really believe that allowing millions more Mexican laborers into our country will benefit the American middle class and not just shareholders of multinational corporations?

Andrés Martinez is a professor at the Cronkite School of Journalism at Arizona State University. Daniel Kurtz-Phelan was an adviser on Secretary of State Hillary Clinton's policy planning staff. Both Martinez and Kurtz-Phelan work for a think tank called New America, which obviously is working against the old America that we knew and loved and toward a new America that international bankers would love.

In our cities and in our schools, it is obvious that we are being transformed into a multicultural nation that shares little in common with our heritage. Go to any elementary school in most parts of the United States and the children of recent immigrants likely outnumber children of parents who can trace their heritage here back more than a generation or two.

The mass immigration proponents would have us believe that our current high level of immigration, the ensuing population growth and our demographic transformation are inevitable. But this is not the case.

Immigration is a policy that can be changed. It has been changed over and over during the course of our history, notably with the Immigration Act of 1924, which sharply curtailed immigration into the United States for 41 years and allowed immigrants to work their way up the economic ladder and allowed their children and grandchildren to fully assimilate into our American culture and economy. This is what must occur again. We need to stop all immigration so the largest immigrant population in our history has time to get an economic footing here without constant economic pressure from below from new immigrants coming in. We need to allow working people some breathing room without constant downward pressure from immigrants coming in and competing for employment with the people already here. We need to stop legal immigration and send illegal immigrants home.

In 2010, Arizona passed an anti-illegal immigration law and Alabama followed suit in 2011. Both states passed laws not to restrict legal immigration but to crack down on illegal immigration—the breaking of our nation's actual immigration laws. Illegal immigrants in both states began to leave, fearing repercussions. The laws proved effective even before they were implemented. But the media and the federal government went on the attack against these states for trying to enforce federal law. That should tell you what the goals of our government really are—that our government and media are not working for the well-being of this nation and will attack Americans who try to enforce laws that are already on the books.

The media and our politicians tell us that it is impossible to deport the millions of illegal immigrants that are here. This is untrue. Arizona and Alabama proved that simply by passing laws at the state level, the illegal immigrants would leave.

The media and the federal government went into full attack mode to ensure that illegal immigration continues into these states. Simple law changes by states can sharply reduce illegal immigration, but our media, our courts and our federal government are formidable obstacles. They will attack if trends turn toward a reduction of immigration. This is because money in our country is controlled by those who want massive amounts of immigration into our nation to continue in order to achieve their goals.

Our government spends billions defending the borders of

Kosovo, South Korea and Afghanistan. We spend billions invading countries on the other side of the world, yet we leave our own borders wide open?

Defending our own borders and ending illegal immigration is a simple matter, especially for a nation as wealthy as ours. A simple fine on employers who hire illegal immigrants would end the influx into our country. Fine each employer $5,000 a day per illegal immigrant. Give half the fine to the person who reports the employer and the other half to pay for enforcement and deportation. The illegals would all be gone in a few months.

Ending the current flood of legal immigrants to our nation would take nothing more than a policy change. But the obstacle is our media, courts and corrupt politicians who are determined to flood us with immigrants until our nation is no more.

The opposition to the Immigration Act of 1924 was fierce. Congressmen who supported the act were smeared as bigots, and every manner of subterfuge was used to block the act from passing. But the Federal Reserve was still in its infancy and our newspapers were not entirely bought out at the time so Americans were still able to hear both sides of the debate. The bill passed and immigration was stopped for a generation.

The proponents of the act had the American people on their side. The act was passed to protect American wages from large influxes of pauperized immigrants and to preserve our national identity and national values at a time when immigrant groups were organized into political blocs that were pursuing ethnic agendas that were often counter to the American national interest—such as involvement in foreign wars that were outside our sphere of interest.

Emmanuel Celler was an outspoken congressman who opposed the Immigration Act of 1924. Celler was patient. He waited until the time was right until he made his move. Forty-one years after the passage of the Immigration Act of 1924, he was still in Congress, and with the money men and the media backing him, he was able to push for the passage of the Immigration Act of 1965 that has been one of the most transformational laws in our nation's history, which is changing the very character of our nation before our eyes, transforming us from a nation of middle class Americans into a nation of poor immigrants, just as the international bankers have long wanted.

The solution to our current situation is simple. The American people must say no more to this deluge of humanity that is flooding onto our shores year in and year out. America is full. All immigration into our nation must end if we are to save our environment, our culture, our freedoms, our safety, our standard of living and the hopes and dreams of our children.

All it would take is a simple vote of Congress to overturn the current immigration quota and instead replace it with zero immigration from here on out.

Of course, there would be much gnashing and wailing of teeth.

When Congress threatened to end the practice of slavery, the slave owners cried out, "If we abolish slavery, who will pick the cotton?" If we were to end immigration, the cheap labor advocates would shriek, "Who will do the jobs that Americans won't do?"

The answer is: No one will do the jobs that Americans won't do. That's because Americans won't toil for hours on end for pauperized wages. But Americans will work for a fair wage. A free human being, an American citizen with rights and responsibilities, should not have to demean himself because of the necessity to earn enough money to eat. An American citizen should be paid well for his work, even if this means the rich man will be a little less rich than he would if he could exploit an impoverished immigrant instead. Americans are perfectly willing to work and toil in harsh and dangerous conditions, as our young infantrymen overseas have proved day in and day out over the last decade. Americans are just not willing to work for subsistence wages and not willing to bootlick for them.

If mass immigration were to end, fast food restaurants would no longer be able to hire middle-aged immigrants raising children to work the stoves and cash registers at minimum wage.

Instead, those jobs will be worked by American teenagers again, just as they were 30 years ago.

The corporate farms that rely on armies of impoverished illegal immigrant labor will go bust, their land will be sold off to small family farmers, which will increase competition and diversity in food production while ending the burden on our social services of having so many impoverished foreigners in our agricultural areas.

Our corporate farms today that employ illegal immigrant labor have more in common with slave plantations of the South or the collectivized farms of the Soviet Union than they do with the family farms of the early Republic. Impoverished peasant farm workers are brought in and paid pauperized wages for large corporate farms financed by banks.

Quigley wrote in *Tragedy and Hope* that the collectivization of farms in the Soviet Union resulted in a drop in agricultural output. As output fell on the large collectivized farms, the Soviet agricultural workers were still growing food on their own private plots. "The output of food from small private plots of the Soviet peasantry, which were presumably worked only in their owners' spare time, produced four or five times the output per acre of the state and collective farms," Quigley wrote. "This was, of course, an indication of the success of private enterprise as a spur in the productive process, a fact which was specifically recognized by Khrushchev in a series of speeches early in 1964."

Stalin taxed away the produce the peasantry had grown on their private plots. That is how much he was for the people.

When people ask today who will pick the crops if the illegal immigrants are sent home, the answer is Americans will in a free enterprise system of small family farms. Under such a system in which small family farms are provided credit through public loan offices, the family farm could flourish again and our free enterprise system could provide us with an abundance of produce from land worked by family farmers and well-paid farm hands. Mechanization will undoubtedly continue, meaning the need for farm labor should decline anyway. We need to recognize as a nation that importing the poor as farm labor for corporate farms does not benefit us as a people, but instead harms us and our communities while enriching corporations that are centralizing our food supply putting it under the control of a handful of people—just as Stalin had collectivized and centralized agriculture in the Soviet Union.

Without a constant influx of more than a million immigrants a year, jobs will open back up to American workers and wages will rise. The wage structure will readjust and we will become a nation where wages are high again. Of course, ethnocentric lobbyists will rage and billionaires will hire immigrant rent-a-mobs by the busload to march and protest and break windows, but as long as the laws are passed and enforced, wages will end their long decline and begin to rise again. Isn't this what we want? A nation where wages are higher than in the Third World?

Obviously, Wall Street does not want this. They want low wages. The corporatists will gnash their teeth and corporate media will wail and the Fed will threaten to raise interest rates at the hint of rising wages. They will trot out every sob story from every sympathetic illegal immigrant to prey on our empathy. That is how we will know that we are on the correct path.

What the media rarely talks about is that not only does mass immigration have negative effects on the United States, it also hurts the home countries of the immigrants. When engineers, scientists, computer programmers and entrepreneurs emigrate here, their home countries experience a brain drain. The very people who would best help develop their own nations instead come here and push down our wages and fill our schools and hospitals with their children when they could be back home building up their home economies. Because of the pull of the American dollar printed out of thin air by the Fed, millions leave their home countries motivated by the dream of bettering themselves and they come here when they should be back home building up their own countries and raising their families in their own cultures instead of causing so much disruption and dislocation in ours.

It is not their fault. They are only trying to better themselves. The fault lies with the international bankers who are responsible for causing so much disruption to our lives.

For the immigrant here in America today, do you want this country to be continually flooded with more than 1 million immigrants a year? Do you want your children to live in an overpopulated nation with a declining standard of living? Do you want us to have a high population density like China and India? Or do you want what America used to be—a land of opportunity and liberty where parents can raise their children to be better off than themselves?

Immigrants come here because they want to have an American standard of living. But our immigration policy is designed to allow immigrants to come here because our leaders want to reduce the American standard of living to Third World standards. To save the American standard of living, we need to end immigration into our country before our standard of living falls any further.

If we continue on our current course, our land of liberty and opportunity will be lost under a flood of humanity. The human Ponzi scheme is going to inevitably collapse into chaos, destitution and bankruptcy. The human Ponzi scheme must end if we are to save America.

This current wave of immigration has been so large and has lasted so long and has been so diverse that it will take generations to assimilate our latest arrivals into the American melting pot. If we are to save our culture and our values, we must allow time for assimilation to take effect. Unlike past waves of Italians, Irish or Germans, who were ethnically and culturally similar to the majority population, this current wave is going to take centuries to assimilate. If our current trends continue, our new immigrants will never assimilate and instead will vote away our nation as they gain in numbers. Just as Texas was overwhelmed by Americans and broke away from Mexico, and the American Indians were overwhelmed by new arrivals and lost their lands, our current immigrants will overwhelm us and we will lose the country that our forefathers fought for and founded. As the immigrants become dominant in numbers over native born Americans, the globalists will use the loss of our national identity to end our sovereignty once and for all. That is a primary purpose of our current immigration policy.

Right now, our immigration policy is leading to the pauperized wage structure that past immigration restrictionists and protectionists were fighting against. Mass immigration leads to wage depression while more profits flow into the hands of the idle rich—the passive-income class—those who do no work but instead feed off of interest, dividends and capital gains. By suppressing wages with cheap labor brought in from abroad, they enrich themselves at the expense of working Americans.

By ending immigration, we can reshape the American wage structure. The rich will be less rich as more of their profits end up in the hands of the people who actually do the productive work of the nation. We can return our wage structure to an earlier time in America when everyone had inside him, like a kind of core, the knowledge that he could earn a decent living, and earn it without bootlicking. We can return America to a time when we were truly free human beings, when life had a buoyant, carefree quality that you could feel, like a physical sensation in your belly, a time before the deterioration in American life that came with the exploiting of cheap immigrant labor.

When you hear a mass immigration advocate blowing smoke about how beneficial immigration is to us and that we are a nation of immigrants, or that the only people who deserve to call themselves Americans are the American Indians, or that you are a bigot if you question mass immigration, remember that you are listening to someone who is deluded and giving you only one side of a complex story, or else you are being manipulated by someone who is seeking to end America as a sovereign, independent and wealthy nation where people are free and prosperous and can earn a living without bootlicking. They will attack you, they will pull on your heartstrings with immigrant sob stories, they will prey on your American tolerance and live-and-let-live tendencies, they will use economic mumbo jumbo to tell you that more immigrants will benefit you financially. They will come at you from every angle. But remember, whether they know it or not, the mass immigration advocate is an agent of international bankers who are seeking your destruction as a free and prosperous American citizen. Remember that whenever the mass immigrationist opens his mouth.

Cheap labor cannot exist without poverty. Our government is importing poverty into our country. The result of mass immigration into the United States is an increase in American poverty. That is what the architects of our immigration policy are working toward.

The tyranny of poverty

Many people are under the misconception that the rich are the enemy of the poor. This is not the case. The rich need the poor. The rich want servants. The poor, by and large, will bow down to the rich for scraps thrown to them.

The poor will quickly trade in a life of want and need to serve the rich. The poor are easily manipulated by politicians who promise handouts, and by radicals who preach class hatred and cloud the minds of the poor with unattainable international utopias. Usually, these radical communists, anarchists and socialists have big money backers who guide these movements not to attack the rich, but to attack the middle class and the sovereignty of nations.

The poor are in a state of want. They are needy by definition. They are prone to bootlick those who offer them scraps, and they easily fall into a state of dependency.

The true enemy of the rich is not the poor but the middle class—the hated bourgeoisie for which both international finance capitalists and international communists have so much contempt. If you own your own home, have strong family support, have savings, perhaps run your own business, or have some source of income other than wages paid by an employer, or you work in a career field where demand for your labor is high and you earn high wages, then you are your own person. You can earn a decent living without bootlicking.

If you are an American citizen and middle class, you are a powerful force to be reckoned with. Although you are not rich, you have rights and assets and you have something to lose. You have numbers and the ability to organize and raise funds to pursue your interests.

The rich have more assets than you but they lack your numbers. You can organize against the rich to pursue your own interests and put your considerable collective assets to work to defeat the rich who are smaller in number. You have voting power.

Currently, our richest Americans have global interests, which are in direct conflict to the interests of the American middle class and the American nation at large. While small in number, the rich are winning in their aims and the middle class is losing. The rich are organized and their goal is clear in their minds—at least in the minds of the richest few who are pulling the strings. These few are in firm control of the media, the government, the banks and the monetary system.

Our current ruling class is made up of extremely rich people who owe their wealth to fractional reserve banking and the current monetary system. Their wealth and power is dependent on the flow of money from the Federal Reserve to Wall Street banks to multinational corporations. The banks and corporations use debt money supplied by the Fed to siphon off the wealth of the people.

The conflict between our current ruling elite and the American middle class is one between people who want a global government in which the elite rules in feudalist fashion over a global proletariat versus those who believe that America is a nation worth saving—that our Constitution, our culture, our heritage, our values and our middle class lifestyle are things worth preserving.

In *1984,* Orwell had an interesting take on the conflict between economic classes.

"Throughout recorded time," Orwell wrote, "and probably since the end of the Neolithic Age, there have been three kinds of people in the world, the High, the Middle, and the Low. They have been subdivided in many ways, they have borne countless different names, and their relative numbers, as well as their attitude towards one another, have varied from age to age: but the essential structure of society has never altered. Even after enormous upheavals and seemingly irrevocable changes, the same pattern has always reasserted itself, just as a gyroscope will always return to equilibrium, however far it is pushed one way or the other. ...

"The aims of these three groups are entirely irreconcilable," Orwell continued. "The aim of the High is to remain where they are. The aim of the Middle is to change places with the High. The aim of the Low, when they have an aim—for it is an abiding characteristic of the Low that they are too much crushed by drudgery to be more than intermittently conscious of anything outside their daily lives—is to abolish all distinctions and create a society in which all men shall be equal. Thus throughout history a struggle which is the same in its main outlines recurs over and over again. For long periods the High seem to be securely in power, but sooner or later there always comes a moment when they lose either their belief in themselves or their capacity to govern efficiently, or both. They are then overthrown by the Middle, who enlist the Low on their side by pretending to them that they are fighting for liberty and justice. As soon as they have reached their objective, the Middle thrust the Low back into their old position of servitude, and themselves become the High. Presently, a new Middle group splits off from one of the other groups, or from both of them, and the struggle begins over again. Of the three groups, only the Low are never even temporarily successful in achieving their aims. It would be an exaggeration to say that throughout history there has been no progress of a material kind. Even today, in a period of decline, the average human being is physically better off than he was a few centuries ago. But no advance in wealth, no softening of manners, no reform or revolution has ever brought human equality a millimetre nearer. From the point of view of the Low, no historic change has ever meant much more than a change in the name of their masters."

In Orwell's book, the ruling class figured out that collectivism could be used to consolidate its wealth and power. "It had long been realized that the only secure basis for oligarchy is collectivism," Orwell wrote. "Wealth and privilege are most easily defended when they are possessed jointly. The so-called 'abolition of private property' which took place in the middle years of the century meant, in effect, the concentration of property in far fewer hands than before: but with this difference, that the new owners were a group instead of a mass of individuals."

In *Animal Farm*, Orwell illustrated through allegory how this process played out in the Soviet Union, where a pig named Napoleon, who was a caricature of Josef Stalin, used a collectivist ideology in which all animals were equal, to organize the animals to overthrow the farmer. Once the farmer was driven away, Napoleon resorted to terror and oppression to consolidate his power and the animals became worse off than before.

In Russia, it was not the working class that overthrew the tsar. It was a revolutionary group of middle and upper class intellectuals, financed by international bankers, who used the working class to overthrow the tsar and Russia's small middle class, who were then murdered in large numbers.

Lenin, who was not of the working class, wrote that working class people were incapable of organizing themselves except in the most basic manner. In *What is to be Done?* Lenin wrote: "The history of all countries shows that the working class, exclusively by its own effort, is able to develop only trade union consciousness, i.e., it may itself realise the necessity for combining in unions, for fighting against the employers and for striving to compel the government to pass necessary labour legislation, etc. ... The theory of socialism, however, grew out of the philosophic, historical and economic theories that were elaborated by the educated representatives of the propertied classes, the intellectuals. According to their social status, the founders of modern scientific socialism, Marx and Engels, themselves belonged to the bourgeois intelligentsia."

Lenin continued explaining that revolution must be led by a small, secret and closed revolutionary elite that guides the working class toward the elite's goals. "The most grievous sin we have committed in regard to organisation is that by our primitiveness we have lowered the prestige of revolutionaries in Russia," Lenin wrote. "A man who is weak and vacillating on theoretical questions, who has a narrow outlook who makes excuses for his own slackness on the ground that the masses are awakening spontaneously; who resembles a trade union secretary more than a people's tribune, who is unable to conceive of a broad and bold plan, who is incapable of inspiring even his opponents with respect for himself, and who is inexperienced and clumsy in his own professional art—the art of combating the political police—such a man is not a revolutionary but a wretched amateur!"

In Lenin's mind, the rough worker, who is clumsy in his speech and incapable of grasping or voicing complicated theories, needs to be led not by members of his own class, but by his intellectual and class superiors—a revolutionary elite from the propertied class.

The revolution in Russia played out as in *Animal Farm*. The revolutionary elite used the working class to overthrow Russia's ruling class. Then the revolutionary elites installed themselves as the ruling class and the working class was just as poor and oppressed as it was under the tsar, even more so.

In America, the process has been more subtle. A revolutionary elite worked behind the scenes to corrupt our politicians with money, seize control of our monetary system, our media and our economic production and slowly transformed our nation not by overthrowing the government, but by infiltrating it and corrupting it. Promises are made to American workers and the American middle class while the elite relentlessly pushes its globalist agenda, signing destructive trade treaties, flooding us with more immigrants and killing off our youth in overseas wars.

The 19th century financier Jay Gould allegedly said, "I can hire one half of the working class to kill the other half."

Working class people and the poor are easily used due to their wants and needs and their lack of education and sophistication. Moneyed interests use revolutionary intellectuals to manipulate the poor and the working class into attacking the middle class.

The current wealthiest class in the United States is pursuing policies that are designed to crush the great American middle class and end it as an economic and political force and submerge us all into the ranks of the poor—to make us all needy, without property, dependent.

Free trade destroys the ability of the middle class to earn a decent living by allowing the rich to move capital out of the United States and around the world to where labor is most oppressed. Mass immigration imports impoverished non-citizen labor in large numbers into the United States which depresses wages and the ability for Americans to earn a decent living and save for the future without falling into debt. Large numbers of immigrants from different nations break up the social cohesion of the middle class reducing the ability of middle class people to organize to protect their interests.

The rich manipulate our culture and economy to break us down and divide us.

Of particular interest to our elites is the American family. Through cultural and economic manipulation the American people are being steered away from the formation of nuclear and extended families. For anyone who has studied elites and power through history, one fact should stand out—family and power are intertwined. From hereditary monarchies to inherited fortunes to political dynasties, the importance of family cannot be denied.

The family is the most basic and foundational unit of human society. The poor tend not to form strong family units. The middle class often forms strong families. The rich are rooted in families, some have passed down fortunes for centuries.

The family is a fragile unit that is easily destroyed, especially by economic hardship. Our current society is rife with temptations, economic upheavals, laws and messages from the media that make it ever more difficult for the traditional family to form and remain intact.

The child who is born into a strong family has an advantage over the child from a broken home. He has social, educational and material support that children from broken homes lack. The single parent has a hard road to follow and often is dependent on handouts from the state. This creates a dependency on the state which leads to subservience and loyalty to those who are providing the handouts. Poverty is generational, inherited by child from adult in a cycle of broken homes and parentless children that can continue for hundreds of years.

It is doubly hard for the child without family to break free from poverty and dependency. It is the rare child that can overcome such disadvantages and break the chains of poverty and dependency and climb up the economic ladder to self-sufficiency and prosperity. Those rare children who have the drive, talent or luck to rise up out of poverty will often found their own family dynasties and pass down their assets and values to the next generation.

Idleness is one of the most destructive vices to the human spirit. Both the poor and the rich are prone to degenerate in their idleness. The unemployed and dependent poor and the hereditary rich can fall into states of idleness in which work is no longer an organizing force in their lives. Without work, they lose the ability and the skills needed to contribute to human society. Idle hands are the devil's workshop, as the saying goes. The idle rich and the idle poor degenerate and easily succumb to substance abuse, crime and debased lifestyles.

In a June 17, 2014 article in *U.S. News and World Report*, Tom Sightings wrote that rich people worry about their children. "Wealthy people know that many a fortune has been squandered by a playboy son or jet-setting daughter," Sightings wrote. "They also know that the prospect of a large inheritance can undermine the ambition, and the dreams, of a child of fortune. Why take on the nasty realities of schoolwork and a job when you have access to a trust fund? Wealthy people, especially those who have made their own fortune, know the answer even if their kids do not: In work there is self-confidence, self-worth and a sense of accomplishment that no amount of money by itself can provide."

In his documentary film, *The One Percent,* Jamie Johnson, an heir to the Johnson and Johnson fortune, revealed the practices and thinking of some of America's wealthiest people. In one scene in the film, Johnson attended a wealth planning seminar in Southern California at which multimillionaire families—people with assets between $300 and $400 million—were planning how to distribute their wealth. The leader of the seminar explained to these people that their goal should be to pass down their wealth to the next five generations of heirs.

These wealthy people were planning to give money to family members who will not be born for another 100 years. Children a century from now will be born into wealth and privilege due to the money and planning of their great-great-grandparents alive today. These heirs, who will not be born for more than 100 years, already have a material advantage over their peers a century from now due to the wealth and planning of their ancestors.

How many poor and middle class people are thinking about the well-being of their great-great-grandchildren who will be born 100 years from now?

The successful family can pass down wealth and power for hundreds of years. However, most fortunes from wealthy families will be widely distributed, diluted and squandered over five generations. Family feuds, incompetent and spendthrift heirs, bad luck, infertility and multiple other reasons will mean most fortunes now will not last another five generations. Those who are not successful in keeping families together and instilling in their heirs the value of work will not pass down wealth and power.

The rich man who is unmarried and childless, or divorced many times over with children from different mothers, will see his fortune vanish and dissipate at his death, taken by lawyers and taxmen and people unrelated to himself.

The *Communist Manifesto* states that the bourgeois family is based on the ownership of private property, on capital and private gain. "The bourgeois family will vanish as a matter of course when its complement vanishes, and both will vanish with the vanishing capital," the book states.

The *Manifesto* states that the communists seek to stop the exploitation of children by their parents. The aim of the communists is to destroy home education and replace it with social education.

"The bourgeois clap-trap about the family and education, about the hallowed co-relation of parent and child, becomes all the more disgusting, the more, by the action of Modern Industry, all family ties among the proletarians are torn asunder, and their children transformed into simple articles of commerce and instruments of labour."

The communists sought the abolition of countries, nations and religions. The communists worked to abolish the bourgeoisie by working to abolish the family. They sought to transform us all into a global proletariat without families and countries, educated by government schools to teach us communist values and the communist historical narrative. Our family and our god were to be the state.

While communism has fallen out of fashion with the economic failure and collapse of the communist bloc in the 1990s, the agenda continues under different names and tactics. The American family, once the cornerstone of social life for the American rich, poor, and above all, the great American middle class, is under relentless assault. Powerful economic and cultural forces are manipulating us to not form strong families. Through inflation, wage competition with immigrants, and overseas economic competition, indebtedness during childbearing years, such as through student loans, it is becoming more and more difficult for middle class people to earn enough income to support nuclear families and to save enough to provide their children with an education and an inheritance. The state is becoming more and more important as the supplier of our needs. Our culture, mainly through the media, promotes promiscuity and alternative lifestyles that are destructive to the formation of families. And our government promotes single parenthood through family law, subsidies and the educational system.

The iron law of government is that you get more of what you subsidize and less of what you tax. Our government subsidizes single parenthood and poverty. It also subsidizes the biggest banks and multinational corporations. Our government taxes wages. It taxes small businesses. It taxes our homes.

The object of government subsidies is not to pull up the poor and help them rise into the middle class, but instead to make their poverty a little more bearable, to make it easier to be a single parent, to keep the poor from being hungry, to make them dependent on others for their right to exist, and to keep the poor firmly in their place and in their station. The purpose of government aid to the poor is not to end poverty but to perpetuate it and grow it.

Orwell said the aim of the high is to remain where they are, the aim of the middle is to change places with the high, while the aim of the low is to create a society in which all men are equal. The ruling class, Orwell said, realized that the only secure basis to perpetuate their oligarchy was to use collectivism to consolidate wealth and power. The threat to the rich is from the middle class—an organized middle class that seizes control of government and uses it to pursue its own interests. The best way to neutralize this threat is to turn the poor against the middle class, strip it of its property, undermine its families, and thus secure the place of the oligarchy permanently. When the middle class has no property and no families to pass down assets and values to, then no new family dynasty can arise from the masses to lead the people and threaten the power of the established ruling families—who today are the family dynasties of the international bankers.

Destroy the middle class family. That's the game. Free trade, immigration and wars are the weapons. Debt is the favored means of enslaving the people.

What was the American Revolution? It was rebellion against monarchy, against a hereditary system where members of wealthy families ruled over the rest. In England at the time, the poor were in a wretched state. But when the poor crossed the ocean to America, often in indentured servitude, they found that land was cheap and abundant and opportunities were plentiful. A poor person through the work of his own hands could own property and become prosperous. The poor became prosperous and formed large and strong families. They married young and had large numbers of children. When the English king tried to put the colonists back in their place, they rebelled and drove the king's armies back across the sea. They then set up a new system that allowed the people to choose their representatives in government. It was a system designed to ensure that leaders were chosen of the people, by the people and for the people—and that positions of power were not inherited and passed down by a few wealthy elites. It was a revolutionary system that was designed to overturn the old conflict between the high, the middle and the low. The high were to be chosen by the voters to ensure that a permanent elite could not form.

The system was designed to ensure that government served the middle and not the high. The system developed over time and produced the wealthiest, freest and most powerful nation in human history—with the world's largest and most prosperous middle class. However, the system was corrupted by money, allowing the high to bend the system toward its will.

The rich today understand the power of the middle, and spend a great deal of effort on propaganda and on clouding our minds so that we go along with their destructive agenda without seizing the reins of power from them. They take advantage of our apathy and our lack of understanding of their methods.

Our current class structure has been evolving toward a tiny population of extravagantly rich and powerful people, a shrinking number of middle class people who are increasingly being squeezed and pilfered, and a growing population of underemployed poor people who are more and more becoming dependents of government.

But this trend is not inevitable. There is a better way. A better class structure would be for there to be a small number of rich people, a small number of poor people with the vast majority of the population being part of a prosperous middle class.

The wealth of the rich should be derived from invention, high-levels of production or organizational skills in business, or from exceptional abilities in productive fields where there is high demand from the people. Passive income seekers whose wealth comes from rents, dividends, speculation and interest payments should be the target of the progressive income tax—not wage earners and active income earners whose activities result in the production of goods and services. Passive income seekers in the upper class should bear the burden of the progressive income tax, not wage earners or small business owners.

Our media and politicians today are constantly telling us that we need to tax the rich. But when they say the rich, they are talking about taxing people with high wages, not taxing passive income streams. They want us to increase taxes on the doctor down the street or the successful small businessman in our hometown, not the fat cat on Wall Street who has an army of lawyers who can protect his wealth through tax loopholes. They want us to tear down our successful neighbors. But what good will this do us? By increasing taxes on wages, does that uplift the poor? Or does it just make the poor feel a little better by bringing their neighbors down closer to their level?

The middle class can be enlarged not by raising income taxes but by ending immigration and enacting tariffs on imported goods and services. The tax system should be reconfigured to end taxes on wage earners and business owners and instead place the tax burden on passive income earners and imports. This will encourage domestic production and employment.

Unfortunately, the poor will always be with us. But if we create an economy in which work is richly rewarded and in demand and where American workers are protected from competition from low-wage, poor nations, our poverty rate will naturally decrease as the poor will be in demand for their labor here in the United States and more opportunity will be available to them. They will be valued for the work they do. We can create a free enterprise economy where poverty is temporary and climbing into the middle class is easily done through work and a little ambition.

Reforming the American wage structure to favor the middle class is a simple task that can be done with just a few policy changes, changes that have already proven effective in our history. The difficulty comes from the moneyed classes who are dependent on our current policies that are resulting in middle class destruction. The rich will fight tooth and nail with all the means available to them to keep those policies in place.

The Tyranny of War

War is a racket.

That was how Marine Corps Maj. Gen. Smedley Butler described it. He would know. He participated in enough of them.

In his book *War is a Racket*, Butler explained that war is sold to the public with idealism and patriotism, but only a small inside group knows what these wars are all about. Butler stated that war is conducted for the benefit of the very few at the expense of the very many, and out of it, a few people make huge fortunes.

Propaganda in the media has always been central to America going to war. In the days leading up to America's entry into World War I, the newspapers were filled with atrocity stories about what wicked, subhuman monsters the Germans were. Stories circulated about how Germans had bayoneted Belgian babies and cut the breasts off nuns. And of course, the Germans were torpedoing ships and killing innocent women and children. Entry into World War I was sold to the American people as a "war to end all wars" and a "war to make the world safe for democracy."

The money men who own the media have always used fear to whip the public into a panic against whatever nation they have targeted for attack. Patriotism, idealism and calls to heroism are used to impel young men to kill and be killed.

The warmongers don't come out and say, hey, we need to go to war because we bought billions in bonds from England and France and if they lose they will default and we will lose our shirts. They don't say, hey, a war will cause the government to spend billions on ships, planes, guns, boots, Humvees, body armor, etc., and we want to sell government bonds to pay for it and we want to earn profits from our stockholdings in the companies that make all that stuff. They don't say, hey, we must go to war to protect the interests of a foreign nation because people from that nation are influential in our Congress and media and helped get the president elected.

No. They say America is under attack. They say, "If you love your family, your hometown, your country and our way of life, you must fight to defend them and to protect democracy and freedom. You are a hero if you go fight overseas for freedom and to liberate the oppressed."

Butler explained that war is an exceptionally profitable business in which enormous sums of money are made by arms manufacturers, chemical companies, ship builders, the steel industry, shoe makers, sugar producers, even the manufacturers of mosquito netting. All of them got enormously rich during World War I. Above all, the bankers raked it in as the war debts mounted and shot toward the stars.

In his book, Butler stated that in World War I a handful of people gained immense profits. He wrote that at least 21,000 new millionaires and billionaires were made during the war. "That many admitted their huge blood gains in their income tax returns," he wrote.

"How many of these war millionaires shouldered a rifle?" Butler asked. "How many of them dug a trench? How many of them knew what it meant to go hungry in a rat-infested dug out? How many of them spent sleepless, frightened nights, ducking shells and shrapnel and machine gun bullets? How many of them parried a bayonet thrust of an enemy? How many of them were wounded or killed in battle?"

Butler explained that the bill that pays the enormous profits made by the war profiteers is shouldered by the general public.

"This bill renders a horrible accounting," he wrote. "Newly placed gravestones. Mangled bodies. Shattered minds. Broken hearts and homes. Economic instability. Depression and all its attendant miseries. Back-breaking taxation for generation and generations."

War is a terrible thing. Most of us already know this. But many Americans still believe the propagandists about good wars, about defending democracy and protecting America from foreign aggressors who seek to kill us and our children.

Our navy patrols oceans and seas on the other side of the planet. Our soldiers and Marines are stationed in countries around the world—from Japan to Germany to Kazakhstan. Our planes and drones bomb people in distant deserts and mountain ranges that most Americans could not find on a map, or even tell you who we are bombing and why.

More than 1.3 million Americans serve as active duty soldiers, airmen, sailors and Marines. Another 850,000 are in the reserve components. Our military has enough nuclear weapons to annihilate any nation on Earth, kill billions of people and poison vast areas of the planet for generations.

Right now, the United States is in possession of the most powerful, far-reaching and destructive military ever to exist in human history. Our military budget for 2013 was more than $600 billion—greater than the next 10 top-spending military nations in the world combined.

Yet, after all this military spending and all the wars we've fought since World War II, the media tells us day in and day out that we are under constant threat. Even with this great and powerful military, we are not safe. Our media tells us that small developing nations on the other side of the world are a threat to our very existence. We are told that ragtag groups of a few thousand thugs on the other side of the planet are a direct threat to our lives and our families. Border conflicts on Russian frontiers or disagreements over uninhabited islands in Asian seas have become a direct military concern for the American people. Some of these border conflicts and disagreements have existed before America was even a country yet today our leaders are willing to send us to war over them.

After all of this military spending and all of these wars, do we feel any safer today than our forefathers felt when we followed George Washington's foreign policy of avoiding entangling alliances? Have all the alliances that we've entangled ourselves in made us safer here at home?

Unlike Russia, India and China, we have no rivals on our borders that are disputing our territory. Our nation occupies one of the most strategically defensible positions on Earth. Yet, our military fights wars on the other side of the planet and defends distant, foreign borders while our own borders are left wide open.

How is it that we are under constant threat from attack, yet our government and media allow our own border to remain so open and porous that millions of foreigners cross it undetected? What kind of nation builds up the most powerful military in history but refuses to patrol its own border?

The Preamble to the U.S. Constitution states: "We the People of the United States, in Order to form a more perfect Union, establish Justice, insure domestic Tranquility, provide for the common defence, promote the general Welfare, and secure the Blessings of Liberty to ourselves and our Posterity, do ordain and establish this Constitution for the United States of America."

When the Founders wrote "provide for the common defence," they meant the common defense of the United States, not the common defense of Europe, Southeast Asia, Ukraine and everywhere else. They did not intend for the U.S. military to be used as a global police force.

Make no mistake. Our military is not providing for the common defense of the American people. Quite the opposite. Since World War II, our military has been used as a world police that is protecting the interests not of the American people, but of the transnational elite that has hijacked our government.

Prior to World War II, the British army and navy were the global force that kept shipping lanes and foreign ports open, invaded foreign nations for oil, diamonds and opium, and sent in gunboats whenever a nation threatened to default on loans owed to the City of London.

But the task was too large for Britain which had been exhausted by two centuries of warfare fought in the interests of a transnational plutocracy. After World War II, America became the hammer and anvil that now enforces their global economic order. Our young men and women are now dying for their interests abroad.

Our military protects the global central banking system that began under the British Empire and expanded greatly since the end of World War II.

Unlike Britain, which often went to war with little public input other than English newspapers howling for blood, America has a very distinct and systematic way of going to war. Britain does not have the checks and balances and separation of powers in its government that we do. The prime minister has the majority party in Parliament behind him. When he wants a war, he goes to war and that's that. But it takes something more to go to war here in the United States.

When the elites set their targets on a nation they want to attack, first, the media is used to prepare the American public for the coming conflict. The media begins to produce story after story about the human rights abuses of the government of the target nation. The stories can begin years before the attack. Story after story is produced in the media telling the public of the evils occurring in said nation. Story after story tells us that said nation is a threat to us and to the world.

Unlike in Britain, demonizing a nation in the media is not enough to get the public to go along with a war. Something more is needed—a catalyzing event—a sneak attack, an atrocity or some dastardly deed that outrages the American public and fills us with fear and anger.

In his autobiography, Ulysses S. Grant wrote about how a catalyzing event was used to start the Mexican War—a war he fought in as a young man but privately opposed.

The newspapers were filled with stories about Mexican aggression at a time when tensions were high due to the American annexation of Texas. American troops were deployed into Texas and then moved provocatively into position to start a war.

"The occupation, separation and annexation were, from the inception of the movement to its final consummation, a conspiracy to acquire territory out of which slave states might be formed for the American Union," Grant wrote.

"The presence of United States troops on the edge of the disputed territory furthest from the Mexican settlements, was not sufficient to provoke hostilities," Grant wrote. "We were sent to provoke a fight, but it was essential that Mexico should commence it."

The goal, Grant wrote, was to provoke Mexico into firing the first shot, which would allow the president to come to Congress and demand war. Because Mexico would be the aggressor, war opponents in Congress would not have the courage to continue their opposition and the war could be prosecuted with vigor.

"Mexico showing no willingness to come to the Nueces to drive the invaders from her soil, it became necessary for the 'invaders' to approach to within a convenient distance to be struck," Grant wrote.

Of course, the rest is history. The Mexicans fired the first shot and lost more than half their nation.

Grant said the outcome of the war was beneficial to the United States and that American soldiers fought heroically and made great sacrifices, but he also said the war should not have been fought and the territory acquired might have been obtained by other means. He opposed the annexation of Texas, which he felt was done to expand the institution of slavery and which set us on a course that led to both the Mexican War and the Civil War, both of which he called "unholy" wars.

"For myself," Grant wrote, "I was bitterly opposed to the measure, and to this day regard the war, which resulted, as one of the most unjust ever waged by a stronger nation against a weaker nation. It was an instance of a republic following the bad example of European monarchies, in not considering justice in their desire to acquire additional territory."

Of course, regardless of how the war began, its outcome was considered a grand success. The method for starting the Mexican War became the blueprint for how America goes to war. First, the media lays the groundwork. Second, the catalyzing event occurs. Third, the nation mobilizes and crushes its opponent with overwhelming force.

This road to war was followed to gain American entry into the Spanish-American War and nearly every big American war since. Before the start of the Spanish-American War in 1898, the *New York World*, owned by Joseph Pulitzer, and the *New York Journal*, owned by William Randolph Hearst, were filled with stories about Spanish atrocities in Cuba. Day after day and week after week, the papers told of one atrocity after another, but there was considerable opposition from Congress, the president and the public to intervening militarily in Cuba. And since the newspaper industry was much more diverse then in its ownership and opinions than it is today, papers across the country argued against intervention in the face of Pulitzer and Hearst whose yellow journalism appealed to emotion.

In early 1898, the U.S.S. Maine was ordered into Havana Harbor. On Feb. 15, 1898, it exploded killing 261 American sailors. The cause of the explosion has never been determined, but that didn't stop the papers from blaming it on Spain.

The press laid the groundwork, the catalyzing event occurred and war was the result. The Spanish-American War transformed the United States into a global empire with conquered lands overseas to rule.

The road to war that America has followed in our past conflicts is well-traveled. It is a road that is quite familiar to war advocates who at this very moment are pushing for new wars.

In September 2012, Patrick Clawson, the director of research at a think tank named the Washington Institute Of Near East Policy (WINEP), gave us a rare and frank moment of clarity during a policy forum when he spoke on some ideas on how government leaders could start a war with Iran.

"I frankly think that crisis initiation is really tough and it's very hard for me to see how the United States president can get us to war with Iran," Clawson told the crowd, "which leads me to conclude that if in fact compromise is not coming, that the traditional way America gets to war is what would be best for U.S. interests."

Clawson continued, "Some people might think that Mr. Roosevelt wanted to get us into World War II, ... you may recall we had to wait for Pearl Harbor. Some people might think Mr. Wilson wanted to get us into World War I, you may recall he had to wait for the Lusitania episode. Some people might think that Mr. Johnson wanted to send troops to Vietnam, you may recall he had to wait for the Gulf of Tonkin episode. We didn't go to war with Spain until the Maine exploded. And, may I point out, that Mr. Lincoln did not feel he could call out the federal army until Fort Sumter was attacked, which is why he ordered the commander of Fort Sumter to do exactly that thing which the South Carolinians had said would cause an attack."

Clawson clearly understands the American road to war.

"So, if in fact the Iranians aren't going to compromise, it would be best if somebody else started the war."

He wants war but knows the public and Congress won't go along if we are seen as the aggressors.

"We could step up the pressure. I mean, look people, Iranian submarines periodically go down, some day one of them might not come up. Who would know why? We can do a variety of things if we wish to increase the pressure."

Clawson tells us that the trick is to covertly provoke the Iranians into firing the first shot so that war can be waged against them.

"We are in the game of using covert means against the Iranians," Clawson concluded. "We could get nastier with that."

Clawson did us a great service by frankly and openly revealing the type of Machiavellian thinking and planning that is coming out of highly funded think tanks in Washington staffed by high-paid academic mercenaries.

In Orwellian fashion, starting a war by killing people and lying about it is called "crisis initiation." The American media has been demonizing Iran for years now. Think tank mercenaries have surely thought up several nasty scenarios that would commence a war with Iran that their benefactors want. Thankfully, at this time the catalyzing event has not occurred.

Niccolo Machiavelli published his book *The Prince* in 1532. In the book, he described tactics that leaders should use to gain and maintain power. Machiavelli told us that men in positions of power must use lies, deception, murder, torture, terror, war, even the false use of religious piety, to survive and attain glory.

In Machiavelli's time when leaders were regularly murdered by rivals, nice guys finished last. Cruelty and a willingness to act immorally were necessary to stay on top. According to Machiavelli, a successful leader must present himself as virtuous and honest to the people while being paranoid and ruthless in practice.

The U.S. Constitution was a direct reaction to the type of leadership described by Machiavelli. The heavy hand of King George resulted in tyranny and rebellion. King George behaved in Machiavellian fashion but was defeated by the American rebels. The victorious American colonists wrote the Constitution to protect themselves against the Machiavellian style of leadership. Checks and balances and a separation of powers were written into law to ensure that no single person could consolidate power and act without oversight. The Bill of Rights was written to protect the citizen from arbitrary Machiavellian cruelties committed by the state. Congress was given the power to declare war to give the people a say in the fights their leaders send them into. The Founders sought to create a transparent government that was accountable to the people to prevent the type of Machiavellian machinations that have been so common in all governments.

Nearly 500 years have passed since *The Prince* was published, but human nature has not changed since then. The Machiavellian mindset persists. While the Revolution and Constitution freed us from hereditary tyrants and clearly defined our rights as Americans, Machiavellian tendencies still exist in the hearts and minds of men in the halls of our government. Good men are destroyed while bad men present themselves as good. Wars are started with lies. Such is human nature. The only defense is an awareness of this fact and a willingness to hold our leaders to the words and spirit of the U.S. Constitution.

Our Constitution explicitly states that Congress has the power to declare war. Yet, just as Congress delegated to the Fed its power to coin money and regulate the value thereof, it has also delegated away its power to declare war.

The Founders gave Congress the power to declare war because it is the branch most accountable to the people. It is the branch where debate is publicly aired. The Founders did not want wars started in secret behind closed doors. They wanted the people to decide.

But we have stood by and allowed Congress to neuter itself while the executive branch has become the ruler of an American empire and our military turned into a global enforcer and occupation force.

While the Founders saw the need for a permanent navy, they were wary of standing armies—many of them believed that maintaining a standing army in times of peace was a danger to liberty.

In 1783, George Washington wrote: "Altho' a *large* standing Army in time of Peace hath ever been considered dangerous to the liberties of a Country, yet a few Troops, under certain circumstances, are not only safe, but indispensably necessary."

Washington said that the country could be protected with a strong navy, a small army with a professional officer corps, and a well-regulated militia.

This is truer today than in Washington's time when the United States was small and surrounded by hostile empires and Indian tribes. Today, we are the richest nation in the world with the world's third largest population. We have one of the most strategically defensible locations on the globe.

Our navy and air force are far and away the world's most powerful. But they are not deployed for homeland defense. They are being used as global policers. Our army does not defend our borders from invasion but instead occupies foreign nations and fights wars overseas.

Our current military is not a defensive force but instead is an offensive one.

If we were to return to George Washington's foreign policy of avoiding foreign entanglements and remaining neutral during foreign wars, we could easily defend the North American continent at a fraction of the cost we are incurring today.

A rational American foreign policy would be to pull back our mighty navy to our own shores instead of having it patrol the coast of China, the Persian Gulf and the Baltic and Black Seas where it provokes foreign powers and puts itself in position to be attacked. Our air bases abroad should be closed and our warplanes brought home and turned over to the Air National Guard which defends our own skies from attack. The Marine Corps should be maintained as a rapid deployment force to defend Americans abroad. And our great army should be brought home and gradually downsized so that it consists of a small force of professionally trained officers and NCOs who maintain their specialization in the art of war.

The defense of the United States today falls on the National Guard, which is perfectly capable of defending the homeland from attack or invasion without the need for a large standing army.

National Guard soldiers and airmen are part-timers. They drill once a month and train two weeks a year while holding down full-time jobs in the civilian sector. They are teachers, police officers, business owners, truck drivers and students. They are not garrisoned on military bases but are our neighbors. They do not spend their entire careers in a military environment moving from place to place around the world. They are part of our communities. And they cost a fraction of what a full-time active duty troop costs.

They also follow in the tradition of the Minutemen and militia men who fought for our independence in the Revolution. They are the defenders of our nation that our Founders envisioned—not the massive military-industrial complex and global behemoth of a military force that we have today.

And with our nuclear arsenal as a deterrent, no nation or collection of nations would ever dare to attack us militarily.

By downsizing the military and reorganizing it for

homeland defense rather than using it as a global police and occupation force, our nation could save vast amounts of money while also reducing the danger of becoming entangled in destructive and expensive wars overseas. We could actually provide for the common defense of the republic rather than having our young men and women used as a global police force for protecting the interests of globalist bankers.

Our annual military budget of more than $600 billion a year could be reduced to around $200 billion and our nation would be safer than it is today and at peace.

Imagine what our country would be like if we reorganized our economy away from massive military spending on armaments and wars and on occupation abroad. Taxes could be lowered. Our government could be put to work not on war production and war but instead on establishing justice, insuring domestic tranquility, promoting the general welfare and securing the blessings of liberty to ourselves and our posterity.

Imagine if our country gave up its role as hegemon and global police force that we took on after World War II. Imagine if all that money spent on the military and war was put to other uses.

Instead of spending billions each year on stationing troops in Japan, Germany and Korea and having our navy patrol the Persian Gulf, our infrastructure could be modernized and improved.

Instead of spending billions on producing long-range nuclear bombers, we could fund the drastic expansion of medical research, medical education, and medical training facilities; the construction of hospitals and clinics; we could spend it on providing the most advanced health care in the world to our citizens.

Instead of spending on wars in the Middle East, we could fund the drastic upgrading of our educational standards and make available to all an attainable educational goal equivalent to what is now considered a professional degree.

Instead of paying for the salaries, housing, healthcare and

pensions for more than a million full-time military troops, those resources could be put to work on creating the conditions to provide clean, comfortable, safe, and spacious housing for all.

Instead of paying for huge military installations around the country and around the world, our government could work toward the establishment of a system of public transportation, making it possible for all to travel to and from areas of work and recreation quickly, comfortably, and conveniently.

With so much of our resources not expended on maintaining a global empire, our government could instead spend on improving the environment, on the development and protection of water supplies, forests, parks, and other natural resources and the elimination of chemical and bacterial contaminants from air, water, and soil.

It could spend on the genuine elimination of poverty in America.

It could spend more on the space program and the exploration and colonization of the solar system, on scientific research, or on any other priority on which the voting public would care to concentrate the resources of the nation.

It could spend on all these things and still spend less than it does today on war and maintaining such a huge military.

Or it could spend on none of these things and instead return that $600 billion a year to the pockets of the American taxpayer.

Before World War II, American military expenditures were a small part of the federal budget except in times of war. After World War II, the globalists seized control of our government and media and have kept us on a war footing ever since. They used the fear of the Soviet Union to compel the American people to spend massive amounts on our military and on wars abroad. With the fall of the Soviet Union, the American people demanded a peace dividend which the globalists feared would cause the United States to give up its role as a global police force. But the War on Terror replaced the Cold War as justification for even more massive military spending and constant intervention abroad.

World War II has been their rallying cry for more war. For the globalists, the bloodletting of that awful war was a turning point in history which allowed them to fulfill their main objectives. It was a "good war" for them and a "necessary war."

They have been flooding us with propaganda in their movies, their books and from their bought-and-paid-for intellectuals and politicians about how it was our duty to fight and die overseas in that awful war. America was brainwashed to believe that we saved the world for liberty and democracy when in fact we saved it for international capitalism and international communism. We saved it for the globalists who used this great crisis to create the beginnings of their world government in the institutions of the United Nations, the World Bank and the IMF, with the Federal Reserve providing the dollars that enrich them while plunging our people into debt and overseas wars.

Our victory in World War II has not brought us peace. It has brought us war after war and is leading us to national bankruptcy.

Today, their system based on American militarism and a Ponzi scheme of Federal Reserve Notes is coming to an end. The globalists have been pushing behind the scenes for another great war, which we must avoid at all costs if we are to survive as a nation.

The tyranny of the draft

A line of argument arises every now and then in our media, from our public officials and in comments in online discussions about a need to revive the draft.

The line goes something like this: A volunteer army places the burden of war on minorities and the poor who volunteer for military service because of economic necessity. Because they are volunteers, the government is more likely to go to war because a volunteer has given his consent to serve and knows that going to war was part of the deal. Because the volunteers are serving, the majority of the country has no skin in the game and will not protest in the streets to prevent wars from occurring or stop them once they start.

Other arguments are also given, such as a draft providing direction and employment for our young people and that through service to their country they are instilled with discipline and patriotism. A draft also brings equity by forcing the children of the rich to serve alongside the poor, making the rich share the burden and the risk of defending the nation.

One line of reasoning that arose during the Iraq War was that a draft might have stopped the war because young people would have felt personally at risk of being sent over there and would have protested. The reasoning went that because there was no draft, young people did not fear being sent over there and didn't rise up in protest to end the war like they did during the Vietnam War when mass antiwar protests were held across the nation.

Just think about this last argument for a moment—that a draft would have ended the war in Iraq like it did the Vietnam War. In Vietnam, we lost 60,000 American lives. In Iraq, we lost about 4,500 American lives. The Vietnam War lasted 19 years with more than 10 times the number of American casualties than in the Iraq War, which lasted eight years.

By 2005, the Iraq War had broken the U.S. Army because of casualties that were a fraction of those in Vietnam. Young people had stopped enlisting. Captains and junior NCOs, the leaders most needed in the fight on the ground, were getting out rather than re-enlisting. Our leaders knew that each new casualty was a liability and that tactics needed to change to reduce casualties. A concern for casualties was high, unlike in Vietnam where conscripted troops were thrown into the meatgrinder by the hundreds of thousands. In 1968 and 1969, more than 500 Americans were killed a month in Vietnam.

The U.S. Army's volunteer force could not sustain anywhere near 500 killed a month and continue the war. Americans have different reasons for volunteering to serve, but one of them is not to go overseas to be killed as cannon fodder. It takes a draftee for that.

The argument that a draft would have prevented the Iraq War or ended it sooner is false on its face. The protests against Vietnam didn't occur until tens of thousands of Americans had been killed after nearly two decades of war. The Iraq War could never have piled up that many bodies with an all-volunteer force.

If the Vietnam War or the Korean War had been fought with volunteers rather than draftees, there is no possibility that the body count would have ever reached the numbers that they did. It was the draft that allowed our government to plow under that many young Americans in World War I, World War II, Korea and Vietnam.

What Vietnam taught us is that our country can expend billions of dollars and plow under 60,000 American boys and still lose a war that was fought to keep a distant nation from turning communist—it taught us that we can lose a war and the communists can take over and the danger to our nation from that is zero. The communists took over Vietnam and the country remained a poor developing nation on the other side of the planet just as it was before. It has never been a threat to us. The Vietnamese communists had allied with the Chinese communists against us, and only a few years after we left they were fighting each other. China invaded Vietnam in 1979 just a few years after we left and they killed 60,000 Vietnamese soldiers in the Sino-Chinese War. It was of little interest to the American people because we had had enough of that place. There was no "domino effect" from our loss in Vietnam. There was no threat to us if the communists took over that country. Communism was always a bankrupt ideology fit only for tyrants and fools. Today, Vietnam is begging for foreign investment from the capitalist countries and asking for an alliance with us.

On July 11, 2014, the *New York Times* published an editorial by a former adviser to communist Vietnamese prime ministers who argued for a U.S.-Vietnamese alliance against China. The writer, Tuong Lai, said that Ho Chi Minh actually admired America, and that the Vietnam War was misguided.

The irony is that Vietnam gained independence and

sovereignty through communism—an ideology that is internationalist, anti-independence and anti-sovereignty. Vietnam allied with communist China to fight America. The communists won and now all these years later Mr. Lai argues from the pages of the *New York Times* that we, his nation's former enemy, should ally with his country against China, his former ally—that America and Vietnam should really be friends. He wants his country to be wealthy like other American allies, such as Japan, Singapore and South Korea. He wants us to defend his nation at our expense.

Vietnam shows us the wisdom of our Founders. When we fight overseas wars, we only entangle ourselves in conflicts that we should stay out of. We squandered so many lives and so much money fighting an enemy that a few decades later wants to be our ally, not for any benefit to our nation, but for its own purposes. For us to entangle ourselves in an alliance with Vietnam would be the height of idiocy and only put our nation in greater danger of conflict with China. The Vietnamese have lived in the shadow of China for millennia. That is their fate. Ours is not to defend them from their neighbor and former ally.

The lessons of Iraq are similar. The media was full of fearmongering after 9/11. Our media told us that Iraq had weapons of mass destruction. The *New York Times* told us through unnamed sources that Saddam Hussein was building a nuclear bomb. Our politicians, both Democrats and Republicans, told us that Iraq was a threat to our nation. Foreign intelligence agencies told us that Iraq was acquiring materials to build weapons of mass destruction. Foreign intelligence agencies even provided our president with falsified documents to make a case for war. Our own intelligence agencies told us that Saddam Hussein was building weapons of mass destruction and that Iraq was a direct threat to our lives.

The argument was made that Saddam Hussein must be stopped for the safety of our people and that if we liberated the Iraqis and gave them democracy all would be well. They would be free of a murderous dictator and we would be safe.

We spent billions, killed thousands and plowed under

4,500 of our own. Iraq was destroyed, no weapons of mass destruction were found, and today more than a decade after the war began, Iraq is in chaos. Our media screams about a new threat in Iraq, from a band of a few thousand ragtag terrorist insurgents. The media and the pundits tell us these insurgents are a threat to us if we don't go back over there and bomb them and fight them. Our politicians, both Democrats and Republicans, say something must be done.

If our media and politicians are to be believed, a small insurgent group on the other side of the planet, unaffiliated with any nation, without an air force or navy, surrounded by countries that want to destroy it, is apparently a threat to the world's richest country that has the most powerful and technically advanced military in the history of the world. Obviously, what happens in Iraq is of little consequence to the average American here in the United States. But it is of great consequence to people over there and to people in our country who have interests there. The fearmongering continues because people who have certain interests want us over there fighting for purposes that have nothing to do with the defense of the American people.

Our intelligence agencies are telling us that we are in danger and that something must be done.

Our intelligence agencies told us that if Vietnam became communist it would be a threat to us. Our intelligence agencies have meddled in the affairs of Latin American nations to such an extent that they have made us hated by our neighbors. Our intelligence agencies did not stop the assassination of President Kennedy. Our intelligence agencies did not see the collapse of the Soviet Union coming, right up until the day of the collapse. Our intelligence agencies did not stop 9/11. Our intelligence agencies told us there were weapons of mass destruction in Iraq. Now they tell us that insurgents in Iraq are a threat to us. Our intelligence agencies are either the most incompetent organizations in human history or they are working against us.

One thing to ponder is the reason our intelligence agencies were founded. The CIA was founded in 1947 in the aftermath of

World War II. The CIA was modeled after British Security Coordination, a foreign intelligence agency tasked to use the black arts of espionage, subversion, propaganda and forgery to bring the United States into World War II in the face of widespread antiwar sentiment. The BSC was tasked to infiltrate and subvert American antiwar groups and undermine and smear antiwar citizens and politicians while working with friendly media outlets to disseminate war propaganda.

In May 2000, a statue of William Stephenson, the Canadian who ran the BCS out of Rockefeller Center in New York City, was presented to CIA executive director David Carey. The Canadian newspaper *Winnipeg Free Press* reported on the presentation, calling Stephenson a top British spy in the Second World War who was involved in the formation of the OSS, the forerunner to the CIA.

"If it hadn't been for his activities prior to and including World War II, there might not be a CIA," CIA spokeswoman Anya Guilsher was quoted in the article as saying about Stephenson. "He realized early on that Americans needed a strong intelligence organization, and lobbied President Roosevelt to appoint a U.S. coordinator to oversee intelligence."

In a Canadian documentary titled *The True Intrepid: Sir William Stephenson*, Stephenson was described as a man whose espionage in the United States was critical to saving Britain in World War II through the use of forgery and propaganda against Americans.

"Long before anybody else came up with it, he had this idea of one world, trading and industrializing countries," former OSS counterspy Betty Lussier said about Stephenson in the documentary.

Our intelligence services today are the direct heir of a foreign intelligence service that was tasked to use the black arts of espionage, forgery and propaganda to subvert and discredit antiwar advocates and bring us into a war for the interests of a foreign nation.

Our service men and women, volunteers all, were ordered

into Iraq believing they were fighting to defend our nation from a ruthless dictator who was building weapons of mass destruction to use against us. They believed they were liberating a nation from tyranny. The CIA, along with foreign intelligence agencies, provided convincing documents disseminated through the media that were used as proof that Saddam Hussein was producing weapons of mass destruction.

Was it true?

We now know that it was not. Documents were forged. The CIA provided false evidence that was used to start a war.

Was the Iraq War worth the loss of a leg or an arm? Was it worth being blinded or maimed? Was it worth the loss of a father, a mother, a husband or a wife? Was it worth the loss of a child?

No. It was not.

What our media, politicians and intelligence agencies told us was untrue. The lesson we should have learned from Iraq was that our media, politicians and intelligence agencies cannot be trusted. They cannot be believed. Now they are telling us we must go back into Iraq. And they have been telling us for years that Iran is a threat.

But they know the fear from 9/11 has dissipated. They know that America is tired of war and that our military is stretched thin. They know that our volunteer military cannot bring peace to the Middle East, face down the Russians and the Chinese and still continue being the police force of the world.

They know this is too much.

Every now and then these days, the call for a draft is repeated. The pundits and politicians make their arguments, which always sound logical and reasonable, as if a draft is in our own best interests as Americans. A draft would solve so many problems, you see, and a draft would be fair.

All of the arguments for a draft are smokescreens for the true purpose of conscription, which is to provide large numbers of young bodies for overseas invasions that our leaders expect will result in large numbers of casualties—invasions that will result in tens of thousands to hundreds of thousands of Americans killed.

Smedley Butler had his thoughts on the draft. "The only way to smash this racket is to conscript capital and industry and labor before the nation's manhood can be conscripted," he wrote.

Butler said if we are going to conscript young men to kill and die, we should also conscript the business owners and laborers who are earning money producing the materials of war. Take the profit out of it. Draft the business owners and laborers who work in the military-industrial complex and pay them the same wages as a soldier. That would be fair.

This makes sense. Every war we've fought has imposed fearful sacrifices in blood and treasure on our nation. War profiteering should be made illegal. Personal profit arising from war should be regarded as treason.

Butler also said only those who are physically able of being drafted should have the right to vote on whether we go to war. "A plebiscite not of all the voters but merely of those who would be called upon to do the fighting and dying. There wouldn't be very much sense in having a 76-year-old president of a munitions factory or the flat-footed head of an international banking firm or the cross-eyed manager of a uniform manufacturing plant—all of whom see visions of tremendous profits in the event of war—voting on whether the nation should go to war or not. They never would be called upon to shoulder arms—to sleep in a trench and to be shot. Only those who would be called upon to risk their lives for their country should have the privilege of voting to determine whether the nation should go to war."

Today, we hear many people saying America should fight this country or that country or get involved in this conflict or that one. We hear them talk and sometimes they sound passionate and make a case that sounds well-reasoned. America should fight to prevent some genocide from happening or to protect some group from aggression. It sounds noble. Yet, these war advocates do not want to go over there themselves and fight. They want other Americans to go over there.

If someone is arguing that we should fight a war overseas but they've never been in the military and have no intention of joining up, then they are essentially arguing for other people to go fight and die without themselves having skin in the game. They believe that war is worth the lives of other Americans but not their own. An American who argues for war but who has no intention of participating is essentially a bloodthirsty coward, or else that person is a foreign agent who is seeking to involve the United States in a conflict overseas for foreign interests. We know foreign interests work hard to involve us in wars overseas, as British Security Coordination proved before World War II. Foreigners will bribe our leaders, use subversion against us, employ agent provocateurs, plant fake news stories in the press, produce fake polls, forge documents and feed our government false intelligence, and even murder us to get us to fight their enemies.

If someone feels passionate about some foreign conflict, they should buy a plane ticket and go over there and join the side of their choice and leave the rest of us out of it. And if someone is arguing for a draft, history shows that this policy has always resulted in tens of thousands of American dead overseas.

America never fought a war with volunteers where more than 10,000 Americans were killed. America never fought a war with draftees where fewer than 30,000 were killed. Our highest casualties far and away came in wars that were fought with drafted troops.

And the draft never brought fairness to any of our wars either. The rich and the connected always found a way to avoid the front lines. For example, former Fed Chairman Alan Greenspan was of draftable age during World War II. He hated fascism and believed the war was worth fighting; however, in his memoirs he described how a doctor found a spot on his lung indicating tuberculosis which prevented him from being drafted. Greenspan spent the war years playing the clarinet in a jazz band in smoky clubs. So, when hundreds of thousands of Americans his age were dying overseas, he was able to stay in the U.S. and tour the country playing the clarinet in jazz clubs because an X-ray showed he might have a fatal pulmonary disease. Once the war ended, the spot cleared up.

The journalist and Rhodes Scholar James Fallows wrote how his draft number came up after he graduated from Harvard while the Vietnam War was raging. He wrote in an article for *Washington Monthly* how he studied Army regulations and decided that he would disqualify himself for service by losing enough weight so that he would not meet the Army's height and weight standards. When he and his fellow Ivy League draftees arrived at the Boston Navy Yard for their medical examinations, they wore red armbands and chanted pro-Ho Chi Min slogans. When Fallows stepped on the scale to be weighed, he was borderline for being underweight. His conscription into the Army came down to a physician's decision. To help ensure the correct decision was made, Fallows told the doctor that he was suicidal. The skeptical doctor then marked Fallows down as unqualified for military service.

"I was overcome by a wave of relief, which for the first time revealed to me how great my terror had been, and by the beginning of the sense of shame which remains with me to this day," Fallows wrote. "It was, initially, a generalized shame at having gotten away with my deception, but it came into sharper focus later in the day. Even as the last of the Cambridge contingent was throwing its urine and deliberately failing its color-blindness tests, buses from the next board began to arrive. These bore the boys from Chelsea, thick, dark-haired young men, the white proles of Boston. Most of them were younger than us, since they had just left high school, and it had clearly never occurred to them that there might be a way around the draft. They walked through the examination lines like so many cattle off to slaughter. I tried to avoid noticing, but the results were inescapable. While perhaps four out of five of my friends from Harvard were being deferred, just the opposite was happening to the Chelsea boys. … We returned to Cambridge that afternoon, not in government buses but as free individuals, liberated and victorious. The talk was high-spirited, but there was something close to the surface that none of us wanted to mention. We knew now who would be killed."

The working class and those with a sense of duty to their nation went to Vietnam and were killed, maimed or psychologically scarred in the tens of thousands. Those who were skilled deceivers and liars stayed home and went on to become the leaders of their generation and our nation. One honest and brave opponent of the war, the great boxer Mohammed Ali, chose not to lie and take the easy way out, but instead flat out refused to fight in Vietnam. Ali went to jail with his head held high and carrying with him a spirit of civil disobedience and did more to end the draft than a thousand Ivy League draft dodgers.

The rich, the crafty and the connected will never be sent to the front lines if they don't want to go. They will fake illnesses or get plush appointments to staff jobs. They will stay in school or fling urine at the draft board. They will always find a way out. The draft scoops up the middle and working classes and those who trust their leaders and believe in the justness of the cause. The draft, through the force of law and the power of propaganda, sends the draftee out to kill and die.

If you can be forced by your government against your will to kill and die for your country, then you are not a free person. You do not live in a free country. Your freedom is a lie. A free people are not drafted.

In a free country, a free people will choose to fight to defend their homes, their families, their communities and their nation of their own free will and self-interest. The Revolutionary War was fought by volunteers who defeated the most powerful empire of their day. Not a single draftee was among them.

If World War II had truly been a necessary war, then there would have been no need for a draft. But there was a draft because not enough Americans were willing to fight and die overseas without being forced to by our government, which sent hundreds of thousands of young American men to their deaths. If you read the press of their day, the American GI didn't know what he was fighting for in Europe. The Japanese had attacked his country, but he was fighting and dying in Africa, Italy and France. It didn't make sense.

Gen. George Patton, our greatest general of the war, wrote about the idiocy of destroying Hitler only to turn over half the world to Stalin. Patton knew that he had been intentionally held back in the fight against Hitler, which caused thousands of unnecessary American deaths in order to allow Stalin time to seize Eastern Europe when Patton knew he could have taken it first. In the aftermath of the war, he began to criticize the actions of our leadership. He wrote to his wife that he was going to resign his commission and come home and reveal what was really going on. Fortunately for the communists and the globalists, he met an untimely death before he ever made it home.

Our elites to this day continue their massive propaganda campaign about that war. Millions of Americans have fallen for it. We want to be proud of our nation and our military and we want the sacrifices of hundreds of thousands of our young men to have been worth it. We want to believe. Our patriotism and our loyalty to our military members is used against us to justify their slaughter and to take us into new wars.

When you hear arguments for a draft, it is a clue that our leaders have a big war in the works. A draft means they want to send a lot of men overseas and they know that casualties will be very high—higher than they could possibly get away with using a volunteer army. The arguments for a draft are all sophistry to get you to go along with the forcible conscription of our youth for wars of invasion that will result in tens of thousands to hundreds of thousands of them being killed.

Don't buy it.

In his *Farewell Address,* George Washington said: "Against the insidious wiles of foreign influence (I conjure you to believe me, fellow-citizens) the jealousy of a free people ought to be constantly awake, since history and experience prove that foreign influence is one of the most baneful foes of republican government. But that jealousy to be useful must be impartial; else it becomes the instrument of the very influence to be avoided, instead of a defense against it. Excessive partiality for one foreign nation and excessive dislike of another cause those whom they actuate to see danger only on one side, and serve to veil and even second the arts of influence on the other. Real patriots who may resist the intrigues of the favorite are liable to become suspected and odious, while its tools and dupes usurp the applause and confidence of the people, to surrender their interests."

Washington said the real patriot who resists foreign wars will be hated by the warmongers and accused of being a traitor. Is that not as true today as it was in his day?

"The great rule of conduct for us in regard to foreign nations is in extending our commercial relations, to have with them as little political connection as possible," Washington said. "So far as we have already formed engagements, let them be fulfilled with perfect good faith. Here let us stop."

Our volunteer army is professional and certainly large enough to defend our nation from attack from any other nation in the world. We are in a much stronger position today to defend ourselves than we were in Washington's time. We do not need a draft for the defense of the United States.

A draft is necessary only for offensive wars of aggression. The only purpose of a draft is to provide cannon fodder for high-casualty wars of invasion—not for defense of our nation.

When you hear someone arguing, quite reasonably and logically for a draft, understand that you are listening to the voice of death. This voice is attempting to convince you that a draft is to defend America, you see. A draft is fair so everyone must share the burden of service to our country. It's to stop genocide. It's to stop evil. It's for your own good. It's for the good of the world.

If you disagree they will call you an isolationist and talk about World War II and Hitler and call you a Nazi.

Don't argue back. Don't try to reason. Just resist. You are an American citizen. No one can tell you to pick up a rifle and go kill and die against your own will. Not if you stand up and say no.

Creating fear in the minds of the American people is necessary to maintain the current military-based economy and our foreign policy of aggressive interventionism abroad.

But the fear is unjustified. No nation could ever invade us and conquer us, even if we were to drastically reduce our military spending. In fact, reducing our military spending, giving up our role as a global police force and instead concentrating on the common defense of the North American continent would enhance our safety and security while also increasing our prosperity and domestic tranquility.

But what would the world look like without the American hegemon? It would definitely be a different place.

Regardless of whether we reduce our military spending and role as world police through choice, through economic collapse or through military defeat, the days of the American hegemon are numbered. Our economy has been destroyed by suicidal trade policies. Mass immigration is reducing us to a Balkanized nation of low-paid corporate wage slaves. Like the British Empire before us, our nation is being buried under a massive debt. China is rising and our days of being the dominant economic and military power in the world will end in our lifetimes if the present course is continued. How we respond to this changing global environment is key to our survival as an independent nation and a free people.

The rise of China

The rapid economic rise of China over the past three decades has been the story of our era. China's continuing economic development and its growing military power will define our century.

In the 1980s, China was an impoverished country with an economy smaller than Belgium. Today, it is a manufacturing powerhouse, the world's workshop, with the world's second largest economy by gross domestic product and largest by purchasing power parity. It is the largest nation in the world by population, with four times as many people as the United States.

With economic power comes military power. With more than a billion people, China, as a global power, will be able to throw its weight around more and more as the century progresses, just as America threw its weight around in the 20th century.

China's standing in the world for the past 300 years has been an anomaly in its long history. For more than a thousand years, China was a dominant global power—economically, militarily and culturally. For centuries, the world hungered for Chinese merchandise. The nations of the East imitated Chinese culture and technology and bowed down before Chinese military might. In the West when Europe was a backward place, Europeans coveted Chinese goods and marveled at stories of China and its advanced civilization.

But in the 1500s, the Chinese government turned inward and China's economy and civilization stagnated. The Europeans began to develop rapidly, in part driven by the desire to reach China and trade for Chinese goods.

By the 1800s, China had been surpassed by Western Europe and Japan in economic and military power. The great Chinese nation was militarily humiliated time and again and was carved up and exploited by foreigners from nations a fraction its size.

Americans should pay careful attention to the Chinese experience. Due to bad leadership, a great nation, powerful and advanced and seemingly invincible, quickly stagnated and fell victim to outsiders who sought to exploit its people and resources. China was looted by foreigners, by opium pushers and sellers of false ideologies. Its wealth and territory were stolen under threat from foreigners in gunboats and armed with bayonets. Foreign financiers funded revolutions and wars that reduced the Chinese people to poverty.

While those of us in the West may be vaguely aware of how China was humiliated over the past few centuries, for the Chinese the harsh lessons of history are burned into their minds. For the Chinese, free trade is a sucker's game. Their memory of free trade is British gunboats arriving with opium. The British killed Chinese for the right to push drugs in Chinese cities. The British had been running a trade deficit with China. British gold and silver were being used to buy Chinese goods while the British had nothing to offer that the Chinese wanted to buy. Opium was their answer and free trade was their justification. Bullets, artillery shells and death were how the British got the Chinese to bend to their will.

The old free trade maxim was proven true time and again by British free traders: If goods don't cross borders, armies will.

The Chinese government refused to allow British opium into its cities so in came the British army and navy; blood was spilled so the goods the British were selling could flood in. The British trade deficit with China turned to a trade surplus and China was impoverished under an opium epidemic that turned millions of Chinese into drug addicts.

Great fortunes were made in the West off the sale of opium. Interestingly, today opium remains one of the world's most lucrative commodities—underground trade of opium is estimated to be worth hundreds of billions of dollars, not subject to taxation with profits laundered through the banking system. In 2000, the Taliban shut down opium production in Afghanistan, the world's leading producer of opium at the time. Within a year of the shutdown, the U.S. military invaded. Since 2001, opium production has skyrocketed in Afghanistan exceeding the production levels from before the arrival of the U.S. military. It's a development that might cause one to ponder the old free trade slogan about armies crossing borders when goods cannot.

Opium left an indelible mark on the thinking of today's Chinese leadership. Today, China is following a nationalistic trade policy of protecting and developing home industries while running up a massive trade surplus with the United States. The goal of Chinese development is to capture industries and technologies to build up Chinese economic power, which can then be translated into military power. The Chinese are well aware that the United States did not rise to become the world's greatest economy by following a free trade policy. They know our great economy was built behind a tariff wall. It wasn't until after we had attained economic dominance that our leaders switched gears to free trade. The Chinese know that we were protectionist when Britain was a free trade nation and our protectionist policies allowed us to surpass Britain in economic power while Britain fell into debt and into dependency on the United States. These are the lessons of history that the Chinese have learned and why they are following our successful development policies of the 19th century while watching us exhaust ourselves in overseas wars, lose our industries and fall deeper into debt to them.

As its power grows, China is reassuming its historical role as the dominant power in Asia. Right now, the dominant power is the United States. The biggest obstacle to China reasserting itself and rectifying what it sees as historical wrongs—such as the loss of Taiwan—is the U.S. Navy.

Just as the U.S. Navy became an obstacle and a target for the Japanese Empire, our navy today will increasingly be seen by China as a foreign menace that must be dealt with.

By patrolling the Chinese coastline, our navy is not protecting us but instead is putting us in grave danger. If China and Japan, or China and Vietnam, or Malaysia, or the Philippines are willing to get in a shooting war over uninhabited rocks in the East and South China seas, should this be a cause for war for the United States? Should our young men and women sacrifice their lives over foreign quarrels over uninhabited rocks? Should our cities face nuclear destruction over border conflicts in Asia?

Any war between China and the United States would be a global disaster. The use of our navy in Asia and the meddling in Asian affairs by our leaders are an existential threat to the American people. It is not in the interest of the American people to be a global police force in Asia.

Japan, Korea, the Philippines and Vietnam were dealing with the Chinese long before the United States came into existence. It is not in our interest to defend Vietnam or Japan or any other nation from the Chinese. They can figure out how to get along with China without us just as they did before we entered our era of international meddling.

Smedley Butler gave his opinion on how the United States can avoid getting drawn into wars that are none of our business.

Butler wrote: "The ships of our navy, it can be seen, should be specifically limited, by law, to within 200 miles of our coastline.

Had that been the law in 1898, the Maine would never have gone to Havana Harbor. She never would have been blown up. There would have been no war with Spain with its attendant loss of life. Two hundred miles is ample, in the opinion of experts, for defense purposes. Our nation cannot start an offensive war if its ships can't go further than 200 miles from the coastline. Planes might be permitted to go as far as 500 miles from the coast for purposes of reconnaissance. And the army should never leave the territorial limits of our nation."

When the 19th century was coming to a close and new powers were rising, the world entered a very dangerous period. Britain was exhausted and buried in debt. Germany and Japan were rising and were challenging the old order. The result was two world wars that brought mass death and destruction. America and the Soviet Union emerged as the new great powers.

The Soviet Union is now gone and America is buried in debt and exhausted. China is rising and will increasingly challenge the old order as its power grows in relation to the United States.

The rise of American power in the 20th century was used not to benefit the American people, but instead to advance the ambitions of a transnational elite that desired global government. These elites rejected the wisdom of our Founders who warned us to avoid foreign entanglements. Instead, these elites plunged us into World War I, World War II, the Korean War, the Vietnam War, the Persian Gulf War, the Afghanistan war, the Iraq war, and countless other interventions around the world.

Are we a safer and freer nation today because of all this bloodshed, death and destruction? Are we more prosperous? Did all that death and destruction make the world a better place?

Today, the world is no closer to peace than it was before we assumed the role of global police force. Our wars and international meddling have made us hated. In fact, we are entering a very dangerous moment in world history—as dangerous, if not more so, than in 1914 or 1939.

As China rises, it will challenge the old order. How America meets this challenge could secure our survival as a free people or it could spell the doom of our nation.

America is in debt and in economic turmoil. We are overburdened by our military spending and our alliances abroad. Yet, our enormous geographic advantages over the world's other great powers remain.

It is time we return to the wisdom of our Founders, reject the propaganda of the internationalist warmongers who are using us for their own ends, and return to a policy of avoiding entangling alliances abroad. We should take advantage of our unique position on the globe to stay out of wars that should not be our business.

China is a great nation but geographically it is in a very difficult spot. Unlike the United States, which is separated from the rest of the world by the Atlantic and Pacific oceans and shares borders with only two nations which are not a military threat to us, China is surrounded by great power rivals.

Its great rival, Japan, is off its coast to its northeast. To the north is Russia. To its southwest is India. And to its west are the Islamic nations of Pakistan, Afghanistan, Tajikistan, Kyrgyzstan and Kazakhstan. It also shares a border with the unstable nations of North Korea, Vietnam, Laos and Myanmar.

It has border disputes with two of the biggest powers in the world—Russia and India, both of which are nuclear powers. In the 20th century, it had border conflicts with both that broke out into open hostilities, and recently it has been riling up the Indians with border incursions into disputed territory in the Himalayas. It also suffers from Muslim unrest on its western frontier and has experienced terrorism from its Muslim minorities.

It has a narrow coastline that is boxed in by South Korea, Japan, Taiwan, the Philippines and Vietnam—all rivals with competing claims in the surrounding seas.

Compared to the United States, China has a complicated and dangerous border that gives its leaders much to worry about. Our situation is strategically superior and easily defended while China is boxed in on all sides.

China is also a nation suffering from enormous internal

imbalances that could lead to social upheaval. Its history is bloody with periodic revolutions and civil wars—some of the worst in history, such as the Taiping Rebellion of 1850-1864 that left 20 million dead, making our own Civil War seem like a minor sideshow in comparison.

As China grows militarily, its rivals will respond. They will take measures to defend themselves or come to an understanding with China, just as they have always done going back centuries.

However, the United States is the wild card in the region, throwing Asia out of balance and causing China's neighbors to act boldly in ways they wouldn't if we weren't in the picture.

Asia is not our neighborhood. Our meddling only increases the likelihood of war, not reduces it. The Asian nations must chart their own path without our meddling and our arrogance in believing we know what's best for billions of people on the other side of the world whose nations have existed before Columbus sailed the Atlantic.

If war were to break out in China on the Russian or Indian frontiers, or with Vietnam or with Taiwan, it would be a travesty. If we were to intervene, it would become our travesty.

It is in the American interest to extricate ourselves from the region and declare neutrality in all Asian conflicts. If India and China were to go to war over some desolate Himalayan peak, or Russia and China were to fight over the changing course of a Siberian river, or Japan and China were to engage in a naval battle over some rocks in the East China Sea, the fighting could quickly escalate and go nuclear, especially if we were to intervene and cause China to feel backed against a wall. Our cities would be set in their sights and face destruction.

Better to follow the advice of our Founders and stay out of foreign wars.

Our national interest is to stay out of Asia and mind our own business rather than make their travesties become ours. The Vietnam and Korean wars were disastrous for our nation. The Iraq War was a tragedy. The Afghanistan war has been an endless quagmire and farce. The lesson learned from those bloody wars is that we should never ever again engage in a shooting war in Asia. Or in Europe, for that matter.

The solution is to pull our troops out of Asia and pull back our navy to our own territories.

We are a nation in debt and exhausted by war. All of our wars in Asia, Europe and the Middle East have not brought world peace and have not made us respected as a nation, but instead have only brought oceans of blood and killed off so many Americans in their youth. We are hated around the world for our interventions and seen as an exploitative imperialist nation. Our so-called allies lobby our government and corrupt our politicians to pull us into their conflicts that have nothing to do with us.

Whether we intervene or not, we will be criticized and hated. We are damned if we do and damned if we don't. We might as well don't, and save American lives and money rather than continuing our destructive interventionist foreign policy that pretends to be for democracy and liberty while in reality is serving the interests of a transnational elite that uses us and our military to protect an international financial system that manipulates the American dollar as a medium for global exploitation.

This is China's era. Let them have their day. China is not a natural enemy of the United States. If we were to pull out and disengage from the region, the Chinese would turn their attention away from us and to more immediate concerns. China has its hands full on its own borders. If we remain strong and united and mind our own business, China will pose no threat to us.

Russia is not a natural enemy of the United States. It also has a long and complicated border with serious security concerns. During the Crimean War of 1853-1856, France, England and Turkey invaded the Crimean Peninsula, which was Russian territory at the time. It was a bloody war that left more than 700,000 people dead. Yet, the United States stayed out of it and the war had no effect on our lives. Russia has been fighting wars on its frontiers from time immemorial. It is not in our interest to take sides. Its neighbors have been part of Russia and have broken away time and again over history. These conflicts will persist and the world will keep turning. Our involvement only increases the danger to ourselves and throws the region out of balance. Europe is a continent that has a larger population than us and is richer than us. If they don't want to fight Russians over Ukraine or Latvia, why should we? Why should Americans fight and die over their backyard? Why should we risk the survival of our own nation over disagreements on the other side of the world?

India and Pakistan are two nuclear nations with serious conflicts with each other. Our interest is to remain neutral and not choose sides. They must resolve their conflicts themselves without Americans intervening with all our arrogance and ignorance of their issues. We only make matters worse. They are nations that must deal with their own problems without American meddling.

The Middle East has been nothing but a quagmire for us. Our wars and meddling have left the region a smoking rubble where our own young people have died in vain for the interests of foreign governments and domestic war profiteers. The Middle East today is no closer to peace than when we first began meddling there in earnest after World War II. We arrogantly believed we could bring them capitalism and democracy and instead we have left the region more of a mess than the imperialist powers of Europe did a century before. The Middle East is boiling with ethnic and religious tensions that go back millennia. At what point will it finally dawn on us that our interventions are destructive not only to the people there but also to ourselves? At what point do we come to the understanding that it is time to forget about trying to fix the Middle East and instead turn our attention to the Midwest where our own people are struggling?

It is time to forget about the Middle East and start taking care of the Midwest. In our own cities, we have violence and gang wars. We have Bloods and Crips and Sureños and Norteños fighting deadly gang wars in our own backyard, and we think we are going to solve conflicts with Shiites and Sunnis, Israelis and Palestinians, Serbians and Albanians, Ukrainians and Russians?

No. Let those people solve their own problems. Let us

worry about our own backyard. Let us attempt to fix our own problems here at home before we meddle in other people's affairs.

What we need is a strong defense that protects us from attack while not entangling us in conflicts abroad that only bring us sorrow and pain.

Don't tread on me

In 1838, a young Abraham Lincoln gave a speech. "We find ourselves in the peaceful possession, of the fairest portion of the earth, as regards extent of territory, fertility of soil, and salubrity of climate," he said. "We find ourselves under the government of a system of political institutions, conducing more essentially to the ends of civil and religious liberty, than any of which the history of former times tells us. We, when mounting the stage of existence, found ourselves the legal inheritors of these fundamental blessings.

"Shall we expect some transatlantic military giant, to step the ocean, and crush us at a blow? Never! All the armies of Europe, Asia and Africa combined, with all the treasure of the earth (our own excepted) in their military chest; with a Bonaparte for a commander, could not by force, take a drink from the Ohio, or make a track on the Blue Ridge, in a trial of a thousand years.

"At what point then is the approach of danger to be expected? I answer, if it ever reach us, it must spring up amongst us. It cannot come from abroad. If destruction be our lot, we must ourselves be its author and finisher. As a nation of freemen, we must live through all time, or die by suicide."

Lincoln recognized in his day when America was still a small country compared to the great empires of Europe that no overseas power could threaten us. He recognized that the danger to America and to our liberty was not from foreign armies. He warned that if we were to be defeated as a nation our defeat would come from within.

Are not our current policies of free trade, mass immigration and endless wars abroad the policies of national suicide? Since the foundation of the Federal Reserve, these policies have been pushed on us relentlessly.

In his autobiography, Gen. Ulysses S. Grant wrote of the prowess of the American fighting man during the Civil War—the enduring resoluteness of the Northerner and the dash and daring of the Southern soldier. "The troops on both sides were American," Grant wrote, "and united they need not fear any foreign foe."

When we are united, no nation abroad is a threat to us. Not China. Not Russia. Not the nations of Europe, or any combination of them.

The true threat to our nation is not foreign nations or some terrorist organization overseas. The true threat is within. The true threat to the American people is from the globalist politicians and bureaucrats who have infested our government and have entangled us in conflicts around the world. In our name, they bomb wedding parties and kill children, they arm revolutionaries who destabilize societies, they meddle in the politics of other countries, they promise American lives to defend countries that we have no common interests with. These politicians and bureaucrats are funded by multinational corporations, international banks and foreign lobbyists. They are putting us all in danger. These people are not loyal to the American people but instead to their benefactors and to the goals of globalist organizations, such as the Council on Foreign Relations, the Trilateral Commission and the Bilderbergers. Their corporate media whips up hatred toward certain nations that the globalists want us to destroy, while presenting favored nations and groups with sympathy. They attach us to foreign nations and obligate us to defend them through treaties that entangle us in alliances that put our own people under threat in conflicts that are none of our business. The globalists are supported in their goals and in their actions by bought-and-paid-for propagandists in the media, while true patriots are shunned or smeared.

"As avenues to foreign influence in innumerable ways, such attachments are particularly alarming to the truly enlightened and independent patriot," George Washington told us. "How many opportunities do they afford to tamper with domestic factions, to practice the arts of seduction, to mislead public opinion, to influence or awe the public councils?"

The source of their power is money. And when you follow the money, it all leads back to the Federal Reserve.

"Our detached and distant situation invites and enables us to pursue a different course," Washington said. "If we remain one people under an efficient government, the period is not far off when we may defy material injury from external annoyance; when we may take such an attitude as will cause the neutrality we may at any time resolve upon to be scrupulously respected; when belligerent nations, under the impossibility of making acquisitions upon us, will not lightly hazard the giving us provocation; when we may choose peace or war, as our interest, guided by justice, shall counsel.

"Why forego the advantages of so peculiar a situation? Why quit our own to stand upon foreign ground? Why, by interweaving our destiny with that of any part of Europe, entangle our peace and prosperity in the toils of European ambition, rivalship, interest, humor or caprice?

"It is our true policy to steer clear of permanent alliances with any portion of the foreign world; so far, I mean, as we are now at liberty to do it; for let me not be understood as capable of patronizing infidelity to existing engagements. I hold the maxim no less applicable to public than to private affairs, that honesty is always the best policy. I repeat it, therefore, let those engagements be observed in their genuine sense. But, in my opinion, it is unnecessary and would be unwise to extend them."

Before World War II, Washington's words guided our foreign policy. Warmongers constantly tried to plunge us into wars but the people remembered his words and attempted to avoid foreign entanglements. In 1898, Washington was betrayed when we were stampeded into the Spanish American War by the yellow press and warmongering politicians. Washington was betrayed again by our entry into World War I. But people still remembered his words and spoke out against the warmongers.

Since World War II, Washington's words have been forgotten and the globalists have been using us as their global police force to their own ends, entangling us in every conflict around the world. They have plunged us into war after war overseas. The cost in blood and treasure to the American people and to the people of the world has been appalling. For the globalists, all the wars we have fought for the past 100 years have been a great boon. The plutocrats have never been richer or closer to their dream of a world government; but for the rest of us it has been an expensive, bloody mess.

It is time to pursue a different course. Let us bring the troops home. Let's bring them home from Europe, the Middle East and Asia. Let's close our air bases abroad and bring the planes and pilots home. Let's pull back our navy to our own coastline.

Let's protect America again. Let's be a republic again and defend our Constitution, our liberties and our prosperity here at home. Let's defend our own borders for a change.

We have sent our young people around the world for more than a century now participating in foreign wars that have plowed under hundreds of thousands of our own and millions of others. Are we loved around the world for all this slaughter? Have we brought the world peace?

No.

Let's pursue a different course. Our country is exhausted. Let's stay home and take care of our own and not be a part of other people's conflicts. Whether we do this or not, there will be more wars in the future. Countries will go to war and people will die like they always have. If we stay out of it, the world will still turn.

"Observe good faith and justice towards all nations; cultivate peace and harmony with all," George Washington told us. "The great rule of conduct for us in regard to foreign nations is in extending our commercial relations, to have with them as little political connection as possible. So far as we have already formed engagements, let them be fulfilled with perfect good faith.

Here let us stop."

Let's heed Washington's words. It is time to return to a policy of avoiding foreign entanglements. We are strong and can defend our own country without being pulled into conflicts abroad. Armed neutrality should be our foreign policy. We should cultivate peace and harmony with all, but stay out of their stupid wars.

The obstacle to this policy is our own warmongering press and politicians who are paid off by globalists and foreign influence. They are the enemies of the American patriot.

When our service members join the military, they hold up their right hands and solemnly swear an oath of enlistment. They state their names and say, "I will support and defend the Constitution of the United States against all enemies, foreign and domestic; that I will bear true faith and allegiance to the same; and that I will obey the orders of the President of the United States and the orders of the officers appointed over me, according to regulations and the Uniform Code of Military Justice. So help me God."

Our officers take a similar oath. They raise their right hands and state their names and say, "I will support and defend the Constitution of the United States against all enemies, foreign and domestic; that I will bear true faith and allegiance to the same; that I take this obligation freely, without any mental reservation or purpose of evasion; and that I will well and faithfully discharge the duties of the office on which I am about to enter. So help me God."

They swear to protect the Constitution against all enemies, foreign and domestic. Those enemies today are not in Asia, Europe or Africa. They are here at home, walking the halls of the Capitol. They are in the boardrooms of international banks and multinational corporations, in think tank conference rooms, in newsrooms, pushing their agenda, planning new trade treaties, planning to submerge us under a deluge of new immigrants, planning new wars.

It is time to turn our attention to the home front where our

Constitution is being destroyed by the enemies of our republic, both foreign and domestic.

No more wars abroad. Let's defend our freedom here at home. Let's defend the legacy handed down to us through the sacrifices of the patriots of 1776.

The Tyranny of the Media

There should be no irony in the fact that the most coveted award in American journalism is named after a warmonger.

When an American journalist wins a Pulitzer Prize, he has achieved the top honor in his line of work. Yet, who was Joseph Pulitzer for whom the award is named?

Pulitzer was an immigrant to our country who had ties to money. He arrived in the U.S. at age 17. After a stint in the Army and a series of jobs, he landed a position as a reporter for a German language newspaper in St. Louis. By the time he was 22, he was appointed to fill a vacancy in the Missouri state legislature. Within a few years, he was buying newspapers. In 1883, he bought the *New York World* from the infamous financier Jay Gould.

Pulitzer's style of journalism became known as yellow journalism. He used sensationalism to sell papers. Today, William Randolph Hearst's name is more closely associated with yellow journalism, but Pulitzer was the master of it a decade before Hearst purchased the *New York Journal*. Hearst modeled the *Journal* after Pulitzer's *World*.

In the late 1890s, Pulitzer and Hearst competed to produce the most sensational stories about Spanish atrocities in Cuba in an attempt to incite the American people to war in the face of strong antiwar sentiment in Congress and in the White House.

Hollywood has branded Hearst as the main culprit behind yellow journalism and many writers have blamed him for the war, while leaving Pulitzer's reputation alone. Pulitzer's name has instead been associated with his prize and what's best in American journalism.

What is often not said is that Hearst visited Cuba during the Spanish-American War and saw firsthand the death his warmongering had wrought. He had a change of heart after seeing the dead and dying and his yellow journalism softened afterward. His papers did not fan the flames of war before World War I and during the 1930s when warmongers were attempting to break American isolationism.

Hearst paid his reporters well and treated them well. He was widely regarded by reporters as a good publisher to work for. Many of Pulitzer's reporters and editors fled to Hearst's paper when the two publishers were engaged in a newspaper circulation war.

Pulitzer was known as a temperamental and volatile tyrant who fired reporters and editors often in a rage. He employed spies to infiltrate Hearst's newsroom to scoop stories. Pulitzer was a strange man who traveled the world on his yacht without his wife or family but with an entourage of single, young men. He became one of America's great plutocrats with a home on Jekyll Island near the homes of J.P. Morgan and John D. Rockefeller.

But because of his prize, he is not remembered for his faults as Hearst is, but instead for the money under his name that still today he holds out as a carrot to reward ambitious reporters who compete for it by attempting to please a board of judges at Columbia University.

More than a century ago, Pulitzer and Hearst made great fortunes in the newspaper business. Today, many people are under the false assumption that the purpose of the media is to make money. But the quickest way to lose a fortune is to go into the media business. Pulitzer had financial backers with deep pockets and Hearst had his father's silver fortune. The reality is the money comes first—you need a whole lot of money if you are going to run a newspaper, a television network or a radio station and play the media game.

The people who run the media do not do so to make money. They go into media because they already have access to a great deal of money and they want to employ it to influence the public.

The power of the press in undeniable. It has the power to start wars, to lose them, to elect politicians and to destroy them. It can turn a business no one has ever heard of into a multimillion-dollar enterprise. It can start fads. It can conduct character assassinations and drag a person's name through the mud without the slightest bit of truth to any of the accusations made. The press can bring down presidents, or overnight it can turn an obscure person into a nationally, even internationally, known figure. It can create and destroy—especially if it speaks with one voice across the board putting out the same themes and messages day in and day out.

Along with control of the monetary system and control of politicians, control of the media is a critical pillar of the power structure that the international bankers stand atop. The media is a weapon of influence and control used to move the thoughts of the people in the direction that the banking elite wants. The media is used to steer the public's attention to matters that the elite deem important and divert the public away from subjects the bankers wish to keep hidden. The purpose of the media is not to inform but to shape public opinion. It repeats day in and day out certain themes to implant them in our heads while suppressing other topics and issues that our betters would rather us not think about. We are kept distracted with trivialities and salaciousness while the bankers' agenda moves forward. The media gives voice to complaints from the public about various government matters, which gives the semblance of freedom of speech while keeping those complaints carefully controlled and on the targets of their choosing. Liberals and conservatives. Republicans and Democrats. Christians, Muslims and atheists. Rich and poor. Black and white. North and South. East and West. Through the press, our passions are excited and inflamed and we are kept in a state of agitation that creates discontent and keeps us divided among ourselves.

By the end of World War II, most American newspapers, the book publishing industry, Hollywood and all of radio and television were in the hands of the international bankers and their agents. From 1945 to the late 1990s, the American media was consolidated and heavily centralized. The wire services, radio stations, publishing houses, television networks and Hollywood studios were controlled by a handful of men mostly out of New

York who have provided the lenses through which Americans have viewed the world.

The lenses from the various outlets may have slightly different tints to appeal to different audiences but they all show us the world that the owners wish us to see. And the owners are a small group of people financed and under the control of fractional reserve bankers.

To understand how the bankers take control, the newspaper industry provides a good illustration of their methods. At one time in this country, newspapers were mainly family-owned enterprises that gave a wide variety of opinions from community to community. In the late 1800s, banking interests began to gobble up paper after paper.

But even after World War II, many newspapers were still privately owned and the editorial pages reflected the opinions of their owners. Cities around the country often had more than one newspaper often with morning and evening editions.

But toward the end of the 20th century, the newspaper business was becoming more and more consolidated by a smaller and smaller group of men.

In the 1980s, a copyeditor named Dean Singleton began buying up newspapers and building a media empire. Singleton was a college dropout from a poor family from the small Texas town of Graham. He had tried his hand at being a reporter which hadn't worked out for him. At age 21, while working as a copyeditor at the *Dallas Morning News,* some entrepreneurs offered him the chance to run a small town weekly newspaper, which he accepted.

Then, at age 34, Singleton began acquiring newspapers and building one of America's biggest newspaper empires, purchasing one newspaper after another around the nation. When he was 36, he spent $150 million to buy the *Houston Post* and another $95 million for the *Denver Post*.

Singleton's game was to use debt to buy struggling newspapers, often from heirs who had inherited the papers from their fathers and did not wish to run them. Singleton would buy these papers and then ruthlessly cut costs by firing reporters, photographers, copyeditors, editors and any personnel that he could. He bought up all the papers he could and consolidated staff and content on a regional basis. Editorial and copy desks were centralized by region to cut expenses. The opinion pages and editorial content were made the same across regions, meaning that where once you could find a variety of opinions from various papers regarding different topics, the same opinions would run across Singleton's MediaNews Group empire. The same politicians would be supported or attacked or ignored and the same issues and topics were covered in the same way. The front pages in Denver, Oakland or Detroit were often exactly the same.

By age 40, Singleton was a wealthy media mogul with a great deal of influence. By 2005, he controlled 56 daily newspapers and over 100 non-dailies in 12 states with a circulation of about 2.5 million. From 2007 to 2012, he served as the chairman of the Associated Press, the world's largest wire service that provides news content to media outlets around the world.

In the many articles on the Internet about Singleton, never is it explained how a small town Texan who was never much of a reporter and not a businessman suddenly rose up meteorically from the copy desk to build and own one of the nation's largest newspaper companies.

Singleton has been described as having a strong work ethic, but his business experience amounted to running a small-town weekly paper purchased with other people's money. Yet by age 36, he had spent $150 million to purchase a metropolitan newspaper in one of the nation's largest cities.

How does one do that?

The answer lies in Singleton's business partner, a man named Richard Scudder.

Scudder, who died in 2012 at age 99, was an interesting character with an obscure past. Not much is written about him online, but unlike Singleton, who is essentially reviled by reporters as having had a negative impact on journalism, Scudder is written about in positive terms. Scudder was an inventor from a family that had long been in the newspaper business on the East Coast. Most articles emphasize that his lineage is distinctly American and traces back to before the Revolutionary War. Articles about him call him the financier who backed the rise of Singleton's MediaNews Group.

What is intriguing about Scudder is that he was a U.S. Army military intelligence officer during World War II. According to the *New York Times,* Scudder was assigned to Operation Annie, Annie being short for anonymous. The operation was an underground German-language radio station that broadcasted misinformation to the German people.

Scudder worked in psychological operations warfare, or PSYOPS for short, which is a military field that specializes in producing and disseminating misinformation and disinformation to persuade, change and influence populations in order to achieve strategic goals.

After the war, Scudder returned to the United States to work in journalism. His connections in the financial industry enabled him to provide Singleton with the money to buy up newspapers around the country, consolidate them and centralize the themes and messages that his papers were using to influence the American population.

Scudder was the money man. He chose Singleton to be his hatchet man and the public face of the company. Singleton is notorious in the field of journalism as a man who was less concerned about the quality of journalism than he was about paying back his creditors. He also had no compunction when it came to laying off personnel. If you were a reporter who worked for a newspaper that was purchased by Singleton, you knew right away that layoffs were coming and there was a good chance you would soon be looking for a new job.

If you read MediaNews Group newspapers with a critical eye, certain themes and messages will become apparent. MediaNews Group newspapers report the day to day news on crime, local politics, sports and so on; but at the macro-level the themes and messages are hard to miss.

First of all, the papers are pro-immigration and very sympathetic to illegal immigrants. MediaNews Group immigration stories are always written with a humanitarian point of view toward immigrants with America presented as a nation of immigrants. Story after story tells us how all these hardworking immigrants face hardships from our xenophobic society. Over and again you read about the honor graduate immigrant child who is fearful that her parents will be deported. You read about the struggling, hardworking father who fears deportation and the breakup of his family. The negative impact of immigration on wages, schools, hospitals, our communities and the crime rate is downplayed or blamed on other things. The irony is that Singleton's reporters who write these pro-immigration stories tend to be liberal with strong pro-labor sentiments. These reporters have been laid off in large numbers, seen their salaries slashed, their health insurance benefits reduced, their 401k matches taken away and their unions crushed under MediaNews Group's harsh anti-labor tactics. All the while MediaNews Group reporters continue to promote diversity and the need for more immigrants never questioning why a company that treats its own workers so harshly is so driven to promote increasing the level of immigration into our country. These pro-immigrant reporters never put two and two together and realize that immigration is a tool the rich use against American labor, especially for the purpose of weakening unions.

Second, the papers are always supportive of free trade. Free trade is mentioned as a net benefit to the nation, while the negative effects, such as job loss, wage stagnation, community disruption, and so on, are downplayed or blamed on other causes. Every now and then the paper's editorial pages will issue warnings about the dangers of protectionism. The ghosts of Reed Smoot and Willis C. Hawley often haunt the editorial pages whenever a whiff of protectionist sentiment is detected in the public.

Third, the papers are supportive of America's interventionist foreign policy. Establishment politicians who advocate for American action against Iran or Russia or anywhere else around the world are portrayed as being mainstream while politicians who do not support America's world police role are portrayed as fringe characters and isolationists. MediaNews Group papers support interventionism abroad, but will harshly criticize actions of our troops overseas or of specific decisions made by interventionist politicians, but the theme that America must take a leadership role in the world using our military remains.

Fourth, the primacy of the Federal Reserve is faithfully supported. Specific actions and actors can be criticized when it comes to monetary policy but the monetary system itself is never questioned. MediaNews Group newspapers always support this system and defend it. For example, on July 27, 2009, during the depths of the housing bust, MediaNews Group newspapers in Northern California ran an opinion piece that was a spirited defense of the Fed. The op-ed stated that Fed Chairman Ben Bernanke was taking criticism from both sides of the aisle in Congress due to the Fed's failure to uncover unsound lending practices by financial firms.

"The Obama administration wants to give the Fed greater authority to oversee financial institutions, something it should have had in the past," the editorial stated. "A particularly troublesome idea that Bernanke is wisely rejecting is a congressional proposal to let the Government Accountability Office audit the Fed. ... It is essential that the central bank remain independent of congressional influence, which could result in financial decisions by the Fed being based more on partisan politics than sound economics. ... The Fed should be given a chance to show that with some additional new authority, it can keep a check on the lending practices of financial institutions without the aid of a new consumer protection bureaucracy and the meddling of Congress."

There you have it in a nutshell. The purpose of buying up all these newspapers in communities from coast to coast was to persuade, change and influence the American people to accept the strategic goals of mass immigration policy, free trade policy, American interventionism abroad, and to protect the independence of the Federal Reserve from democratic reforms. The Fed must remain independent and free to control the monetary system without the interference of our elected representatives and the democratic process.

Politicians who support mass immigration, free trade, America's world police role and the power of the Fed are presented as mainstream, while politicians who stray from the mainstream line are presented as bigots, xenophobes, protectionists, isolationists, wingnuts or conspiracy theorists.

Now, some people might think this is just how capitalism works, that Singleton and Scudder were buying up newspapers in an industry undergoing change and that they were doing what they could to make a buck in the good old American capitalist spirit—that Singleton's empire is an example of the creative destruction the economic theorists tell us about, and that Singleton and Scudder were providing a greater good by buying up struggling newspapers and reorganizing them during a period of change to make them profitable once again. But this was demonstrably not the case.

In 2010, MediaNews Group filed for Chapter 11 bankruptcy. According to a March 19, 2010 article in the *Denver Business Journal*, Singleton and Scudder had lost hundreds of millions of dollars during the course of purchasing their empire. They had borrowed nearly a billion dollars and had squandered almost all of it.

Under a reorganization plan, MediaNews Group was allowed to reduce its debt from $930 million to $165 million. The creditors agreed to reduce the debt in exchange for equity in the company. The two biggest creditors were Wells Fargo and Bank of America, which received the lion's share of the equity. The plan specified that Singleton would receive a base salary of $994,000, plus 6 percent of the restructured company's stock and annual bonuses of up to $500,000 if the company hit earnings targets. The plan specified that the president of the company, Joseph Lodovic, would earn a salary of $1 million and annual bonuses of as much as $500,000, and receive 3 percent of the restructured company's stock. Lodovic had received a $500,000 bonus for his work on the restructuring and for initiating the bankruptcy proceedings and received another $250,000 more when the bankruptcy plan was approved.

So, essentially, Singleton racked up nearly a billion dollars in debt from big banks to buy up newspapers around the country. He couldn't pay back the debt so the banks basically cut their losses of $765 million while continuing to pay Singleton around $1 million a year for his work for them.

Is this the free enterprise system?

Apparently, money wasn't the object here, at least not for the banks when it came to financing Singleton and Scudder. The banks were willing to hand over hundreds of millions of dollars to them and they lost most of it, but the banks were still happy enough with the outcome to continue paying Singleton nearly $1 million a year despite the massive monetary losses.

Do you think an aspiring owner of a small newspaper can compete in the marketplace with the likes of Singleton who is backed by nearly a billion dollars and does not have to make a dime of profit?

In 2013, Singleton retired a very wealthy man at age 62. He is physically weak and his hands shake from multiple sclerosis, which he had been battling for 26 years while building his empire. But his work for the banks is done and he now lives on a large ranch in Colorado.

The Singleton story is not unique to the United States. The international bankers spend millions and are willing to lose it all to put their people in control of the media. After all, it's just money they are spending, and money is just numbers on a screen or pieces of paper printed off a printing press. When you control the system that creates money then you can always make more of it. And the media is a crucial resource that must be controlled if you are going to maintain control of that system and push an agenda that will destroy the sovereignty of nations and impoverish the middle and working classes.

Two of the most widely read newspapers in America are

the *New York Times* and the *Wall Street Journal*. The *Times* is said to lean left while the *Journal* is said to lean right. One is said to be liberal and the other conservative. The two papers are often thought of as being opposed to each other, with the *Times* appealing to Democrats and liberals and the *Journal* to Republicans and conservatives.

But when it comes to the issues that matter to the bankers, the two papers line up and promote the interests of the banks, although they take different angles and approaches. When it comes to immigration, the *Times* takes a humanitarian view, producing sob story after sob story about immigrants who are suffering all manner of hardship and how the government must do something to protect and help them. For the *Journal*, immigration is more of an economic than a humanitarian matter. Immigrants start new businesses, fill labor shortages and bring economic growth, if you believe the line the *Journal* is pushing. Both papers push for more immigration. Both push for free trade. And both push for interventionism abroad.

The papers also line up on other issues that the banking elite are pushing, such as gay marriage, global warming and gun control.

As an aside, Carroll Quigley had an interesting theory about guns and weapons. In *Tragedy and Hope,* Quigley stated that authoritarian eras arise when weapons are expensive to use and take specialized skills and training, such as the feudal era of knights in armor on horseback, or our present era of tanks, aircraft carriers and jet fighters. Eras of democracy and freedom arise when weapons are easy to use and cheap to attain by the average person, such as the era of the Springfield musket and the Colt 45.

"Thus, mass armies of citizens, equipped with these cheap and easily used weapons, began to replace armies of professional soldiers, beginning about 1800 in Europe and even earlier in America," Quigley wrote. "At the same time, democratic government began to replace authoritarian governments (but chiefly in those areas where the cheap new weapons were available and local standards of living were high enough to allow people to obtain them.)"

Quigley stated: "In 1830 democracy was growing rapidly in Europe and in America. At that time the development of weapons had reached a point where governments could not get weapons which were much more effective than those which private individuals could get. ... As a result governments in Europe in 1830 hardly dared to oppress the people, and democracy was growing; but in the non-European world by 1930 (and even more by 1950) governments did dare to, and could, oppress their peoples, who could do little to prevent it."

In our media today, gun control is presented as being necessary for public safety, especially the safety of our children. Yet, gun control places restrictions on law-abiding gun owners, while doing little to stop illegal gun ownership. The main target in recent years has been AR-15 owners. It is the illegal gun owners who commit the vast majority of gun violence in the United States while the AR-15 is so rarely used in crime as to be statistically negligible.

Ask yourself why the media is pro-gun control.

Do you think it is because the media wants to protect us, or because it wants to protect the owners of the media from us?

If you are a homeowner with a gun, you can protect yourself from criminals. If you do not have a gun, you are dependent on the police for your protection. Ask yourself how this affects your views on government and on how you vote.

If you have an agenda to take away the sovereignty of a nation and implement a world government, would you be pro-gun control or pro-gun ownership?

Do you think the plantation owners allowed their slaves to own guns?

Returning to the *New York Times,* it led the way when it came to war propaganda in the lead up to the Iraq War. Its front page blared headlines about Iraqi weapons of mass destruction that could kill thousands or even millions of us. The *Times* ran these stories based on information provided from anonymous government officials who were either entirely incompetent or else criminally lying to start a war in which thousands of Americans and tens of thousands, if not more, Iraqis were killed. These anonymous sources peddled their fearmongering in the pages of the *Times,* mainly in the articles of reporter Judith Miller.

As soon as the war was underway, the *New York Times* became one of the biggest critics of the way it was fought. So the paper helped propagandize us into war and then criticized the actions of the men and women who were fighting and dying in it.

The *New York Times* happens to be one of the world's leading proponents for globalization, free trade, immigration and interventionism abroad. It also pushes a line that the more debt the U.S. government accrues, the better. Government debt equals economic growth, if the writers in the *Times* are to be believed. That is the purpose of the paper, to push the agenda of the international bankers, and the *Times* has been at it for over a hundred years.

The *New York Times* was purchased in 1896 by Adolph Ochs, the son of immigrants. Today, the publisher is Ochs's great grandson Arthur Ochs Sulzberger Jr. The *Times* has been pushing the same agenda spanning three centuries and multiple generations from the same wealthy dynasty.

In 2009, the Mexican multibillionaire Carlos Slim, who was the second richest man in the world in 2015, lent the *Times* $250 million. As of 2011, he controlled 8.1 percent of Class A shares in the New York Times Company. So you have a Mexican plutocrat financing one of America's most influential newspapers. And the *Times* is a major proponent for Mexican immigration and amnesty for illegal immigrants. Any guess as to why? Why, purely for humanitarian reasons, of course.

You should ask yourself why day in and day out both the *New York Times* and the *Wall Street Journal* and so many other American media organizations spend so much time, money and effort producing stories about the Middle East and why they are always telling us how important this region is to us and how we must do this and that over there and spend so much American money and so many lives in a region on the other side of the planet.

The interest of the American people is not to go bankrupt and lose our young people fighting in wars in the Middle East. Our true interest is to keep out of quarrels that have been going on for millennia and that we are not ever going to solve. But the bankers have interests over there so they are going to keep telling us not to be isolationists and that we must send our children to fight and die over there and we must pay our taxes to send them there.

The *Times* told us through anonymous sources from various intelligence agencies that Iraq had weapons of mass destruction. We know that the *Times* purveyed false information that was part of a propaganda push to start a war that resulted in the deaths of thousands of people. If this newspaper could do such a thing, how could any thinking or feeling person ever trust it again?

To understand how the mainstream media operates and who it works for, one only need look at the case of the reporter Gary Webb. Webb was an investigative reporter who worked for the *San Jose Mercury News*. He was a passionate believer in the importance of journalism and in the power of the press to bring corruption to light. In 1996, the *Mercury News* published Webb's *Dark Alliance* series of articles which reported that the CIA was associated with drug smugglers who were smuggling cocaine into American inner cities. According to his articles, the CIA was working with Contra rebels who were smuggling drugs into the U.S. to pay for their war against the Nicaraguan government. The drug smugglers had CIA handlers who had full knowledge of the drug smuggling operation. Webb's articles were released in the early days of the Internet and were one of the first instances of information going viral. People around the world were reading Webb's series.

The articles began to have an impact with the public, especially in the African American community, which had been devastated by the crack epidemic. As the articles gained traction, the mainstream media went into attack mode. The *New York Times,* the *Washington Post* and the *Los Angeles Times* all attacked and attempted to discredit Webb's reporting. The *Mercury News* was criticized and put under pressure by the larger establishment media outlets. Its management couldn't take the heat and began putting pressure on Webb. Webb was transferred by management to a smaller bureau far from his home and was eventually forced out of his job. However, he continued his work, releasing a book based on his *Dark Alliance* reporting. He also took a job in Sacramento helping to uncover corruption in the California state government. He had become a legendary figure who was respected by large segments of the public. By leaving newspaper journalism, he had freed himself from the need to earn a salary and continued his work unhindered by the watchful eyes of his former editors.

Unfortunately, his work came to an end in 2004 when he was found dead in his apartment with two bullets in his head. The coroner called it a suicide.

Despite the attacks from the mainstream media that ended Webb's career at the *Mercury News,* his reporting on CIA involvement in smuggling cocaine into the United States was vindicated. A later government investigation concluded that CIA assets had smuggled cocaine into the United States with the knowledge of CIA agents.

Before his death, Webb wrote an article, titled *The Mighty Wurlitzer Plays On,* about his belief in journalism and how it had changed after the *Dark Alliance* series was released.

"If we had met five years ago, you wouldn't have found a more staunch defender of the newspaper industry than me," Webb wrote. "I'd been working at daily papers for seventeen years at that point, doing no-holds barred investigative reporting for the bulk of that time. As far as I could tell, the beneficial powers the press theoretically exercised in our society weren't theoretical in the least. They worked.

"I wrote stories that accused people and institutions of illegal and unethical activities. The papers I worked for printed them, often unflinchingly, and many times gleefully. After these stories appeared, matters would improve. Crooked politicians got voted from office or were forcibly removed. Corrupt firms were exposed and fined. Sweetheart deals were rescinded, grand juries were impaneled, indictments came down, grafters were bundled off to the big house. Taxpayers saved money. The public interest was served. ... Bottom line: If there was ever a true believer, I was one.

"And then I wrote some stories that made me realize how sadly misplaced my bliss had been. The reason I'd enjoyed such smooth sailing for so long hadn't been, as I'd assumed, because I was careful and diligent and good at my job. It turned out to have nothing to do with it. The truth was that, in all those years, I hadn't written anything important enough to suppress."

What happened to Webb is a good illustration of how our media actually works. Reporters are mostly low paid, overworked, idealistic individuals who truly are trying to serve the public interest. The owners of their organizations allow these reporters to uncover corruption on their local city council, or on the local police force, or in business, or in any other areas where the true power in this country is not concerned. But when the moth flies too close to the flame, as Webb did, it gets burned. The power of the press is then used to suppress information that is deemed to be harmful to the interests of the international bankers. Make no mistake, the press is beholden to the money power in this country, which is centralized and flows directly from the Fed to the banks to the people in charge of the media. These people have an agenda and the press is a means for them to fulfill it.

The people at the very top of the largest media outlets are often members of the Trilateral Commission and the Council on Foreign Relations, or else are closely associated with these groups. Media moguls and reporters attend the Bilderberg Conference every year but never divulge what is discussed at that mysterious assemblage of agents for the global plutocracy.

To understand their end game, one only need listen to the words of Walter Cronkite during an award acceptance speech at the World Federalist Association in 1999. Cronkite served as the anchorman for CBS Evening News from 1962 to 1981 and was often called "the most trusted man in America." Each night during an extremely tumultuous time in American history, Cronkite told Americans the news in a friendly, paternal, yet authoritative style. He told Americans that President Kennedy had been shot, that Americans had landed on the moon, that the Vietnam War was a lost cause and that President Nixon was a crook.

After his retirement from journalism, the World Federalist Association presented him with the Norman Cousins Global Governance Award for his support for a world government. In his acceptance speech, Cronkite told the crowd that when he was starting out in his career he had been asked to be a spokesman and Washington lobbyist for the cause of world government. He said he had been honored to have been made the offer but instead he decided to become of reporter. He explained that he had been an advocate of world governance but his calling had been in the world of journalism.

"I did my best to report on the issues of the day with as much fairness as I possibly could in an objective a manner as possible to achieve," he told the crowd after accepting the Global Governance Award. "When I had my own strong opinions, I tried to put them aside for the moment in the interest of fairness. I didn't communicate my hope to my audience. Now, however, my circumstances are considerably different. I'm in a position to speak my mind and by God I'm going to do it."

Cronkite then went on to tell the crowd about those strong opinions that he kept from his audience while reading them the news.

"First, we Americans are going to have to yield up some of our sovereignty," he said. "That's going to be to many a bitter pill. ... Today, we must develop federal structures on a global level. To deal with world problems, we need a system of enforceable world law, a democratic world government."

He goes on to quote Alexander Hamilton, and then frames

his calls for the United States to surrender its sovereignty in idealistic American terms of liberty, peace and justice. He uses American ideals that appeal to so many of us, but twists them around to make it appear as if the American revolutionaries were not fighting for independence, sovereignty, self-rule, and to protect their liberty from tyrants abroad. Instead, Cronkite makes it sound as if the Founders had set up a system for the purpose of federalizing the planet to create a world government.

Cronkite then quotes a passage from a book by evangelist Pat Robertson about world government being the work of the devil.

"Well, join me," Cronkite said jokingly. "I'm glad to sit at the right hand of Satan."

Cronkite's speech was followed up by a speech from Hillary Clinton who praised Cronkite with the highest flattery for his career as a news reader. "For decades you told us the way it is," Clinton said, "but tonight we honor you for fighting for the way it could be."

Clinton's speech was followed by a speech from the actor Michael Douglas.

So here you had together one of the country's most influential journalists; the First Lady of the United States who went on to become a senator, a presidential candidate and the secretary of state; and, one of the world's highest paid actors; all speaking to an organization which advocates for the surrender of American sovereignty to a world government.

One might think that these are talented people who rose to influential positions who just happened to hold certain views about world government. However, the opposite is the case. These people were recognized for their talents early on and selected for influential positions because of their views and their willingness to support a certain agenda. They were selected to be placed in influential positions to promote that agenda.

Cronkite worked for CBS which was founded and owned by a man named Bill Paley. Paley's father was an immigrant to the United States from Ukraine who became wealthy running a cigar business. The older Paley bought a radio network in the 1920s and tasked his son Bill to run it. Bill Paley expanded the small radio network into the national giant known as CBS.

Bill Paley used his power over the airwaves to advocate for certain causes, such as U.S. entry into World War II. The reporter Edward R. Murrow worked for Paley to create sympathy for the British and antipathy for the Germans during the early days of the war before the U.S. had gotten involved. Once the U.S. was in the war, Paley worked as a psychological operations (PSYOPS) officer and was given the rank of colonel.

At CBS, Paley hired talented journalists, such as Cronkite and Murrow, to work for him because they were on board with his agenda, which was pro-immigration, pro-interventionism abroad, pro-free trade and pro-Federal Reserve. Paley was an internationalist through and through.

The people who are supplied the money to finance such capital intensive operations as CBS are always on board with the internationalist agenda. That is why they receive their funding. Never in our modern era is a person who supports immigration restrictionism, non-interventionism, tariffs to protect American businesses and workers from foreign competition, and the abolishment of the Federal Reserve, supplied with the money to finance a media outlet. People who advocate for American interests rather than internationalist ones are not handed a megaphone to promote such views. Instead, the megaphone is used to attack and smear them.

Fox News presents itself as being patriotic and attempts to appeal to those who feel a love of country. Yet, the founder of Fox News, Rupert Murdoch, is a foreigner who took American citizenship at age 54 to satisfy a law that said only American citizens could own television stations. Murdoch is the son of an Australian newspaper owner. As a young man, Rupert had a hand in running his father's newspaper business. Like Dean Singleton, Murdoch began acquiring newspapers in rapid fashion, buying them up and building an Australian newspaper empire, then moving offshore to expand into New Zealand. By 1968, he was buying newspapers in the United Kingdom. His papers used a mix of patriotism, raunchiness, sensationalism, celebrity tabloidism, even nudity, to attract large numbers of readers. He then moved into the cable TV business in the UK with Sky Television.

By the 1970s, he was buying up newspapers in the United States. In the 1980s, he was buying up American television stations. In the 1990s, he moved into Asia buying up Hong Kong-based Star TV.

Murdoch built his empire with debt. He was given access to a bottomless well of money that he used to buy up media outlets around the world. His creditors saw in him a talent for attracting audiences that were being neglected and felt alienated by the mainstream media and who viewed Murdoch's style as an alternative point of view.

But is it?

Like the media owners whose media outlets he seemingly opposes, Murdoch is an internationalist through and through. His newspapers and television stations may present themselves as being patriotic, whether they are in Australia, England or the United States, but Murdoch's patriotic style is being used to push the same old internationalist agenda—immigration, interventionism and free trade, just as MSNBC, CNN, and all the other networks do. Murdoch pretends to be an opposing voice while pushing the same agenda, just with a different style and voice.

The international bankers would not have supplied Murdoch with billions in loans if he was not on board with the agenda.

It is interesting to look at the backgrounds of the different journalists who rise to the top of the media game. Some have ties to the intelligence agencies, many are members of the Council on Foreign Relations and the Trilateral Commission. Top media owners and top reporters are attendees of the annual Bilderberg Conference every year where the richest and most influential people in the world meet behind closed doors.

Many people today are unaware that the Republican Party

was the party of non-interventionism, protectionism and immigration restrictionism for most of its history. The man who helped transform the party into the interventionist, mass immigration, free trade party it is today was a journalist named William Buckley, who founded the *National Review* in 1955. The mainstream media made Buckley the voice of conservatism in America, and Buckley used his media megaphone to discredit non-interventionists, immigration restrictionists and protectionists in the Republican Party. Buckley was a member of the elite Skull and Bones society and was an FBI informer while attending Yale. After college, he worked for the CIA in Mexico.

Another media personality who worked for the CIA is CNN anchor Anderson Cooper. Cooper is a descendent of the 19th century robber baron Cornelius Vanderbilt. During college, Cooper interned at the CIA for two summers and then decided to go into journalism after earning his degree.

Another interesting CNN anchor is Wolf Blitzer. Blitzer was born abroad. He began his career working for the British wire service Reuters in its Tel Aviv bureau in Israel. He then became a reporter for the *Jerusalem Post*. In the 1970s, he worked for the American Israeli Public Affairs Committee (AIPAC), the influential lobby that advocates for the interests of the nation of Israel. So one of CNN's top anchors was a lobbyist working for the interests of a foreign government.

Fareed Zakaria, who has a show on CNN and wrote for *Newsweek*, *Time Magazine* and the *Washington Post*, among other media outlets, was born in Mumbai, India, and got his start in journalism while at Harvard by writing for *Foreign Affairs*, a magazine published by the Council on Foreign Relations. He serves on the CFR board, has attended a Bilderberg Conference and was a trustee on the Trilateral Commission.

The American media is a collection of so-called reporters who are intelligence agency assets, foreigners and lobbyists who work for capital intensive operations financed by a clique of international bankers who have a long-term goal of dissolving the United States as a sovereign nation. The international bankers did not buy up the American media to keep the public informed. Quite the opposite. They bought it up to shape public opinion and move it in the direction of their choosing.

In his autobiography *Memoirs,* the international banker David Rockefeller wrote, "For more than a century, ideological extremists at either end of the political spectrum have seized upon well-publicized incidents such as my encounter with Castro to attack the Rockefeller family for the inordinate influence they claim we wield over American political and economic institutions. Some even believe we are part of a secret cabal working against the best interests of the United States, characterizing my family and me as 'internationalists' and of conspiring with others around the world to build a more integrated global political and economic structure—one world, if you will. If that is the charge, I stand guilty, and I am proud of it."

David Rockefeller, former CEO and chairman of Chase Manhattan Bank and scion of the great John D. Rockefeller who amassed one of the world's great fortunes in the 19th century through oil and banking, has been a key player in the globalization of America over the second half of the 20th century.

Over his lifetime, Rockefeller has served as chairman of the Council on Foreign Relations, co-founded the Trilateral Commission with Zbigniew Brzezinski, and serves on the advisory board of the Bilderberg Group. In addition, he has maintained longstanding ties to the CIA with close friendships with agents and directors, some of whom worked for him at Chase.

The United Nations headquarters building was built on land that was owned and donated to New York City by the Rockefeller family. A Rockefeller architect designed the U.N. building.

The Rockefellers and their international banking fraternity have worked for generations to internationalize our country's foreign policy, to discredit that old American tendency to mind our own business in foreign affairs and stay out of other people's wars. Hundreds of thousands of us have died overseas as a result.

These international bankers have done much to internationalize our economy and discredit our old protectionist tendency that favored American small business and American workers over multinational corporations and pauperized labor. They have replaced the old economic trade policies of our constitutional republic with those of the British Empire. As a result, we have seen businesses and jobs flee our shores, our wages have stagnated and the American dream has become more and more ephemeral. These bankers have done much to internationalize our population by flooding us with immigrants from all over the world, pushing down wages and diluting our culture and heritage. We are being transformed from a common people with a common culture and language into a United Nations multicultural stew of confusion and alienation.

Perhaps these bankers believe they are actually creating a utopia on Earth. Or perhaps they are nothing more than imperialists and empire builders, who, unlike Alexander the Great or Caesar, cower behind closed doors and do their work in secret because they know their plans for a global empire are unpopular and that their power is derived not from leadership and military prowess but from mere trickery and the illusions of fractional reserve banking, which could be neutered overnight by an act of Congress if it were impelled by the insistence of a mass movement of the public for a fairer and more rational monetary system.

What is certain is that the international bankers will not stop. They will continue forward with their agenda until we the people stop them. They will continue telling us that free trade is good for us even after all our jobs have been shipped overseas and chronic unemployment is the norm; that immigration is good even after wages have fallen to Third World levels and our middle class has died; that interventionism must continue after so many of our children have been killed abroad and our nation has been bankrupted. They will continue to propagandize for their agenda and continue to work for it as long as they remain in control of the power to create money out of thin air.

Media organizations, especially capital intensive ones like

television and radio networks and Hollywood studios, are entirely dependent on banks for credit, which is their lifeblood. Whether it is Fox News or MSNBC, the *New York Times* or the *Wall Street Journal,* the *Nation* or the *National Review,* or even the alternative media, they all depend on money coming from "investors" who can cut off the money flow if a message is put out that is detrimental to the agenda.

The media is no friend of the American people. It is working now to get us into the next war and to discredit the so-called neo-isolationists of our day who want to prevent it.

While the bankers are firmly in control, over the past decade and a half we have been living through an incredible period of information freedom. While the mainstream media and most of the alternative media are in the hands of the bankers, the Internet has allowed those without access to large amounts of capital to present different points of view. New narratives about history, economics, monetary policy and current events are presented on millions of different websites allowing people to question the narratives put out by the big media outlets.

But the bankers are working relentlessly to take control of the Internet. Billions are being spent on search engines, social media sites and other information platforms to bring them under control and align them with the agenda. Bills are being pushed through Congress to take control of the Internet and end the information freedom we are experiencing today. In a way, the Internet offers the bankers a new means of control, allowing them to track our beliefs, behaviors and even our location at any given time to an unprecedented degree. We live in an interesting time when freedom and tyranny are in the balance. How things will turn out depends on how the people react to the new controls the bankers are attempting to put in place.

The Tyranny of Public Education

What is the purpose of getting an education?

Most people will give you the same answer to that question. You get an education so you can get a good job.

That is how the system has been set up over the past 130 years or so. We go to school to learn how to be employees. The American educational system teaches us how to show up on time and learn a few skills so we can be employees who earn salaries from employers—and employers are essentially rich people, or corporations whose stockholders are rich people, who are seeking profits from the labor of employees.

The American educational system is not teaching our children how to be good, knowledgeable American citizens who are self-sufficient and free. It is teaching them how to be human capital for capitalists who have access to money created by banks. And our educational system is doing such a lousy job at this that employers have been abandoning the American worker for foreign labor.

If you have a child in school today, you are probably aware that multiculturalism is a big part of our current educational system. Our kids are being indoctrinated to be "global citizens" in a multicultural nation. They are being taught about the evils of isolationism, protectionism and nativism. They are being taught the bankers' narrative of history.

What they are not taught is how to be prosperous, free citizens in a constitutional republic. They are hardly taught civics these days and about our Constitution and the rights and liberties the Founders fought for and handed down to us.

America is the richest country in the world but poverty and want is all around us, and the number of Americans living below the poverty line is growing. If one of the purposes of our educational system is to reduce poverty, then our children would be taught in school about money. The cause of poverty is the lack of money, yet how much time is spent in school teaching our students about the importance of money and how to manage it? Money rules our world and determines if we live in a nice home or under a bridge, yet kids learn little about money in school.

Imagine if from an early age children were taught the importance of keeping a budget—of tracking how much money they are earning and how much they are spending and what they are spending it on. Imagine if children were taught the importance of staying out of debt and how debt can lead to hardship and poverty and can reduce their chances of getting ahead in life. Imagine if they were taught what the main causes of poverty are in America—single parenthood, substance abuse, sloth, criminality. Imagine if they were taught how to buy a house or a car and how interest rates increase the amount of money they pay for these things over time. Imagine if they were taught about the importance of starting to save for retirement at an early age. Imagine if they were taught about how the monetary system really works and how fractional reserve banks pyramid debt upon debt beyond what can be paid with the actual supply of money in an economy and how this system causes the boom-and-bust cycle that inevitably leads to inflationary asset bubbles followed by deflationary busts that result in bankruptcies and unemployment.

Children are taught little of this in school. They will graduate and will go out into the world with very little knowledge of money and personal finance. The media bombards them with consumerist messages about all the things they need to buy. The banks throw credit cards at them to allow them to buy these things at high interest. Some will go to college where they will be offered easy-to-get student loans. Many of these kids will start off their working lives buried in debt, paying a good portion of their earnings from their labor to usurers. The whole system is designed to put them in debt. The education system is designed today to put them in massive debt for decades.

Money will rule their lives and will determine if they are rich or poor, yet their schools did not educate them about best practices on how to manage money.

Our teachers overwhelmingly are dedicated and hardworking and genuinely care about the future of their students. But one of the great weaknesses of our educational system is that the teachers who teach our children have very little life experience outside the public education system. They graduate from high school, go to college, get a teaching credential and then start teaching. The body of knowledge they acquire and pass down to our kids does not come from life experience but from text books selected by the public education system. These books are produced by a small cartel of book publishers. These books say that America is a land of immigrants, Smoot-Hawley caused the Great Depression, the New Deal turned things around, that Americans fought against evil in World War II and that large scale government and international action must be taken to stop anthropogenic global warming.

Teachers teach math and science but more often than not have never applied these subjects in the real world of the American economy and cannot explain why they are teaching these subjects beyond needing to know them to get a job. In a sense, our teachers are the blind teaching the blind.

In past societies, our elders who had a wealth of life experience taught the youth and passed down the knowledge they had accumulated. The purpose of getting an education was not to get a job but to learn how to lead a good and meaningful life.

You learn a job and a trade through experience. The best way to learn a job is as an apprentice working alongside a mentor and learning by doing. Yet, our employers these days do not want to train their employees. They have been off-loading the training of employees onto the public educational system and onto the taxpayer. We pay taxes to fund an educational system that provides employees to corporations.

Why not pay taxes to support a school system that educates our children to learn not how to be an employee for a corporation but instead how to build companies that will compete with those corporations? Why not let the corporations train their own employees at their own expense rather than at ours?

Imagine if in school children were taught how to run their own businesses and earn money for themselves. Imagine if they could take classes on navigating all the complexities and difficulties our government has put in place for running a small business and how corporations are gaming the economy through tax loopholes, immigration policy, free trade agreements and access to credit from the Federal Reserve System. Imagine if kids went to school not to get a job and earn a salary from an employer but instead to learn how to be self-employed or to run their own business and be financially independent. Instead of going to school with the aim of someday being a corporate drone, essentially a wage slave on a corporate plantation, they went to school to learn how to be a rugged individual, a pioneer, like the family farmers from the early days of our history who were beholden to no boss or corporation.

Of course, that type of focus for an educational system might be a threat to the powers that be. After all, it was the family farmer who rebelled when the British king became tyrannical.

Our children are not taught in school how to be free and prosperous citizens because our current educational system was set up to serve the beneficiaries of our current monetary system. Those beneficiaries want us divided, in debt and dependent on salaries from corporations for our right to live. They do not want us to be prosperous citizens free of debt who are economically independent and do not need jobs from the rich to earn a living. In short, they want us to be corporate drones—wage slaves dependent on them for our livelihoods. They want us dependent on them, working on the corporate plantation rather than being like the independent family farmer from the early days of the republic, or the small businessman, like Ben Franklin.

Education is important. But our current educational system is mis-educating our children. A better system would be one that taught our kids not to be corporate wage slaves but instead to be free, prosperous and financially independent American citizens.

Re-awakening the American Spirit

The international bankers and their globalist project are doomed to failure. But the damage they are causing to our nation is reaching a critical point. To save our country, we must strip them of power—and their power is derived from fractional reserve banking and control of the monetary system. Monetary reform is the answer to the destruction and wreckage they are causing in our country and around the world.

The international bankers are working relentlessly generation after generation toward their globalist vision to end the nations of the world and put in place a world government. They are doing this in secret and behind closed doors because what they are creating is an Orwellian nightmare—a world ruled by usurers; a soulless world where international bureaucrats make decisions behind closed doors; a world where our republic and our rights as American citizens have been lost. Their direct object is the establishment of an absolute tyranny over all the world.

The end state of their vision is one in which the United States of America is no longer an independent and sovereign nation. Our borders will be open and the world's poor will flood in and the American people will be submerged under an impoverished global proletariat. Our culture, language, traditions and heritage will be lost forever. We will no longer be American citizens with rights protected by our Constitution, but instead global citizens. Our globalist rulers will not view us as American citizens but instead as labor, a commodity to be purchased at the lowest possible price.

The purpose of our military will not be to protect American interests but instead to protect the interests of global institutions. Our young people will be sent around the world as part of an international force to crush opposition to globalist goals. This international force will even be sent into our own communities to suppress opposition to the globalist agenda. Our every move will be watched and recorded under the surveillance state that they are building around us. There is no peace in their vision. Only oppression, poverty, unemployment, the loss of our rights and liberties, the loss of our country, and more war. The Age of Usury culminates in an Age of Darkness that will descend on the planet once the usurers have achieved their ultimate aims.

But there is a better way. Our Founders offered us a different vision. They fought and defeated a king and an empire and gave us a republic founded on the principles that that all men are created equal, that we are endowed by the Creator with certain unalienable rights, that among these are life, liberty and the pursuit of happiness. They believed that a government should derive its powers from the consent of the governed.

Our current government has been hijacked by globalists and has become destructive to the principles of the Founders.

The Founders ordained and established our Constitution in order to form a more perfect union, establish justice, insure domestic tranquility, provide for the common defense, promote the general welfare, and secure the blessings of liberty to ourselves and our posterity.

But since the establishment of the Federal Reserve in 1913, our money supply, our government, our media and our economy have been hijacked by international bankers who have been working relentlessly to undo the liberties and independence of 1776.

We Americans have been disposed to suffer under the tyranny of our globalist elites, under their booms and their busts, their violations of our independence and our sovereignty, their police and surveillance state, their taxes and their debt, their theft of our prosperity and their deconstruction of our economy and our nation. We have been killed in the hundreds of thousands in their wars. But their evils are still sufferable, and we have not felt sufficient spirit to right our country by abolishing the institutions and practices to which we have grown accustomed. However, because of the long train of abuses and usurpations that are designed to reduce us to absolute despotism, it is our right, it is our duty, to throw off such institutions, and provide new guards for our future security. We must seize the reins of government from these globalist hijackers and institute a new monetary system, laying its foundation on such principles and organizing its powers in such form that will be most likely to affect our safety and happiness. We have suffered patiently under the injuries and usurpations of the international bankers; and such is now the necessity to reform our monetary system and return our government to the principles laid down in our Declaration of Independence and our Constitution.

It is time to end the Age of Usury. We must organize a new Abolitionism in America to once and for all cure us of the evils of usury. We must abolish fractional reserve banking, the practice of usury and the Federal Reserve Bank and put in place a new monetary system under American principles. The Federal Reserve System must be replaced with a new system designed to secure our rights to life, liberty and the pursuit of happiness. A new monetary system must be designed under the American principles of transparency and accountability to the people; a system that works to form a more perfect union, establish justice, insure domestic tranquility, provide for the common defense, promote the general welfare and secure the blessings of liberty to ourselves and our posterity.

The Federal Reserve must be replaced with a U.S. Monetary Council that is operated transparently, subject to checks and balances, accountable to the people and under the authority of Congress. We must retire the Federal Reserve Note and replace it with the U.S. Note that is not backed by debt but instead is issued and regulated by the Monetary Council. We must establish public loan offices in each congressional district. These public loan offices should directly lend U.S. Notes to home buyers and small businesses. The interest from these loans will not be profit for usurers but instead must be re-circulated into the communities from which it is collected and put to work for the public good.

Money could be re-directed away from Wall Street and onto Main Street. We could create a new economy based on the free enterprise system. We could re-awaken the American entrepreneurial spirit and create a new, diversified and vibrant economy in which wages are high and unemployment is unknown. By enacting tariffs on foreign imports, we could bring production back to America and revive our ailing economy. Public loan offices could provide sufficient credit in our communities to build the new businesses and industries that will drive innovation and production and create new prosperity in our country. By ending immigration, downward wage pressure will end and wages will rise. Our wage structure will change to one of high wages where workers are highly compensated for their contributions to the wealth of their employers and communities. With wages high and unemployment low, our middle class could expand again and grow prosperous. The wealth structure in America would be altered so that there are very few to no billionaires, numerous millionaires, a large and prosperous middle class, and limited poverty that is temporary.

Instead of sending our military abroad to spread capitalism and democracy under threat of bomb and bullet, we could keep our young service members at home to protect our own nation. Rather than being an invader and an occupier whose military is used to bend other nations to the will of our elites, we should strive to build a better nation here at home, one that is prosperous and free and can serve as an example that others would want to follow.

We are truly fortunate to live in this land. America is a beautiful country. America is a great country. It is a country worth saving. We should defend her, fight for her and not let her slip from our fingers. We must change course or else the international bankers will steal her from us forever. The Founders fought with muskets and bayonets to give us freedom. They put their lives and fortunes on the line for us. They handed down to us a system that allows us to make changes from within merely by political organization rather than through bullet and bayonet. With the proper vision and the right policies we can save our country.

We don't have to continue to allow the deterioration in

American life that has come with free trade, wars abroad and the exploitation of cheap immigrant labor at home. We must fight to save America because right now our birthright is being stolen from us due to our own apathy and our lack of understanding of the financial, political and psychological methods that are being used against us.

We can be a nation with clean streets, safe communities and excellent schools. We can be a nation that is friendly to parents raising children. We can be a nation that gives all of its citizens the opportunity to pursue their dreams and reach their full potential. We can be a nation where everyone can be prosperous through the work of their own hands. We can be a high-wage nation where all of us can be prosperous and free to enjoy the bounty and beauty of this land. As American citizens, this is our birthright.

We can live in a country where democracy, equality, and comradeship are not remote ideals, but something that exists in front of our eyes. We can live in an America where everyone is free and equal, where there is no permanently submerged class. Everyone can have inside, like a kind of core, the knowledge that we can earn a decent living, and earn it without bootlicking—like Mark Twain's Mississippi raftsmen and pilots, or Bret Harte's Western gold-miners—like what we used to be. We can be free human beings. Life can have a buoyant, carefree quality that all of us can feel, like a physical sensation in our bellies. We can be America again.

What is to be done?

We must return to normalcy. Like in the 1920s, we can again reject the British System and return to the American System, albeit a perfected American System that corrects that system's fatal flaw, which is the use of a fractional reserve central bank to supply credit for the economy. In the 1920s, interventionism and entangling alliances were rejected, tariffs were raised and immigration was restricted, ushering in a decade in which the American middle class expanded and experienced prosperity unrivaled in the world. But that decade ended in disaster caused by the Federal Reserve and fractional reserve banks that created speculatory bubbles followed by a contraction of the money supply.

By returning to the American System and perfecting it by reforming the monetary system, we can usher in the Roaring 2020s, minus the speculatory bubbles, and begin a new era in which American middle class prosperity is the new normal and made permanent. Prosperity and liberty can be what define us as American citizens.

We must give up our role as a world police force and bring our troops home. Our foreign policy must return to the wisdom of our Founders. We must avoid entangling alliances. Foreign wars and foreign meddling must be recognized as destructive to our liberty and safety here at home. Our defense strategy should consist of a muscular and vigorous defense of our borders and coastline. Our destiny as a nation is not to remake the world in our image through force. Our destiny is to defend life, liberty and the pursuit of happiness here at home and serve as an example for the people of the world—to show that it is possible for mankind to live in freedom and prosperity.

We must abandon our current free trade policy that we inherited from the British Empire. This is the policy of multinational corporations and international bankers and serves to break down our sovereignty, our economic independence and our prosperity by encouraging the offshoring of American economic production to low-wage nations while reducing the ability of Americans to form businesses or earn decent wages here at home. Free trade is the policy of globalists who want to end the United States as an independent nation. The goal of the free traders is to merge our economy and government into a supranational entity ruled by international organizations, much like what was done to the nations of Europe that have lost sovereignty to the European Union. Instead, we must return to a traditional and constitutional trade policy of protecting American economic productivity and independence through tariffs. Free trade agreements must be scrapped and replaced with bilateral trade treaties that are mutually beneficial to both sides of the trade agreement. Our goal should be to create an economy based on productive work and the domestic production of goods and services to maximize employment and increase the prosperity of the American people.

We must end mass immigration once and for all. The population of the United States is over 316 million people. We are legally importing more than 1 million foreigners into our country every year, and untold numbers of illegal immigrants. Unemployment is high while wages have been stagnant for more than 30 years. Our national cohesion is dissolving and we are being Balkanized into a cacophony of ethnic interests, many of which are destructive to the interests of the American people at large. We rank only behind China and India in population—we have the third largest population in the world. We have no labor shortage. The purpose of mass immigration is to drive down American wages to Third World levels and divide the American people into ethnic groups that are alienated from one another by language, culture, religion, heritage and values. Mass immigration is a tactic being used to divide and conquer us as a nation and reduce us to poverty. It is the policy of multinational corporations, international bankers and corporatist billionaires who are seeking to destroy us as a nation and a people.

Ending immigration into the United States is a simple matter of policy, an act of Congress, and easily attained merely by allowing for the enforcement of existing laws. The obstacle comes from the media and the richest people in our country who use their money to stir up unrest and relentlessly attack anyone who speaks out about our suicidal immigration policy. Immigration has been restricted before in our history and the results are clear—rising wages. The only way we can achieve these results again is by electing congressional representatives who push hard to pass immigration restriction bills in Congress.

In the early 1920s after the traumatic experience of World War I, the United States rejected entangling alliances and involvement in foreign wars. Antiwar and anti-conscription advocates who were imprisoned by the Wilson administration were freed. We ended mass immigration. The income tax was slashed and tariffs were raised. The results were dramatic. America entered a period of full employment, rising wages and widespread prosperity. The American people were the most modern and prosperous people in the world.

While Congress and the president ended foreign entanglements, mass immigration and free trade, they left the Federal Reserve and the fractional reserve system in place. The reforms that had been made returned American to prosperity and peace but the fractional reserve bankers were still working their old tricks behind the scenes. The Federal Reserve inflated real estate and stock market bubbles with easy credit and then suddenly raised rates and contracted the money supply ending the prosperity of the nation for 12 years and allowing a new elite to confiscate the wealth of the nation. The Great Depression ended only when we were plunged into the most destructive war in human history that killed off more than 400,000 American men.

Without monetary reform, the fractional reserve bankers will continue their old game of inflation, deflation and confiscation. It is what they do. We can change our foreign policy, our trade policy and our immigration policy but any positive results will be temporary as long as the fractional reserve bankers are in control of our money supply. We will continue traveling down the banker's road of boom and bust as long as they have the power to create debt money out of thin air.

The monetary reforms that are needed are simple. First, we must fully audit the Federal Reserve to find out where the money is going and to whom. If any criminality is discovered during the audit, the suspects must be arrested and prosecuted. Second, the Federal Reserve must be closed down and shuttered forever. The Fed has failed as an institution in its stated purpose and instead has concentrated great wealth and power in the hands of a few while reducing the prosperity of the American people at large. It has become a threat to the very existence of our nation and our people. Third, a U.S. Monetary Council must be created by Congress under the American principles of transparency, checks and balances and representative democracy. It should be given the constitutional responsibility to control the issuance and volume of debt-free U.S. Notes. This commission must be made answerable to the electorate through the Congress and the states. The council's purpose must be to regulate the American money supply with the intent of facilitating commerce and the needs of the American people. Money should not be an instrument of debt used to enrich international bankers. It should be a medium of exchange that facilitates the trade of goods and services. We must overturn the current system in which Wall Street banks determine how much money is created and who gets it first. Instead, we must form public loan offices that supply money to the people for the purpose of purchasing homes and starting businesses in their local communities. Usury must be abolished because it is destructive to society and to the human spirit. Instead, the collection of interest should only be allowed by public loan offices as a replacement for taxation and a means to circulate the currency in local communities for the public good.

"Washington Crossing the Delaware"
by Emanuel Leutze.

Saving the republic

Jesus of Nazareth entered the temple and was angered by what he saw. He overturned the tables of the moneychangers and cast out all who bought and sold in the temple. Jesus said to them, "It is written, my house shall be called the house of prayer; but ye have made it a den of thieves."

The scribes and the chief priests heard him and sought how they might destroy him for they feared him because all the people were astonished at his doctrine.

In our day, anyone who walks the Mall in Washington, D.C. and comes upon the Federal Reserve building might notice it looks remarkably like a temple. The building is constructed of white marble in a neo-classical style.

This building is a temple of usury and greed—a den of thieves. The people inside present themselves as modern scribes and economic priests and masquerade as public servants while they rob the nation and the American people of our prosperity and undermine our Constitution, our liberty and our independence.

What is needed today is a modern-day Jesus to enter the temple and overturn the tables of the moneychangers and cast out all those who buy and sell the wealth of our nation using the trickery of fractional reserve banking. We need reformers who breathe fire and brimstone who are not afraid of the wailing and gnashing of teeth of the moneychangers, the speculators and the usurers—who do not fear the moneychanger media and who see rightly the bought-and-paid-for politicians as the traitors of the republic that they are.

Our nation produced such a reformer before. President Andrew Jackson, for all his faults, was tough as nails, able to take a bullet, and was never hesitant to cause the bankers to wail and gnash their teeth.

Jackson rooted out the den of thieves and killed the Second Bank of the U.S. But he did not go far enough.

It is not enough to end the Fed. A central bank is the consolidation and centralization of the power of the international bankers. But the source of their power is fractional reserve banking—the ability to use other people's money for the purpose of usury to create pyramids of debt that exceed the money supply in the economy.

Jackson killed the bank. It took the bankers more than two generations until they were able to re-establish another central bank in the Federal Reserve. The international bankers are transnational and they have an agenda that is transgenerational. They were patient and relentless in their efforts and were able to wait until the time was right and once again seized control of the American money supply. Since 1913, they have hijacked our country to their own ends. They are using us. But only because most of us are blind to it and we allow it through our ignorance and our apathy toward it.

The choice we have today is to accept their goals and watch our sovereignty erode, our independence fade, our prosperity wither and our Constitution made subservient to international law and international institutions that are controlled by a clique of these international elites.

Our current path is leading us into more wars overseas, economic decay, the loss of our culture and heritage and the loss of the liberties and freedoms that our forefathers passed down to us.

What we need today more than ever are leaders to rally the people and once again awaken the Spirit of 1776. Just as the Founders stood up to the British Empire and defeated it at great cost and effort, we must once again stand up and tear down the forces of tyranny and replace them with liberty. Our nation has produced some of the world's greatest leaders who conquered the continent and shaped world history. Where are they today? They are dormant while corrupt politicians and Wall Street bankers rule over us.

Leadership is vital in the shaping of human events. The bankers realize this. They are always on guard to marshal all their resources to destroy any person with leadership qualities who is a danger to their agenda. They have carefully selected corrupted personalities that they control to fill the positions of leadership in our nation. These personalities pander to us, whether on the left or the right, while pursuing the agenda of the financial elites.

But America is filled with greatness. We were founded by great men and women and their legacy lives on inside us. In a sense, our task today is much easier than theirs. They left us with a system that allows revolution to occur peacefully. What is needed is merely leadership and a plan. What we need to do is merely vote in politicians to our Congress who we can trust will enact the correct policy changes that will save the republic from the agenda that the bankers have been implementing.

The solutions to stop their rot and restore the republic are simple:

1. End immigration into the United States and begin a new high-wage era of slow to no population growth.
2. End America's world police role and instead follow an American foreign policy of avoiding foreign entanglements, remaining neutral in foreign conflicts and maintaining a strong

national defense of the republic and for the republic only. War should be seen as it is—a desperate measure that results in death, destruction and the loss of national treasure. War should only be declared by Congress as our Constitution specifies and should only be declared as a last resort in times of national peril. War should never, ever be a source of profits and enrichment for individuals, businesses or industries. Profits made in the military-industrial complex should be banned and war profiteering should be made illegal. We should recognize the merchants of death for who they are and see clearly without self-deception the blood on their hands.

3. End free trade and replace it with a trade policy that favors domestic production and domestic employment. Shift the burden of taxation off the backs of American workers and business owners and back onto the importers of foreign-made goods. Use the tariff as the main form of taxation as specified in the Constitution.

4. End all taxes on wages and on the profits of small businesses. The earnings from productive work, from providing goods and services, should not be taxed. Instead, apply the progressive income tax to unearned or passive incomes—to capital gains, dividends and rents. Since small businesses are the main employer of American citizens, small businesses should be run tax free without the constant heavy hand of the IRS on their backs and in their pockets. Instead, shift the tax burden onto multinational corporations, onto importers of foreign goods and onto passive income earners.

5. Ban the destructive and corruptive practices of fractional reserve banking and usury. These practices produce destructive boom-and-bust cycles and concentrate wealth into the hands of the few while impoverishing the many. These practices amount to modern day slavery and should be seen as criminal, exploitative and destructive to our prosperity, liberty and sovereignty as a nation.

6. Audit and close the Federal Reserve Bank. Replace the Fed with a U.S. Monetary Council that regulates the money supply. Monetary Council members should be appointed by Congress and the state legislatures to represent the interests of the nation at large, the people and the states. This council should be accountable to

the people and subject to democratic controls, checks and balances, and its monetary decisions should be made fully transparent. Unlike the Federal Reserve that serves the needs of international banks and multinational corporations, the monetary council should serve the needs of the American people and small business.

7. The U.S. Monetary Council should issue U.S. Notes that are not instruments of debt but instead serve the needs of commerce and the people. The purpose of our currency should not be to facilitate lending and the collection of interest for profit by banks—usury—but instead should serve as a measure of value and an intermediary of exchange. The Monetary Council should determine the volume of the money supply based on the population of the country and the productivity of the economy. The goals of the council should be to ensure that the currency provides a stable measure of value, facilitates commerce and exists in sufficiency to serve the needs of the American people.

8. Create public loan offices in each congressional district to supply credit to home buyers and businesses. The public loan offices should issue loans as a means to circulate money in the local economy, with interest collected serving as a replacement for taxation. The interest collected from loans should fund the operations of loan offices, and, importantly, should be spent into the local economy in the public interest as a means to enhance commerce and increase quality of life.

These simple policy changes could reorganize our economy to favor productive work and employment over speculation and usury. For much of our history, we did not have a central bank, nor the income tax, nor free trade, nor mass immigration nor a globalist foreign policy. Those things were actually considered un-American and anti-American—the policies of imperialism. We could return to our roots by perfecting the American System. We could once again become a democratic republic, although a better one and a freer one, with a more rational monetary system that discourages debt and encourages work, entrepreneurship and prosperity.

We could create a society where work is richly rewarded and

speculation and usury are punished. We could create a society with a large, inclusive and prosperous middle class that is easily entered through nothing more than a willingness to work for a living. Unfortunately, due to human nature, the poor will always be with us because of circumstance and misfortune, but we should strive to create a society in which poverty is temporary and easy to overcome through a little personal initiative and a willingness to work. We could create a society where the rich are made up not of financiers, bankers and other swindlers and rent seekers, but instead of inventors, entrepreneurs and exceptional performers in their fields who add value to our lives rather than attempting to siphon off our savings and earnings.

We should strive to create a society in which the American people are free and secure in their constitutional rights—a society where we all have the rights to life, liberty and the pursuit of happiness, where each one of us is the master of our fates and the captains of our souls, where each of us can direct the course of our lives as we see fit as a free people.

The bankers are small in number but unified in their aims. They are driving forward in a global effort to tear down the nations of the world and create a world system of financial control in their hands which dominates the world and rules over us in feudalist fashion. Their efforts are bringing oppression, poverty, war and tyranny to us all. For us, as Americans, they are working to strip us of our sovereignty, our heritage, our prosperity and of the liberties that our forefathers have passed down to us.

Their vision is for America not to be an independent republic of free and prosperous citizens, but instead merely part of a larger economic bloc with open borders—where a few millionaires and billionaires run the show and the rest of us are part of an impoverished, multicultural global proletariat.

But it is not too late to save the republic that was born of the Revolution of 1776. We have the numbers and the smarts, and collectively, the money. If we, the American people, were to form a united front against them to enact the policies that will save us, the bankers can be cast out of power and defeated.

Of course, they will wail and gnash their teeth. Their media will attack relentlessly. Their bought-and-paid-for politicians, like pied pipers, will pander to us and speak as if they want what's best for us while attempting to lead us over the cliff.

Our problem, as the great American middle class, is that we lack leadership and direction. The bankers are small in number and focused, while we are large in number and unorganized. We are a slumbering giant that is difficult to awaken.

Leadership is vital in the shaping of human events. To know which leaders are not bought-and-paid-for pied pipers of the financial oligarchy, we should listen to their words while paying careful attention to their actions and to the people behind the scenes who are backing them.

If a politician says nice things that you agree with, but behind the scenes works toward increasing immigration, toward more free trade agreements, toward more wars overseas and meddling in the affairs of other nations, toward increasing the power of the Federal Reserve, then that politician is working against us as a people and as a country.

If someone is a Rhodes Scholar, has ties to the Trilateral Commission, the Council on Foreign Relations, the Bilderberg Conference, the IMF, the World Bank, the WTO, international banks, the mainstream media, the IRS, the CIA, the NSA or the FBI, then that person is working against you, whether he knows it or not. That person is working toward our national destruction.

The road ahead leads either to darkness or light. The great leaders among us who are willing to stand up against the bankers and reawaken the Spirit of 1776 are out there and can lead us to the light of liberty, prosperity and independence.

God has blessed America. We are a blessed people. Like our forefathers, we must stand up for what is right, drive the international bankers out, and reclaim our birthright. God is on our side.

America is worth saving. We must save her. Together, it can be done.

Made in the USA
Columbia, SC
24 March 2023